Rethinking Anthropological Perspectives on Migration

UNIVERSITY PRESS OF FLORIDA

Florida A&M University, Tallahassee
Florida Atlantic University, Boca Raton
Florida Gulf Coast University, Ft. Myers
Florida International University, Miami
Florida State University, Tallahassee
New College of Florida, Sarasota
University of Central Florida, Orlando
University of Florida, Gainesville
University of North Florida, Jacksonville
University of South Florida, Tampa
University of West Florida, Pensacola

RETHINKING ANTHROPOLOGICAL PERSPECTIVES ON MIGRATION

* * * * * * * * * * * *

EDITED BY

GRACIELA S. CABANA

AND JEFFERY J. CLARK

University Press of Florida

Gainesville · Tallahassee · Tampa · Boca Raton
Pensacola · Orlando · Miami · Jacksonville · Ft. Myers · Sarasota

First cloth printing, 2011
First paperback printing, 2020

25 24 23 22 21 20   6 5 4 3 2 1

LIBRARY OF CONGRESS CATALOGING-IN-PUBLICATION DATA
Rethinking anthropological perspectives on migration / Graciela S. Cabana and
Jeffery J. Clark, [editors].
p. cm.
Includes bibliographical references and index.
ISBN 978-0-8130-3607-6 (cloth : alk. paper)
ISBN 978-0-8130-6819-0 (pbk.)
  1. Pueblo Indians—Migrations. 2. Uto-Aztecan Indians—Migrations.
3. Human remains (Archaeology) 4. Emigration and immigration. I. Clark, Jeffery J.
II. Cabana, Graciela S.
E99.P9R36   2011
304.80979—dc22   2010054047

The University Press of Florida is the scholarly publishing agency for the State University
System of Florida, comprising Florida A&M University, Florida Atlantic University, Florida
Gulf Coast University, Florida International University, Florida State University, New
College of Florida, University of Central Florida, University of Florida, University of North
Florida, University of South Florida, and University of West Florida.

University Press of Florida
2046 NE Waldo Road
Suite 2100
Gainesville, FL 32609
http://upress.ufl.edu

Contents

Tables

Figures

Preface

The primary goal of this volume is to break down subdisciplinary boundaries within anthropology in migration research. This aspiration extends well beyond migration research. We would not be the first to voice concern that anthropology has fallen into a "fragmentation trap" where the exploration of new theories is restricted by subdisciplinary boundaries at the expense of the traditional "four-field," or holistic, approach (c.f., Knudsen 2003). Anthropology departments throughout the United States have taken different paths in dealing with the discipline's fragmentation, ranging from physical and intellectual segregation of subdisciplines to half-hearted calls for an integrated anthropology that more often than not fall on deaf ears.

This volume is the culmination of a symposium held at the December 2005 American Anthropological Association meetings in Washington, D.C. This was followed by a two-day workshop held at Arizona State University in November 2006. Since then numerous e-mail exchanges and phone conversations between the editors and participants have greatly enriched the contributions herein. Before you is the outcome of this long and fruitful dialogue. However, this volume is not intended to be the final word on this subject. Rather, our intention is to open up a new dialogue within anthropology about migration that crosscuts the various subdisciplines. And maybe, just maybe, this dialogue will result in a holistic model for studying migration in anthropology.

The contributors to this volume are a diverse lot. Although most of us can be placed into one of the four anthropological subfields, we also provide unique perspectives on migration within our respective subfields. We came together with the common understanding that the discipline of anthropology allows for multiple voices on what migration means and why it is important while at the same time concurring that "migration" is an extremely important research topic.

Beyond that, we agreed to disagree about exact definitions of "migration," and the best methods for assessing its scale and impact. Instead we laid a foundation for a fresh approach to migration studies by presenting work by current researchers. We also willingly engaged in some "creative destruction" of previous time-honored assumptions and vested interests. We make no claims in succeeding to have built a consensus in studying migration across and even within anthropological subdisciplines. However, we hope that with time the diverse chapters in this volume will inspire others both within—and outside of—the discipline to continue moving toward this worthy goal.

We have several people and entities to thank for helping us along the way. Our workshop took place at Arizona State University, with the help of Sander E. van der Leeuw and the School of Human Evolution & Social Change (SHESC), Arleyn W. Simon and the Archaeological Research Institute (ARI), Charles L. Redman and the Global Institute of Sustainability (GIOS), and the College of Arts & Sciences Dean's Office. The University of Tennessee's Department of Anthropology in Knoxville and William Doelle, CEO of the Center for Desert Archaeology in Tuscon, generously provided additional funding to help defray publication costs. We are grateful to Dean R. Snow and John H. Relethford for their thoughtful reviews, and to Brannon I. Hulsey, Frankie L. Pack, and Linda Gregonis for their detailed proofreading and indexing.

Reference

Knudsen, C.
2003 The Essential Tension in the Social Sciences: Between the "Unification" and "Fragmentation" Trap. In *The Evolution of Scientific Knowledge*, edited by H. S. Jensen, L. M. Richter, and M. T. Vendelø, pp. 13–36. Edward Elgar Publishing, Northampton, Mass.

◇◇◇◇◇◇◇◇◇◇◇◇◇◇◇◇◇◇◇◇◇◇◇◇◇◇◇◇◇◇◇

I

◇◇◇◇◇◇◇◇◇◇◇◇◇◇◇◇◇◇◇◇◇◇◇◇◇◇◇◇◇

Setting the Stage

Introduction

Migration in Anthropology

Where We Stand

GRACIELA S. CABANA AND JEFFERY J. CLARK

As anthropologists we pride ourselves on our holistic approach to studying culture and society, past and present; we explore the human condition from multiple perspectives using a variety of data sources. Unfortunately this strength is also a weakness, as this multivariate approach can also lead to fragmentation, dispute, and reductionism. What keeps us together, then? We know that being human involves biology, culture, language, and so forth. Is it possible to consider all these human facets within one methodology, theory, or paradigm? To stitch our fragmented subdisciplines together and realize our holistic aspirations in the context of migration studies we start with two basic questions: What is migration and why is it important?

Why Do We Care?

Migration is a fundamental part of being human. While movement is not exclusive to humans, we are unique from other species in the way we migrate and how we adapt to our new settings. Human migration is not merely physical movement from point A to point B but also entails a complex swirl of biological, sociocultural, and linguistic activities. Human migration, past and present, is important to what it is to be human. Yet myriad behaviors influence human behavior, and not every one is deemed to be an important research domain.

So really, why do we care? Those of us interested in prehistoric[1] migrations study changes in the distributions of various traits and attributes with the goal of reconstructing "history" in the absence of written documents. From the mid-nineteenth century to the mid-twentieth, anthropologists used migrations as pivotal points in history, seeing various racial, cultural, and/or linguistic groups ebbing and flowing across the landscape. They associated these groups "with various genes, material items, and languages." Who was where when became the essential research question. Migration and the subsequent replacement of one group by another was the universal explanation for change. At the mid-twentieth century, the culture-historical approach was supplanted by the neo-evolutionary paradigm. Elucidating universal processes that explained both stasis and change became the primary goal in anthropology. With this theoretical shift, researchers viewed both cultures and societies as self-contained systems, thereby focusing attention on internal change and adaptation at the expense of "external" forces, not realizing that "internal" and "external" are simply matters of scale. Migration was deemed an external historical accident that was unpredictable and hence uninteresting. However, the pendulum has swung back toward migration during the past two decades. We now see population movement in a new light as a process with predictable motivations and outcomes. At the same time, new methodologies have been developed within the various anthropological subdisciplines to reliably track migrations and identify immigrants among indigenous populations at high resolution. If migration is considered both a process and an agent of change in each anthropological subdiscipline, then we have identified a research domain that is worth studying from as many angles as possible.

From a contemporary perspective, a glance at the daily headlines reminds us why we should study migration. Migration is pervasive in our globalized and multicultural world. Depending on context and referent group, we see it as either an ominous threat or a great opportunity. Heightened attention to migration issues has forced us to both reconsider and push the boundaries of anthropology beyond its focus on traditional societies. Past migrations have relevance in the modern world, but in an age when new transportation and communication technologies have exponentially increased interaction and interconnnectivity, we are forced to ask how they are relevant.

In this context, as anthropologists interested in migration we want to know the answers to these questions: What are alternative ways of viewing and characterizing migration? Who moves, how do they move, and what motivates them? How does movement impact individuals and groups as well as their cultures and languages in both homeland and destination areas? How do these variables play out in the short and long term? Are there interesting aspects of human movement that have not yet been explored by anthropologists?

Migration: A Minimal Definition

During the multidisciplinary discussions leading up to this volume, it became apparent that at this early stage, the various researchers could not readily agree on a common definition of migration. Rather, we reached a consensus on having an open perspective on migration and its potential correlates and impacts. This perspective has to be true to our collective understanding of migration and its importance without elevating one anthropological subdiscipline over another in our pursuit of a unified approach to migration studies.

In response to our collective concerns, we developed a minimal definition of migration as a starting point to set us on the right path in thinking about who or what was moving rather than falling into the entrenched habits of studying migration within each subdiscipline. For example, biological anthropologists using a genetic perspective might be tempted to talk about genes moving, divorced of their human carriers. Archaeologists interested in the distribution of artifacts sometimes forget that such items are only portable, not ambulatory, and that processes other than migration can distribute these items. In addition, considering the generally poor resolution of the archaeological record, migration and change is often viewed from the perspective of large social groups over decades or centuries rather than from the perspective of individuals who made decisions over the course of days that led to collective action. Similarly, historical linguists may elide linguistic groups with culture groups, distancing themselves from the actual process of cumulative movements of individuals—along with their languages.

A minimal definition is a safeguard against treating genes, tools, culture, and language as moving independently of people while realizing that at least some of these objects of study can move without migration. We also want to avoid treating social groups as highly integrated systems instead of collections of independent decision makers.

Our minimal definition is a *one-way residential relocation to a different "environment" by at least one individual*. This working definition should be viewed as the lowest common denominator with which anthropologists in each subdiscipline can concur, but many would further embellish it. It is not meant to be the ultimate or even the penultimate definition of migration.

The movement of multiple individuals can occur in two fundamental ways: (1) as a series of individuals (or small groups) acting independently based on common motives; or (2) as a large social group whose actions are coordinated by a central authority. A migration event must minimally consist of an individual moving from origin to destination. A migration event also must be a residential relocation that is relatively permanent. Thus, visits (which by definition are temporary) and seasonal rounds that are cyclical are not migration. A "return" migration back to the place of origin is viewed as a separate, but related, migratory event. The move must be to a destination that is in some way different from the origin point but not necessarily "new" to the emigrant(s) in the sense that he or she (or they) has (or have) no prior knowledge about the destination area.

Migration can be a crossing of an empirically visible material or geophysical boundary. It can also be a movement across a conceptual or cognitive boundary that is empirically invisible, including spiritual or mythical movements. Migration, then, is movement between two "places" that are *conceived of* as different because some sort of real or perceived boundary has been traversed. This view of migration underscores the fact that this movement is not just a physical act and that social and cultural aspects of human migration make it unique from that of other species. As Darling (this volume) show us, it is possible to access both the cognized and geospatial realms of migration. The fact that we rarely have access to the cognitive component of migration does not mean that we should not consider this possibility in our definitions and models.

Building on the Minimal Definition: Key Variables

One reason to create a minimal definition is to encourage open, creative thought on all that may encompass migration, using this definition as starting point. Table I.1 provides a list of broad variables that can be used to build on that definition. Which variables will be used and how they will be used depends on the researcher, on the research question, and on myriad context-specific factors.

Structure and Scale: Is this a physical or a symbolic migration? Who and how many are migrating and what kind of boundary is being traversed (geographic, ecological, social, spiritual or religious, and/or ideological)? What is the tempo and pace of migration? Is there a rigid structure or is the pattern more random and expedient? What is the size, composition, and organization of the migrant units? For example, are members of certain kin groups migrating or members of certain economic classes? Are families moving or is it primarily men or women?

Motivation: Why are people moving? What are the social, biological, or economic "pushes" from the origin and "pulls" toward the destination that are influencing migratory behavior? Are motivation and structure related and do common motives produce broad patterns? Can we really talk about migration as a predictable process?

Impact: How does migratory behavior affect immigrants and the receiving community(ies)? In what ways? Can impact be predicted if certain key variables are known? Are migrations to sparsely populated frontiers qualitatively

Table I.1. "Minimal definition" of migration and accompanying variables

Minimal Definition	Minimal Unit	Variables	Notes on Variables
One-way residential relocation to a different "environment"	Individual	Structure and scale	How many migrants in total? How are individual migrant groups organized? What is the pace and tempo of migration?
		Motivation	Social and economic pushes from homelands and pulls toward specific target destinations. Does motivation affect migration structure and scale?
		Impact	On both migrating and receiving community, including short- and long-term socioeconomic consequences. Salient factors include relative size of migrant and local populations, relative technological and organizational levels, migration motivation (e.g., are migrants conquerors, colonists, or refugees?), migration tempos (1,000 people arriving in one week or 1,000 over a decade).
		Distance	• geographic • environmental • social • linguistic • genetic
		Mode and technology	Mode of transportation is dependent on available technology and affects the rate of migration and physical distance traveled.

different from migrations to areas with large indigenous populations? Does a migration have to have a significant impact to be worth studying?

Distance: How "far" do migrants move in a migratory act? Distance can be measured geographically (5 versus 500 miles), ecologically (from desert to woodlands), socially (from natal group to ethnic group), linguistically (from Uto-Aztecan- to Numic-speakers), and/or genetically (from one set of allele frequencies to another).

Mode of Migration: How do social complexity and technology affect migrations? Ritually, with the help of a mind-altering substance? Physically, with domestic animals and other nonpedestrian conveyances? Does technology alter migration only in a quantitative sense (i.e., more people can travel farther faster), or do qualitative changes make modern models of migration inappropriate for prehistoric cases?

Why a Minimal Definition Is Necessary

The minimal definition of migration offered here purposely makes no assumptions about causes or consequences. By proposing such a definition and variables that expand on it, we are directing research to begin with a very basic conception of migration and asking researchers to assess its correlates within the context of the research agenda of their anthropological subdisciplines. This is opposite of the traditional approach, which is to start with the observed impact and infer migration from this, working backward to identify and characterize immigrant groups. This traditional approach has led to a narrow definition of migration as a movement of people en masse to very different social and geographic environments (e.g., Rouse 1986). These are the most dramatic movements, but we would argue that these are rare relative to other migrations. This view of migration prevents us from thinking about other equally interesting migrations, such as cases where different groups coexist or one group assimilates into another as a result of migration.

Points to Consider

In considering the ramifications of this minimal view of migration in the case studies that follow, three ideas should be kept in mind. First, migration is an inherently social act or process. At least one individual must be involved for migration to occur, but that individual is embedded in a social and economic context. Individuals make decisions and act within this context, whether they are moving individually or not. We often cannot "see" individual migrants in the prehistoric record, but we emphasize that migration is ultimately a socially bounded process undertaken by individuals, regardless of motivation and organization. This is a point Anthony (1990) argues vigorously.

Second, migration is transgressive. It is about crossing perceived and real boundaries that are socially, culturally, and/or linguistically constructed. Economic boundaries may have also been crossed in terms of differences in wealth or subsistence strategy. These boundaries may or may not have clear physical manifestations. Unless the individual crosses such a boundary, he or she is considered to be in the same place and has not emigrated. The boundary type varies based on what the researcher is analyzing and what the immigrant deems important. For example, from the perspective of national immigration officials, you are not an immigrant until you have physically crossed an international border, even if you have moved all the way from Wisconsin to Texas (see Tsuda, this volume). From the perspective of a cultural or a physical anthropologist, this would be considered a migration, but perhaps a linguistic anthropologist would not see it as such (unless dialect is considered). More important, are the boundaries perceived by the immigrants and the receiving communities themselves, or are they boundaries imposed by nation-states or inferred by anthropologists from their data? This raises the possibility that cases existed in the past that would not fit into our modern anthropological conception of migration. For example, archaeologists may not consider population movements based on postmarital residence patterns as migration, but the society under study might have done so. In other words, the subject society dictates what is and what is not migration, as difficult as this is to assess when the society no longer exists. Defining boundaries and thus migration from both emic and etic perspectives challenges us to make a compelling argument for the presence or absence of such boundaries. In turn, we force ourselves to empirically establish that a migration occurred instead of simply assuming that it did and to assess the impact in a second subsequent step (see Clark, this volume).

A third and final important point is that migrants may be crossing more than one boundary and that those boundaries exhibit different permeabilities. For example, in prehistory the Great Basin area of North America was home to several Native American tribes that maintained considerable social and linguistic distance from each other, despite the fact that they occupied similar ecological environments. Yet social distance did not preclude individuals from mating with each other, such that genetic-distance analyses may show closer relationships than are revealed in ethnographic accounts (Fowler, this volume).

Rationale of This Volume

The goal of the volume is to infuse anthropological studies of past migration with new questions and new approaches that emerge from the collective effort of researchers in the various subdisciplines. The volume attempts to accomplish this in two ways: (1) by demonstrating new methodologies to identify past migration; and (2) by addressing innovative topics and themes about migration, especially its impact, using biological, archaeological, and linguistic data. We asked the volume's contributors to consider the minimal definition and the philosophical approach outlined above so that they would be working within common parameters and a shared conceptual framework. The basic level of this definition and this framework permits a high degree of interdisciplinary flexibility and context-dependent freedom. The resulting papers engage with the common definition and vocabulary of variables presented above, directly or indirectly.

The contributions herein range from theoretical treatments of migration to specific case studies. The authors explore migration at multiple scales, from the individual to the population, from the intrasettlement to the macro-regional level. Geographically, the chapters cover indigenous populations from the Americas, Southeast Asia, and Africa.

Following from this Introduction, the volume opens (Part I) with a philosophical piece that problematizes the concept of migration through a historical analysis of the relationship between migration and "culture change." Graciela S. Cabana argues that current definitions and uses of "migration" were developed to answer questions specific to anthropology, suggesting that perhaps migration has since functioned as a handmaiden to studies of culture change. The challenge presented, then, is to divorce ourselves from our immediate academic concerns in order to think epistemologically about what migration is and how to best approach it in prehistoric studies.

The bulk of the volume is organized according to traditional anthropological subdisciplines, beginning with studies that emphasize archaeological approaches to migration (Part II). This is followed by migration studies that focus on archaeolinguistic approaches (Part III). In many ways the strengths and weaknesses of both approaches are comparable. Part IV presents ethnolinguistic case studies, each with very different conclusions and levels of confidence with regard to assessing the scale and impact of migration. Part V includes current genetic and geochemical studies of migration in bioanthropology. These perhaps have more in common with the physical sciences than the social sciences, although such studies increasingly consider social implications. The volume concludes with a chapter that examines prehistoric migration studies from a contemporary perspective.

Archaeological approaches are highlighted in the volume for several reasons. First, more than any other anthropological subdiscipline, archaeology has actively engaged with migration, whether it be to embrace or reject it. The existence of this volume is largely due to archaeology's enthusiasm in bringing the topic back to the forefront through new methods and revised theories (Anthony 1990). This includes a conscious effort to incorporate the findings of contemporary migration studies. Further, because much of the pioneering work has been conducted in recent years by anthropologists working in the southwestern United States, this region is well represented throughout the volume.

In Chapter 2, Wesley R. Bernardini demonstrates how the consideration of oral histories invites a reconceptualization of migration as consisting of discrete social units. Bernardini argues that movement and moving actors in the ancient landscape were instead fluid. A case study of the Hopi that combines archaeological research and oral history shows how migrant units tended to be core households whose heads controlled the use of powerful ceremonial objects. Thus, one could argue that while tracking the movement of the ceremonial objects in prehistory is a relatively straightforward process, the identity of the migrant units is not, because control over the ceremonial objects shifted over time.

In Chapter 3, Severin M. Fowles discusses our modern bias toward giving primacy to stability, or stasis, and toward viewing movement as aberrant in light of the Pueblo mindset, which emphasizes residential mobility. Such movement pervades the normative worldview of Pueblo peoples and challenges the basic premises put forth in this introductory chapter regarding the causes and impacts of migration and even the minimal definition. Fowles offers the various ways that movement imbues Pueblo thought and behavior.

In Chapter 4, J. Andrew Darling further develops the idea of the cognitive embeddedness of migration among the O'odham in the U.S. Southwest and how this group establishes the interrelationships between landscape, cognition, and social ritual. In particular, he shows how song traditions among the O'odham can be used to help individuals cognitively and behaviorally accommodate to geographic surroundings.

In Chapter 5, Jeffery J. Clark summarizes a two-part methodology that he and his colleagues have been developing over the last decade to detect signatures of migration and assess their impact on receiving communities. He compares and contrasts two migrations into one valley in the U.S. Southwest that had very different consequences. One advantage of this methodology is that it can be used to detect migration in the absence of significant or obvious signs of culture change and impact in the destination area. The methodology itself is validated through ethnohistoric and ethnoarchaeological case studies outlined in Clark (2001).

In chapter 6, Scott G. Ortman develops a new and compelling methodology using theory and method from cognitive linguistics and archaeology to both identify past migrations and understand their social impacts. His approach is based on the cognitive process of conceptual metaphor: when it is linked with archaeology and language, it can be used to trace the migration of speech communities. He applies his methodology to the depopulation of the Mesa Verde region in the U.S. Southwest in the thirteenth century A.D.

In Chapter 7, Christopher S. Beekman and Alec F. Christensen build upon their previous (2003) work, which emphasizes multidisciplinary approaches to diagnosing past migrations and assesses their impacts in northern Mesoamerica during the Classic and post-Classic periods. The authors make the case that identifying migration within complex societies with institutionalized inequalities can be extremely difficult. To argue their perspective, they discuss the archaeolinguistic and biological evidence for migration occurrence as well as the impact of migration on complex societies.

Jane H. Hill's chapter (Chapter 8) stresses that although linguistic evidence alone is not sufficient for identifying the causes or social impacts of migration, it can be used to evaluate the occurrence of migration and assess its impact on speech communities. Through her well-documented Uto-Aztecan case study, Hill demonstrates the utility of the comparative method of historical linguistics in informing and complementing archaeological inquiry.

In Chapter 9, Catherine S. Fowler makes the related point that despite decades of debate and a barrage of multidisciplinary studies, we still have little to say about whether a prehistoric migration in the Great Basin of the present-day United States occurred and if it did, at what scale, from where, and by whom. She argues that we desperately need to enhance our temporal and spatial resolution. Fowler predicts that should this occur, our picture of Great Basin prehistory will be much more nuanced and complex, demonstrating migrations of multiple groups in different times and places throughout the area. In contrast, Christopher Ehret (Chapter 10) presents a more optimistic view in his case study of the Maa peoples of eastern Africa. Here, Ehret employs the word-borrowing method of historical linguistics in conjunction with archaeological evidence to reconstruct aspects of Maa history and prehistory in remarkable detail.

The authors of Part V use a much broader temporal scale, going back to the emergence of *Homo sapiens* (or even earlier). This is largely due to their different view of migration from that of researchers in other anthropological subdisciplines. Biological anthropologists tend to align their view of migration with that of biologists and geneticists, who see "migration" largely in terms of "gene flow," with no temporal (or social) strings attached.

Kelly J. Knudson's work in Chapter 11 highlights an emerging methodological development of biogeochemistry, whose application to prehistory quite literally allows us to catch migrants in the act. In her case study, Knudson demonstrates the adoption of nonlocal Tiwanaku identities by indigenous groups in Andean prehistory. Interestingly, the resolution afforded by biogeochemistry opened the door to the social-theoretical inquiry into identity. Knudson and colleagues (as well as many others) have begun to enter the realm of social theory to inform their bioarchaeological studies (see Knudson and Stojanowski 2009), though these ideas are not specifically developed in this volume.

Chapters 12 (Alan G. Fix) and 13 (Deborah A. Bolnick) are closely related in that they both offer historical and contemporary perspectives on the field of anthropological genetics, especially its ability to reconstruct migration. Fix's case study of the Semai Senoi of Southeast Asia provides a vehicle for discussing the potential misinterpretations of genetic inference of population origins and movement, particularly when researchers do not take all evolutionary forces of a population into account. Bolnick contemplates similar questions and shows how increasingly sophisticated computer simulation and mathematical modeling have—to an extent—helped resolve some of the concerns expressed by Fix.

Susan R. Frankenberg and Lyle W. Konigsberg (Chapter 14) and Keith L. Hunley (Chapter 15) tackle migration at broader scales. Frankenberg and Konigsberg ask what happens when we model two extreme migration scenarios that are the most likely to be detected in the present day. Can we actually detect migration, and if we can, under what circumstances? In their exercise they consider the genetic parameters of multiple populations and offer scenarios in which migration could be reliably detected as long as additional supporting evidence is considered. Hunley also uses sophisticated modeling and statistical approaches to infer migration over the entire course of human history. But as Hunley admits, some historical "details" might remain obscure if we use genetic data alone.

The final chapter in the volume, by Takeyuki (Gaku) Tsuda, compares and contrasts prehistoric and modern migration studies, both methodologically and theoretically. This seems to be an appropriate conclusion considering the reliance of Anthony (1990) on modern migration studies twenty years ago in resurrecting migration in archaeology. The observant reader will note that most authors in some way reference this seminal article. Anthony showed that the modern migration literature of the 1980s could be used to identify key processes and variables in prehistoric migration studies. Because migration never truly lost its cachet as a potential explanatory framework, migration studies quickly reemerged in the disciplinary mainstream.

However, as Tsuda notes, the migration literature that tends to be cited in the literature on prehistory is now outdated and modern migration scholars have since developed new ideas and insights. Tsuda brings these new ideas to the table but also takes an informed outsider's view of prehistoric migration. Like Beekman and Christensen (Chapter 7), Tsuda raises the question of whether migration in more contemporary societies in any way mirrors that of the past, but he also wonders how much apparent discrepancy may actually reflect differences in methodology rather than the real differences between past and present migrations. He also discusses the importance of scale: whereas modern migration scholars may assess migration from the perspective of a few years or centuries, a prehistorian is evaluating data representing centuries, if not millennia.

No grand synthesis is offered at the end of the volume. The lack of consensus among—and even within—the anthropological subdisciplines on migration research is evident from the chapters in this volume. Therefore an attempt at a synthesis would be premature at this stage; it would be overly reductionist at best and more likely ill conceived. Instead, we believe that the minimal definition and identification of key research topics in migration studies in this introduction are first steps toward a synthesis, or at least toward interdisciplinary dialogue and cross-fertilization. The ensuing chapters are designed to be an intellectual *meze,* a representative sample of migration studies currently being conducted in each subdiscipline. These studies provide ample food for thought as we move beyond the detection of migration occurrence to address the more interesting questions of short- and long-term impacts.

Notes

1. The volume emphasizes periods of time or case studies in which the dominant source of information comes from nondocumentary sources, although in some cases that information is complemented with written records or oral histories. In this light, the term "prehistory" should be understood as synonymous with "past."

References

Anthony, D. W.
1990   Migration in Archaeology: The Baby and the Bathwater. *American Anthropologist* 92:895–914.

Beekman, C. S., and A. F. Christensen
2003   Controlling for Doubt and Uncertainty through Multiple Lines of Evidence: A New Look at the Mesoamerican Nahua Migrations. *Journal of Archaeological Method and Theory* 10:111–164.

Clark, J. J.
2001   *Tracking Prehistoric Migrations: Pueblo Settlers among the Tonto Basin Hohokam.* Anthropological Papers of the University of Arizona no. 65. University of Arizona Press, Tucson.

Knudson, K. J., and C. M. Stojanowski
2009   *Bioarchaeology and Identity in the Americas.* University Press of Florida, Gainesville.

Rouse, I.
1986   *Migrations in Prehistory: Inferring Population Movement from Cultural Remains.* Yale University Press, New Haven, Conn.

1

The Problematic Relationship between Migration and Culture Change

GRACIELA S. CABANA

For more than a century, anthropologists have been pursuing "migration" as a topic of inquiry: if people moved from one area to another at some point in prehistory, did that movement precipitate changes in behavior, language, and material culture? The answer to this question has important implications. If the answer is "yes," then identifying past large-scale migrations potentially allows us to identify significant patterns and processes in human cultural and biological evolution. A study of migration therefore holds the promise of opening large windows into the past, and for this reason migration has reemerged as a hot topic among prehistorians over the past two decades.

In the course of exploring migration as a subject of anthropological inquiry, I began to realize that anthropologists (including myself) are invested in a certain migration worldview. That worldview puts a heavy premium on the investigation of "culture change." Pursuing these interests has led to a dead end. I devote this chapter to an analysis of the historical relationship between prehistoric migration and change within anthropological archaeology, because it is within this realm that migration studies tend to be most heavily pursued. Although biological and linguistic anthropologists also research the topic, archaeological theory provides the basis for many of these studies. My comments are reserved for migration studies within North American anthropology, though anthropologists working in other contexts may find them of interest as well.

Migration in Archaeology

Traditionally, the archaeological view of "migration" is significant population movement such that "the people of one area expands [sic] into another area replacing the latter's population" (Rouse 1986:13). "Migration" as a concept refers directly to "migration theory," a term first coined by Adams et al. (1978)

to embrace the numerous individual cases in which migration has been used as an ad hoc explanation for culture change. Although migration has never been hailed as a grand theory of change for human history and prehistory, archaeologists have invoked migration so frequently that an unspoken set of assumptions remains in archaeological thought about the nature and effects of migration on material. One major assumption has been that "migration"—or significant population movement—accounts for abrupt changes in the material culture patterns that constitute the archaeological record. For a long time, archaeologists treated such abrupt changes as evidence for the arrival of a new "culture" and hence a new "people" (Adams 1968; Adams et al. 1978; Binford 1972 [1965], 1972 [1971]; Trigger 1968). The concepts of migration and culture change have enjoyed an intimate relationship within archaeological thought, to the point that when theoretical approaches to culture change shift, anthropological migration studies are drastically affected. Historically, archaeological approaches have existed in tension with scientific method and theory, ranging from a tentative embrace to a firm rejection.

That tension has played itself out quite dramatically in the arena of what historically has constituted acceptable "explanation" in archaeological research (see Fogelin 2007 for a recent analysis). "Explanation" can mean a description or an accounting of events. Additionally, "explanation" can incorporate prediction (Trigger 1989). A predictive explanation accounts not only for past events but also for future events if all the appropriate conditions are met. This latter interpretation derives from the deductive-nomological enterprise Hempel described (the covering-law model of explanation; Hempel 1942) that was adopted by many archaeologists beginning in the 1960s (e.g., Watson et al. 1984), such that "explanation means implicitly or explicitly showing how particular events and processes are covered by general theories and laws" (Trigger 1989:275).

As the emphasis on different explanatory modes has shifted in archaeology, so has the approach to culture change. Accordingly, for many archaeologists in the 1960s and 1970s, explanation in terms of culture change involved understanding internal mechanisms leading to cultural evolution. These mechanisms were to be understood by uncovering the regularities and universal laws that shaped human behavior.

In turn, the status of migration studies has depended heavily on whether or not the discipline demands specific or universal explanations for culture change. When the discipline's scale of inquiry has been on the particular and the contingent, or "historical," explanation, archaeologists initiate migration studies. Conversely, when the discipline has been primarily concerned with universal explanation, in particular the Hempelian covering-law model of universal explanation, migration studies have suffered.

Below, I explore the changes over time in the popularity of migration as an explanation in archaeology within the discipline's broad ideological movements of the twentieth and twenty-first centuries. These range from culture historical to processual and postprocessual archaeologies, which I review in chronological order of initial appearance. These do not characterize all of North American archaeology, and they are not mutually exclusive; variants of culture history and processualism continue to be practiced in today's postprocessual climate. The intention of this structure is to provide a convenient frame for discussing migration theory in Western archaeology.

The Culture Historical Approach in Archaeology

In the culture-historical approach of the early twentieth century, migrationist explanations dominated historical reconstructions. This is in large part because culture historians inherited a worldview that assumed that migrations were part of history. As Adams (1978:1) states, "migration theory is as old and as widespread as tribal mythology."

In general, culture historians envisioned human history as constructed through the ebb and flow of populations and their associated ideas and cultures through diffusion, migration, invasion, and conquest. Culture historians who took part in nationalist agendas (Trigger 1989) traced the ancestries of modern populations through their movements to legitimize the claims of contemporary populations and their institutions. Historical reconstruction involved the archaeological documentation of population movement (migration) as well as the movement of ideas (diffusion).

Accordingly, culture historians assigned archaeological sites to cultures, races, and ethnic groups, often within nationalist agendas. They did this by following a chain of assumptions: first, that artifact assemblages were proxies for archaeological "culture groups"; and second, that these culture groups were "the material expressions" of real cultures and ethnicities. Another way to phrase this is artifact assemblage = culture = people. This simple equation allowed culture historians to reconstruct which peoples were where when and what happened to them over time (e.g., Childe 1925, 1950; Clark 1970; Lamb 1958; Parker 1916; Steward 1940).

Culture historians invoked migration freely and interchangeably with material culture change. Yet neither migration nor change was an object of inquiry for culture historians. Instead, change and the mechanisms producing change—such as migration, diffusion, and innovation—were implicit in the definition of these terms. The task of the archaeologist, especially beginning in the twentieth century, was to distinguish between migration and diffusion when faced with material culture change. Thus, migrationist explanations were situational because they were invoked on a case-by-case basis. At the same time, culture historians applied migration to so many cases that migration became a universal explanation for change, despite the fact that it was never formally proclaimed as such. This monolith of migrationist "explanations" was subsequently challenged by processual archaeologists.

In the upcoming set of discussions I follow Kosso (1991) in treating Lewis Binford and Ian Hodder as symbolic representatives of the New Archaeology and postprocessual schools. Note that while these are now considered to be synonymous, postprocessualism is a much broader category that accommodates a variety of poststructuralist, neo- or post-Marxist, and postmodern approaches as well as Hodder's contextual (later "interpretive") versions.

The New Archaeology

Migration studies floundered in the 1960s and 1970s, during the time when the New Archaeology (Caldwell 1959) dominated North American archaeological thought most strongly. During the early New Archaeology (later termed processual archaeology) period, the issue that migration once explained—change—became the new object of inquiry. It was hoped that once the mechanisms of change became clear, these would fill the explanatory void that migration once occupied and more—that they would provide insights into general trends or even universal explanations.

Binford, a dominant proponent of the New Archaeology paradigm, often stated that the goal of archaeology was to study "problems dealing with cultural evolution or systemic change" (1972 [1962]:31). As a neo-evolutionist, Binford believed that human culture and human behavior consisted of regularities that were the result of internal processes such as adaptation (Trigger 1989). In turn, regularities that were hypothesized be consistent through time and space either confirmed or were themselves candidates for law-like, universal explanations. Archaeologists at this time sought a concept or concepts that could give the discipline much of what the concept of natural selection gave the natural sciences; that is, one or a few universal processes underlying cultural change and fueling cultural evolution.

Early processual archaeologists viewed migration as no more than a descriptor of historical events and not as a mechanism that "explained" these events. In contrast, culture historians evoked migration on an ad hoc basis (Adams et al. 1978) to identify traditions and chart their movements in time and space, thus describing the course of specific events. Many New Archaeologists instead sought explanations that were predictive and therefore universal. Referencing migrationist explanations in archaeology, Binford states:

> Specific "historical" explanations . . . simply explicate mechanisms of culture process. They add nothing to the explanation of the processes of culture change and evolution. If migrations can be shown to have taken place, then this explication presents an explanatory problem; what adaptive circumstances, evolutionary processes, induced the migration? (1972 [1962]: 22)

Here Binford downgrades "historical" explanations (statements about specific events) and emphasizes internal "adaptive" and "evolutionary" explanations (predictive statements); migration falls into the former category of explanation. Because migration was so closely tied to the culture-historical approach to explanation, it was ignored in subsequent processualist studies of culture change (Adams et al. 1978; Anthony 1990).

This raises the question of why processualists did not simply adapt the concept of migration into a predictive explanation of culture change. One possible answer could be found in the processualist emphasis on studying bounded systems. A systems approach reinforced the idea that explanation had to be predictive. Systemic approaches in archaeology were tied to the Hempelian philosophy of science that emphasized generalized law-like or universal statements. As a general approach, these "covering laws" emphasized the dependence of hypotheses upon universal statements so that any explanatory hypothesis would ultimately refer to universal statements and have a predictive quality. As already discussed, migration, which at that time was considered to be a historical event, was not considered to be suitable for such explanations. Second, in order to be an analytically and scientifically powerful explanatory tool (in the predictive sense), the systems approach kept its focus on the inner workings of systems (Trigger 1989). Migration, on the other hand, was seen as external to the system being studied, although "external" is merely a scalar issue since system boundaries are often arbitrary (Anthony 1990; Cameron 1995).

The approach allowed for human behavior, including human culture, to be analytically modeled as internally coherent systems that interact with other systems. These other systems can consist of both cultural and noncultural phenomena, such as other cultural groups, environmental zones, or trade networks (Flannery 1967). Most important, for a systems model to provide testable hypotheses, systems must assume self-regulation. Self-regulation in a systemic context assumes that systems usually respond to minor variations in one or more of the systems articulating with it through equilibrating mechanisms. Assuming self-regulation, if the system is always confronted with the same input, it will regulate itself in the same way each time. In other words, explanation in a systemic context is predictive as well as descriptive.

A systemic view of how change took place excluded migration except as an occasional possibility. Change was fundamentally internal: change within systems could be induced by external stimuli, or "perturbations," but the genesis of change came from within the system. Cultural systems most often reacted to perturbations by maintaining an overall steady state (Trigger 1989). Occasionally, systems responded in a "deviation-amplifying" way, meaning that changes in one part of the system resulted in more changes so that the system moved farther away from its original state (Maruyama 1963). Herein lies the possibility for cultural evolution. Focusing on the internal dynamics of systems meant that processualists looked for regularities (or patterns) in the *mechanisms* of change rather than in the ultimate *effects* of change. Migration, from a systems perspective, is an external disruptive force that is not predictable from within a system. Therefore migration was not amenable to a systems approach.

Some processual archaeologists rejected migration as an explanation for culture change (e.g., Chapman 1997) or simply ignored it (e.g., Renfrew 1987). Certainly processualists did not consider migration to be worthy of study. As mentioned above, migration was such an integral part of culture historical "explanation" that migration studies became discredited along with the entire approach. Others add that these migrationist explanations proved equivocal at best (Chapman 1997; Renfrew 1987; Rouse 1986). Finally, from an internal and systemic point of view, migration could not regularly predict culture change and therefore could not fulfill the demanded role of general explanation.

Postprocessual Archaeology

Beginning in the 1980s, archaeologists—particularly postprocessualists— rarely concerned themselves with migration per se. Nevertheless, postprocessualism dramatically affected migration studies simply by critically questioning the evolutionary and functionalist assumptions underlying processualism.

Postprocessualists challenge processualism's conviction that archaeological knowledge consists of universal laws and general processes (Shanks and Tilley 1987). They argue that there is more to human behavior than causal relationships and that the neo-evolutionary approach to culture and society is flawed. In this light, universal explanations, as inevitable cause-effect relationships, are too limiting. Instead, explanation can be situational. In the late 1980s, Hodder referred to this as "historical explanation," which tries to "limit the dependence on general statements" (1987:1). In the 1990s, Hodder developed this further as "interpretation" (Hodder 1991, 1999), an approach that involved a greater emphasis on "discerning whether a particular case *is* an instance of a general pattern" and on "re-interpreting general understanding in a specific context" (Hodder 1999:70). The overall effect of postprocessual critique on migration studies has been to free migration from the crushing responsibility of providing a universal mechanism of change; instead, migration once again can be applied on a case-by-case basis.

The advent of postprocessual archaeology has also inadvertently nurtured migration studies through its insistence on its own diversity: "Unlike processual archaeology, [post-processual archaeology] does not espouse one approach or argue that archaeology should develop an agreed-upon methodology. This is why post-processual archaeology is simply 'post-.' . . . It involves diversity and lack of consensus" (Hodder 1986:170). Nevertheless, it does pursue some common themes (meaning, agency, history, multivocality, to name a few). Additionally, there is room for multiple levels and scales of explanation in modern archaeological studies, in that it "does not oppose such [historical] description to explanation and general theory" (Hodder 1987:2). Thus, recent migration studies have experienced postprocessual critique (e.g., Champion 1990; Chapman and Hamerow 1997) and processual reevaluation (e.g., Anthony 1990; Cameron 1995; Clark 2001) or some combination of both, which Hegmon (2003) terms "processual plus" (e.g., Bernardini 2005; Burmeister 2000).

In sum, migration's tie to culture change has affected the popularity and rigor of migration studies in archaeological explanation. Early in the twentieth century, migration was assumed to produce historical change. During the New Archaeology of the 1960s and 1970s, only studies that seemed to lead directly or indirectly to general explanations of culture process were considered; migration was ignored. In spite of this dismissal, the New Archaeology laid the foundation for future migration studies after the 1970s.

Processual studies of migration are presently flourishing in today's postprocessual, diversified, and multivocal climate. David Anthony's high-impact paper "Migration in Archaeology: The Baby and the Bathwater" (1990) broke the ice. Anthony insisted that although migration may be a complex phenomenon, it is a structured process with predictable motivations and therefore a tractable field of study. Several recent migration studies use processual methods in an attempt to identify migration indirectly by identifying migrants through their material idiosyncracies (Clark 2001; Lyons 2003). Most recently, archaeologists have been incorporating theoretical approaches to social identity into migration studies (Bernardini 2005; Burmeister 2000; Duff 2002; Neuzil 2008).

Despite recent advances, migration studies continue to be hampered by their historical attachment to explaining culture change. For better or for worse, archaeologists have tended to be interested in migration only if it could explain culture change. A presumed tie between migration and culture change is usually the default starting point for archaeological migration studies. This means that we assume what migration is and that whatever migration is, it leads to culture change. Moreover, we assume to know the *nature* of the relationships among migration, material remains, and the archaeological record. In reality, however, we do not know that any of these relationships exist.

The lack of an explicit definition of migration perpetuates this chain of assumptions. If the only goal of migration studies is to explain culture change, then we lose our ability to both understand migration for its own sake and track other potentially interesting archaeological associations with migration, such as urbanization, industrialization, agricultural strategies, family structure, gender roles, and ideology (Anthony 1990).

Migration is not well understood, yet archaeologists in increasing numbers are reconsidering migration in their explanations of culture change. But what is "migration"? Much of the time, either migration is not defined and implicitly assumed to cause culture change or it is defined in such a way as to maximize the likelihood that migration explains culture change in the desired archaeological context. Early in the history of archaeological research, Rouse's (1986) definition of migration as essentially population replacement reflected a general consensus. More recently, with few exceptions, the term migration subsumes multiple forms of population movement (Champion 1990; Kristiansen 1989) in the hope that at least one of those potential forms leads to culture change. If migration indeed includes multiple processes, then the effects of these processes as detected archaeologically will be confounded, making any claim to an explanation of culture change suspect.

Why Culture Change?

So far this chapter has developed the idea that identification of migration is seen as an end rather than a means of identifying change in prehistory. It is clear that archaeologists have placed a research premium on culture change. Why is that? More specifically, why do we conduct our analyses of prehistory in terms of change? Silliman (2005, 2009) suggests that this focus on change (and its presumed converse, continuity) arises from the acculturation models that have informed North American archaeology from its inception, the core ideas of which we retain. Acculturation models tend to view cultures as distinct, bounded units (see Bernardini, this volume) that either donate or receive cultural traits but do not do both. In this view, a predefined culture will change (or not) as a result of contact with another culture. Often, the arrival of the contacting culture is hypothesized as a migration.

In many ways this lens on the past is convenient for the practice of archaeology. North American archaeologists are trained to look for changes in material culture traits (e.g., pottery styles, point types, architectural features). These documented changes allow us to characterize a site diachronically, over the long term. If the changes seem abrupt enough, we may then hypothesize that a migration caused them. In many cases, we see cultures as bounded units moving from point A to point B, from time X over to time Y, and movement as producing significant material (and probably biological and linguistic) changes in the receiving area B. If we follow this recipe of archaeological explanation, then the project of historical reconstruction becomes relatively easy.

This recipe has been changing somewhat. Among archaeologists of the U.S. Southwest in particular, migration is no longer viewed as population replacement but as population mixing (see Clark, this volume): "cultures" break up during large migration processes with myriad small migrant units moving to multiple destinations, generating numerous co-residence contexts with local groups. This mixing brings socially distant groups into close proximity, requiring new social institutions that are more encompassing (either consensual or hierarchical/coercive) in order to form viable communities (Crown 1994; Clark 2001; Lyons 2003; Neuzil 2008). In this light, the "new" migration is almost an evolutionary force that leads to either increasing complexity or collapse. Even now, though archaeologists see migration in very different light than they did 50 years ago, it is very much viewed as an agent of change.

But what if, following Silliman (2005), we conceptualize change and continuity as the *same* process? Doing so would suggest a radical reconception of the past: instead of a past as peopled by essentialized identities (e.g., "the Anasazi") or impersonal migrant units, imagine it filled with actors "strategically surviving," acting in ways to maintain, mobilize, or entrench rather than "acculturate" to incoming cultures. Historical reconstruction would then become an extremely difficult task. Additionally, the normative practice of archaeology would have to be reconfigured: what do we look for when we excavate a site? How do we characterize it in our site reports and research projects? Clearly, if we assess our assumptions concerning the concepts of "culture change" and "migration" as well as the presumed relationship between these two ideas, archaeological anthropology has a lot to lose—yet we cannot afford not to reevaluate.

Conclusions

I have advanced the general argument that within the anthropological discipline, our historical bias toward explanation of change, particularly cultural change, has severely limited prehistoric migration studies. Although I paint a picture of a field of study that is hampered by dated disciplinary concerns, the landscape of possibilities within migration studies is rapidly changing as anthropologists embrace new methodologies, technological innovations, and conceptual foci (as this volume attests). Nevertheless, we presently lack an integrated theory of migration that is able to address issues of biological, linguistic, and/or (material) cultural change and move beyond these issues.

While it is true that multiple researchers have often come together to contribute ideas, resulting in compendium volumes that tackle migration from archaeological, biological, and linguistic perspectives (for recent examples, see Bellwood and Renfrew 2003; Friedlaender 2007; Jablonski 2002; Pawley et al. 2005; Renfrew and Boyle 2001; Sagart et al. 2005), more often than not the results of such endeavors are at best equivocal. For any particular area or time period, researchers cannot reach a consensus when documentary evidence is lacking. Nevertheless, such multidisciplinary efforts continue and are inspired by the scientific ideal of converging lines of evidence (see Rouse 1958): if enough sources of evidence point to the same thing—in this case, migration— then we have confirmed a hypothesis. Yet we have not reached agreement as to what would constitute evidence given the question or why we might or might not expect any particular line of evidence to converge and in what way. Hence, we have a need for migration theory or theories in anthropology, particularly for investigations into the past. Rather than a *multidisciplinary approach*, what is needed is a true *interdisciplinary approach* in which teams of researchers are equally invested partners in investigating and elucidating past migrations and their causes, consequences, and correlations.

References

Adams, W. Y.

1968   Invasion, Diffusion, Evolution? *Antiquity* 42:194–215.

1978   On Migration and Diffusion as Rival Paradigms. In *Diffusion and Migration: Their Roles in Cultural Development. Proceedings of the Tenth Annual Chacmool Conference*, edited by P. G. Duke, J. Ebert, G. Langemann, and A. P. Buchner, pp. 1–5. University of Calgary Archaeological Association, Calgary, Canada.

Adams, W. Y., D. P. Van Gerven, and R. S. Levy
1978   The Retreat from Migrationism. *Annual Review of Anthropology* 7:483–532.
Anthony, D. W.
1990   Migration in Archaeology: The Baby and the Bathwater. *American Anthropologist* 92:895–914.
Bellwood, P., and C. Renfrew (editors)
2003   *Examining the Farming/Language Dispersal Hypothesis.* Cambridge University Press, Cambridge, Mass.
Bernardini, W.
2005   *Hopi Oral Tradition and the Archaeology of Identity.* University of Arizona Press, Tucson.
Binford, L. R.
1972 [1962]   Archaeology as Anthropology. In *An Archaeological Perspective*, edited by L. R. Binford, pp. 20–32. Seminar Press, New York.
1972 [1965]   Archaeological Systematics and the Study of Culture Process. In *An Archaeological Perspective,* edited by L. R. Binford, pp. 195–207. Seminar Press, New York.
1972 [1971]   Mortuary Practices: Their Study and Their Potential. In *An Archaeological Perspective*, edited by L. R. Binford, pp. 208–243. Seminar Press, New York.
Burmeister, S.
2000   Archaeology and Migration. *Current Anthropology* 41(4):539–567.
Caldwell, J. R.
1959   The New American Archaeology. *Science* 129(3345):303–307.
Cameron, C. M.
1995   Migration and the Movement of Southwestern Peoples. *Journal of Anthropological Archaeology* 14:104–124.
Champion, T.
1990   Migration Revived. *Journal of Danish Archaeology* 9:214–218.
Chapman, J.
1997   The Impact of Modern Invasions and Migrations on Archaeological Explanation. *British Archaeological Reports International Series* 664:11–20.
Chapman, J., and H. Hamerow (editors)
1997   *Migrations and Invasions in Archaeological Explanation.* British Archaeological Reports International Series 664.
Childe, V. G.
1925   *The Dawn of European Civilization.* Kegan Paul, London.
1950   *Prehistoric Migrations in Europe.* Instituttet for Sammenlignende. Kulturforskning (Oslo), Ser. A: Forelesninger 20.
Clark, J. D.
1970   *The Prehistory of Africa.* Praeger, New York.
Clark, J. J.
2001   *Tracking Prehistoric Migrations: Pueblo Settlers among the Tonto Basin Hohokam.* Anthropological Papers of the University of Arizona, Number 65. University of Arizona Press, Tucson.

Crown, P.

1994   *Ceramics and Ideology: Salado Polychrome Pottery*. University of New Mexico Press, Albuquerque.

Duff, A.

2002   *Western Pueblo Identities: Regional Interaction, Migration, and Transformation*. University of Arizona Press, Tucson.

Flannery, K. V.

1967   Culture History v. Cultural Process: A Debate in American Archaeology. *Scientific American* 217(2):119–121.

Fogelin, L.

2007   Inference to the Best Explanation: A Common and Effective Form of Archaeological Reasoning. *American Antiquity* 72(4):603–625.

Friedlaender, J. S. (editor)

2007   *Genes, Language, & Culture History in the Southwest Pacific*. Oxford University Press, New York.

Hegmon, M.

2003   Setting Theoretical Egos Aside: Issues and Theory in North American Archaeology. *American Antiquity* 68(2):213–243.

Hempel, C. G.

1942   The Function of General Laws in History. *The Journal of Philosophy* 39:35–48.

Hodder, I.

1986   *Reading the Past*. 2nd ed. Cambridge University Press, Cambridge.

1987   The Contribution of the Long Term. In *Archaeology as Long-Term History*, edited by I. Hodder, pp. 1–8. Cambridge University Press, Cambridge.

1991   Interpretive Archaeology and Its Role. *American Antiquity* 56(1):7–18.

1999   *The Archaeological Process: An Introduction*. Blackwell Publishers, Oxford, England.

Jablonski, N. (editor)

2002   *First Americans: The Pleistocene Colonization of the New World*. University of California Press, Berkeley.

Kosso, P.

1991   Method in Archaeology: Middle-Range Theory as Hermeneutics. *American Antiquity* 56(4):621–627.

Kristiansen, K.

1989   Prehistoric Migrations: The Case of the Single Grave and Corded Ware Cultures. *Journal of Danish Archaeology* 8:211–225.

Lamb, S. M.

1958   Linguistic Prehistory in the Great Basin. *International Journal of American Linguistics* 24(2):95–100.

Lyons, P. D.

2003   *Ancestral Hopi Migrations*. University of Arizona Press, Tucson.

Maruyama, M.

1963   The Second Cybernetics: Deviation-Amplifying Mutual Causal Processes. *American Scientist* 51:164–179.

Neuzil, A.

2008 *In the Aftermath of Migration: Renegotiating Ancient Identity in Southeastern Arizona*. Anthropological Papers No. 73. University of Arizona Press, Tucson.

Parker, A. C.

1916 The Origin of the Iroquois as Suggested by Their Archaeology. *American Anthropologist* 18:479–507.

Pawley, A., R. Attenborough, J. Golson, and R. Hide (editors)

2005 *Papuan Pasts: Cultural, Linguistic and Biological Histories of Papuan-Speaking Peoples*. Pacific Linguistics, Canberra, Australia.

Renfrew, C.

1987 *Archaeology and Language: The Puzzle of Indo-European Origins*. Cambridge University Press, Cambridge.

Renfrew, C., and K. Boyle (editors)

2001 *Archaeogenetics: DNA and the Population Prehistory of Europe*. McDonald Institute, Cambridge, UK.

Rouse, I.

1986 *Migrations in Prehistory: Inferring Population Movement from Cultural Remains*. Yale University Press, New Haven, Conn.

Rouse, I. (editor)

1958 *The Inference of Migrations from Anthropological Evidence*. University of Arizona Bulletin 29. University of Arizona Press, Tucson.

Sagart, L., R. Blench, and A. Sanchez-Mazas (editors)

2005 *The Peopling of East Asia: Putting Together Archaeology, Linguistics and Genetics*. Routledge/Curzon, New York.

Shanks, M., and C. Tilley

1987 *Reconstructing Archaeology*. Cambridge University Press, Cambridge.

Silliman, S. W.

2005 Culture Contact or Colonialism? Challenges in the Archaeology of Native North America. *American Antiquity* 70(1):55–74.

2009 Change and Continuity, Practice and Memory: Native American Persistence in Colonial New England. *American Antiquity* 74(2):211–231.

Steward, J. H.

1940 Native Cultures of the Intermountain (Great Basin) Area. *Smithsonian Miscellaneous Collections* 100: 445–502.

Trigger, B. G.

1968 *Beyond History: The Methods of Prehistory*. Holt, Reinhart and Winston, New York.

1989 *A History of Archaeological Thought*. Cambridge University Press, Cambridge.

Watson, P. J., S. A. LeBlanc, and C. L. Redman

1984 *Archaeological Explanation. The Scientific Method in Archaeology*. Columbia University Press, New York.

II

Archaeological Approaches

2

Migration in Fluid Social Landscapes

WESLEY R. BERNARDINI

The minimal definition employed in this volume describes migration as "one-way residential location to a different 'environment.'" This definition conceptualizes migration as a transgressive phenomenon involving the crossing of social boundaries. But what if both social boundaries and the groups we envision crossing them are less discrete than we had imagined? This chapter presents a cautionary note regarding boundedness in migration studies based on ethnographic and archaeological data from the U.S. Southwest, where precontact social borders were relatively fuzzy, units of migration were small and surprisingly unstable over time, and migration consisted not of singular disruptive "events" but rather a multigenerational sequential process. These conditions characterize what I term "fluid" social landscapes, and they present an analytical and conceptual challenge to even the minimal definition of migration utilized in this volume.

Normative Models

Migration is often assumed to occur in a social landscape with firm political boundaries and well-established ethnic identities. Prehistoric populations are understood to have had clear notions of "us" and "them," of a homeland and "foreign" territories. Yet many ancient landscapes were more politically and ethnically continuous than discontinuous, complicating normative views of migrating groups and the process of movement (Bernardini 2005a).

The notion that prehistoric social landscapes were divided into territorial blocks occupied by distinctive cultures has been common in both North American and European archaeology, though the origins of these normative models were slightly different. The emphasis in early European archaeology on finding ancestors of modern (state) populations and on tracing the cultural developments leading to modern ethnic/national groups led to widespread use of migration (and diffusion) as means of spreading "peoples" across the landscape. Such "wave-of-advance" models (Ammerman and Cavalli-Sforza

1984) were used to explain the spread of a material culture, the presence of which was generally assumed to mark the spread of a known group of people (Clark 1994). In North America, in contrast, the view of indigenous populations as holdovers from the Stone Age led researchers to focus on defining the geographic boundaries of these timeless cultural units (Trigger 1989). That is, Native American tribes were viewed as "social fossils" whose development had stagnated at an early stage of cultural evolution and whose cultures and territories had persisted essentially unchanged across the centuries. Nevertheless, the end result in both the Old and New Worlds was similar, in that archaeological reconstructions depicted well-bounded culture areas often assumed to be equivalent to modern tribes (Duff 2002).

In North America, then, much early twentieth-century archaeology was primarily descriptive and classificatory. In the U.S. Southwest (Figure 2.1), cultural taxonomy became not just a method but a set of assumptions about the nature and scale of human social organization as behavioral characteristics (common language, ideology, esprit de corps) were assigned to the populations of culture areas. Duff (2000, 2002) has charted the development of taxonomic concepts in the American Southwest, demonstrating that although researchers who first defined culture areas rarely made explicit statements about economic, social, or political integration of the populations living within them, subsequent researchers often assumed that a culture area was the prehistoric equivalent of a tribe. In a landscape partitioned by quasi-tribal boundaries (e.g., "Anasazi"[1] or "Mogollon"), migration was conceptualized primarily as the movement from one culture area to another. The discovery of apparently intrusive "Anasazi" settlements in central Arizona (e.g., Haury 1958) provided support for this view.

Culture areas were an important heuristic early archaeologists of the Southwest developed for establishing order in an ancient landscape about which very little was known at the time. They were not, however, explicitly designed for the purposes of investigating issues of cultural identity and population movement, at least as these questions are posed today. Assumptions about clear social boundaries between populations with deep historical roots are increasingly in conflict with data that demonstrates the fluidity of the prehistoric southwestern social landscape. Researchers have found, for example, that site-unit intrusions such as the classic example described by Haury (1958) were the exception rather than the rule in the long history of southwestern population movements (Cordell 1995). Much more common was the incremental movement of smaller groups of immigrants who did not express their identity in overt material culture at their destinations (Adams 1996; Cameron 1995; Dean 1970; Kintigh 1996; Lipe 1995; Marshall and Walt 1984; Reid 1989;

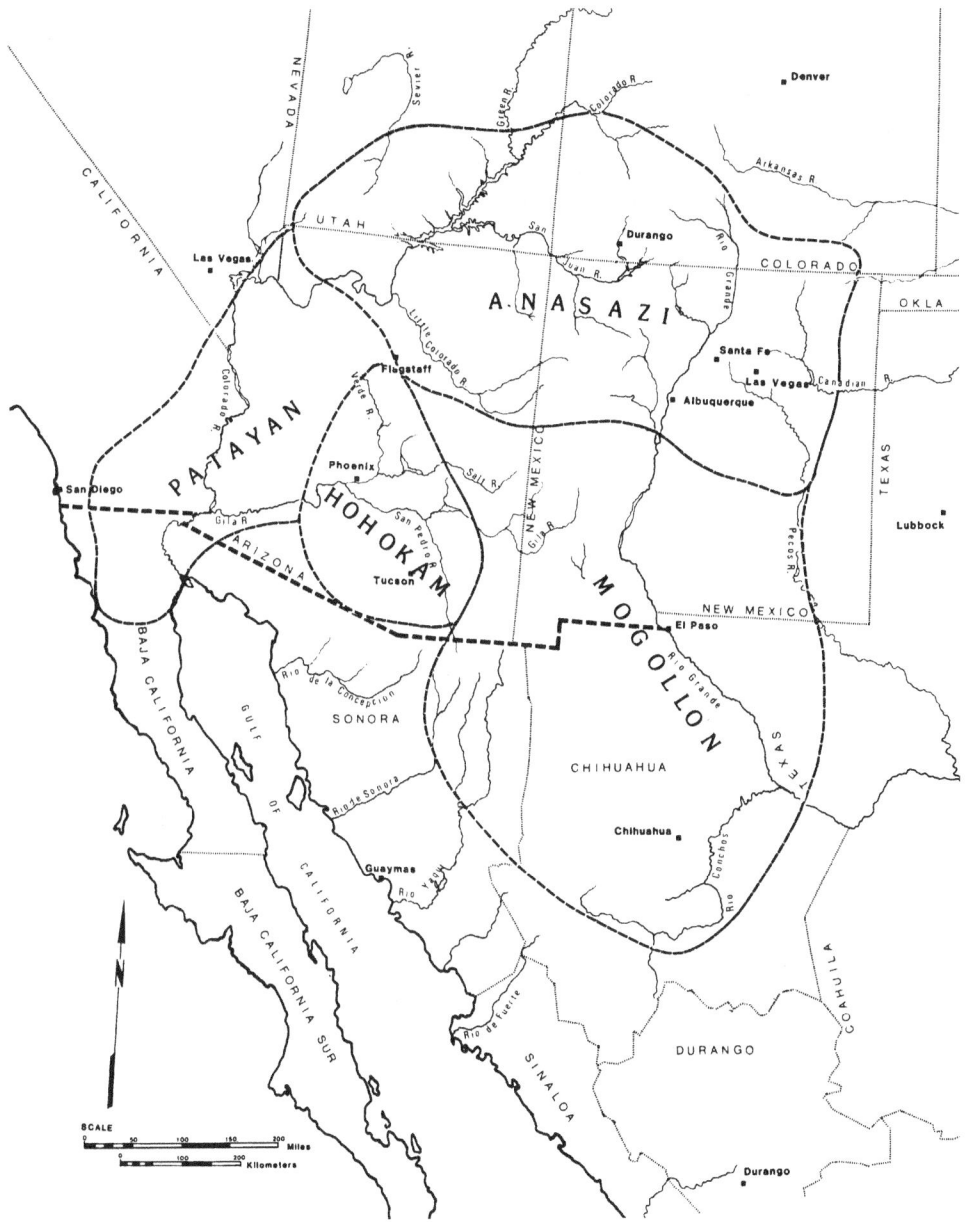

Figure 2.1. Major culture areas of the American Southwest, ca. A.D. 1000–1300 (after Cordell 1984:Figure 1.5).

Zedeño 1994), at least not for more than a few years after migration (Hegmon 1998).

Taking culture areas as the de facto groupings for addressing questions about prehistoric social behavior also fails to capture the multiple, even overlapping scales at which identity and group membership operate. The culture area approach cannot, for example, capture the nested nature of identity expressed by a member of the Hopi tribe who described himself as a Parrot Clan member first, a member of his village second, and then a Hopi (Whiteley 1988). Nor are culture areas well suited for describing the history of an individual whose multigenerational migration history placed his ancestors within the boundaries of several culture areas at different points in time, giving him ties to multiple antecedent groups (Dongoske et al. 1997; Moore 2001).

Demography

Southwestern archaeologists have long noted the demographic instability of Puebloan populations. More than 70 years ago, Gladwin and Gladwin commented that "the fundamental character of a nomadic people is shown repeatedly in the willingness of the Basketmakers and the Pueblos to abandon their homes on the slightest pretext. The region where they lived is pock-marked with ruins, many of which could have been occupied for only a few years, and it is rare to find a site which will yield evidence of successive occupations" (1935:276).

The Gladwins' impression of "short-term sedentism" (Nelson and LeBlanc 1986) is well supported by chronological data from village sites. For example, tree-ring records from 119 well-dated archaeological sites in Arizona and New Mexico[2] (Hantman 1983) indicate a median site occupation length of just 50 years. There is only a weak relationship in these data between site size (number of rooms) and occupation length (Pearson's $r = .40$, $r^2 = .16$), revealing that both large and small sites often had short occupations spans. Close examination of well-documented growth patterns of large villages reveals that already short occupation spans were often bookended by periods of growth and decline, leaving relatively few years of stable peak population levels (Bernardini 2005a). Thus, it was typical for ancestral Puebloans to spend no more than a single generation at a given village.

A review of U.S. southwestern demographic patterns in late prehistory (ca. A.D. 1250–1450) identified only two regions—Hopi and Zuni—with large concentrated populations that exhibited internally focused interactions (that is, with relatively few imports) (Duff 2002) (Figure 2.2). The combined population of the remaining six regions outside Hopi and Zuni was less than either

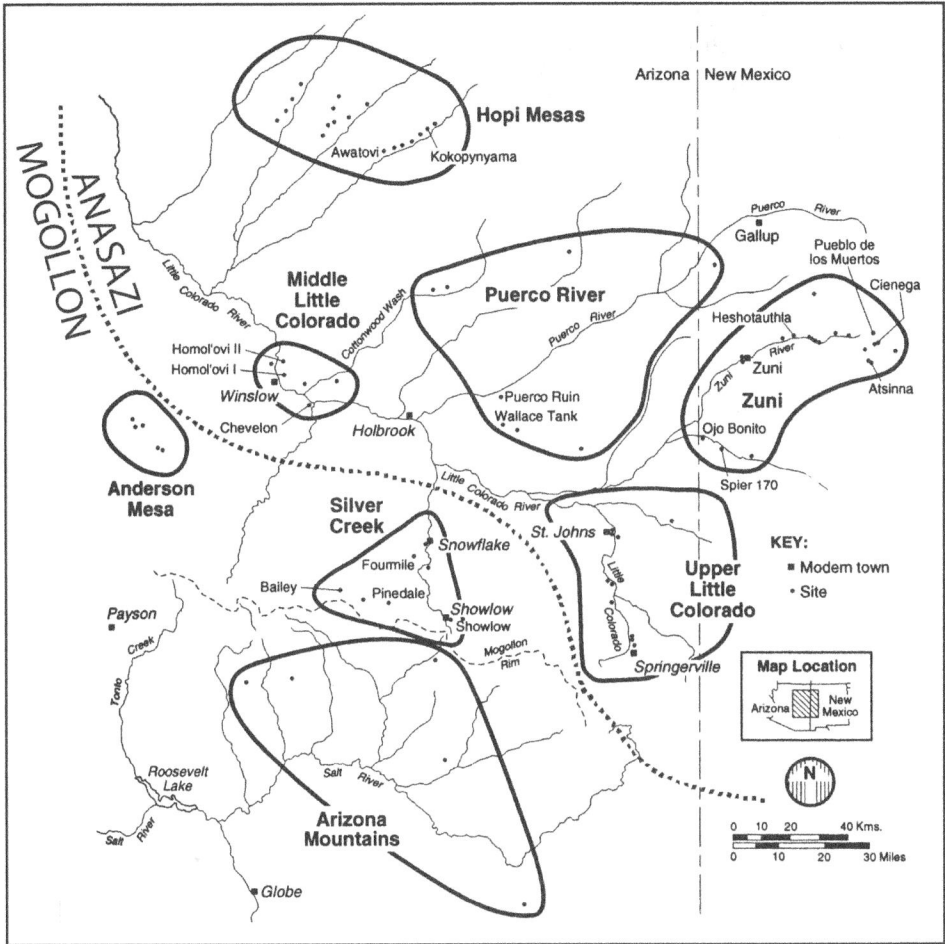

Figure 2.2. Regions of the Western Pueblo area of the American Southwest, ca. A.D. 1250–1400 (after Duff 2002:Figure 4.3).

Zuni or Hopi alone and occupied an area seven to ten times the size of either group (Duff 2002). Duff questions whether regions outside Hopi and Zuni contained sufficient population to sustain internally focused interactions and suggests that "we should consider [these regions] a single interaction sphere characterized by crosscutting relationships among distant sites" (2002:44). Thus, only a distinct minority of southwestern regions appear to conform to "idealized notions of material and social coherence" (Duff 2002:43).

In a complementary analysis, Schachner (2007) emphasizes the role of "population circulation"—frequent movements that were small in scale (both socially and geographically) within and between regions (see Chapman and Prothero 1985; Prothero and Chapman 1984)—in the apparent "fuzziness" of both social groups and social boundaries evident in some landscapes. Ethnographic studies reveal that societies with high rates of population circulation are characterized by social fluidity in residence, group membership, and leadership and by language and traditions permeated by themes of mobility (Chapman and Prothero 1985). Schachner's case study of the Zuni region reveals that even in this relatively dense area there was considerable fluidity of population (with most pueblos, even large aggregates, occupied for less than 25 years) and few stable boundaries. Schachner argues that "frequent population circulation actively undermines many of the defining characteristics of archaeological definitions of community, including stable, well-defined membership, territorial control, shared identity, internally focused social ties, and permanence. At a fundamental level, studies of population circulation also question whether social phenomena equivalent to what archaeologists commonly term communities necessarily existed" (2007:30).

In light of these studies, the culture area concept may be a problematic heuristic device for modeling identity and movement in the American Southwest and perhaps in middle-range societies elsewhere. This model assumes that interaction is concentrated within a culture area, producing a zone of relative cultural homogeneity (the existence of which then creates boundaries that help clarify and perpetuate differences among the residents of different culture areas). Frequent movements by small social groups that crosscut culture area boundaries, however, would inhibit the long-term development of stable regional identities implied by the culture area model. Landscapes in perpetual demographic flux must have been characterized by different units and processes.

Units of Migration

If culture areas and social boundaries are somewhat suspect in the American Southwest, what of the migrating groups themselves? If the culture areas of earlier research are unreliable units of identity, can we instead trace migrating groups themselves across space and time? A close look at archaeological data, oral tradition, and ethnographic data suggest that the answer is yes but that the process by which migrating groups reproduced themselves over time is more complex than it first appears.

Southwestern archaeologists have used the fine-grained architectural and chronological record of Pueblo ruins to reconstruct ancient migrating units in some detail (e.g., Clark 2001; Lyons 2003). Most studies have concluded that the household or small multihousehold groups were the most common migrating unit in Pueblo prehistory (Adams 1996; Dean 1970; Duff 1998; Lipe 1995; Kintigh 1996; Reid 1989), though some regions feature notable movements by communities (e.g., Adams 2004; Kintigh 1985).

Some archaeologists (e.g., Bernardini 2005b; Lyons 2003) have found it productive to consider migration as it is recounted in Native American oral traditions, seeing in this resource a potential model for the migration process. The migration traditions of the Hopi tribe, for example, feature small multi-household groups called clans, which function as the primary decision-making and migrating unit. The migration pathways described in clan migration traditions were complex, overlapping, and irregular because clans regularly fissioned and fused. Cosmos Mindeleff described clan migrations as "a little trickling stream of humanity, or rather many such streams, like little rivulets after a rain storm, moving here and there as the occurrence of areas of cultivable land dictated, sometimes combining, then separating, but finally collecting to form the pueblo groups as we now know them" (1900:645). Movement was frequent in this migration period, often occurring on a subgenerational frequency (Bernardini 2005a; Parsons 1939). A tradition of movement remains deeply ingrained in Pueblo thought (Naranjo 1995), which conceptualizes life as a journey on a road (echoing the characteristics of societies with high levels of population circulation noted above) (Parsons 1939). In fact, the Hopi conceptualize ancestral territories in ways similar to those of hunter-gatherer groups, as linear pathways of travel rather than as two-dimensional geographical blocks (Bernardini 2005a, 2005b; cf., Ingold 1980). Elsewhere (Bernardini 2005b) I have coined the term "serial migration" to describe this process of regular small-scale movement.

Debate rages over the historical validity of the particulars of oral traditions (e.g., Echo-Hawk 2000; Mason 2000, 2006; Whiteley 2002), but for present purposes we may concern ourselves with whether the *process* of migration as described in Hopi clan traditions provides a useful model for ancient population movements. The clan model of migration offers some clear benefits over the culture area approach in that it features small decision-making groups that appear to correlate with the scale of decision-making evident in the archaeological record. The fact that oral traditions discuss the fissioning and fusing of clans also encourages us to think about migrating groups as dynamic entities rather than as static units that persist through generations.

Yet a closer look at ethnographic data suggests that Hopi clans are even more dynamic than once suspected, and this dynamism provides important hints about how identity is produced and reproduced during the migration process.

The Reproduction of Hopi Clans

Hopi oral traditions describe the clan as the decision-making and migration unit. But contemporary Hopi clans are unilineal exogamous descent groups that cannot move as units, since they are bound to other descent groups through marriage (e.g., Aberle 1970). Further, it seems unlikely that consanguineal units on the order of a few dozen people could have survived the whims of fertility and mortality for the 800-plus years covered by clan migration traditions (e.g., Gaines and Gaines 1997). As Whiteley (1985, 1986) has shown, however, clans are not corporate groups united in their control of land and ceremony. Rather, a clan consists of a core household surrounded by a number of other household groups in an "orbital" arrangement of dependence and support (Connelly 1979). Offices and privileges are thus held "not in the clan as a whole, but in a maternal family or lineage in the clan" (Parsons 1933:23). These "core households" of clans are distinguished primarily through their control of ceremonial objects (*wiimi*) used in the clan's proprietary ceremony, most important of which is the "fetish," or badge of office (Parsons 1969). It is possession of the fetish that legitimizes control of a ritual by the core segment of a village clan. Thus, clan mothers are important "not because they perpetuate the clan but because in their houses they look after the fetishes of the ceremonies" (Parsons 1936:231).

The reproduction of Hopi clans is complicated by the fact that although inheritance of the *wiimi* ideally remains within the genealogical line of the core household, the *wiimi* can and does pass out of the controlling household without losing legitimacy in the eyes of the community, for it is the object that conveys authenticity upon the group, not the reverse. In fact, there are no actual totems of Hopi clans (e.g., a crane figurine for the Crane Clan) "because the fetish is primarily associated with the ceremony and only derivatively with the clan" (Parsons 1936:231). Possession of the clan fetish is so critical to the performance of ceremony and therefore to the existence and identity of the clan that the "tradition of provenience accompanies the *wiimi* and *is more reliable than tradition of clan provenience or origin*" (Parsons 1939:970, emphasis added). Thus, "when a Hopi refers to migration of clan he is really referring to a migration by a fetish-holding maternal family" (Parsons 1922:289, 1933:37).

Orientation of a descent group around durable objects linked to the performance of public ritual provided a social identity that could be readily transferred as communities formed, dissolved, and reformed (Bernardini 2008). The prehistoric social landscape was thus populated by durable fetishes and ceremonies that were owned by descent groups with fluctuating composition, size, rules of membership, symbolic affiliation, and relationships to other descent groups. Thus, for example, the fetish-holding core segment of what is now known as the Snake Clan may have been known as the Lizard Clan or the Cactus Clan in the past (segments that today are considered to be "orbiting" the core Snake segment), yet the fetish and the esoteric knowledge at the core of the fetish-ceremony complex could have persisted relatively unchanged. This situation allowed the traditional knowledge held by fetish-holding groups to persist for far longer than it would have if it was transmitted genealogically.

The implications of this revised understanding of clans for reconstructions of prehistoric migration are significant. Clans must be understood to have been even smaller and even more dynamic social units than was previously recognized (e.g., Bernardini 2005a). The movement of a clan's fetish from one village to another would have been a time of considerable negotiation and reorganization as orbiting groups vied for strategic position relative to the core household. Migration events may have presented opportunities for clans to grow in size and importance in a new village or may have presented challenges from competing/redundant ceremony-controlling groups that threatened its size and prominence in a new social setting. For example, one of the events that precipitated the famous factional split of the Hopi village of Orayvi in 1906 was the arrival of 52 people from Songoopavi in the spring of that year (Whiteley 1988). The Songoopavi group allied itself with the "Hostile" faction at Orayvi and attempted, unsuccessfully, to overthrow the existing Bear Clan chief before the entire Hostile contingent was expelled from the village. The Hostile challenge at Orayvi included the staging of parallel ceremonial performances, each claiming exclusive legitimacy (Titiev 1944; Whiteley 1988).

Conclusions

The fluid social landscapes described in this study complicate attempts to draw normative culture area boundaries comprising populations with similar identities stemming from their protracted co-residence and common history. Migration in this type of landscape was not an event but an ongoing process (Duff 1998) in which *the most recent place of residence would be a relatively narrow description of a person's identity*. That is, labeling an immigrant as an "Anasazi," or a "Silver Creek" person or even a "Cottonwood Pueblo person" would be of little use in summarizing his or her identity because as little as a generation ago he, his parents, or his grandparents likely lived in a different (possibly even several different) village, region, and culture area. It is for this reason that the Hopi tribe does not find culture areas to be meaningful units of identity when tracing their history (Ferguson and Lomaomvaya 1999).

Instead, immigrants and their successive hosts and neighbors would have understood identity in terms of the small social groups through which day-to-day social and ritual status was reckoned in each village and through which a named, possibly totemic affiliation was held and transmitted.

Yet we cannot simply substitute "clans" for culture areas without critically examining clans as a social unit or we risk transferring assumptions about clear boundaries, homogenous decision-making units, and discrete social identities to a smaller social scale. Close consideration of ethnographic material reveals that Hopi clans are much less corporate than was once thought (Whiteley 1985, 1986) and that clan migration was an opportunity for renegotiating social relationships as much as it was a movement of a discrete social unit. If, however, we define clans in relation to objects linked to widely recognized rituals and ritual knowledge, it is possible to see how both social identity and social knowledge could persist across villages and generations even in the face of unstable group membership. Ideas and memories are often what move and persist in migration, more so than groups of people (Bernardini 2008).

Thus, there were at least two different kinds of migrants (or, perhaps, a continuum) in the ancestral Puebloan landscape—those with control of objects and associated knowledge that were the currency of identity and those without. The former arrived in a new location with a publicly recognized and tangible social identity. The latter—the majority of migrants—left home with a much fuzzier idea of who they would be upon arrival.

It is not hard to see that such complex processes of movement and social reproduction could have implications for studies of ancient migration. Analyses that trace movement through physical characteristics (strontium, DNA, etc.), for example, typically assume a level of coherence and intergenerational stability in migrant group membership that may not always be justified. What is more, in areas of the world without high-resolution chronological control, it may be difficult to even "see" the actual decision-making groups who migrated, given the relatively short time frames for which they persisted. Thus, analyses may group as a single unit individuals who participated in several distinct serial events or who cycled in or out of group membership over time. Reconciling variation in physical/genetic markers with instability in socially reproduced identities is a significant challenge facing migration studies.

Finally, it is important to conclude by noting that frequent movement need not come at the expense of durable cultural identities in the contemporary political landscape. In fact, for the Hopi tribe of Arizona, it is precisely the complexity and uniqueness of a clan's sequential migrations that enables this history to be used as a mnemonic for curating and legitimizing a clan's social identity. That is, the history of migration itself can serve as a form of institutional memory. Those of us studying ancient migrations must strive to accommodate both change and persistence in our reconstructions of the past.

Notes

1. Archaeologists have rightly abandoned use of the term Anasazi in favor of Ancestral Puebloan. I employ the term Anasazi here only to refer to historical usage by archaeologists.

2. The data are a subset of sites analyzed by Hantman (1983:Table 5), focusing on sites with at least ten dates, a potential cutting date, and date samples from at least two contexts. Two cave sites with long but intermittent occupations and 13 sites counted twice in the original analysis were excluded from the present study.

References

Aberle, D.
1970 Comments. In *Reconstructing Prehistoric Pueblo Societies*, edited by William Longacre, pp. 215–223. University of New Mexico Press, Albuquerque.
Adams, E. C.
1996 The Pueblo III-Pueblo IV Transition in the Hopi Area, Arizona. In *The Prehistoric Pueblo World, A.D. 1150–1350*, edited by M. A. Adler, pp. 48–58. University of Arizona Press, Tucson.
2004 Homol'ovi: A 13th–14th Century Settlement Cluster in Northeastern Arizona. In *The Protohistoric Pueblo World, A.D. 1275–1600*, edited by E. C. Adams and A. Duff, pp. 119–127. University of Arizona Press, Tucson.
Ammerman, A., and L. L. Cavalli-Sforza
1984 *The Neolithic Transition and the Genetics of Populations*. Princeton University Press, Princeton, N.J.
Bernardini, Wesley
2005a *Hopi Oral Tradition and the Archeology of Identity*. University of Arizona Press, Tucson.
2005b Reconsidering Spatial and Temporal Aspects of Prehistoric Cultural Identity: A Case Study from the American Southwest. *American Antiquity* 70(1):31–54.
2008 Identity as History: Hopi Clans and the Curation of Oral Tradition. *Journal of Anthropological Research* 64:483–509.
Cameron, C.
1995 Migration and the Movement of Southwestern Peoples. *Journal of Anthropological Archaeology* 14:104–124.
Chapman, M., and R. Prothero (editors)
1985 *Circulation in Population Movement: Substance and Concepts from the Melanesian Case*. Routledge and Kegan Paul, London.
Clark, G. A.
1994 Migration as an Explanatory Concept in Paleolithic Archaeology. *Journal of Archaeological Method and Theory* 1(4):305–342.

Clark, J. J.

2001   *Tracking Prehistoric Migrations: Pueblo Settlers among the Tonto Basin Hohokam.* University of Arizona Press, Tucson.

Connelly, J. C.

1979   Hopi Social Organization. In *Handbook of North American Indians,* vol. 9, edited by A. Ortiz, pp. 539–543. Smithsonian Institution, Washington, D.C.

Cordell, L. S.

1995   Tracing Migration Pathways from the Receiving End. *Journal of Anthropological Archaeology* 14(2):203–211.

Dean, J. S.

1970   Aspects of Tsegi Phase Social Organization. In *Reconstructing Prehistoric Pueblo Societies,* edited by W. A. Longacre, pp. 140–174. University of New Mexico Press, Albuquerque.

Dongoske, K., M. Yeatts, R. Anyon, and T. J. Ferguson

1997   Archaeological Cultures and Cultural Affiliation: Hopi and Zuni Perspectives in the American Southwest. *American Antiquity* 62(2):600–608.

Duff, A. I.

1998   The Process of Migration in the Late Prehistoric Southwest. In *Migration and Reorganization: The Pueblo IV Period in the American Southwest,* edited by K. A. Spielmann, pp. 31–52. Anthropological Research Papers 51, Arizona State University, Tempe.

2000   Scale, Interaction, and Regional Analysis in Late Pueblo Prehistory. In *The Archaeology of Regional Interaction: Religion, Warfare and Exchange Across the American Southwest and Beyond,* Proceedings of the 1996 Southwest Symposium, edited by M. Hegmon, pp. 71–98. University Press of Colorado, Boulder.

2002   *Western Pueblo Identities: Regional Interaction, Migration, and Transformation.* University of Arizona Press, Tucson.

Echo-Hawk, R. C.

2000   Questions of Evidence, Legitimacy, and the (Dis)Union of Science. *American Antiquity* 65(2):227–238.

Ferguson, T. J., and M. Lomaomvaya

1999   *Hoopoq'uaqam niqw Wukoskyavi (Those Who Went to the Northeast and to the Tonto Basin): Hopi-Salado Cultural Affiliation Study.* Hopi Cultural Preservation Office, Kykotsmovi, Arizona.

Gaines, S. W., and W. M. Gaines

1997   Simulating Success or Failure: Another Look at Small Population Dynamics. *American Antiquity* 39(2):683–697.

Gladwin, H., and W. Gladwin

1935   *The Eastern Range of the Red-on-Buff Culture.* Medallion Papers 16, Gila Pueblo, Arizona.

Hantman, J. L.

1983   *Social Networks and Stylistic Distributions in the Prehistoric Plateau Southwest.*

Unpublished Ph.D. dissertation, Department of Anthropology, Arizona State University, Tempe.

Haury, E.

1958 Evidence at Point of Pines for a Prehistoric Migration from Northern Arizona. In *Migrations in New World Culture History*, edited by R. H. Thompson, pp. 1–8. University of Arizona Press, Tucson.

Hegmon, M.

1998 Technology, Style, and Social Practices: Archaeological Approaches. In *The Archaeology of Social Boundaries*, edited by M. Stark, pp. 264–279. Smithsonian Institution Press, Washington, D.C.

Ingold, T.

1980 *Hunters, Pastoralists and Ranchers*. Cambridge University Press, Cambridge.

Kintigh, K.

1985 *Settlement, Subsistence, and Society in Late Zuni Prehistory*. Anthropological Papers of the University of Arizona no. 44, University of Arizona Press, Tucson.

1996 The Cibola Area in the Post-Chacoan Era. In *The Prehistoric Pueblo World, A.D. 1150–1350*, edited by M. Adler, pp. 131–144. University of Arizona Press, Tucson.

Lipe, W. D.

1995 The Depopulation of the Northern San Juan: Conditions in the Turbulent 1200s. *Journal of Anthropological Archaeology* 14:143–169.

Lyons, P.

2003 *Ancestral Hopi Migrations*. Anthropological Papers of the University of Arizona no. 68. University of Arizona Press, Tucson.

Marshall, M. P., and H. J. Walt

1984 *Rio Abajo, Prehistory and History of a Rio Grande Province*. New Mexico Historic Preservation Program, Historic Preservation Bureau, Santa Fe.

Mason, R.

2000 Archaeology and Native North American Oral Traditions. *American Antiquity* 65(2):239–266.

2006 *Inconstant Companions: Archaeology and North American Indian Oral Traditions*. University of Alabama Press, Tuscaloosa.

Mindeleff, C.

1900 Localization of Tusayan Clans. In *Nineteenth Annual Report of the Bureau of American Ethnology to the Secretary of the Smithsonian Institution, 1897–98*, Part I, pp. 635–653. Government Printing Office, Washington, D.C.

Moore, J.

2001 Ethnogenetic Patterns in Native North America. In *Archaeology, Language, and History: Essays on Culture and Ethnicity*, edited by J. Terrell, pp. 31–56. Bergin and Garvey, Westport, Conn.

Naranjo, T.

1995 Thoughts on Migration from Santa Clara Pueblo. *Journal of Anthropological Archaeology* 14:247–250.

Nelson, B., and S. LeBlanc
1986   *Short-Term Sedentism in the American Southwest: The Mimbres Valley Salado.* University of New Mexico Press, Albuquerque.

Parsons, E. C.
1922   Contributions to Hopi History. *American Anthropologist* 24:253–298.
1933   *Hopi and Zuni Ceremonialism.* American Anthropological Association Memoirs 39. Menasha, Wis.
1936   The House-Clan Complex of the Pueblos. In *Essays in Anthropology Presented to A. L. Kroeber,* edited by R. H. Lowie, pp. 239–231. University of California Press, Berkeley.
1939   *Pueblo Indian Religion.* University of Chicago Press, Chicago.

Parsons, E. C. (editor)
1969   *Hopi Journal of Alexander M. Stephen.* AMS Press, New York.

Prothero, R., and M. Chapman (editors)
1984   *Circulation in Third World Countries.* Routledge and Kegan Paul, London.

Reid, J. J.
1989   A Grasshopper Perspective on the Mogollon of the Arizona Mountains. In *Dynamics of Southwestern Prehistory,* edited by L. Cordell and G. Gummerman, pp. 65–97. Smithsonian Institution Press, Washington, D.C.

Schachner, G.
2007   *Population Circulation and the Transformation of Ancient Cibola Communities.* Unpublished Ph.D. dissertation, Department of Anthropology, Arizona State University, Tempe.

Titiev, M.
1944   *Old Oraibi: A Study of the Hopi Indians of Third Mesa.* University of New Mexico Press, Albuquerque.

Trigger, B. G.
1989   *A History of Archaeological Thought.* Cambridge University Press, Cambridge.

Whiteley, P.
1985   Unpacking Hopi "Clans": Another Vintage Model out of Africa? *Journal of Anthropological Research* 41(4):359–374.
1986   Unpacking Hopi "Clans," II: Further Questions about Hopi Descent Groups. *Journal of Anthropological Research* 42(1):69–79.
1988   *Deliberate Acts: Changing Hopi Culture Through the Orayvi Split.* The University of Arizona Press, Tucson.
2002   Archaeology and Oral Tradition: The Scientific Importance of Dialogue. *American Antiquity* 67(3):405–415.

Zedeño, M. N.
1994   *Sourcing Prehistoric Ceramics at Chodistaas Pueblo, Arizona: The Circulation of People and Pots in the Grasshopper Region.* Anthropological Papers of the University of Arizona no. 58, University of Arizona, Tucson.

3

Movement and the Unsettling of the Pueblos

SEVERIN M. FOWLES

Everyone's on the move, and has been for centuries: dwelling-in-travel.
—James Clifford (1997:2)

You have a connection to everything, especially if it's along the route of migration.
—Leigh J. Kuwanwisiwma, Greasewood Clan, Paaqavi
(quoted in Ferguson and Colwell-Chanthaphonh 2006:148)

An interesting story appeared in the newspapers a few years ago about London cab drivers and their brains. The outlines of the story are as follows.

A study had been undertaken in which the relationship between brain development and the length of time on the job among cab drivers was explored (Maguire et al. 2000). The research appears to have been premised upon two assumptions: that downtown London is a vast and convoluted tangle of streets confounding all rational spatial logic (a true observation, if ever there was one) and that navigating this web in an automobile requires Herculean cognitive efforts (also a true observation, particularly for Americans, but also, I suspect, for British neophytes). The hypothesis built upon these assumptions, then, was (1) that London cabbies, whose job it is to internalize the street system so as to move through it smoothly and efficiently, must be constantly exercising those portions of the brain related to spatial representation, mental mapping, and navigation; and (2) that the results of this cognitive exercise should be evident over time in the physical development of their brains. Remarkably, the researchers did discover a relatively clear positive correlation between the length of time cabbies had been on the job and the relative size of their posterior hippocampi, where spatial representations appear to be stored.

As did those reporting on it, I find this study truly striking in its tangibility. Is it not odd that spatial smarts can be so vividly depicted as differently sized lumps of gray matter? We seem to be presented with satisfyingly graphic and quantifiable evidence that Pierre Bourdieu was correct, that habitual practices do, quite literally, lead to a kind of embodied knowledge. Indeed, rather than simply relying on claims that the practice of spatial navigation inculcates a vague sort of "cabbie habitus," we now need only consult MRI scans!

I am being slightly facetious, of course, but I do find it intriguing that neural research appears to be reinforcing the commonplace notion that itinerancy leads to a special kind of mental acuity not found in more sedentary individuals. We use terms such as "provincial" and "staid" to refer to both spatial rootedness and mental dullness. By contrast, explorers, expatriates, and those who navigate ever-changing environments are regarded as "worldly" in the sense of being both well traveled and knowledgeable. Movers and shakers—they are the ones with the ideas. In a popular sense, then, we accept that people on the move think differently. (Indeed, we might now go so far as to say they have different *brains*.)

Insofar as spatial rootedness can be said to have pejorative associations when used in reference to thought, it is ironic that the situation is quite the reverse when we turn to consider the evolution of human societies. In prehistoric studies, sedentism—not movement—has the clear cachet, marking as it does the revolutionary moment when nomads ceased their migrations, laid claim to landed property, and established the territorial foundation upon which, eventually, the nation-state was constructed. It has long been viewed thus. Speculating on human origins, for instance, Rousseau conjured up the image of a primordial Savage who spent his time "wandering about in the forests, without industry, without speech, *without any fixed residence*" (1967 [1755]:207; emphasis added). It was sedentism that made the Savage civil: "The first man, who after enclosing a piece of ground, took it into his head to say, *this is mine . . .* was the real founder of civil society" (1967:214). Rousseau's "first revolution," then, was the construction of permanent architectural anchors, fixed property that the individual both possessed and was possessed by. Sir Henry Maine (1861) elaborated, famously arguing that the birth of government lay in the shift from personal ties to territorial ties. And within contemporary archaeology, this same imagined moment of geographic tethering continues to be viewed as a, if not *the*, pivotal event in human prehistory, a profound moment when hunter-gatherers finally "settled down" in villages and opened the door to agriculture, surplus, and social complexity.

But how sure are we that those undertaking this "first revolution" necessarily embraced sedentism? The popular image, perhaps, is of a fatigued nomad breathing a sigh of relief, having finally found respite from the endless relocations that had burdened his ancestors for thousands of years—the marathon runner finally arrived at his finish line. It is typically assumed, in other words, that hunter-gatherers would have remained migratory only if they had no other choice. Sedentism, so the story goes, would have been adopted wholesale and without hesitation once it became economically viable.

Of course, some anthropologists have gone to great lengths to construct evolutionary counternarratives. Marshall Sahlins (1972), more than anyone, worked to defend the nomad with his remarkably influential image of "the original affluent society" (the critiques notwithstanding), but others have contributed to this project as well. Salzman (1980) observed that twentieth-century efforts to settle nomadic groups in Sub-Saharan Africa often met with vigorous resistance, despite the fact that these groups were given land, agricultural training, and equipment to sustain themselves. And in his analysis of the Basseri of Iran, Barth (1965:135) demonstrated that far from being burdensome to society, frequent migrations were instead viewed as moral imperatives; movement, in this ethnographic case, attained a quasi-religious status and was vigorously defended. Indeed, the anthropological critique of sedentism's supposed desirability might be traced all the way back to the fourteenth century, when Ibn Khaldun (for some, the first anthropologist) offered his own passionate defense of nomadism, arguing that sedentary life in fact "constitutes the *last* stage of civilization and the point where it begins to decay." Nomads, he stated bluntly, "are closer to being good than sedentary people" (Ibn Khaldun 1967 [1377]:Part 2:4). This position is not entirely lost on archaeologists, some of whom have argued that increasing occupational permanence would have been adopted only very reluctantly in prehistory and that returns to nomadism would have been a common strategy of those seeking to escape the social inequalities and systems of dependency that inevitably arise in settled towns (Fowles 2010).

Nevertheless, it remains difficult not to theorize the emergence of village life without a tinge of teleology, without the sense that a human prophecy of sorts was fulfilled each time ephemeral brush shelters were replaced with masonry walls. This is the point Brian Boyd (2006) recently made in a provocative essay that challenges the traditional notion of sedentism in the very place of its supposed birth: the Early Natufian villages of the Levant some twelve millennia ago. (Had Rousseau the archaeological evidence of today, he would have undoubtedly envisioned a Natufian for his "first man," the early architect of both permanent residences and civil society.) "Building in stone at these places," writes Boyd (2006:171), "may well seem (to us) to 'fix' those locales but it does not follow that the people who carried out those acts of construction then became similarly fixed." Rather, he envisions an Early Natufian landscape punctuated by newly marked and cognized places through which moved migratory—or at least "semi-mobile"—groups who were in no hurry to settle down and adopt a "sedentary" or "Neolithic" mindset.

If London's cab drivers demonstrate that high mobility leads people to think differently today, would this not have been all the more pronounced among the yet more mobile peoples of the Early Natufian? Would there not have been vastly different minds at work throughout the world among pre- and proto-Neolithic peoples who were constantly on the move, dwelling-in-travel? The interpretive challenge before us is to learn to think like a nomad and to read the archaeological record accordingly. It is toward this end that I offer the following thoughts on the relationship of movement to cognition, spirituality, and identity among the Pueblo communities of the American Southwest.

Pueblo, Place, and Non-Place

The Pueblos present us with an especially interesting example because our image of their relationship to movement is so fraught with inconsistency and paradox. This has been the case since the sixteenth century, when European impressions of the Southwest first began to be constructed. Indeed, the relative degree of mobility of the various New World peoples was, in many respects, a major colonial concern, and historic documents make it clear that the Spanish conquistadors were originally attracted to the native villagers of New Mexico and Arizona because—in contrast to the highly nomadic foragers that surrounded them—the Pueblos were perceived to be refreshingly sedentary. Immobility lent the Pueblos a certain respectability in European eyes. More importantly, immobility held the promise of controllability: Pueblo villages were viewed as dense, possessable human resources that could be mined for their labor and saved from pagan damnation en masse.

The Spanish quickly learned just how incorrect their first impressions were, however. Yes, the Pueblos lived in large villages of up to a few thousand souls or more, but these were not "sedentary" communities like those the Spanish had left behind in Europe. Time and again, the conquistadors arrived at Pueblo villages only to find them vacated, the population having used an established tradition of long-distance residential mobility as a form of resistance to slip through the fingers of their would-be masters. Reflecting upon this tradition, anthropologists would later refer to the Pueblos—those of the pre-reservation period, at least—as "urbanized nomads" (Fox 1967:24). More recently, archaeologists have described their ancestral settlement patterns as characterized by "short-term sedentism" (Nelson and LeBlanc 1986) or "serial migrations," as Wes Bernardini (2005) so nicely puts it. Regardless of the terms used, the general conclusion is that we must not permit the deep stability of Pueblo architecture to fool us into thinking that Pueblo *people* were equally stable.

I am particularly fond of the phrase "urbanized nomads" because it not only implies a complicated settlement dynamic but also references a distinctive personality or character: that of the village-dwelling migrant. Superficially, of course, this would seem to be a contradiction in terms, for how could one both live in a village and yet still consider oneself a migrant? Parsons (1996:14) explains it this way: "The early Pueblos were nomads in terms not of days or seasons but of decades or centuries." That is to say that while the stationary periods may have been longer and the "base camps" more impressive architecturally, they were nevertheless merely extended pauses in a fundamentally nomadic life, a life in which migration was viewed (in the long run) more as the rule than the exception.

Many contemporary Pueblo people have offered their own statements to this effect. "Movement is a part of us. . . . Without movement, there is no life," explains Tessie Naranjo (1995:250), a Tewa scholar reflecting on the itinerant habits of her ancestors. Today, as in the past, movement is a fundamental motif in Pueblo philosophy. Migrations from one world to the next, from one landscape to the next, from one settlement to the next—these are viewed as natural and, to a certain extent, ritually mandated aspects of traditional Pueblo life.

How can we incorporate such a perspective into our archaeological analyses? To pose this question is not to request additional studies of the structural effects of migrations on Pueblo social or political organization, valuable though these may be.[1] Rather, it is to demand new ways of talking archaeologically about the manner in which serial migration left its mark on Pueblo ideology and identity as well. How might we investigate movement as a *religious* phenomenon no less than a social, political, or economic phenomenon? How, in other words, might we complement Anthony's (1990:895) insistence that migration is structured behavior by also exploring the way in which migration is structured thought?

Clearly our first step should be to avoid the conceptual pitfall of the conquistadors who assumed that, like the Europeans, the Pueblos also privileged residential stasis as a normal or desired state of affairs. Geographic fixity is an especially "state" state of affairs, tied to a systematic commodification of the landscape that tethers individuals and nations to particular, owned places. Plenty of population relocations may occur within state societies, of course. However, when land is individually owned, when landed property is a basis of power (and especially when a group's identity is tied to control of "the homeland"), movement away is typically viewed as a threat to the social order. Similar assumptions that geographic stasis is normal and desired and that residential mobility is therefore a disruption exist within much anthropological work on migration among small-scale village societies. Migrations are viewed as responses to "pushes" and "pulls" (Anthony 1990), external forces that dislodge social groups from their naturally sedentary state.

The question is whether or not these assumptions at all approximate the way societies in the past would have conceptualized the situation, particularly those societies engaged in periodic or serial migrations through time. Might it have been the case that for such groups, residential *stasis* was understood as the disruption or pause within a normal state of perpetual movement? This latter position is closer to contemporary Pueblo philosophy. Consider the following statement by Naranjo (1995:249): "Specific [geographic] boundaries are not the important elements because as the people moved, their mountain boundaries also moved. The idea was to have boundaries to create a place—to fix a place—temporarily within a larger idea of movement." Within the ontology of the Pueblos, movement is naturalized and place-fixing or residential stasis is the phenomena in need of explanation. Rather that asking why a group migrated, in other words, we are led to ask why they stayed put as long as they did.

The modern Pueblo village, of course, is a fixed "place," an architectural symbol of the group around which elaborate cosmologies are constructed. To borrow from Basso (1996), it is very much a place in which wisdom sits. However, within the oppositional thought of the Pueblos (see Naranjo 1995:249) there is also room, I suspect, for viewing the village as a "non-place" of sorts. Augé (1995:77–78) defines "non-places" as follows: "If a *place* can be defined as relational, historical and concerned with identity, then a space which cannot be defined as relational, or historical, or concerned with identity will be a *non-place*." This is a term Augé uses to explore the condition of supermodernity, and his classic example of a contemporary non-place is an airport where one waits or pauses while in the midst of a trip. Despite hours of sedentism at the gate (or longer, depending on flight delays), one nevertheless thinks of oneself as being in the midst of "traveling."

Might the ancestral Pueblos have viewed themselves similarly: ever in the midst of migrating or moving, even during the years or decades spent at a given village? Might villages have been conceived as mere way stations within the larger journey—waiting rooms, airports, non-places?

Perhaps this would seem a gross misreading of native sentiment, for alongside the aforementioned philosophy of movement, each contemporary pueblo is also quite heavily invested in the specific natural and built landscape within which its members dwell (see Fowles 2009). The tourist visiting Taos Pueblo, for instance, confronts this deep attachment to place immediately. Upon entering the pueblo, he is handed a brochure prefaced with the following declaration: "We have lived upon this land from days beyond history's records, far past any living memory, deep into the time of legend. The story of my people and the story of this place are one single story. . . . *No man can think of us without thinking of this place.* . . . We are always joined together" (emphasis added).

Could there be a clearer statement of the modern village's "placeness," of the manner in which it is "relational, historical and concerned with identity"? Indeed, let us suppose the visitor to Taos Pueblo took brochure in hand and walked through the village. He would immediately be impressed by the Rio Pueblo, the sacred river that flows through the center of the plaza, dividing the community into north and south architectural complexes that mirror the moiety relations that in turn underlay much of Taos's ceremonial life. To the north of the river, he might notice a conspicuous wooden pole, the axis mundi that embodies the connection between past and present worlds and is the focus of an important village-wide ritual during the fall. And on the western side of the village, he would certainly take note of the dramatic ruins of the early historic Catholic church with its piles of wooden crosses that memorialize the generations of Pueblo individuals buried there. "No man can think of the Taos people without thinking of this *place*," he would undoubtedly concur.

But as always, one must read between the lines. The brochure statement quoted above was, in fact, originally made in court as part of Taos Pueblo's appeal to regain territory that had long figured prominently in its ceremonial life. It is, in other words, a legal statement born of modern land claims cases that are themselves born of the U.S. reservation system, the Spanish system of *congregación*, and centuries of (often-violent) colonial lockdown on Pueblo mobility. This is not to say that the statement is in any way insincere; only that the situation would have been quite different in the past.

The *precolonial* ideology of place at Taos and at most other pueblos was probably much more similar to that expressed in a Tewa statement recorded by Ortiz (1969) regarding the relationship between the spirits and the stone shrines where they were venerated. Ortiz was told that the spirits did not permanently reside in the shrines; on the contrary, spirits were constantly in flight (they traveled in the sky as clouds). To clarify the point, his informant offered a metaphor quite similar to the one considered above: the spirits, he suggested, were like planes flying overhead and the shrines were like airports where the spirits landed and paused in their travels.

Whether or not this metaphor can be extended to the relationship between Pueblo village and villager—whether or not we are willing to envision villages as immense flight delays built of adobe, stone, and wood—it is essential to acknowledge that Pueblo identity is first and foremost vested in the route itself and that the shifting landscape through which groups move is as much a "place" as the way stations (i.e., the sites) that archaeologists study. In other words, there would have been no phenomenological thinness to the larger Puebloan landscape, for it was in passing through this landscape that the Ancestral Pueblo people built a sense of who they were (see also Bernardini 2008). Following Bender (2001), we might say that these were societies in which being on-the-move was indeed a way of being in place.

Moving Rituals

If Pueblo identity was linked to movement—if, in some sense, it was a *product* of a tradition of serial migrations—then this raises the question of how Pueblo identity was maintained during the decades spent sojourning at prehistoric villages. How did one stay a nomad when all or most of one's life was spent in residence at a single place? Indeed, an even larger question is how this ideological focus on movement has been maintained historically across centuries of life spent tethered to reservations.

To begin with, we need to note that village life itself was probably never entirely sedentary within the precolonial Pueblo tradition. Seasonal residential movements away from the home village to be closer to agricultural fields, long-distance logistical expeditions for hunting or trade, the movement of individuals between villages as a result of intermarriage, and many other processes would have led communities to continuously traverse the landscape. But these are not examples of "migrations," properly so called, which for present purposes we can define in Pueblo terms as *a residential move that leads to the establishment of a new spiritual center or middle place as well as the redefinition of a group's major cosmological boundaries* (again, see Naranjo 1995).[2] So let us narrow our inquiry, then, and ask how this more specific idea of migration was kept alive during extended periods of stasis. How did Pueblo groups deal with the challenges of staying put while still maintaining their identity as migrants? How did they weather sedentism?

One answer to this question seems very clear: through ceremony. The most frequently cited example, of course, is the Pueblo tradition of memorizing and retelling the earlier migration pathways of a clan or kiva society during ritual events. The story of a movement from lower world to upper world, followed by an ambulant journey from settlement to settlement in search of the center or middle place—this is the formulaic Pueblo account of migration, the result of which is a "topogeny" (sensu Fox 1997) that is to space what genealogy is to time. We need hardly look further for evidence of the fundamental ongoing link between Pueblo identity and movement. Recitations of topogenies were cognitive lines of flight that kept migration constantly in mind.

But origin stories merely scratch the surface. Innumerable other aspects of Pueblo ceremonialism might be interpreted as rituals of movement, and it is significant that many seem designed to set the body no less than the mind in motion along a past or potential migration pathway. Among the Tewa, for instance, a boy, sitting in the kiva, or ritual chamber, may listen in passive immobility to an elder's account of the migrations of his ancestors. But when the history lesson is over and he begins to climb the ladder to exit the kiva, he finds that another migration exercise has just begun, for the ladder is itself a kind of symbolic pathway, each of its twelve rungs referencing the twelve stops made by the ancestral Tewa on their journey south from the point of emergence to the present homeland (Naranjo 2009). In fact, the very movement up and out of the kiva is doubly referential, for it also replicates the cosmic coming into being of the Pueblo peoples as they traveled from the lower world to the present upper one.

Physical reenactments of a history of migration were undertaken at larger scales as well. Until recently, pilgrimages to ancestral sites and/or to major shrines were common among the Pueblos and involved the explicit retracing of a previous migration from one center place (the village of the living) to another center place (often the place of emergence or the residence of the ancestors). In some cases, pilgrimages were undertaken over long distances of up to a few hundred miles or more (see Ellis and Hammack 1968). In this way, pilgrims developed extensive familiarity with the larger landscape that no doubt facilitated future residential relocations—a ritual philopatry that built and perpetuated a kind of nomadic knowledge. Indeed, it is probably correct to say that the physical movement of pilgrims through the landscape was a way of actively rehearsing and maintaining migration as a meaningful cultural model, an ever-present social option. Traditionally, all the Pueblos also engaged in long-distance running rituals (Nabokov 1981) that led young boys and men through a similarly extensive landscape marked by shrines (both natural and manmade), each of which was conceived of as its own center place of sorts. Such running rituals appear to have operated, on some level, as embodied reenactments of origin stories, as migrations in fast forward.

Ritualized relay races of shorter duration but with much greater visibility further underscore the religious centrality of migration. Among the Northern Tiwa, these relays take place along formal racetracks oriented east-west to mirror the path of Father Sun in the sky. Indeed, the sun is viewed in many ways as the ideal Pueblo individual: a consummate nomad, forever on the move across the sky (the sky of this world and of the underworld, alternately), all the time working for the good of his children. And relay racers, in turn, run as a way of helping the sun in his migration. Interestingly, Father Sun is thought to pause in his travels only briefly during winter solstice when the position of the setting sun on the horizon appears unchanged for a number of days. This is the time of "standing still," a precarious period marked by a large number of taboos, and it is the duty of the entire ritual community to help the sun father reinvigorate his celestial migrations. Symbolically, then, sedentism is associated with weakness and danger.

Pueblo dance—in which bodily movement itself becomes a form of prayer—must be considered yet another ritual of movement. Dances vary from village to village and sometimes even from group to group within a given village (again, movement defines identity), but all treat movement in a characteristic manner. Consider Collier's description of Taos Pueblo's nighttime dance along the banks of Blue Lake, the sacred destination of their annual pilgrimage:

> Here . . . moved scores, hundreds of ghosts. They moved like masses of smoke, like wind made visible, like masses of cloud. . . . No casual motion, no gesture of one to another, ever appeared; all was a mass rhythm; but an evolving rhythm which changed a hundred times during the night. (Collier 1962 [1949]:127)

Let us underline this notion of an evolving or ever-changing rhythm—*of a motion that is itself in motion*—for this also aptly describes the more public Pueblo dances undertaken within the walls of the village. Such dances typically are performed in sequential fashion, the same movements being repeated in each of the plazas or kivas of the pueblo (see Brown 1989; Earle and Kennard 1938; Ortiz 1969). Movement, in other words, is complexly layered: at an intimate level, there is the continuous movement of dancers, even though the overall ritual might be temporarily stationed in a particular plaza. And at a larger level, this internally dynamic congregation itself engages in a kind of metamovement, shifting from place to place, from plaza to plaza, from kiva to kiva, *from center to center*, recreating a deep history of serial migration across the greater southwestern landscape. Dances, in other words, are migrations in microcosm.

Not only humans engage in ritual dances; the kachina, or spirits, do as well, and it is in these latter dances that one finds a powerful statement not only of the centrality of continual movement but also of the deep link between specific movements and one's social (and spiritual) identity. The following description of kachina dances at Hopi demonstrates this nicely:

> Sometimes the entire line [of kachina dancers] will pause, at others two or more steps will be executed in rapid succession. These variations are usually accompanied by gestures with the arms and head,—the right arm raised and the head turned in that direction, followed by the same movement of the left arm and the head. Another variation occurs in the

turning of the line. At certain points in the song the entire line changes, but the manner in which the turn is executed tends to be distinctive for each Kachina. Angakchina twists his body half way to the right and then turns completely to the left. Tasap Kachina extends the right arm, shakes the rattle, and then turns with the rattle held over the head. Other Kachinas turn one after the other, the movement flowing down the line and back. These differences in dance steps serve to distinguish one Kachina from another; they become as essential characteristics as the painting and decoration of the mask. (Earle and Kennard 1938:11)

The turn of the head, the quickness of step, a twist or a shake: all are subtle movements that speak volumes about the spirits being impersonated. Just as each kiva or clan group has its own distinctive oral history of migrations throughout the landscape, so too do the spirits have their own distinctive sequence of movements. In both cases, identity is defined through motion, through a trajectory, rather than through place.

A great many additional rituals of movement from the ethnographic record might be drawn upon to illustrate this point. But what of the archaeological record? What are the material signatures of such rituals?

An Archaeology of Urbanized Nomads

Some are relatively subtle. For instance, during the excavation of an early fourteenth-century kiva at T'aitöna (Pot Creek Pueblo) some years ago, I encountered a pecked stone shrine installed high in the kiva's fill (Fowles 2009). The stratigraphic position of the shrine as well as the discovery of an early historic sherd not far away suggested that the shrine had been constructed as part of ceremonial journeys back to the site following its abandonment. The pilgrims in this case were almost certainly from either Taos or Picurís, the two nearby Northern Tiwa villages, both of whom trace their ancestry to the site and who have continued to revisit it in recent decades. There is no reason to think T'aitöna was exceptional in this regard. Indeed, while on survey a few hundred kilometers to the north, I located a smaller thirteenth-century settlement with another stone shrine—this time, a large stone displaying ground cupules—seated atop its mounded remains (Fowles 2004). This shrine, like that at T'aitöna, was clearly constructed by individuals who had retraced the path of a migration back to a place they or their ancestors once occupied.

Other material signatures of ritualized movement are more dramatic. The monumental Chacoan roads of the eleventh and twelfth centuries provide the most striking pre-Columbian example. The roads are wide, straight, and in

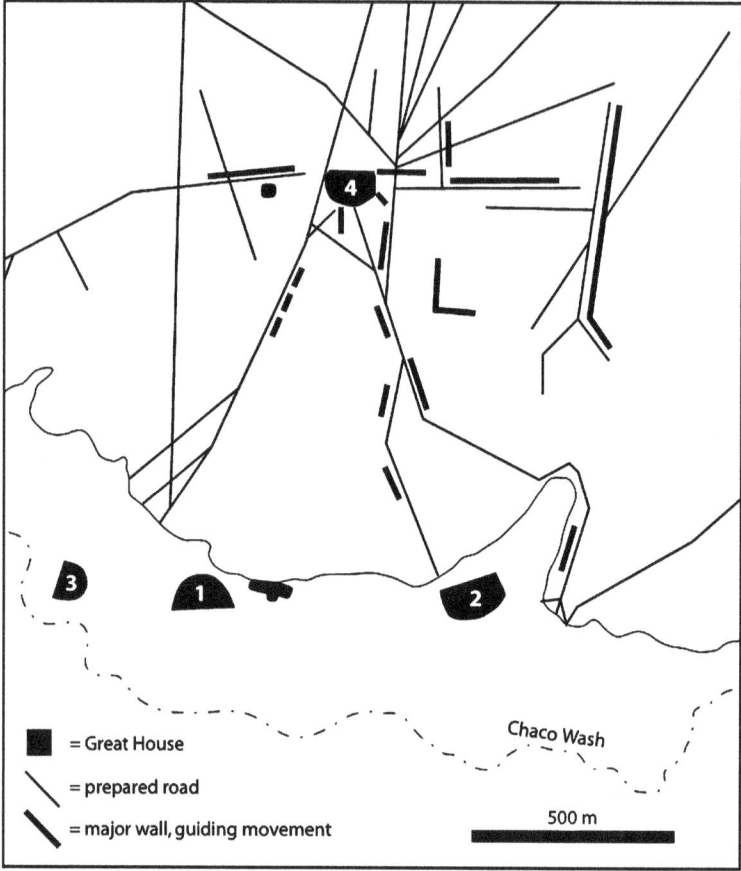

Figure 3.1. Elaborate prepared roads in the vicinity of Pueblo Alto, Chaco Canyon (based on Holley and Lekson 1999:40, Fig. 3.1). 1 = Pueblo Bonito; 2 = Chetro Ketl; 3 = Pueblo Arroyo; 4 = Pueblo Alto.

some cases banked by linear mounds or low walls (Figure 3.1), but by far their most remarkable aspect is the fact that they were not constructed according to an obvious economic logic. They were not, in other words, constructed to assist the efficient transport of people and goods between settlements. Rather, the Chacoan roads seem to represent strategies of formalizing or ritualizing a traveler's movement through the landscape toward important locations, be they ancestral great houses or natural geographic features (see Marshall 1997; Van Dyke 2007).

Chacoan roads also have an excessive quality that is curious: in some cases, a traveler would have had the option of walking any one of a number of roads when a single route would seem to have sufficed. In other cases, single roads split like a bamboo stalk into two or four closely parallel routes (Sofaer et al. 1989), again presenting the traveler with multiple options of how to move through the landscape. In this sense, they are similar to the subtler fifteenth- and sixteenth-century "gateway trails" in the Tewa area recently described by Snead (2002; 2005:83–84; 2008:113–132). Gateway trails appear to have marked the formal entrance to a pueblo, and like the Chacoan roads—albeit now in the idiom of "understated sacredness" (Swentzell 1997) that has come to distinguish the post-Chacoan Pueblos—they are characterized by excess in the sense that multiple trail and staircase segments are found alongside one another (Figure 3.2). Snead reasonably suggests that such redundancy marks

Figure 3.2. Narrow, parallel "gateway trails" marking the approach to Tsankawi Pueblo, Bandelier National Monument. Photo credit: Severin M. Fowles.

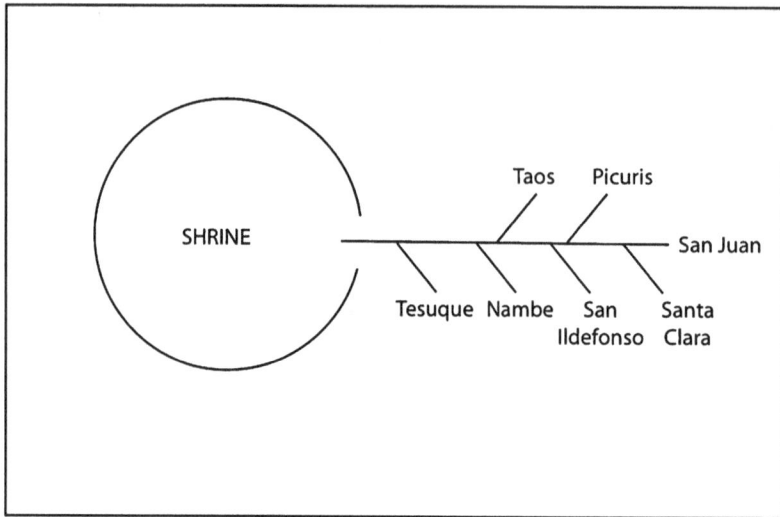

Figure 3.3. Schematic representation of the World Quarter Shrine and associated "roads" atop Mt. Tsikomo (based on sketch by Tewa member in Parsons 1974 [1929]).

a ritual concern with repetition and periodic renewal (Snead 2008:126–127). However, I am more inclined to interpret this redundancy as a materialization of the strong Pueblo link between movement and identity. Indeed, there is much to learn about both Chacoan roads and Tewa gateway trails through a comparison with the even smaller paths found in association with certain shrines that remain in use in many parts of the Pueblo world.

Take, for instance, the important Tewa shrine atop Mt. Tsikomo. This is a large circular rock shrine with an opening to the east from which—or, rather, *to* which—extend a series of short, rock-lined "roads." As drawn in schematic form by a Tewa informant (Figure 3.3), these roads designate specific routes that supplicants from the various Tewa and Northern Tiwa pueblos must follow when approaching the shrine and the spirits who dwell within.[3] Pueblo shrines, ancestral Tewa villages, and Chacoan great houses all were and are important "places," of course. But the paths taken to these places did not involve movement through "non-places" in Augé's sense. Rather, we find clear emphases on marking movement itself and on linking social identities to particular pathways, particular ways of traversing the landscape—different roads for different peoples.

If life for the Pueblos is premised on movement, then it is probably also accurate to say that movement is in turn premised on the existence of *roads*. Road metaphors within Pueblo religion are pervasive. Parsons (1996:18) noted, for example, that "all spirits or sacrosanct persons have a road of corn

Figure 3.4. The Mother of the Katsina creating a cornmeal "road" for the Katsina chief of Nambé Pueblo. (Tewa illustration, from Parsons 1974 [1929]:105).

meal or pollen sprinkled for them when their presence is requested" (Figure 3.4). Celestial bodies travel along formal roads in the sky. Rivers and irrigation canals are also conceptualized as sacred roads. And, as we have already seen, Pueblo shrines and other sacred places frequently have their own roads as well. In short, Parsons was not exaggerating when she concluded that, for the Pueblos, "life *is* a road" (ibid., emphasis added). Or as Tessie Naranjo of Santa Clara puts it: "Movement, clouds, wind and rain are one. Movement must be emulated by the people" (quoted in Anscheutz 2006:67). As in other nomadic cultures, Pueblo ontology stressed routes over roots (Clifford 1997; also Bender 2001).

This fundamental ontology is elegantly rendered iconic in Pueblo rock art, where road imagery is common. Recently, for instance, I recorded a large boulder in the Rio Grande gorge near Taos on which two long parallel lines of dots had been pecked (Figure 3.5). Conversations with a consultant from Taos indicated that a common Pueblo way to think about such lines of dots was as material mnemonics to aid in the recounting of ancestral movements through time and space. As the dots were pecked in linear succession, the stories moved from location to location along a historical path of ancestral migrations. Similar sorts of devices have been used in kivas at Zuni, where corn kernels would apparently be placed on the floor in linear sequence as clan histories were told (cf., Cushing 1979). At a much larger geographic scale, the Hopi are known to have pecked clan symbols at periodic locations along trails as they undertook

Figure 3.5. A migration petroglyph in the Rio Grande Gorge, just north of Pilar, New Mexico. Photo credit: Severin M. Fowles.

their migrations; today these clan symbols, like beads on a string or dots in a line, continue to be revisited during ceremonial trips that trace the movements of the ancestors (Ferguson and Colwell-Chanthaphonh 2006). In the case of the rock-art panel in Figure 3.5, however, we might speculate further, for here we find two parallel lines of dots that would seem to indicate dual movements, the histories of two groups perhaps, running in parallel just as pre-Columbian roads sometimes ran in parallel as they approached villages, shrines, or other sacred locations on the landscape. We might even relate this imagery more specifically to the oral history of the nearby Tewa, which details the ancestral movements of the Summer People and the Winter People (the two moiety groups comprising Tewa communities) as they moved south in parallel fashion on either side of the Rio Grande, making twelve stops en route to the present villages (see Ortiz 1969). As archaeologists, we may spend much of our time thinking about each of these stops or dots in isolation. But the Pueblos, it seems, have always been more interested in the larger lines of flight they collectively define.

Implications

The Pueblo rituals of movement we have been considering are quite different from the dominant rituals of more sedentary cultures with developed notions of landed property and strong national or imperial boundaries. Consider, for instance, the primary actions of a Christian during Mass: he sits in his pew, he stands up, sits down, kneels, sits again—all the while staying *in place*. This pattern of anchored ritual praxis, I suggest, may be thought of as appropriate to a Western sociopolitical tradition in which geographic stasis and permanent control of land is viewed as the normal way of things. (Westerners, significantly, always hold *seats* of power.) And let us remember that in the Jewish tradition, when the story of the Exodus is recounted, emphasis is placed on the trials and tragedies that forty years of wanderings "lost in the wilderness" entailed. Jewish identity may have been forged in the great migration out of Egypt, but the final lesson was that one must return to claim one's homeland and remain fixedly in control of it at all costs. The lessons of Pueblo theology move entirely counter to this. The Pueblo congregation, as we have seen, is a moving congregation, a *migrating* congregation, and its politics are that of the nomad who stands ready to vote with his or her feet.

One way to understand this migration mentality, as I have suggested, is to look to its historical development. Tilley (1994:28) emphasizes that "movement through space constructs 'spatial stories,' forms of narrative understanding." This is undoubtedly true not only of a De Certeau–like walk through a city but also of the more episodic serial migrations of the Pueblos that occurred over decades or centuries. We see the evidence of this deep history even today. The long-term spatial narratives or topogenies constructed during the Pueblo people's time as urbanized nomads continue to be expressed through such things as relay races, dances, pilgrimages, the construction of roads, and the like. Migration, in other words, has structured Pueblo religious thought and ritual action.

But should we conclude our analysis there, with the suggestion that migration rituals were merely the ideological *product* or residue of a deep history of life on the move?

Undoubtedly it was more complicated than this, particularly in the Pueblo world prior to European colonialism and the imposition of state systems of sedentism. During precolonial times, migration rituals would have stood in a much more prominent position vis-à-vis actual patterns of residential mobility. Indeed, while functionalist interpretations may be unfashionable today, let me offer one such reading here: the ritualization of movement may well have played an essential role in keeping migration on the table as a behavioral option or model to be activated when the need arose.

Cases in which such needs were both felt and quickly acted upon abound in the historic record (see Schroeder 1979). The migration of Tewa families westward to the Hopi mesas (Dozier 1954) and of Laguna families to Isleta Pueblo (Ellis 1979) are the best-studied examples of recent population movements between villages. Lesser-known, but no less dramatic, migrations were undertaken by Pueblos who left their villages to join yet more nomadic non-Pueblo peoples. During the mid-seventeenth century, for instance, Taos Pueblo responded to the oppressive presence of the Spanish by simply vacating their village stronghold and traveling eastward to join the Apache in modern-day Kansas. Sometime afterward they were forcibly escorted back to Taos by Spanish troops. In 1696, Picurís Pueblo migrated onto the Plains for similar reasons; ten years later, they too were gathered up by the military and returned to their former home. Movement is politics, a fact that was lost on neither the Pueblos nor their Spanish wardens (Fowles 2010).

In earlier times, episodic migrations to and from villages would have been much more common, as many have observed. This is evident not only in the overall occupation spans of most large precolonial villages (typically only a few generations) but also in the more detailed studies of site chronology that frequently reveal extended periods of settlement abandonment followed by subsequent reoccupation (e.g., Adler 2002; Creamer 1993)—clear traces of a nomadic way of life "in terms not of days or seasons but of decades or centuries" (Parsons 1996:14). Of course, one could view (and many have viewed) the recurrent site abandonments as failures of sedentization. Given the evidence at hand, however, it seems just as likely that the ancestral Pueblos would have viewed *residential permanence* as a failure of *nomadism*.

Taking a cue from the London cabbies, then, let me suggest that ritual may have served as a sort of cognitive gymnasium in which ancestral Pueblo peoples kept their hippocampus muscles toned and in shape—a way of keeping migration in mind and on the table as a social option. "Every group will entrust to bodily automatisms the values and categories which they are most anxious to conserve," writes Connerton, and "they will know how well the past can be kept in mind by a habitual memory sedimented in the body" (1989:102).

What remains to be considered is whether this strategy also had a recursive aspect. Might there have been a way in which Pueblo religion *propelled* or was responsible for the very migratory patterns it was so heavily influenced by? In his remarkable study of the pre-Columbian trails on the Pajarito Plateau, Snead (2008:131) concludes that while "human intent and action created the trail . . . ultimately the trail imposed its own order on human experience." Such is the rebounding effect of human engagement with the material landscape, and it is no less the case with ritual practice. To what extent, we might ask, were the migrations of the Pueblo past prompted by religious imperatives? Might the abandonment of villages or even whole regions have had little at all to do with the relative merits of the intended destination (the pushes and pulls) and much more to do with the revival of movement itself? I leave these questions for another paper. Here, my goal has simply been to point to the material signatures of a nomadic mentality in what is often portrayed as having been a more-or-less sedentary tradition.

Notes

1. Alongside the relatively recent (i.e., post-Anthony [1990]) studies of migration's social implications by McGuire and Saitta (1996), Cameron (1995), Clark (2001), Bernardini (2005), and others, I have offered my own consideration of the structural implications of migration and ethnic co-residence vis-à-vis the emergence of Eastern Pueblo moiety organization (Bernardini and Fowles 2011; Fowles 2005). Moieties, I suggest, were used as a way of conceptualizing the historic confrontation of post-Chacoan migrants and autochthonous Rio Grande communities during the fourteenth century.

2. Traditionally, each Pueblo individual regarded his or her village as the center of the world, as the place where north, south, east, west, up, and down all converged on a single point. Each village, in turn, was surrounded by a nested series of landscape features (mountains, lakes, canyons, springs, caves, shrines, etc.) that bounded the cosmos and gave physical definition to this notion of centeredness. "Migration" as an analytical concept must be understood in relation to such indigenous perceptions of space. Hence, movement to and from one's village or within a community's existing cosmic boundaries was not "migration." Nor were temporary excursions to foreign lands. Rather, a "migration" was when the center of the world shifted, when new cosmic landmarks were adopted. Pueblo oral histories provide us with a clear sense of this when they recount how each migration of the ancestors was prompted by a realization that some existing place was not, in fact, the center of the world and that a new center must be sought by moving (migrating) elsewhere.

3. The Mt. Tsikomo shrine even includes a separate road entering from the west to accommodate the Navajo who occasionally visited as well.

References

Adler, M.

2002 The Ancestral Pueblo Community as Structure and Strategy. In *Seeking the Center Place: Archaeology and Ancient Communities in the Mesa Verde Region*, edited by M. D. Varien and R. H. Wilshusen, pp. 3–23. University of Utah Press, Salt Lake City.

Anscheutz, K. F.

2006 Tewa Fields, Tewa Traditions. In *Canyon Gardens: The Ancient Pueblo Landscapes of the American Southwest*, edited by V. B. Price and B. H. Morrow, pp. 57–73. University of New Mexico Press, Albuquerque.

Anthony, D. W.

1990 Migration in Archaeology: The Baby and the Bathwater. *American Anthropologist* 92(4):895–914.

Augé, M.

1995 *Non-Places: Introduction to an Anthropology of Supermodernity*. Verso Books, London.

Barth, F.

1965 *Nomads of South Persia: The Basseri Tribe of the Khamseh Confederacy*. Humanities Press, New York.

Basso, K.

1996 *Wisdom Sits in Places: Landscape and Language among the Apache*. University of New Mexico Press, Albuquerque.

Bender, B.

2001 Landscapes On-the-Move. *Journal of Social Archaeology* 1(1):75–89.

Bernardini, W.

2005 *Hopi Oral Tradition and the Archaeology of Identity*. University of Arizona Press, Tucson.

2008 Identity as History: Hopi Clans and the Curation of Oral Tradition. *Journal of Anthropological Research* 64(4):483–509.

Bernardini, W., and S. Fowles

2011 Becoming Hopi, Becoming Tiwa: Two Pueblo Histories of Movement. In *Movement, Connectivity, and Landscape Change*, edited by M. Nelson. University of Colorado Press, Denver.

Boyd, B.

2006 On "Sedentism" in the Later Epipaleolithic (Natufian) Levant. *World Archaeology* 38(2):164–178.

Brown, D.

1989 Dance as Experience: The Deer Dance of Picuris Pueblo. In *Southwestern Indian Ritual Drama*, edited by C. Frisbie, pp. 71–92. Waveland Press, Prospect Heights, Illinois.

Cameron, C.

1995 Migration and the Movement of Southwestern Pueblos. *Journal of Anthropological Archaeology* 14:104–124.

Clark, J. J.
2001   *Tracking Prehistoric Migrations: Pueblo Settlers among the Tonto Basin Hohokam.* Anthropological Papers of the University of Arizona no. 65. University of Arizona Press, Tucson.

Clifford, J.
1997   *Routes: Travel and Translation in the Late Twentieth Century.* Harvard University Press, Cambridge, Mass.

Collier, J.
1962 [1949]   *On the Gleaming Way.* Swallow Press, Chicago.

Connerton, P.
1989   *How Societies Remember.* Cambridge University Press, Cambridge.

Creamer, W.
1993   *The Architecture of Arroyo Hondo Pueblo, New Mexico.* School of American Research Press, Santa Fe.

Cushing, F. H.
1979   *Zuni: Selected Writings of Frank Hamilton Cushing.* University of Nebraska Press, Lincoln.

Dozier, E. P.
1954   *The Hopi-Tewa of Arizona.* University of California Press, Berkeley.

Earle, E., and E. A. Kennard
1938   *Hopi Kachinas.* J. J. Augustin, New York.

Ellis, F. H.
1979   Laguna Pueblo. In *Handbook of North American Indians*, vol. 9, *Southwest*, edited by A. Ortiz, pp. 438–449. Smithsonian Institution Press, Washington, D.C.

Ellis, F. H., and L. Hammack
1968   The Inner Sanctum of Feather Cave. *American Antiquity* 33(1):25–44.

Ferguson, T. J., and C. Colwell-Chanthaphonh
2006   *History Is in the Land: Multivocal Tribal Traditions in Arizona's San Pedro Valley.* University of Arizona Press, Tucson.

Fowles, S. M.
2005   Historical Contingency and the Prehistoric Foundations of Moiety Organization Among the Eastern Pueblos. *Journal of Anthropological Research* 60(1):25–52.

2009   The Enshrined Pueblo: Villagescape and Cosmos in the Northern Rio Grande. *American Antiquity* 74(3):448–466.

2010   A People's History of the American Southwest. In *Ancient Complexities: New Perspectives in Pre-Columbian North America*, edited by S. Alt. University of Utah Press, Salt Lake City.

Fox, J. J.
1997   Genealogy and Topogeny: Towards an Ethnography of Rotinese Ritual Place Names. In *The Poetic Power of Place: Comparative Perspectives on Austronesian Ideas of Locality*, edited by J. J. Fox, pp. 91–102. Australian National University, Canberra.

Fox, J. R.
1967   *The Keresan Bridge: A Problem in Pueblo Ethnology*. London School of Economics Monographs on Social Anthropology no. 35. Athlone, London.

Holley, G. R., and S. H. Lekson
1999   Comparing Southwestern and Southeastern Great Towns. In *Great Towns and Regional Polities in the Prehistoric American Southwest and Southeast*, edited by J. E. Neitzel, pp. 39–44. University of New Mexico Press, Albuquerque.

Ibn Khaldun
1967 [1377]   *The Muqaddimah: An Introduction to History*, translated by F. Rosenthal. Princeton University Press, Princeton.

Maguire, E. A., D. G. Gadian, I. S. Johnsrude, C. D. Good, J. Ashburner, R. S. J. Frackowiak, and C. D. Frith
2000   Navigation-Related Structural Change in the Hippocampi of Taxi Drivers. *Proceedings of the National Academy of Sciences, U.S.A.* 97(8):4398–4403.

Maine, H. S.
1861   *Ancient Law: Its Connection with the Early History of Society, and Its Relation to Modern Ideas*. John Murray, London.

Marshall, M. P.
1997   The Chacoan Roads: A Cosmological Interpretation. In *Anasazi Architecture and American Design*, edited by Baker H. Morrow and V. B. Price, pp. 62–74. University of New Mexico Press, Albuquerque.

Marshall, Y.
2006   Introduction: Adopting a Sedentary Lifeway. *World Archaeology* 38(2):153–163.

McGuire, R. H., and D. J. Saitta
1996   Although They Have Petty Captains, They Obey Them Badly: The Dialectics of Prehispanic Western Pueblo Social Organization. *American Antiquity* 61(2):197–216.

Nabokov, P.
1981   *Adobe, Pueblo and Hispanic Folk Traditions of the Southwest*. Office of Folklife Programs, Smithsonian Institution, Washington, D.C.

Naranjo, T.
1995   Thoughts on Migration by Santa Clara Pueblo. *Journal of Anthropological Archaeology* 14:247–250.
2009   Discussant comments. New Mexico Archaeological Council Meetings, November 14, Hibben Center, University of New Mexico, Albuquerque.

Nelson, B. A., and S. A. LeBlanc
1986   *Short-Term Sedentism in the American Southwest: The Mimbres Valley Salado*. University of New Mexico Press, Albuquerque.

Ortiz, A.
1969   *The Tewa World: Space, Time, Being, and Becoming in a Pueblo Society*. University of Chicago Press, Chicago.

Parsons, E. C.

1974 [1929]   *The Social Organization of the Tewa of New Mexico.* Memoirs of the
American Anthropological Association no. 36. Kraus Reprint Co., Millwood,
NJ.

1996   *Pueblo Indian Religion.* Vol. 2. University of Nebraska Press, Lincoln.

Rousseau, J.-J.

1967 [1755]   Discourse on the Origin of Inequality. In *The Social Contract and
Discourse on the Origin of Inequality*, pp. 148–258. Washington Square Press,
New York.

Sahlins, M.

1972   *Stone Age Economics.* Aldine Transactions, Chicago.

Salzman, P. C.

1980   *When Nomads Settle: Processes of Sedentarization as Adaptation and Response.*
Praeger, Berlin.

Schroeder, A. H.

1979   Pueblos Abandoned in Historic Times. In *The Handbook of North American
Indians*, vol. 9, *The Southwest*, edited by A. Ortiz, pp. 236–254. Smithsonian
Institution, Washington, D.C.

Snead, J.

2002   Ancestral Pueblo Trails and the Cultural Landscape of the Pajarito Plateau,
New Mexico. *Antiquity* 76(293):756–765.

2005   Ancient Trails of the Pajarito Plateau. In *The Peopling of Bandelier*, edited by R.
P. Powers, pp. 79–85. School of American Research Press, Santa Fe.

2008   *Ancestral Landscapes of the Pueblo World.* University of Arizona Press, Tucson.

Sofaer, A., M. Marshall, and R. Sinclair

1989   The Great North Road: A Cosmographic Expression of the Chaco Culture of
New Mexico. In *World Archaeoastronomy*, edited by A. G. Aveni, pp. 365–376.
Cambridge University Press, Cambridge.

Swentzell, R.

1997   An Understated Sacredness. In *Anasazi Architecture and American Design*, edited by B. H. Morrow and V. B. Price, pp. 186–89. University of New Mexico
Press, Albuquerque.

Tilley, C.

1994   *A Phenomenology of Landscape: Places, Paths, and Monuments.* Berg, Oxford.

Van Dyke, R.

2007   *The Chaco Experience: Landscape and Ideology at the Center Place.* School for
Advanced Research Press, Santa Fe.

4

S-cuk Kavick

Thoughts on Migratory Process and
the Archaeology of O'odham Migration

J. ANDREW DARLING

> A comparable approach is called for today, an approach which would analyze not things in space but space itself, with a view to uncovering the social relationships embedded in it.
>
> (Lefebvre 1991:89).

> The real knowledge that we hope to attain would have a retrospective as well as a prospective import. . . . It will help us to grasp how societies generate their (social) space and time—their representational spaces and their representations of space.
>
> (Lefebvre 1991:192).

This chapter is the fourth in a series of essays that examine O'odham ideology and archaeology to consider various aspects of the anthropology of Native infrastructure, mobility, and indigenous landscape analysis (see Darling 2009; Darling and Lewis 2007; Darling et al. 2004). In this chapter, I wish to develop an idea of migration in terms of the relationship between landscape and spaces in which infrastructure—as the association of facilities and ideas that allow societies to function—mediates between the two. I wish to consider migratory dislocations or relocations and their ideological implications, including the processes implied by the translation of conceptual or cognitive spaces (landscape ideologies) to new areas. One way that cognitive geography is expressed is through traditional song practices. I consider the impact of migration on cognitive geography and its implication for song transformation in light of archaeological evidence of O'odham migration during the historic period.

Among the O'odham, migration has legendary and historical significance, and their meanderings take place over a regionally extensive landscape that encompasses the expanse of desert known as the Pimería Alta—that portion of the Arid Southwest below the Mogollon Rim extending across the international border into northern Sonora, Mexico (Figure 4.1; cf. Bahr et al. 1994).

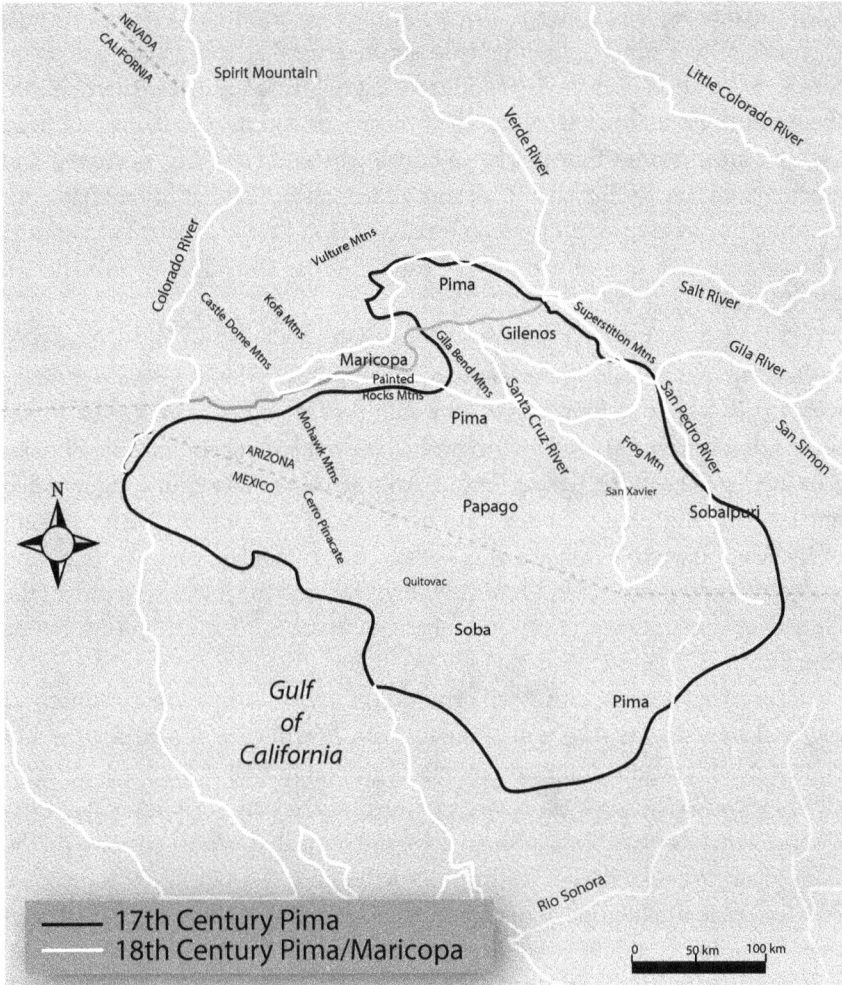

Figure 4.1. Map of Pimería Alta showing tribal territories (after Fontana 1983; Harwell and Kelly 1983).

Within this vast area, rivers, waterholes, mountain ranges, and a diversity of desert-adapted plants and animals provide the natural backdrop in which O'odham peoples subsisted. This is further supplemented by a vast infrastructure of trail networks linking resource areas, water resources, settlements, and sacred places (Darling 2009; Darling and Eiselt 2009).

I began studying O'odham mobility by looking at the continuity of settlement from prehistory to the historical present while focusing on one aspect of Piman mobility—*village drift*, a process whereby a settlement may change its location gradually by several kilometers over a period of years. Paul H.

Ezell introduced this concept to explain the dispersed character of Akimel O'odham (River Pima) settlements in south-central Arizona and to account for the frustration of historians endeavoring to locate historic settlements on the ground. He attributed village drift to several Akimel O'odham practices: "[1] . . . the custom of destroying a house where a death had occurred and erecting another for the survivors some yards away, [2] that of married sons building houses in proximity to their parents, and [3] the practice of building a house near new land when it was brought under cultivation" (1961:110–111; see also Darling et al. 2004:282).

For Ezell (1963), village drift provides a useful explanation for the dispersal of O'odham peoples along the length of the middle and lower Gila River valley from central Arizona to its confluence with the Colorado River. Ezell also observed that drift could account for gradual movement of people in the Pimería Alta during the historic period (before A.D. 1950), as well as more-punctuated and larger-scale population dislocations. Such dislocations include movement of the Maricopa, an amalgam of Colorado River peoples, who over a period of decades, if not centuries, ultimately migrated into the lower west end of the Gila River Indian Community and northeast to the Salt River Pima-Maricopa Community.[1]

Where I take issue with Ezell's important early work is the ascription of regional movements of populations to drift. For this author, drift does not constitute migration. From an archaeological standpoint, individual farmsteads (*rancherías*) or sites have their own spatial and temporal qualities. Components or loci within sites represent repeated reoccupations of the same location over a moderate time period, neither short term nor long term, that resemble oscillations of occupation and abandonment within a confined space (Darling et al. 2004; Dewar and McBride 1992). Over several decades, dispersed settlements gradually shift, or "drift," as inhabitants abandon land, occupy new land, and reoccupy old land within confined settlement districts. This may result in the appearance of extensive archaeological deposits (horizontal stratigraphies). Districts, however, do not drift and instead encompass the wider area in which *rancherías* move. O'odham settlement districts prior to 1920 along the middle Gila River encompassed between two to six square miles and were complexes of one to four *ranchería* settlements (Darling et al. 2004).

As organizational and spatial units, settlement districts are significant. O'odham identify districts by name. Districts also tend to delineate shared language dialects recognizable as communities or associations of relatives or clans. This is especially true for the Tohono O'odham Nation in southern Arizona, where the nine administrative or political districts roughly coincide with dialect groups. An individual's group is of great importance to self-identification, the identification of relatives, and the recognition of shared colloquialisms, history, and traditions (Spicer 1949). Similar patterns pertain to the Akimel O'odham living along the Gila River. Individuals identify where they come from on the basis of named, dispersed communities corresponding closely to districts, for example Blackwater (U'us Koek), Sacaton Flats (Ha-shan Koek), Komatkĭ, or Lone Butte (S-cuk Kavic). Such names identify an area or district, which in turn references the area's history and way of speaking and the families known to live there.

Three general points can be garnered from this revised approach to understanding village drift:

Village mobility and drifting is linked to landscape features, particularly along the Gila River. These include geomorphology, flood cycles, landscape change, and O'odham response to changing conditions.

Settlement districts traditionally define O'odham concepts of localization and self-identification. They tend to delimit dialect areas and territory administered by a council of elders or headmen. Finally, settlement districts define the limit that villages could drift without actually migrating.

Territorial marking within or between districts served to identify the areas where *rancherías*, or portions of a village, could feasibly drift. The most apparent evidence of territorial marking includes the regular spacing of cemeteries on ground above the limit of regular flooding. Cemeteries could serve as mnemonic landscape features that solidified land claims or resolved potential disputes, particularly during instances of land reoccupation by drifting villages (Darling et al. 2004).

Where district organization provides some limit to *ranchería* mobility, O'odham migration, at minimum, is the movement of a segment of the population outside its district. Village structure and the social relationships within a newly occupied region or landscape were reestablished. Migration can also be envisioned as a response to changing conditions or opportunities affecting existing populations. As such, when economic opportunity, the destructive forces of a catastrophic flood, or other socioeconomic conditions were not addressed by drifting, migration was a likely alternative.

Migration, therefore, is a district-level process in which individual families move to a location where they have established connections or a group of families might occupy a previously unoccupied area where a new district might be created. Drift, on the other hand, is household change on the level of individuals in families.

Numerous examples of migration can be described that include the Maricopa and Halchidhoma migrations from the lower Gila and Colorado rivers as well as smaller-scale moves by the Gila River Pima to the Salt River during periods of drought (Cameron 1994; Ezell 1963; Spier 1933; Wilson 1999). However, based on oral history research within the Gila River Indian Community, I believe that migration was as frequent a phenomenon as drifting.[2]

O'odham Mobility at the Regional Scale

A comprehensive examination of the record of O'odham migration within the Pimería Alta awaits further research. However, one case study is worth considering in light of this discussion.

As part of the Pima-Maricopa Irrigation Project (P-MIP)[3], two late historic archaeological sites, GR-649 and GR-1104, were excavated along a portion of canal reach WS-IC in the northern portion of the Gila River reservation known as the Broadacres. These sites were established as a result of several historical processes, including the use of the Broadacres area for commercial woodcutting. Following the 1906 revision to the Dawes Act, also known as the Burke Act, new incentives emerged to create non-Indian corporate farms on the reservation through the leasing of Indian allotments and canal construction. This included the creation of the Fowler Ranch in the Broadacres area in 1918. The ranch depended on the Fowler Ditch, a canal that was fed by runoff irrigation water from cotton farms in the city of Tempe to the north. Sites GR-649 and GR-1104 were established at roughly the same time and provided labor to the Fowler Ranch and the nearby Lone Butte Ranch. Each site represented clearly distinctive settlements. GR-649 was a traditional O'odham *ranchería* consisting of six to ten small dispersed square houses; *vatos*, or shade structures; a variety of trash-pit features; thermal roasting pits; and a probable elder's meeting house (*Je: n Ki*) in the traditional round house style. GR-1104 was an early reservation labor (work) camp that consisted of several one-room houses built on cement slabs, prefabricated outhouses, a camp store, a cistern, and showers. The camp was supervised by a non-Indian foreman. While GR-1104 certainly plays a role in settlement of the area after 1918, it is GR-649 and the emerging settlement district known as S-cuk Kavick that interests us here (Figure 4.2).

Labor opportunities in conjunction with the traditional use of this part of the reservation for gathering firewood for sale soon led to the establishment of as many as thirteen to fifteen traditional O'odham *rancherías* within only a few years. Settlement of the newly created district centered on the lease farms, the canals, and a prominent peak known as Lone Butte, or S-cuk Kavick. In time, a local entrepreneur established a store in a location identified as Drugstore Village (Amadeo Reo, personal communication), where he offered store credit

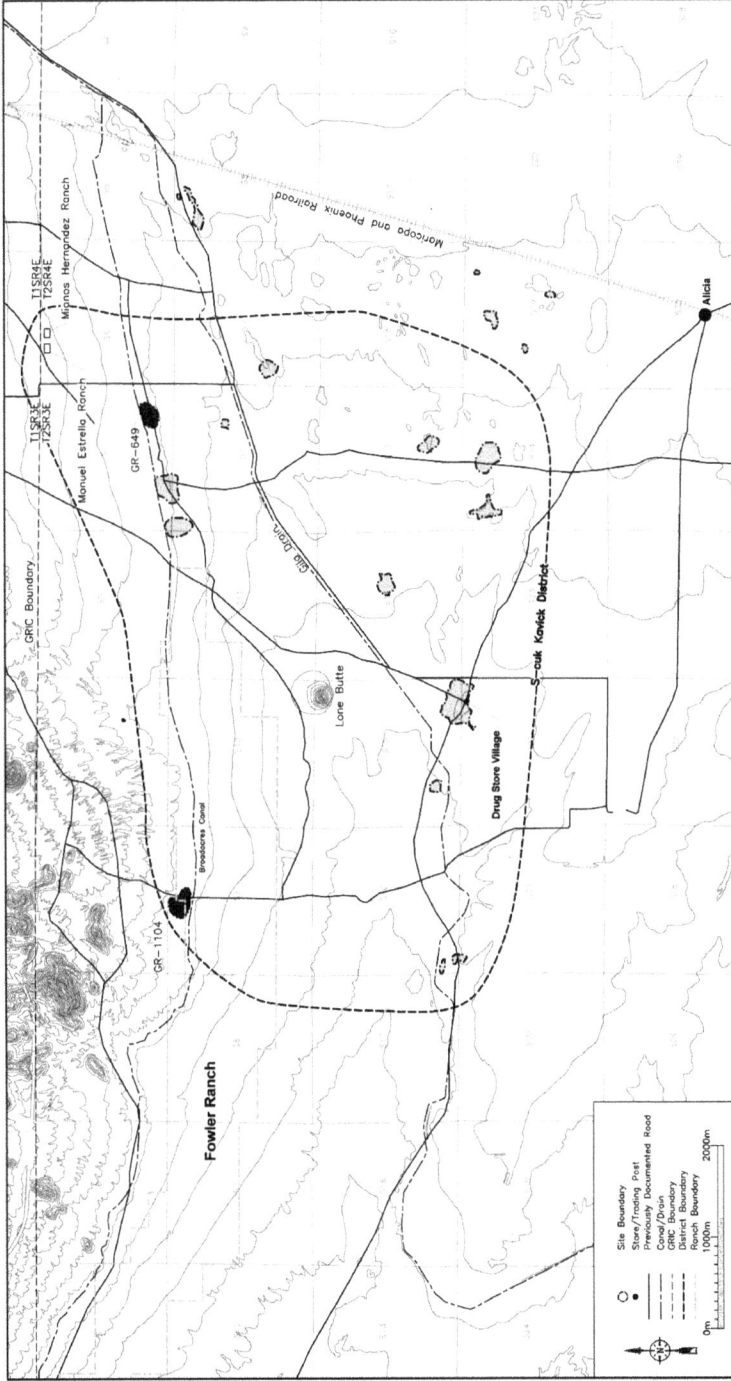

Figure 4.2. S-cuk Kavick and GR-649 in central Arizona.

in return for cut green wood, which he could later sell in Phoenix and Tempe to the north.

Of interest to the discussion of migration is the general recognition by Gila River Indian Community elders that S-cuk Kavick was settled by Tohono O'odham (Papago), who had earlier migrated to the west end of the community in the vicinity of Komatkĭ, St. Johns, and Santa Cruz. These O'odham established earlier wood-cutting camps in the S-cuk Kavick area prior to the creation of the lease farms that became more permanent as farming and labor opportunities developed. Oral history and genealogies also suggest that many of the O'odham who came to the west end and ultimately to S-cuk Kavick originated in communities located south of the international border. These included towns and villages with large O'odham populations such as Caborca, Quitovac, and Cuñ Ge: sh (Rabbit Falls). Elders sometimes refer to them as Je: kum O'odham, or Mexican Pimas. Initially, many of them settled in the St. John's area of the reservation in a place identified as Papago Hill and were known as Hiatup O'odham (roughly translated as "Sand Dune People"). Hiatup O'odham were often stigmatized for their use of the Spanish language and their dialect of the *O'odham niok* (Pima language). They also were identified in terms of distinctive patterns of material culture, including their use of adobe architecture.

Other associations with the Hiatup O'odham were religious in nature. This included their involvement with the Catholic Church, which was more tolerant of traditional practices of singing and curing. As a result several O'odham migrants from the south in the late nineteenth and early twentieth century are remembered as *mamakai*, or medicine people. They not only served the O'odham in traditional curing practices but also were sought out for medicine by Yaqui newcomers from Mexico living in the community of Guadalupe near Tempe. Finally, syncretic musical and dance traditions associated with the Catholic Church including *pascola* and *matachina* dancing were introduced at various times to the Catholic O'odham community living in the west end.

Many of these same practices associated with O'odham of Papago Hill extended to the S-cuk Kavick district and those who lived there seasonally. Oral history identifies many of the individuals who lived at GR-649, which became a center of social activities, particularly for celebrations such as Independence Day. Rodeos, foot races, traditional O'odham singing, and *pascola* and *matachina* dancing were featured attractions at celebrations. Yaqui relatives and friends from Guadalupe would also participate.

Gila River elders attribute a two-room adobe house to a man named Ge'e Sadivan ("Big Pants"), also known as Raymond Pablo. Raymond Pablo, who was likely Mexican Pima, also lived in the west end in Papago Hill, where he built similar adobe brick houses. Raymond Pablo is remembered both as a traditional *pascola* dancer and as the principal organizer of the celebrations at S-cuk Kavick. These were attended by other west-end O'odham with southern roots, including Don Thomas and Juan Chiago—both singers—as well as a patriarch and medicine man, Manuel Estrella (also known as "Curly Manol," or "old man Manuel"), and Mianos Hernandez, his kinsman (both migrants from Mexico and residents of S-cuk Kavick). Mianos Hernandez was remembered as a cowboy, a violin player, and a specialist in making musical bows.

The late Leonard Pancott, an elder and O'odham cowboy, participated in the rodeos organized by "Big Pants" and recalled both his adobe house and the celebrations (as told by Leonard Pancott to Gordon Domingo, July 23, 2003):

> LP: I know quite a few people (when they live), and for some reason, I don't care how hard up we are, we always find enough meat to put on a dance. [Laughs.] Yep! And the last celebration they had here is . . . I can remember it now . . . is in 1940, no . . . '41. Forty-one cuz, aah, I'm born and raised in Casa Blanca, or Bapchule, right around St. Peter's Mission. And them Catholics, [when] they came up this way, they had the Fourth of July celebration. And I was involved into other things and I went to Sacaton, where they had the rodeo. And some of the guys from my circle came up this way to make a horse race here. They had a trail there . . . race track . . . right in here someplace, about a half a mile. They run the horses, and on foot, during the celebration. And, I went to Sacaton on that day too, that Fourth of July. How I remember is, I won the saddle bronco there and I got seven dollars and fifty cents. [Laughs.] The next day I take off to Phoenix! I was a rich Indian!

Leonard Pancott also recalled the house (Feature 1) associated with Raymond Pablo (Big Pants):

> GD: And this feature here, we were talking about it and being that it is brick, you know, he kinda figured that maybe it wasn't Pima. Maybe the Mexicans migrated here before that time, you know and had built this and it was just occupied at the time that he was talking about the festivities because this isn't the style that we live in at that time. Like he said, he grew up in a arrow-weed frame. . . .
>
> LP: There is some people that are building but mostly it was originated from the Papagos. There's a lot of adobe houses but I never have seen . . . I've never, after I got big enough where I should be helping them, and running off some place. So I never got to see how they do it, how they build, and I often wondered what they do to make the foundation.

Within the last thirty years or so, forty years, it was, you know, they put an adobe house but they use cement foundations. Before that, I don't know what they do. They just level the ground and start it from there with a foundation, I don't know.

Many elders who remember S-cuk Kavick recall the gatherings of families to sing songs and socialize and remember that many of those who gathered there were related to or had family members still living on the border or in Mexico.

Spiritual Mountains and Dream Journeys

From the standpoint of migration, it is clear that in many ways, the Hiatup O'odham living in the west end of the Gila River Indian Community transported their lifestyles from their original homelands to the south. These traditions were subsequently tailored to the local landscape and social conditions, although many of the differences were perpetuated, particularly linguistic practices, several generations after the move. Archaeologically this is manifested in architectural house styles and in certain details of the material culture, although for historic Pima archaeology, we are only beginning to get a sense of these subtle differences. Certain elders from the west end, for example, continue to have a keen sense of the differences between Papago and Pima pottery, although this has not been put to the test with actual collections.

In terms of settlement and mobility, it is interesting that migration to the north did not imply that ties with family members to the south were severed. Elders remember short-term visits to the south for social and religious reasons, including memories of trips along wagon roads and trails connecting the western districts of Gila River with communities to the south as far as Sonora. Other trips include livestock drives from the St. Johns area to Ventana on the Tohono O'odham reservation. This suggests that Papago ranching or cowboy traditions influenced or were even introduced to the Gila River Indian Community. This is a point I will return to below.

Song practices were also transported to the north, although with the exception of dance traditions such as *pascola* and *matachina*, it is unclear how traditional songs were received in new social environments. In an earlier essay (2009), I was able to demonstrate how O'odham song cycles, which typically feature a detailed account of a journey, can in some circumstances be related to very specific geographic referents and identifiable trails. This was especially true of the Akimel O'odham (Pima) version of the Oriole songs as recorded by Don Bahr and Vincent Joseph (Bahr et al. 1997). In my interpretation of Bahr's translation, I found that this version of the Oriole song series clearly identifies a route of the O'odham Salt Journey particular to the Akimel O'odham.[4]

In my subsequent discussions, however, O'odham singers and elders pointed out that alternate versions of the Oriole songs exist and were performed in other locations. As they noted, it can be problematic for singers from different districts or reservations to sing the same songs together because of different understandings of the song geography. As Amadeo Rea has noted (in personal communication), the itinerary of the journey expressed in traditional O'odham song may have to be negotiated by the singers, particularly if they come from different O'odham traditions or geographic regions. This implies that song details reflect the district of origin and are therefore not universal. In Vincent Joseph's rendition of the Oriole songs, the point of origin is in his home district in Hashan Koek district (Gila River District 2). Alternate versions of the Oriole songs have yet to be examined in a comparative sense but should reflect geographical contrasts.

The Woodpecker Song Story

How, then, are song traditions adjusted to new geographic surroundings following migration, and is this adjustment indicative of cognitive adjustments by groups settling a new area? I find that one story from S-cuk Kavick describes the origin of the Hikvik (Woodpecker) songs and may addresses the issue directly. The story was told by an elder who grew up at S-cuk Kavick, but the event actually takes place in the west end and involves the singer Ron Chiago, who performed the Woodpecker songs during celebrations with Don Thomas.

> The story concerns a singer who knew the songs but no longer sang them correctly:
> A woodpecker builds a nest under the eaves of the singer's *vato* (shade). The singer is intrigued and keeps an eye on the nest until one day he reaches up and pulls out the woodpecker. As he stands there looking at the bird in his hand, a cat comes and carries the woodpecker off. Soon the singer becomes ill and an infection causes a small wound or hole in the back of his head to open up. As the singer lay on his bed with a fever, the woodpecker spirit comes to him and carries him on a journey. During the journey, the woodpecker instructs the singer in the correct performance of the songs.

The Hikvik story has many possible interpretations or meanings, and certain elders would interpret it as a story of cultural loss for which the singer suffers the consequences. However, I would propose that his re-learning of the songs also speaks of a process of revision in which the songs are recast in a new geographical environment after migration and resettlement. This is entirely speculative, since a translation of the Woodpecker songs is not available to me. However, elders acknowledge that songs change over time. Even suggesting that songs can be revised suggests that geographical revisions are possible as new lands are occupied through migration and that known songs may not be directly relevant in the new environment. Such processes as those demonstrated by the Hikvik story suggest a way that core principles shared by O'odham broadly may be perpetuated while expressions of cognitive geography (senses of space or places) may be adjusted to new landscapes and social conditions.

As a final example, traditions relating O'odham devil spirits (*jiavul*) and cowboys have been well documented by Kozak and Lopez (1999) for the Tohono O'odham and include shrines and topographic features thought to be associated with spirits and devil sickness. While devil associations occur at various locations in the Gila River Indian Community, associations between cowboy culture and devil songs seem to predominate in the west end as a result of recent Mexican O'odham and Tohono O'odham migration. Lone Butte, a volcanic remnant also known as Black Butte by the O'odham, has similar associations. I suggest that these associations between cowboys and devils as well as other traditions relate to the development of the S-cuk Kavick district during the early twentieth century.

As Leonard Pancott observes in his conversation with Gordon Domingo:

> GD: Yeah. The title of the whole area, that particular butte, is, ah, S-cuk Kavick, Black Butte. In the Pima we call it S-cuk Kavick.
>
> LP: And that according to the legend, that Black Butte was the third one to come up. South Mountain, the River, then this one, and the fourth one, way on the other hand, fourth mountain came up, which was on the edge of Estrella Mountain, where the lightning falls . . .

Damon Burden, field director on the excavations at S-cuk Kavick, interjects with the following question:

> DB: Would that be Pima Butte?
>
> LP: Yeah, it was Pima but it was the fourth one that came up, when this planet was made. I'm getting too deep, you guys wouldn't understand.

Leonard Pancott is referring to a song that discusses the origins of these mountains, which for some O'odham is a parallel story to the longer stories of creation. It is currently impossible to determine if the origin story of the

Lone Butte precedes the devil associations, which Pima cowboys may have introduced. Nevertheless, I feel that it has the potential to describe the ways that landscape concepts may be reformed to new environments without being totally abandoned.

Summary and Discussion

I have attempted to address the phenomenon of O'odham migration in two ways. First, migration, as a social process above the level of *rancherías* organized in settlement districts, was contrasted with local mobility defined as village drift or movements of individuals or families within districts. Second, through the example of an archaeological and oral history investigation of the origins of the S-cuk Kavick district after 1918 on the Gila River, I sought to demonstrate the ways that migrants proceeded from Mexico and the southern O'odham reservations to the west end of the Gila River community and subsequently established S-cuk Kavick in response to labor opportunities on newly leased farms.

I considered the implications for material cultural expressions in the archaeological context. More important, I addressed the ideological implications of settlement in a new area. I discussed O'odham song traditions as an expression of the ideological side of infrastructure and landscape ideology in light of these migratory processes. In particular, I wanted to consider or speculate on the potential impact of migration on cognitive expressions of geography through song. Accommodation and revision of song geographies without changing the basic structure of the songs is suggested by the story of the origin of the Woodpecker songs in the west end of the reservation. In this particular case, instead of abandoning songs or creating a new series, song geography appears to have been revised.

I feel there is enormous potential in the study of song geography for the very reason that with sufficient data on songs, directional patterns based on revisions as well as overlapping spatial geographies can be related to conceptual frameworks or cognitive geographies that can be further related to actual facilities such as trail networks on the ground.

Finally, O'odham migration can be summed up in terms of mobility above the level of settlement districts, which was not random but was shaped by existing infrastructure, including trail networks and other ideological and social networks such as song traditions. In the O'odham world, migration was also nondirectional, and while much of the oral historical record reviewed thus far suggests that many O'odham moved from south to north, this may also be indicative of historical conditions, including ethnic persecution, that contribute to large-scale migrations such as the Yaqui diaspora. It is interesting, however, to observe how migratory events may result in adjustments in geographical conceptualization and traditional song practices while other traditions such as the *pascola* and *matachina* dances may have been introduced and reintroduced into the northern Pimería Alta on several occasions. Social processes such as these provide ample room for considering larger-scale movements among Uto-Aztecans throughout north and west Mexico and into the Arid Southwest.

Conclusion

Elders invoke the metaphor of a spider web in describing the many migrations of O'odham throughout the Arid Southwest. This metaphor is used in much the same way that Henri Lefebvre (1991: 173) uses it. He does not use the spider-web image to answer Marx's question "Do spiders work?" Instead, Lefebvre asks whether the spider's web creates space in the same way that societies generate spaces through spatial practices. I would say that societies do operate in this way.

The ideas expressed in this essay have been inspired in their entirety from conversations with elders about migration and its relation to an archaeological record.[5] O'odham theorizing about their world contributes to this essay and to migration theory in general. Leonard Pancott provided his remembrances of S-cuk Kavick on July 23, 2003, approximately one year before his passing. His sensibilities are as valuable as French sociology and are directly relevant to understanding the past in O'odham terms. It was our loss in those moments when we could not "understand" that he would switch from English to speaking O'odham.

> Gordon Domingo (laughing): Well, that about covers it.
> Leonard Pancott: Yeah, that about covers it. Let's get out of here. I see that you think I'm pretty much bullshit. [Laughs.] Like I keep telling them, you know I can go back. I was born in 1919. I can remember when I was at least ten years old.
> GD: It's getting hot.
> LP: Yeah, it's getting to be that time. I want to go watch the damn cartoons.

Notes

1. Ezell's recognition of gradual versus larger-scale (in terms of population) migratory processes precedes similar distinctions recognized by Bernardini (2005), who, among others, emphasizes the archaeological limitations involved in migratory events that are hard to see archaeologically versus migratory processes involving smaller incremental moves.

2. O'odham migration was a frequent occurrence in the first half of the twentieth century, when the Arizona cotton boom perpetuated and expanded upon traditional migratory labor patterns associated with the harvest of wheat and other crops (Dobyns 1989; Waddell 1969).

3. P-MIP is a long-term tribal self-governance project sponsored by the Bureau of Reclamation on the Gila River Indian reservation to build and design a water-delivery system consisting of more than 80 miles of mainstem canal.

4. The Tohono O'odham Salt Journey route is well documented (Lumhotz 1912; Underhill 1946).

5. Interpretations and misinterpretations of fact are mine alone and do not represent the official views of O'odham communities or Tribal members living in the United States or Mexico. I am grateful to elder consultants, Gordon Domingo especially, who provided their input, while working on behalf of the Cultural Resource Management Program of the Gila River Indian Community.

References

Bahr, D., L. Paul, and V. Joseph
1997   *Ants and Orioles: Showing the Art of Pima Poetry.* University of Utah Press, Salt Lake City.
Bahr, D., J. Smith, W. S. Allison, and J. Hayden
1994   *The Short Swift Time of Gods on Earth.* University of California Press, Berkeley.
Bernardini, Wesley
2005   *Hopi Oral Tradition and the Archeology of Identity.* University of Arizona Press, Tucson.
Cameron, L.
1994   Estrella Dawn: The Origin of the Maricopa. *Journal of the Southwest* 36(1): 54–75.
Darling, J. A.
2009   O'odham Trails and the Archaeology of Space. In *Landscapes of Movement: Trails, Paths, and Roads in Anthropological Perspective*, edited by J. E. Snead, C. L. Erikson, and J. A. Darling. University of Pennsylvania, Philadelphia.
Darling, J. A., and B. S. Eiselt
2009   Trails Research in the Gila Bend Area. In *Trails, Rock Features and Homesteading in the Gila Bend Area: A Report on the State Route 85, Gila Bend to Buckeye Archaeological Project*, edited by J. C. Czarzasty, K. Peterson, G. E. Rice, and J.

A. Darling, pp. 199-227. Anthropological Research Papers no. 4 (Arizona State University Anthropological Field Studies no. 43), Gila River Indian Community, Sacaton, Az.

Darling, J. A., and B. V. Lewis

2007 Songscapes and Calendar Sticks. In *The Hohokam Millennium*, edited by S. K. Fish and P. R. Fish, pp. 130–139. School for Advanced Research Press, Santa Fe, N.M.

Darling, J. A., J. C. Ravesloot, and M. R. Waters

2004 Village Drift and Riverine Settlement: Modeling Akimel O'odham Land Use. *American Anthropologist* 106(2):282–295.

Dewar, R., and K. McBride

1992 Remnant Settlement Patterns. In *Space, Time, and Archaeological Landscapes*, edited by J. Rossignol and L. Wandsnider, pp. 193–226. Plenum Press, New York.

Dobyns, H. F.

1989 *The Pima-Maricopa*. Chelsea House Publishers, New York.

Ezell, P. H.

1961 *The Hispanic Acculturation of the Gila River Pimas*. Memoirs of the American Anthropological Association 90. American Anthropological Association, Menasha, Wisc.

1963 *The Maricopas. An Identification from Documentary Sources*. University of Arizona Anthropological Papers no. 6. University of Arizona Press, Tucson.

Fontana, B. L.

1983 Pima and Papago: Introduction. In *Handbook of North American Indians*, vol. 10, *Southwest*, edited by A. Ortiz, pp. 125-136. Smithsonian Institution, Washington, D.C.

Harwell, H. O., and M. C. S. Kelly

1983 Maricopa. In *Handbook of North American Indians*, vol. 10, *Southwest*, edited by A. Ortiz, pp. 71–85. Smithsonian Institution, Washington, D.C.

Kozak, D. L., and D. I. Lopez

1999 *Devil Sickness and Devil Songs*. Smithsonian Institution Press, Washington, D.C.

Lefebvre, H.

1991 *The Production of Space*. Blackwell Publishing, Ltd., Oxford.

Lumhohltz, C.

1912 *New Trails in Mexico*. Charles Scribner's Sons, New York.

Spicer, R. B.

1949 People on the Desert. In *The Desert People: A Study of the Papago Indians of Southern Arizona*, edited by A. Joseph, R. B. Spicer, and J. Chesky, pp. 3–93. University of Chicago Press, Chicago.

Spier, L.

1933 *Yuman Tribes of the Gila River*. Cooper Square Publishers, New York.

Underhill, R. M.
1946 *Papago Indian Religion.* Columbia University Press, New York.
Waddell, J. O.
1969 *Papago Indians at Work.* Anthropological Papers of the University of Arizona no. 12. University of Arizona Press, Tucson.
Wilson, J. P.
1999 Peoples of the Middle Gila: A Documentary History of the Pimas and Maricopas, 1500s–1945. Manuscript on file. Cultural Resource Management Program, Gila River Indian Community, Sacaton, Ariz.

5

Disappearance and Diaspora

Contrasting Two Migrations in the Southern U.S. Southwest

JEFFERY J. CLARK

Since the publication of David Anthony's seminal article in 1990, archaeologists of the U.S. Southwest—particularly those working in the late precontact period (A.D. 1200–1500)—have returned to migration in their explanations of material culture change (e.g., Adams and Duff 2004; Adler 1996; Bernardini 2005; Cameron 1995; Ciolek-Torrello 1997; Clark 2001; Crown 1994; Lyons 2003; Neuzil 2008; Rice 1998; Riggs 2001; Spielmann 1998). This resurgence of migrationist explanations is ironically fitting, considering that the U.S. Southwest was the epicenter of processual, or New, Archaeology, which initially threw the migration baby out with the cultural historical bathwater (although a few Southwest archaeologists never abandoned migration during this era [see, e.g., Lindsay 1987; Longacre 1976; Reid 1989]). Beginning in the mid-1990s, the topic reentered mainstream archaeology with a vengeance.

Definition

To study migration systematically, the term must be defined and differentiated from other forms of human movement. My perspective on migration is derived from the precontact U.S. Southwest, when the region was likely populated by small- to medium-sized agricultural communities dependent on pedestrian travel. In this region, migrations were typically organic movements by small groups rather than colonizations and forced resettlements directed by a centralized political authority (Cameron 1995). From this vantage point, I define migration as *a long-term residential relocation by one or more social groups across community boundaries in response to spatially uneven changes in social and economic conditions.* While this definition has an intentional degree of ambiguity, particularly with the use of such terms as "long-term residential relocation," "community boundaries," and "social groups," it excludes short-term visits and movements by individuals, including those attributed to post-marital residence patterns (Herr and Clark 2002). It also excludes localized and scheduled movements such as seasonal rounds by hunter-gatherers and other nonsedentary groups.

This definition of migration includes many elements of the minimal defi-nition presented in the introduction of this volume. For a migration to oc-cur, some measurable boundary must be traversed and this movement must be relatively permanent (i.e., one way). However, my definition raises the minimal emigrant unit from the individual to the social group. Such groups could include scouting parties, households, small suprahousehold groups, and larger social formations. Regardless of the distance and boundaries traversed, the movement of a single individual is not migration, although that individ-ual could still be considered an emigrant. Also, in my definition, the type of boundary traversed is explicitly that of a community rather than a more ge-neric "environment." Here, a community is defined in the traditional archaeo-logical sense as co-residence of groups (typically households) that interact frequently at social, economic, and political scales based on spatial proxim-ity and shared history (Fish et al. 1992; Murdock 1949; Rohn 1971; Wills and Leonard 1994). Implicit in this definition is the notion that the community is a sedentary or semi-sedentary organization that occupies a circumscribed geographic space and possesses some concept of territoriality.

This definition has a number of advantages for the archaeologist. First, it excludes many small-scale movements that are beyond archaeological detec-tion and focuses attention on those that are more likely to have a significant impact. Second, the definition emphasizes the rational motives behind mi-gration (Anthony's [1990] often-cited "pushes" and "pulls"). Identifying these motives enables archaeologists to study migration as a predictable process instead of a historical accident or random event.

Finally, the definition emphasizes the spatial and temporal "discreteness" of social groups when examining the impact of migration processes in local contexts at maximum resolution. As is evident in the fine-grained archaeo-logical record of the U.S. Southwest (Clark 2001; Haury 1945, 1958; Lyons 2003; Neuzil 2008; Riggs 2001), migrations do not occur in continuous waves but as point-to-point movements across the landscape (Anthony 1990). The uneven discontinuous movements by immigrants generate numerous microcontexts in which immigrant and local groups can interact cooperatively or competi-tively. In the late precontact Southwest, the postmigration social map becomes increasingly complex as more data allow for finer resolution. If the old view of migration was as a "culture replacer," the new view is of migration as a "social mixer." As such, migration can be a potent force for change because new social institutions are required to integrate local and immigrant groups. Previously rigid social structures can be rapidly transformed under the pressure of immigration, leading to collapse or reorganization. Consequently, the postmigration world is often a structurally fluid setting, ripe for change by human agents.

Breaking Down Migration

As per Herr and Clark (1997), archaeological migration can be partitioned into four broad research categories: (1) detection of occurrence and scale; (2) motivation; (3) logistics/organization during migration; and (4) impact in homeland and destination areas. Here I will focus on the first and last topics, detection and impact. Motivation is a topic already extensively covered in Anthony (1990) and will not be addressed further here. The remaining topic, logistics/organization during migration, is difficult to address with archaeological data given the ephemeral character of emigrant settlements on the move and so will also not be discussed in this chapter.

Detection of Occurrence and Scale

Although largely a methodological issue, evaluating the occurrence and scale of migration in the archaeological record is perhaps the most important of the four categories. When consensus cannot be reached on this basic issue, subsequent debate often devolves into polemical quagmires. Over the past fifty years, the related concepts of culture drift (Binford 1963), isochrestic variation (Sackett 1977, 1985, 1986), technological style (Lechtman 1977), and low-visibility style (Carr 1995) have been used by archaeologists to reliably demonstrate migration. These various concepts are all related to an "etic" dimension of style that is low in message content but still provides valuable information on cultural background and settlement history. The messageless dimension tends to be more conservative within groups and less easily copied by other groups than the more visible and iconographic emic dimension that is consciously produced to convey social messages (Wiessner 1983; Wobst 1977). More recently the messageless dimension has been linked to Bordieu's (1977) concept of habitus (Burmeister 2000; Stone 2003), or the underlying rules that structure interaction within a society. These rules are passed between generations at the family and community levels through socialization.

The optimal archaeological correlates of "style without a message," or habitus, are attributes of tools, textiles, architecture, and cuisine with low contextual and physical visibility that also reflect culturally dictated choices made during production (Carr 1995). These choices yield unique *technological styles* (Childs 1991; Lechtman 1977; Lemonnier 1986; Stark et al. 1998) that provide information about the producer's cultural background, learning framework, and community of practice. Technological styles can be found in mundane artifacts used in domestic settings such as bedding, clothing, utilitarian ceramics, and flaked and ground stone implements (J. Adams 2002; Newton 1974; Sackett 1982; Stark et al. 1998; Webster 2007). Technological styles can also be found in walls, domestic installations, the organization of domestic space, and food recipes (e.g., Baker 1980; Collett 1987; Diehl et al. 1998; Ferguson 1992; Wegars 1991). Correlating these styles with specific social groups and mapping their spatial and temporal distributions has allowed archaeologists to track movements of the associated groups with reasonable confidence (e.g., Carr and Maslowski 1995; Clark 2001; Clark et al. in press; Lyons 2003; Mills 1998; Neuzil 2008). Furthermore, use of these datasets to detect the occurrence of migration and pinpoint immigrant enclaves is supported by ethnographic, ethnohistoric, and ethnoarchaeological data (Clark 2001).

Evaluating the Impact of Migration

The impact of migration is perhaps the most interesting of the four topics from an anthropological perspective. While displacement of one group by another is possible, archaeological studies in the precontact U.S. Southwest indicate that migrations more often resulted in the co-residence of different immigrant and local groups within communities, settlements, and even houses (E. C. Adams 2002; Bernardini 2005; Cameron 1995; Clark 2001; Mills 1998; Neuzil 2001; Riggs 2001).

Once immigrants and locals have been identified through the low-visibility dimension of style discussed above, changes in settlement pattern and site layout (or lack thereof) reveal how immigrants and locals are getting along. In addition, patterning between immigrant and local groups in highly visible forms of material culture such as ceremonial architecture, design elements and symbols on any media, and various luxury goods can be used to reconstruct the social and economic relations in the postmigration setting (Carr 1995; Clark 2001). These material culture types and attributes have a high message potential that reflects differences of status and wealth. They also inform about whether known cultural differences, identified using low-visibility style, are being suppressed, actively displayed, or mediated.

In migration processes, the chain of movement, co-residence, and subsequent movement can generate a complicated social map. While immigrant and local groups may have had contact prior to movement, after contact they are forced to "share" resources and interact more frequently. Such interaction may be cooperative, resulting in multicultural networks and integrative institutions (Crown 1994; Lyons and Lindsay 2006), or competitive, resulting in sporadic violence and organized conflict (Rice and LeBlanc 2001; Wilcox et al. 2001). In symmetrical immigrant-local power relationships, this interaction may lead to the formation of new religions and identities and even to ethnogenesis (Crown 1994; Haury 1945; Williams 1992). In asymmetrical relationships, interaction can lead to assimilation, replacement, displacement, and even genocide.

Immigrants from the same origin that move to different locations can maintain long-distance networks based on their shared heritage and origin. These networks may develop into diasporic communities if the immigrant identity is sufficiently developed to persist across generations (Clifford 1994; Cohen 1997; Orser 1998; Safran 1991). Goods and ideas can move within these decentralized communities that provide immigrants and their descendants with opportunities unavailable to local groups. Diasporic communities are often transformed in exile as immigrant descendants are caught between maintaining traditions and assimilating within local contexts (Clifford 1994:311–312). Archaeological signatures of diasporic communities include stylistic horizons and exchange networks associated with immigrants and their descendants (Orser 1998).

Considering the broad range and spatial variability of immigrant-local interaction, a bottom-up approach that reconstructs this interaction at local scales (in the U.S. Southwest, this would be within individual valleys and basins) is required to make sense of the complicated postmigration world. Following the careful reconstruction of local culture histories in areas potentially impacted by migration, the archaeologist can step back to identify common themes. These themes and the variation within them are equally important in reconstructing migration processes.

Ancestral Puebloan Immigration in the Lower San Pedro Valley

To demonstrate the two-step methodology in detecting the occurrence/scale and evaluating the impact of migration, as discussed above, I will draw on a well-documented case study from the southeastern Arizona during the late precontact period (Figure 5.1). Within this region, the Center for Desert Archaeology (Tucson, Arizona) has conducted extensive survey and test excavations in the northern or "lower" San Pedro Valley (Clark and Lyons 2011). This research, combined with earlier work accomplished primarily by the Amerind Foundation (Di Peso 1958; Gerald 1975), has led to the subdivision of the lower San Pedro into four districts based on differences in settlement pattern and

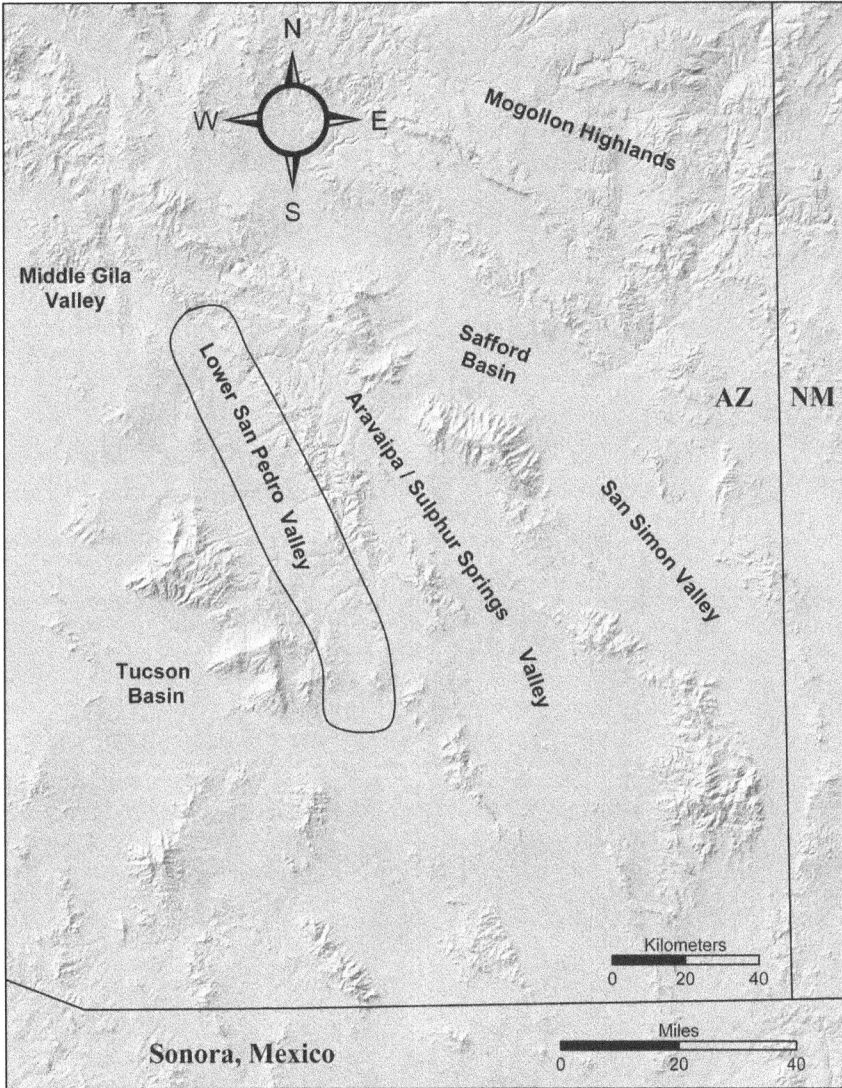

Figure 5.1. Lower San Pedro Valley study area, southeastern Arizona.

material culture (Figure 5.2). Recent chronological refinements in ceramic and architectural classifications (Lyons 2004, 2011) have allowed us to further subdivide the late precontact period (from A.D. 1200 to A.D. 1450) into four intervals, each 50 to 75 years long (Clark et al. forthcoming).

Through much of the precontact sequence, the local population of the lower San Pedro Valley was part of the Hohokam world, which was centered on the Phoenix Basin (Masse et al. forthcoming). "Hohokam" is a traditional

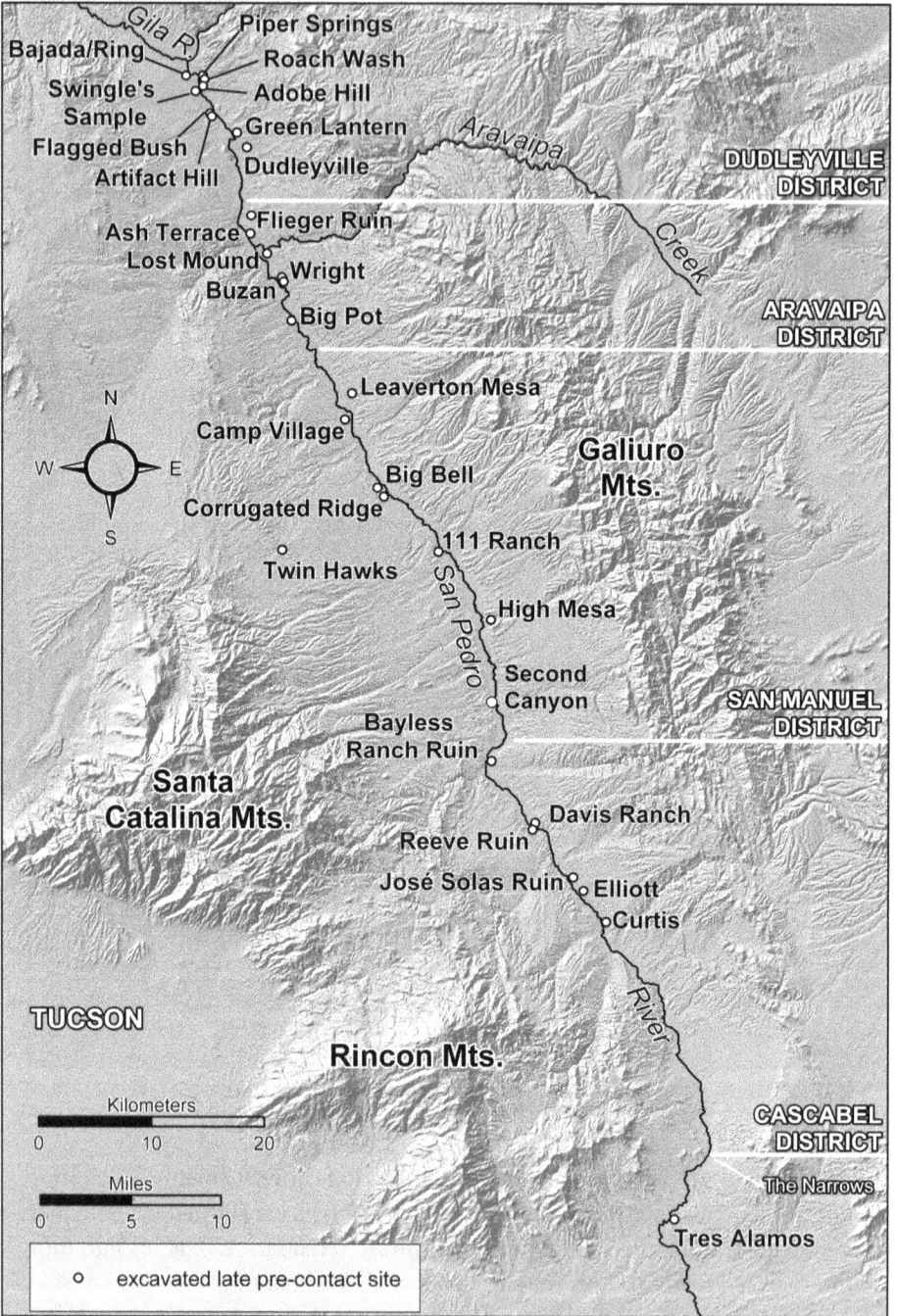

Figure 5.2. Excavated sites in the lower San Pedro Valley, with district boundaries.

U.S. Southwest "culture area" with artifacts, architecture, and settlement patterns that have been associated with economic, cultural, and religious institutions that focused on irrigation agriculture (Abbott 2000; Crown and Judge 1991; Doyel 1987; Haury 1976). By A.D. 1200, a number of Hohokam communities had developed within the few river valleys that dissect the semi-arid Sonoran Desert. Many of these communities can be traced back for at least 500 years (and some perhaps longer than a millennium), as social groups were tethered to the relatively few locations in the river valleys where sustainable canal systems were possible (Abbott 2000; Clark and Gilman forthcoming; Craig and Clark 1994; Gregory 1991; Masse et al forthcoming; Tuthill 1947). This fostered deep sedentism and long-term community stability that stands in stark contrast to the residential mobility of Ancestral Puebloan communities to the north (see Bernardini, this volume; Fowles, this volume).

Mogollon Highland Immigration and Subsequent "Disappearance"

Based on the available evidence, two migrations from the Ancestral Puebloan world in northern and central Arizona into the lower San Pedro Valley can be identified. The first occurred during the late 1100s and early 1200s. This initial migration is indicated primarily by low-message attributes: the distribution of utilitarian corrugated pottery manufactured using a coil-and-scrape technological style generally associated with Ancestral Puebloan groups. This technological style can be contrasted with local Hohokam-influenced styles that include paddle-and-anvil manufacture and a polished nontextured surface treatment.

A plot of corrugated ceramic density in the utilitarian ceramic assemblages recovered from 256 systematically sampled sites in east-central Arizona dating primarily from A.D. 1150 to 1300 shows a corrugated-ceramic "corridor" penetrating the northeastern flank of the Hohokam world (Figure 5.3; Clark and Lengyel 2002). This corridor extends through the Safford Basin, cuts through the central portion of the lower San Pedro Valley, and finally ends in the Tucson Basin.

Increasing the resolution to the terminus of this corridor, we find corrugated ceramics in quantity only within the San Manuel District of the lower San Pedro (Figure 5.4). Sites in the central portion of this district have over 50 percent corrugated wares in their utilitarian ceramic assemblages. West of this district, the 10 and 20 percent contour intervals extend over Redington Pass, where the distribution abruptly ends in the northeast Tucson Basin. Petrographic analysis of sand temper in corrugated ceramics indicates that these were locally produced throughout this area, excluding trade as a mechanism for their distribution (Heidke 1996; Lyons 2011; Neuzil 2008).

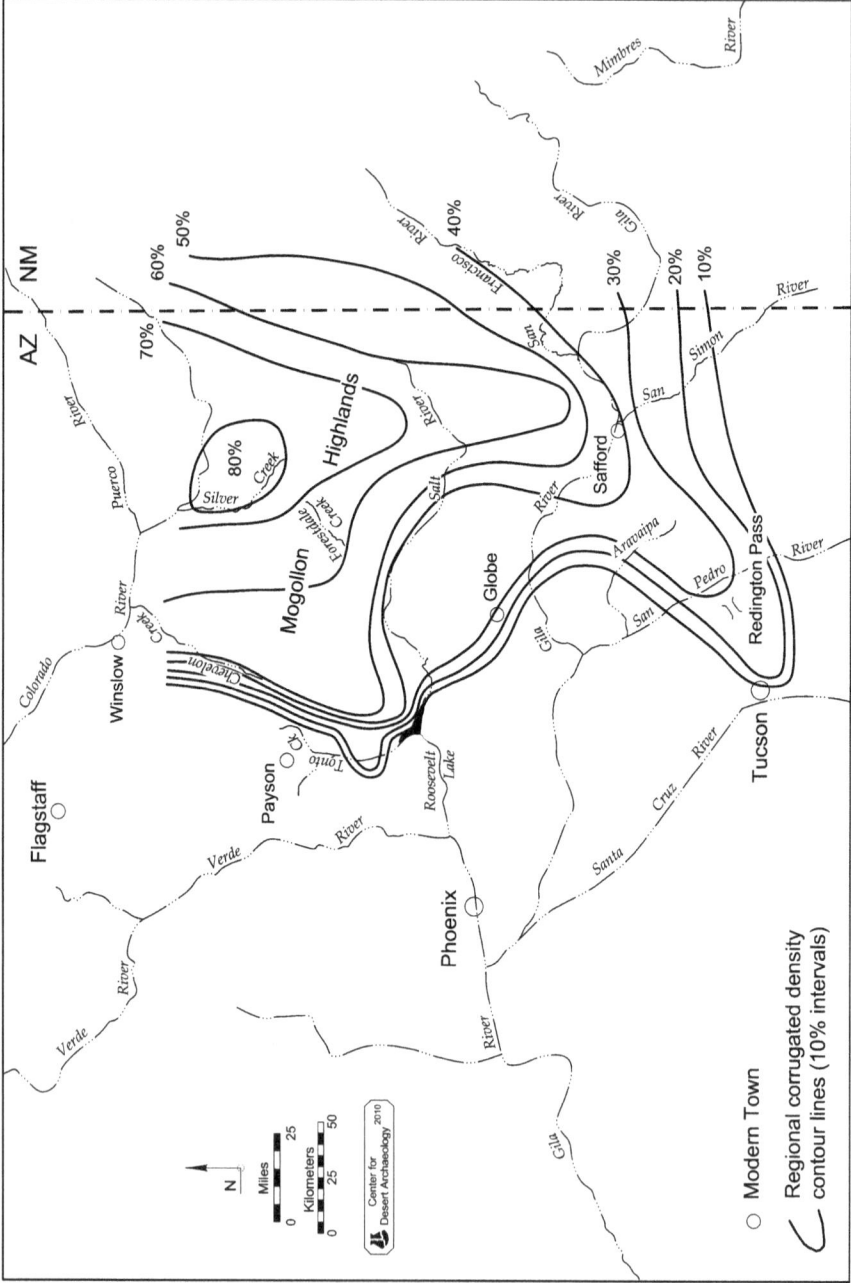

Figure 5.3. Percentages of corrugated ceramics in utilitarian ceramic assemblages in east-central Arizona, plotted as isobars (ca. A.D. 1150 to 1300).

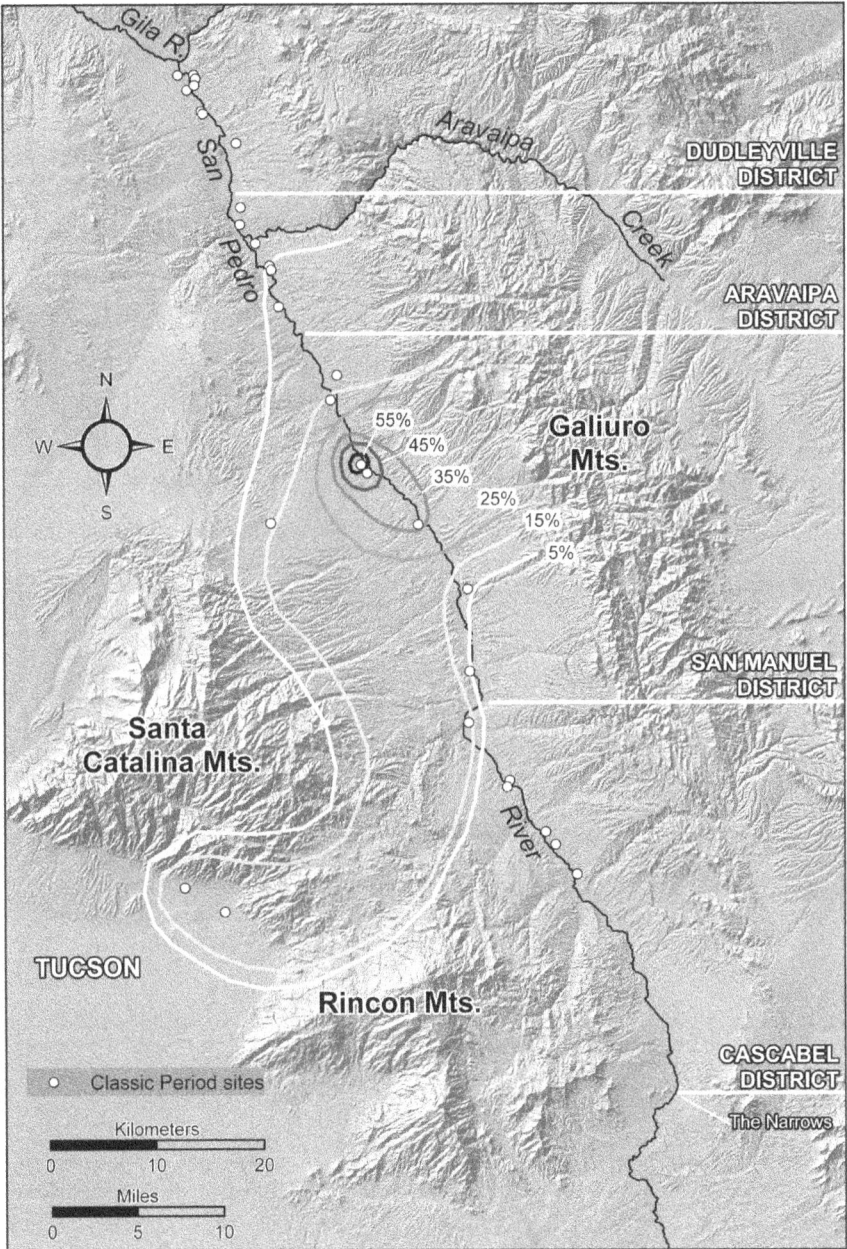

Figure 5.4. Plot of corrugated ceramic percentages in lower San Pedro Valley utilitarian ceramic assemblages. Note that corrugated ceramics are found in quantity only in the San Manuel district.

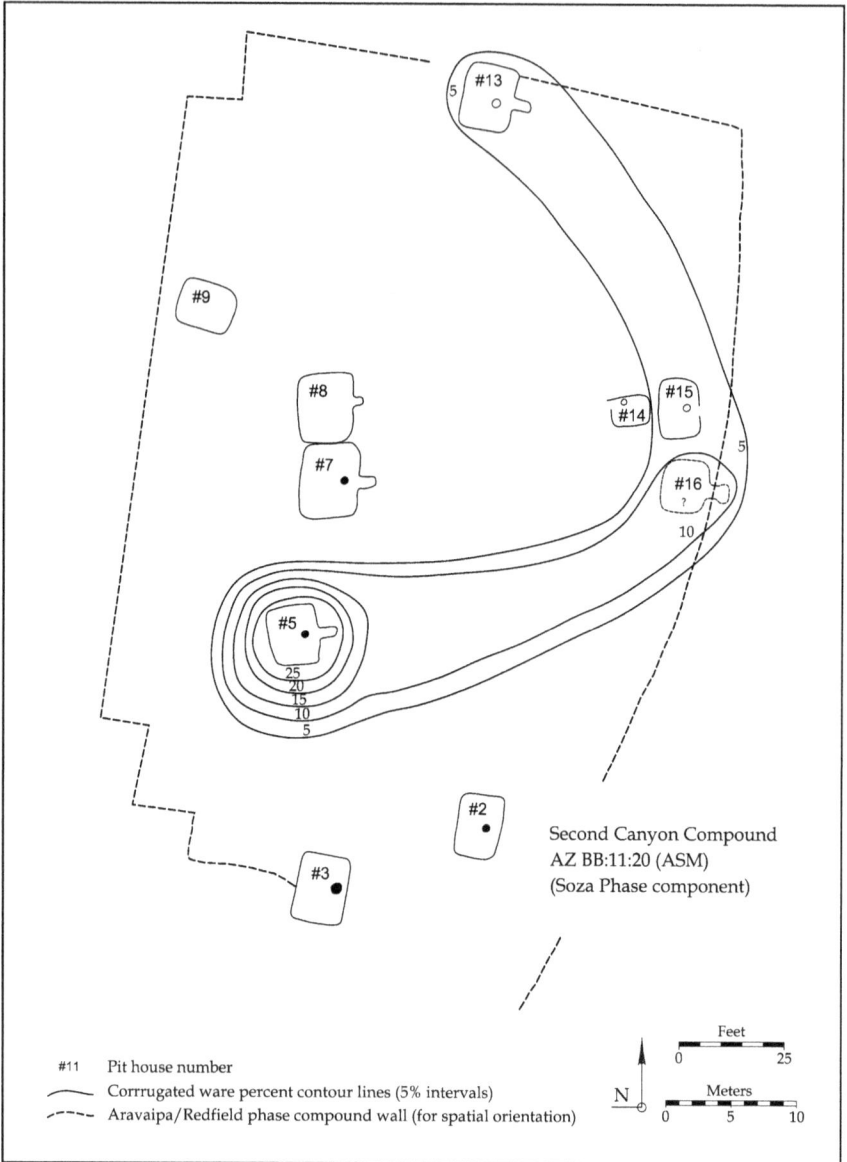

Figure 5.5. Second Canyon, located on the southern edge of the corrugated corridor, lower San Pedro Valley.

Further increasing resolution to the settlement level, Second Canyon lies on the southern edge of the corrugated corridor in the lower San Pedro Valley. In the thirteenth-century component of the site, corrugated wares are concentrated in one pithouse (Figure 5.5). This highly uneven distribution suggests that the inhabitants of this structure or nearby groups that used it as a trash dump had substantially more corrugated vessels in their domestic assemblage than other resident households.

At all three levels of resolution, the distribution of corrugated ceramics is consistent with the migration of Ancestral Puebloan households (probably from the nearby Mogollon highlands in east-central Arizona) into the northeastern portion of the Hohokam world. The inhabitants of the San Manuel District appear to have been more tolerant of these immigrants than those in other districts. As the evidence in Second Canyon indicates, immigrants were allowed to settle in local villages, suggesting close interaction and minimal tension.

The density of corrugated ware in the San Manuel District suggests that the scale of migration was appreciable at least in this area. However, it is likely these newcomers were a minority in all but the most dense areas. With the exception of early experimentation with masonry construction techniques, few other changes are noted in the material culture of local settlements during this interval. Throughout the lower San Pedro the dispersed settlement pattern that characterized the previous interval continued. Although this migration can be detected using ceramic technological styles, the social and economic impact as expressed in settlement pattern and high-visibility material culture was minimal. Immigrants integrated closely with local groups in the San Manuel District and "disappeared" archaeologically by A.D. 1300, when corrugated pottery production tapered off in the region. Thus, in this example, although a migration can be detected, it apparently had minimal impact on the local population.

The Kayenta Diaspora

The exodus from the Four Corners area by Kayenta and Tusayan groups in the late 1200s can be contrasted with this earlier migration (Figure 5.6). The Kayenta region, in particular, was almost completely depopulated, and emigrants from this region dominated the eastern migration stream that ultimately reached the lower San Pedro Valley. This diaspora, one of the most intensively examined migration processes in the ancient Southwest (Di Peso 1958; Haury 1958; Lindsay 1987; Lyons 2003; Lyons and Lindsay 2006; Reid 1989; Riggs 2001), was in part triggered by the so-called Great Drought indicated in the tree-ring record. Problems created by this environmental downturn were

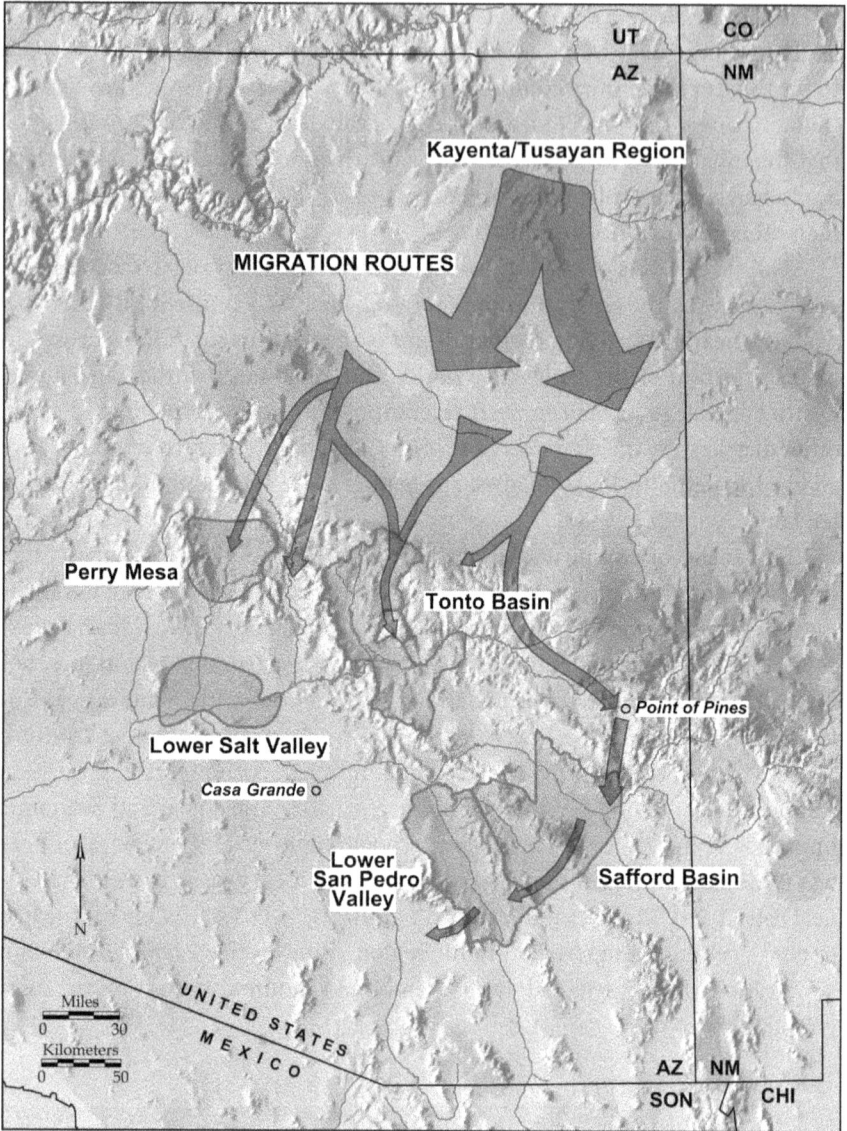

Figure 5.6. Migrations of Kayenta and Tusayan groups into central and southern Arizona in the late 1200s and early 1300s A.D.

exacerbated by social factors, leading to the complete collapse of communities in this region (Dean 1996). These economic refugees took advantage of earlier migration routes and social networks that accommodated them once they reached the Mogollon highlands, allowing them to ultimately move into the Safford Basin (Neuzil 2008; Woodson 1999) and the lower San Pedro Valley

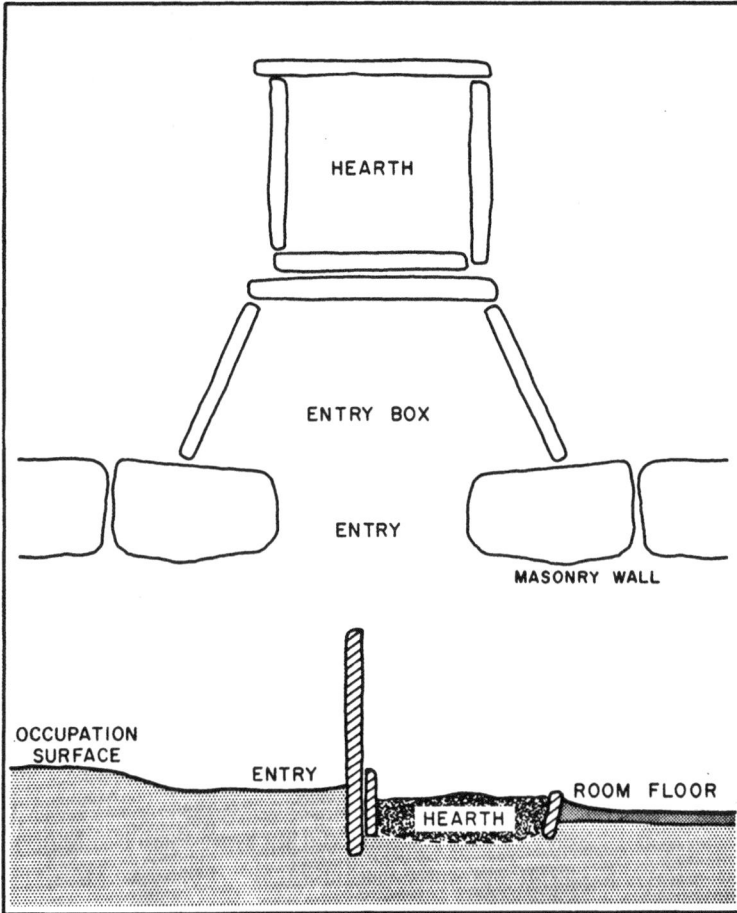

Figure 5.7. A slab-lined entry box, accompanied by a square hearth also lined with stone, is a marker of Kayenta immigrants in the lower San Pedro Valley. Top: plan view; bottom: cross-section.

(Clark et al. in press). Unlike the earlier Mogollon highland immigrants, Kayenta groups possessed a well-developed identity and decorated-ceramic tradition. They soon became powerful minorities in each of their destination areas, maintaining connections with Kayenta groups in other regions and ultimately forming a diasporic community.

In the lower San Pedro, Kayenta immigrants settled primarily in the Cascabel District during the late thirteenth century and early fourteenth centuries, and they soon became the dominant population there (see Figure 5.2). Their presence is indicated by a high density of distinctive domestic installations such as entry boxes (Figure 5.7; Lindsay et al. 1968) and utilitarian ceramic forms such as perforated plates (Lyons and Lindsay 2006). Both entry boxes and perforated plates are concentrated at Reeve Ruin and Davis Ranch. They are also found at other enclaves along the migration route (Lyons and Lindsay 2006; Woodson 1999). Prior to this interval, these distinctive markers were found only in the Kayenta region.

Shortly after the arrival of the first Kayenta immigrants, dramatic changes occurred in the lifeways of the local inhabitants. In terms of high-visibility material culture, the immigrants brought their distinctive decorated ceramic tradition with them, reproducing it using local raw materials (Maverick Mountain Series). At approximately the same time, the local red-on-brown tradition ceramic tradition was revived in the Aravaipa District to the north. This tradition was influenced technologically and stylistically by earlier and contemporaneous Hohokam ceramic traditions in the Phoenix and Tucson basins. While immigrant-decorated ceramics are found in substantial quantities at immigrant settlements in the Cascabel District and in limited quantities at local settlements, red-on-brown ceramics are virtually absent from immigrant settlements. This distribution suggests that the newcomers overtly expressed their identity on decorated ceramics shortly after their arrival. This expression triggered a response in kind by local groups, illustrated by the revival of the local decorated ceramic tradition.

Differences in conspicuous material culture between local and immigrant groups were not restricted to decorated ceramics. Early Kayenta immigrants built kivas such as the example at the Davis Ranch site excavated by the Amerind Foundation (Di Peso 1958). This suggests that ancestral Puebloan religion survived intact at least initially in their destination areas. However, this kiva was abandoned, filled with trash, and used as a burial area during the occupation of the settlement, indicating that the descendants did not continue the religious traditions of their immigrant parents.

Partially in response to the immigrant "threat," local groups constructed platform mounds using a template borrowed from the Hohokam in the Phoenix Basin. Although San Pedro Valley mounds were much smaller than their Phoenix Basin counterparts, they were nonetheless visible territorial markers of first-comer status and the long history of local groups in the area in the face of a burgeoning immigrant population. Mound construction was probably part of a strategy to legitimize claims of local groups to the best agricultural land in the lower San Pedro floodplain. This scenario is supported by the fact that the largest concentration of platform mounds is in the Aravaipa District, the most fertile region in the valley. In addition, platform mounds were constructed in every major settlement within the San Manuel District. As expected, no mounds were built in the Kayenta-dominated Cascabel District and no kivas have been identified outside this district.

Another indicator of the substantial impact of Kayenta immigration is the dramatic change in the settlement pattern of local groups shortly after the arrival of these immigrants. Nucleated and planned villages replaced the dispersed farmsteads and hamlets that had characterized the previous interval. Although the causes of this aggregation have not been fully established, elevated social tensions and perhaps overt conflict with Kayenta immigrants probably played an important role. Evidence that supports this scenario includes the fact that immigrant and local settlements near the boundary between the groups were built in defensible positions that were further enhanced by architectural construction. These fortified settlements may have served as refuges for the inhabitants of less-defensible settlements in the vicinity during times of trouble.

After a generation or two of interaction between immigrant and local groups, material culture patterns indicated that initially well-demarcated social boundaries began to dissolve, although both groups maintained aspects of their identity. During the early 1300s, the distinctive and potentially divisive immigrant and local decorated-ceramic traditions were replaced by a new tradition associated with Salado polychromes. This replacement occurred not only in the lower San Pedro but also throughout much of the Hohokam world. In the lower San Pedro, petrographic sourcing suggests that the Kayenta immigrants and their descendants made much of this pottery.

Salado polychromes have close stylistic and technological parallels to Kayenta decorated pottery in the homeland (Lyons 2003). However, these vessels differ from Kayenta pottery in the use of an exterior red slip that resembles red wares produced by local potters. This change may represent a conscious attempt to increase its appeal to local groups. Salado polychromes not only dominate the decorated assemblages of Kayenta enclaves in the Cascabel District, they are also the prevalent decorated types found in local platform mound villages to the north. This exchange suggests close interaction between local and immigrant groups in which the latter remained a powerful minority. However, changes in ceramic decoration and the abandonment of kivas and associated ideology suggest that Kayenta identity had also been substantially transformed.

In addition to decorated ceramics, Kayenta immigrants and their descendants controlled much of the obsidian trade in the lower San Pedro. Obsidian, ideal for making sharp stone tools, is rarely encountered in assemblages that predate the arrival of Kayenta groups. Immigrant enclaves in the Cascabel

District are associated with much higher densities of obsidian than that of contemporaneous local villages. However, the latter were still associated with substantially higher obsidian frequencies than local settlements that predate Kayenta immigration.

Energy Dispersive X-Ray Fluorescent (EDXRF) sourcing reveals that the vast majority of lower San Pedro obsidian was obtained from the Cow Canyon and Mule Creek formations east of the Safford Basin, another destination area for Kayenta immigrants (Neuzil 2008; Woodson 1999). This evidence also supports the existence of a Kayenta diasporic community that included immigrants in the lower San Pedro. Long-distance connections associated with this community allowed immigrants and their descendants to exploit differences in resources such as obsidian between valleys and basins.

Despite the evidence for increased interaction between local and immigrant groups during the fourteenth century, both populations remained aggregated. Overall population decline is indicated in the lower San Pedro, a trend throughout the southern Southwest (Hill et al. 2004). The causes of this precontact decline are the subject of considerable debate. By A.D. 1400, only a few villages at the northern end of the Lower San Pedro were occupied. These villages display a bewildering mix of Kayenta and local attributes, suggesting that both groups inhabited them. Of note, no obvious ceremonial architecture such as kivas or platform mounds are found in these late settlements, and ideology was expressed primarily on Salado polychromes that increase in density (Crown 1994). In the face of declining numbers, this remnant population may have formed a new "Salado" identity that selectively incorporated aspects of both traditions in a last-ditch attempt to maintain viable communities in the area. This Salado identity was short lived, since these last villages were probably depopulated by A.D. 1450. The final inhabitants either moved elsewhere with some heading north in a return migration or changed their lifeways in such a way as to render them archaeologically invisible for the next 200 years.

Concluding Remarks

At a macro-regional scale, migration should be viewed as a directed process with predictable outcomes. From this perspective, order can be found in seemingly chaotic movement of myriad households and small suprahousehold groups by reconstructing the common socioeconomic factors that "pushed" groups out of one region and "pulled" them into another.

However, the scale and impact of each migration should be assessed one valley and basin at a time. At this fine scale of resolution, emphasis should be placed on the spatial and temporal unevenness of the migration process. This permits the study of a wide range of co-residence outcomes among immigrants and locals. Although some migrations have little impact, others result in conflict, new integrative institutions, diasporic communities, and even new identities, underscoring the transformational potential of migration as a social mixer.

Advances in method and theory over the past decade permit archaeologists to assess the scale and impact of migration separately by partitioning stylistic variability into high- and low-visibility categories. In the lower San Pedro Valley, two minority migrations from the Ancestral Puebloan world were identified using low-visibility domestic material culture. Settlement pattern and conspicuous material culture suggest that the earlier short-distance migration from the Mogollon Highlands of east-central Arizona had little impact. These immigrants were assimilated after several generations to such an extent that they disappeared archaeologically. The later long-distance migration from the Kayenta region of northeastern Arizona resulted in a diasporic community that dramatically impacted lives of local groups. Kayenta influence can be traced to the end of the precontact archaeological sequence.

Migration had an important place in archaeological explanation during the opening decades of the previous century. In returning to migration at the beginning of this century, I believe we are moving not in circles but forward in the direction of increasing resolution, sophistication, and anthropological relevance. An old explanation is not necessarily a bad one, so now that the baby's back let's see it through to maturity and finally realize the enormous research potential of migration in archaeology.

References

Abbott, D.
2000 *Ceramics and Community Organization Among the Hohokam.* University of Arizona Press, Tucson.
Adams, E. C.
2002 *Homol'ovi: An Ancient Hopi Settlement Cluster.* University of Arizona Press, Tucson.
Adams, E. C., and A. Duff (editors)
2004 *The Protohistoric Pueblo World.* University of Arizona Press, Tucson.
Adams, J.
2002 *Ground Stone Analysis: A Technological Approach.* University of Utah Press, Salt Lake City.
Adler, M. (editor)
1996 *The Prehistoric Pueblo World A.D. 1150–130.* University of Arizona Press, Tucson.

Anthony, D.

1990   Migration in Archeology: The Baby and the Bathwater. *American Anthropologist* 92:895–914.

Baker, V.

1980   Archaeological Visibility of Afro-American Culture: An Example from Black Lucy's Garden, Andover. In *Archaeological Perspectives on Ethnicity in America: Afro-American and Asian American Culture History*, edited by R. Schuyler, pp. 29–37. Baywood Publishing, New York.

Bernardini, W.

2005   *Hopi Oral Tradition and the Archaeology of Identity.* University of Arizona Press, Tucson.

Binford, L.

1963   "Red Ocher" Caches from the Michigan Area: A Possible Case of Cultural Drift. *Southwestern Journal of Anthropology* 19:89–108.

Bourdieu, P.

1977   *Outline of a Theory of Practice.* Cambridge University Press, Cambridge.

Burmeister, S.

2000   Archaeology and Migration. Approaches to an Archaeological Proof of Migration. *Current Anthropology* 41(4):539–567.

Cameron, C. M.

1995   Migration and the Movement of Southwestern Peoples. *Journal of Anthropological Archaeology* 14(2):104–124.

Carr, C.

1995   A Unified Middle-Range Theory of Artifact Design. In *Style, Society, and Person: Archaeological and Ethnological Perspectives*, edited by C. Carr and J. Neitzel, pp. 171–258. Plenum Press, New York.

Carr, C., and R. Maslowski

1995   Cordage and Fabrics: Relating Form, Technology, and Social Processes. In *Style, Society, and Person: Archaeological and Ethnological Perspectives*, edited by C. Carr and J. Neitzel, pp. 297–343. Plenum Press, New York.

Childs, S. T.

1991   Style, Technology, and Iron Smelting Furnaces in Bantu-Speaking Africa. *Journal of Anthropological Archaeology* 10:332–359.

Ciolek-Torrello, R.

1997   Prehistoric Settlement and Demography in the Lower Verde River Region. In *Vanishing River: Landscapes and Lives of the Lower Verde River Valley*, edited by S. Whittlesey, R. Ciolek-Torrello, and J. Altschul, pp. 531–595. SRI Press, Tucson.

Clark, J. J.

2001   *Tracking Prehistoric Migrations: Pueblo Settlers Among the Tonto Basin Hohokam.* Anthropological Papers of the University of Arizona no. 65. University of Arizona Press, Tucson.

Clark, J. J., and P. Gilman
Forthcoming   Persistent and Permanent Pithouse Places in the Northeast Sonoran Basin and Range. In *Southwest Pithouse Communities, A.D. 200–900*,
edited by L. Young and S. Herr. University of Arizona Press, Tucson.

Clark, J. J., and S. Lengyel
2002   "Mogollon" Migrations into Southeastern Arizona. Paper presented at the 12th
Mogollon Conference, October 18th and 19th, Las Cruces, New Mexico.

Clark, J. J., and P. Lyons (editors)
2011   *Migrants and Mounds: Classic Period Archaeology of the Lower San Pedro Valley*.
Anthropological Papers no. 45. Center for Desert Archaeology, Tucson.

Clark, J. J., P. Lyons, J. B. Hill, S. Lengyel, and M. Slaughter
Forthcoming   Migrants and Mounds in the Lower San Pedro Valley, A.D. 1200–
1450. In *The Archaeology of a Land Between*, edited by H. Wallace. University of
Arizona Press, Tucson.

Clifford, J.
1994   Diasporas. *Cultural Anthropology* 9(3):302–338.

Cohen, R.
1997   *Global Diasporas: An Introduction*. University of Washington Press, Seattle.

Collett, D.
1987   A Contribution to the Study of Migrations in the Archaeological Record: The
Ngoni and Kololo as a Case Study. In *Archaeology as Long-Term History*, edited
by I. Hodder, pp. 105–116. Cambridge University Press, Cambridge.

Craig, D., and J. J. Clark
1994   The Meddler Point Site, AZ V: 5: 4/26 (ASM/TNF). In *The Roosevelt Community
Development Study: Meddler Point, Pyramid Point, and Griffin Wash Sites*, by M.
Elson, D. Swartz, D. Craig, and J. J. Clark, pp. 1–198. Anthropological Papers no.
13(2). Center for Desert Archaeology, Tucson.

Crown, P.
1994   *Ceramics and Ideology: Salado Polychrome Pottery*. University of New Mexico
Press, Albuquerque.

Crown, P., and W. J. Judge (editors)
1991   *Chaco and Hohokam. Prehistoric Regional Systems in the American Southwest*.
School of American Research Advanced Seminar Series. School of American
Research Press, Santa Fe.

Dean, J.
1996   Kayenta Anasazi Settlement Transformations in Northeastern Arizona, A.D.
1150–1350. In *The Prehistoric Pueblo World, A.D. 1150–1350*, edited by M. Adler,
pp. 29–45. University of Arizona Press, Tucson.

Diehl, M., J. Waters, and J. H. Thiel
1998   Acculturation and the Composition of the Diet of Tucson's Overseas Chinese
Gardeners at the Turn of the Century. *Historical Archaeology* 32(4):19–33.

Di Peso, C.

1958   *The Reeve Ruin of Southeastern Arizona.* The Amerind Foundation no. 8. Dragoon, Arizona.

Doyel, D.

1987   *The Hohokam Village: Site Structure and Organization.* American Association for the Advancement of Science, Southwestern and Rocky Mountain Division, Glenwood Springs, Colorado.

Ferguson, L.

1992   *Uncommon Ground: Archaeology and Early African America, 1650–1800.* Smithsonian Institution Press, Washington, D.C.

Fish, S., P. Fish, and J. Madsen (editors)

1992   *The Marana Community in the Hohokam World.* Anthropological Papers of the University of Arizona no. 56. University of Arizona Press, Tucson.

Gerald, R.

1975   Drought-Correlated Changes in Two Prehistoric Communities in Southeastern Arizona. Unpublished Ph.D. dissertation, Department of Anthropology, University of Chicago.

Gregory, D. A.

1991   Form and Variation in Hohokam Settlement Patterns. In *Chaco and Hohokam: Prehistoric Regional Systems in the American Southwest,* edited by P .L. Crown and W. J. Judge, pp. 159–194. School of American Research Press, Santa Fe.

Haury, E.

1945   *The Excavation of Los Muertos and Neighboring Ruins in the Salt River Valley, Southern Arizona.* Papers of the Peabody Museum of American Archaeology and Ethnology no. 24(1). Harvard University, Cambridge, Mass.

1958   Evidence at Point of Pines for a Prehistoric Migration from Northern Arizona. In *Migrations in New World Culture History,* edited by R. Thompson, pp. 1–8. Social Science Bulletin no. 27. University of Arizona, Tucson.

1976   *The Hohokam, Desert Farmers and Craftsmen: Excavations at Snaketown, 1964–1965.* University of Arizona Press, Tucson.

Heidke, J.

1996   Qualitative Temper Characterization of Potsherds from the Gibbon Springs Site. In *Excavation of the Gibbon Springs Site: A Classic Period Village in the Northeastern Tucson Basin,* edited by M. Slaughter and H. Roberts, pp. 259–266. Report no. 94–87. SWCA, Tucson.

Herr, S., and J. J. Clark

1997   Patterns in the Pathways. *Kiva* 62(4):365–389.

2002   Mobility and the Organization of Prehispanic Southwest Communities. In *The Archaeology of Tribal Societies,* edited by W. Parkinson, pp. 123–154. International Monographs in Prehistory, Archaeological Series 15. Ann Arbor, Mich.

Hill, J. B, J. J. Clark, W. Doelle, and P. Lyons

2004   Prehistoric Demography in the Southwest: Migration, Coalescence, and Hohokam Population Decline. *American Antiquity* 69(4):689–716.

Lechtman, H.

1977   Style in Technology—Some Early Thoughts. In *Material Culture: Styles, Organization, and Dynamics of Technology*, edited by H. Lechtman and R. Merrill, pp. 3–20. West Publishing, New York.

Lemonnier, P.

1986   The Study of Material Culture Today: Towards an Anthropology of Technical Systems. *Journal of Anthropological Archaeology* 5:147–186.

Lindsay, A., Jr.

1987   Anasazi Population Movements to Southern Arizona. *American Archaeology* 6(3):190–198.

Lindsay, A., Jr., R. Ambler, M. A. Stein, and P. Hobler

1968   *Survey and Excavations North and East of Navajo Mountain, Utah, 1959–1962.* Museum of Northern Arizona Bulletin no. 45, Glen Canyon Series no. 8. Northern Arizona Society of Science and Art, Flagstaff.

Longacre, W.

1976   Population Dynamics at the Grasshopper Pueblo, Arizona. In *Demographic Anthropology*, edited by E. Zubrow, pp. 169–184. School of American Research Advanced Seminar Series. University of New Mexico Press, Albuquerque.

Lyons, P.

2003   *Ancestral Hopi Migrations*. Anthropological Papers of the University of Arizona no. 68. University of Arizona Press, Tucson.

2004   Cliff Polychrome. *Kiva* 69(4):361–400.

2011   Ceramic Typology, Chronology, Production, and Circulation. In *Migrants and Mounds: Late Prehistoric Archaeology of the Lower San Pedro River Valley, Arizona*; edited by J. J. Clark and P. Lyons. Anthropological Papers no. 45. Center for Desert Archaeology, Tucson.

Lyons, P., and A. Lindsay, Jr.

2006   Perforated Plates and the Salado Phenomenon. *Kiva* 72(1):5–54.

Masse, W. B., L. Gregonis, and M. Slaughter

Forthcoming   Corridor, Frontier, Melting Pot, or Autonomous Systems: The Lower San Pedro Valley, A.D. 600–1275. In *The Archaeology of a Land Between*, edited by H. Wallace. University of Arizona Press, Tucson.

Mills, B.

1998   Migration and Pueblo IV Community Reorganization in the Silver Creek Area, East-Central Arizona. Arizona. In *Migration and Reorganization: The Pueblo IV Period in the American Southwest*, edited by K. Spielmann, pp. 65–80. Anthropological Research Papers no. 51. Arizona State University, Tempe.

Murdock, G.

1949   *Social Structure*. MacMillan, New York.

Neuzil, A.

2001   Ceramics and Social Dynamics: Technological Style and Corrugated Ceramics during the Pueblo III to Pueblo IV Transition, Silver Creek, Arizona. Unpublished M.A. thesis, University of Arizona, Tucson.

2008   *In the Aftermath of Migration: Renegotiating Ancient Identity in Southeastern Arizona.* Anthropological Papers no. 73. University of Arizona Press, Tucson.

Newton, D.

1974   The Timbara Hammock as a Cultural Indicator of Social Boundaries. In *The Human Mirror*, edited by M. Richardson, pp. 231–251. Louisiana State University Press, Baton Rouge.

Orser, C., Jr.

1998   The Archaeology of the African Diaspora. *Annual Review of Anthropology* 27:63–82.

Reid, J. J.

1989   A Grasshopper Perspective on the Mogollon of the Arizona Mountains. In *Dynamics of Southwestern Prehistory*, edited by L. Cordell and G. J. Gumerman, pp. 65–97. Smithsonian Institution Press, Washington, D.C.

Rice, G.

1998   Migration, Emulation, and Tradition in Tonto Basin Prehistory. In *A Synthesis of Tonto Basin Prehistory: The Roosevelt Archaeological Studies, 1989–1998*, edited by G. Rice, pp. 231–241. Roosevelt Monograph Series 12, Anthropological Field Studies 41. OCRM, Arizona State University, Tempe.

Rice, G., and S. LeBlanc (editors)

2001   *Deadly Landscapes.* University of Utah Press, Salt Lake City.

Riggs, C.

2001   *The Architecture of Grasshopper Pueblo.* University of Utah Press, Salt Lake City.

Rohn, A.

1971   *Mughouse.* Archaeological Research Series 7-D. United States National Park Service, Washington, D.C.

Sackett, J.

1977   The Meaning of Style in Archaeology: A General Model. *American Antiquity* 42:369–380.

1982   Approaches to Style in Lithic Archaeology. *Journal of Anthropological Archaeology* 1:59–112.

1985   Style and Ethnicity in the Kalahari: A Reply to Wiessner. *American Antiquity* 50:154–159.

1986   Isochrestism and Style: A Clarification. *Journal of Anthropological Archaeology* 5:266–277.

Safran, W.

1991   Diasporas in Modern Societies: Myths of Homeland and Return. *Diaspora* 1(1):83–99.

Spielmann, K. (editor)

1998   *Migration and Reorganization: The Pueblo IV Period in the American Southwest.* Anthropological Research Papers no. 51. Arizona State University, Tempe.

Stark, M., M. Elson, and J. J. Clark

1998   Social Boundaries and Technical Choices in Tonto Basin Prehistory. In *The Archaeology of Social Boundaries*, edited by M. Stark, pp. 208–231. Smithsonian Institution Press, Washington D.C.

Stone, T.

2003   Social Identity and Ethnic Interaction in the Western Pueblos of the American Southwest. *Journal of Archaeological Method and Theory* 19(1):31–67.

Tuthill, C.

1947   *The Tres Alamos Site on the San Pedro River, Southeastern Arizona*. The Amerind Foundation 4. Dragoon, Arizona.

Webster, L.

2007   Mogollon and Zuni Perishable Traditions and the Question of Zuni Origins. In *Zuni Origins: Toward a New Synthesis of Southwestern Archaeology*, edited by D. Gregory and D. Wilcox, pp. 250–317. University of Arizona Press, Tucson.

Wegars, P.

1991   Who's Been Workin' on the Railroad? An Examination of the Construction, Distribution, and Ethnic Origins of Domed Rock Ovens on Railroad-Related Sites. *Historical Archaeology* 25(1):37–65.

Wiessner, P.

1983   Style and Social Information in Kalahari San Projectile Points. *American Antiquity* 48:253–276.

Wilcox, D., G. Robertson, Jr., and J. S. Wood

2001   Organized for War: The Perry Mesa Settlement System and Its Central Arizona Neighbors. In *Deadly Landscapes*, edited by G. Rice and S. LeBlanc, pp. 141–194. University of Utah Press, Salt Lake City.

Williams, B.

1992   Of Straightening Combs, Sodium Hydroxide, and Potassium Hydroxide in Archaeological and Cultural-Anthropological Analyses of Ethnogenesis. *American Antiquity* 57:608–612.

Wills, W. H., and R. Leonard (editors)

1994   *The Ancient Southwest Community*. University of New Mexico Press, Albuquerque.

Wobst, H. M.

1977   Stylistic Behavior and Information Exchange. In *Papers for the Director: Research Essays in Honor of James B. Griffin*, edited by C. Cleland, pp. 317–342. Anthropological Papers no. 67. Museum of Anthropology, University of Michigan, Ann Arbor.

Woodson, M. K.

1999   Migrations in Late Anasazi Prehistory: The Evidence from the Goat Hill Site. *Kiva* 65(1):63–84.

III

Archaeolinguistic Approaches

6

Using Cognitive Semantics to Relate Mesa Verde Archaeology to Modern Pueblo Languages

SCOTT G. ORTMAN

In this chapter I develop a new approach to integrating archaeology and language in the study of ancient migrations. The very existence of language families implies that the movement of speech communities has been a common feature of human history, even if such movements are rare today. Rouse (1986:175–180) recognized this in distinguishing population movements—which involve the colonization of a previously uninhabited area or the absorption/displacement of indigenous people by newcomers—from immigration—which involves an intrusion of individuals or small groups into an already-populated area. My approach focuses on cases in which the present-day speakers of a language live in a different area than past speakers, and in this sense it focuses on archaeolinguistic traces of past population movements.

The approach I develop here focuses on a cognitive process called *conceptual metaphor*, which is a common denominator of material culture and language. Previous studies have shown that the conceptual metaphors of ancestral speech communities are embedded in the documented languages of their descendants. Recent archaeological research shows that these metaphors are also expressed in archaeological material culture. Based on these findings I suggest it is possible to relate archaeological complexes to protolanguages by correlating conceptual systems as they are expressed in the archaeological record and in potentially related languages. I will first review current methods for relating archaeology and language and discuss their strengths and weaknesses. Then I will introduce conceptual metaphor as an additional basis for linking archaeology and language, show how one can reconstruct protometaphors from linguistic and archaeological evidence, and apply these methods in a case study that traces the migration of a specific speech community from its homeland in the Mesa Verde region of the U.S. Southwest.

Background

The essays in this and other recent edited volumes (e.g., Blench and Spriggs 1997, 1998, 1999a, 1999b; Bellwood and Renfrew 2003; Madsen and Rhode 1994) illustrate that there is widespread interest in the integration of archaeology and language. My own interest in bringing these fields together stems from an awareness of the quantum leap in understanding that typically follows decipherment of ancient scripts. One only need compare Thompson's *Maya History and Religion* (1970) with Friedel, Schele, and Parker's *Maya Cosmos* (1993) to appreciate the revolution in understanding that occurs once the language spoken in archaeological sites is known. It is obvious that if we can agree on the language or languages spoken at archaeological sites, we can obtain a much deeper understanding of the culture that created these sites by integrating the precise spatial, chronological, and behavioral data of archaeology with the rich conceptual data embedded in language.

The benefits of such integration have yet to be widely felt for nonliterate societies because for such societies our only option is to relate archaeological complexes to protolanguages reconstructed using the comparative method. Kirch and Green (2001) provide an exemplary study of this process for Polynesia, but the case they examine is relatively straightforward because all Polynesian languages are genetically related and most islands are still inhabited by descendants of their original colonizers. Most other regions of the world have experienced longer and more complex histories of human occupation that involve migration, admixture, ethnogenesis, and language shift in addition to demic expansion and phylogenesis (Moore 1994, 2001). In these more complex situations it is not safe to assume that ancestral forms of present-day languages were spoken in the archaeological sites of a region or that the language of these sites was ancestral to any documented language.

Although Kirch and Green show that it is possible to integrate archaeological and linguistic prehistory, current methods for doing so do not always provide clear or definitive answers, as debates over the Numic expansion (Fowler, this volume; Madsen and Rhode 1994), the proto–Indo European homeland (Anthony 2007; Mallory 1989, 1997; Renfrew 1987), and the language of Teotihuacan (Dakin and Wichmann 2000; Kaufman and Justeson 2007) attest. Nevertheless, there is too much to be gained from successful integration for us to ignore the challenge.

Existing Methods for Correlating Archaeology and Language

In the recent archaeolinguistic literature a variety of methods are used to re-late protolanguages to archaeological complexes. Each of these methods can produce plausible correlations, but in many cases there are disagreements over results or results differ depending on the method used. In the following para-graphs I outline these methods and offer some observations on their strengths and weaknesses.

The first method focuses on pattern matching: speech-community histories generated from application of the comparative method are fitted to culture-historical sequences generated from archaeological study. An excellent ex-ample is provided by Ross (1998), who relates a series of speech-community events (SCEs) in the history of the Austronesian languages of central Papua to the archaeological record of this region. Ross (1997) also provides the most lucid discussion I have seen on the types of SCEs that trigger language change, how and why language changes occur, and how these events can be recon-structed using the comparative method. Ross argues that all SCEs (such as differentiation, division, and contact) are manifestations of overall change in social interaction networks and therefore should influence material culture sequences in a region as well.

There is no reason to doubt that the kinds of events that bring about a change in speech communities should also exert some influence on material culture, but whether there are necessary relationships between SCEs and ma-terial culture patterns is not at all clear. In fact, the archaeological literature on material culture and social identity (Carr 1995; Clark 2001; Stark 1998) suggests that any such relationships will be more complex than a superficial analysis can reveal. In addition, glottochronology has proven to be more mis-leading than helpful in dating SCEs, so the pattern-matching approach cannot consider the timing of events in matching up linguistic and archaeological se-quences. In fact, Ross (1997) advocates dating SCEs using archaeological cor-relations. Given these problems, the chance of incorrect correlations based on superficial similarities between linguistic and archaeological event sequences appears to be relatively high, especially in cases where the archaeological re-cord is poorly known, material culture is poorly preserved, or the social his-tory of an area is complex.

The second technique is referred to by Campbell (1998) as linguistic migra-tion theory. This technique combines two principles to estimate the geograph-ical area in which a protolanguage was spoken. The first principle is called the "center of gravity" principle (Sapir 1949 [1916]): the homeland of a lan-guage family tends to be in the area where the most members of higher-order subgroups of a language family occur, and the distribution of lower-order subgroups reflects the direction of later migration or spread of speech communities in the family. The second principle is known as the "least moves" principle: the homeland is also most likely to be in the area that would require the fewest number of migrations to produce the resulting distribution of languages and dialects. The underlying assumption of both principles is that when a language family diversifies, the various daughter languages are more likely to stay close to the region where they diversified as opposed to moving very far or very frequently (Campbell 1998).

Linguistic migration theory has been used to postulate the homeland of the Athapaskan (Sapir 1949 [1916]) and Austronesian (Bellwood 2005) language families, but it may be misleading in the case of the Uto-Aztecan (Fowler 1972; Hill 2001; Lamb 1958; Miller 1986), Kiowa-Tanoan (Davis 1959; Hale and Harris 1979; Ortman 2009; Trager 1967), and Indo-European (Anthony 2007; Mallory 1989; Renfrew 1987) families, depending on one's point of view. Given these conflicting results, Campbell (1998) cautions that "it is not difficult to imagine rather straightforward situations in which linguistic migration theory would fail to produce reliable results" (359–360). Also, linguistic migration theory can only be applied to diverse language families for which the branching pattern is clear, and it does not deal with time depth. One must use other methods to determine how long ago the protolanguage was spoken and thus which archaeological complex in the homeland area was most likely created by the speakers of this language.

A third technique used for determining linguistic homelands is known as the "words and things" approach. In this method, reconstructed terms for plants and animals are related to their natural ranges and the homeland of the protolanguage is inferred to lie in the area where these ranges overlap (e.g., Fowler 1983; Kirch and Green 2001; Mallory 1989). With the homeland thus defined, one then looks for an archaeological culture of an appropriate age for the protolanguage, as in the maximum diversity method. The "words and things" method can be more persuasive than the pattern-matching method because it does not require linguistic and cultural phylogenies with similar structures. However, there are still difficulties (see Renfrew 1987), including the possibility of climate change or human activity influencing the distributions of plants and animals, the tendency of humans to apply old words or loanwords to new things, and the problem of estimating the age of a protolanguage. There is also a more subtle and thorny problem caused by the fact that the real-world referents of words change over time, and as a result it is often difficult to determine whether a reconstructed morpheme refers to a specific species, a category of plants or animals, or even a more abstract concept derived from the characteristics of a plant or animal.

The final method used to relate protolanguages to the archaeological record is a variant of the "words and things" approach in which protolexicons for technological innovations such as maize agriculture, horse domestication, wheeled transport, or metallurgy are related to their manifestations in the archaeological record (e.g., Anthony 2007; Hill 2001; Mallory 1989). The attraction of this method is that it seeks out *interpenetrating evidence*, by which I mean something in the actual content of a language that is also expressed in material culture: the dating and spatial locations of archaeological finds are used in combination with reconstructed words for those objects to determine where and when a protolanguage was spoken. A recent controversial example is Jane Hill's (2001) work on Proto-Uto-Aztecan (PUA), which places this speech community in southern Mexico based on proposed reconstructions of PUA maize-farming vocabulary combined with archaeological evidence that maize was first domesticated in this region (see Beekman and Christensen [2003] and Merrill et al. [2009] for dissenting views).

Despite its attractive features, even this method has its shortcomings. First, it relies upon a fairly complete knowledge of archaeology and language across a broad area. Hill's (2001) placement of PUA in southern Mexico, for example, relies on accurate reconstruction of subgroups and lexicons across a far-flung language family and on archaeological evidence suggesting that maize was first domesticated in this region. Second, even when a given innovation is reconstructible to a protolanguage, this does not necessarily mean that the innovation was invented among speakers of this language. For example, Hill (2007) argues that much of the PUA maize vocabulary derives from contact with Oto-Manguean-speakers; thus we cannot associate the PUA speech community with the archaeological sites where the oldest domesticated maize has been found. So even if Hill's model is correct, it does not necessarily tell us which archaeological sites were occupied by PUA-speakers.

Linguists have used each of the methods reviewed above to correlate archaeology and language, and it is clear that each method can produce plausible results in certain situations. However, these methods have conspicuously failed in situations where a number of ethnic groups speaking unrelated languages have occupied a homogeneous physiographic and ecological region and shared similar technologies. The Pueblo region of the U.S. Southwest is a quintessential case of this situation, where none of the methods reviewed above have produced convincing links between archaeology and language. Indeed, despite nearly a century of effort (Davis 1959; Ellis 1967; Ford et al.

1972; Gregory and Wilcox 2008; Hale and Harris 1979; Mera 1935; Reed 1949; Trager 1967; Wendorf and Reed 1955) and despite the relatively shallow time depths involved, no consensus exists about how Pueblo languages relate to various Ancestral Pueblo archaeological complexes in the southwest. To tackle situations like this, we need a method that seeks interpenetrating evidence that is strongly conserved in language, is not determined by environment or technology, and is expressed directly in material culture. I suggest that conceptual metaphors can provide such evidence.

What Is Conceptual Metaphor?

In the subfield of linguistics known as cognitive linguistics, metaphor is a cognitive process through which an abstract concept is understood in terms of more a concrete concept (Kövecses 2002; Lakoff 1987, 1993; Lakoff and Johnson 1980, 1999). Metaphors are motivated by correspondences in the image-schema structure of two domains of experience that lead to a mapping of entities, properties, and relations from the more concrete *source domain* to the more abstract *target domain*. This mapping makes it possible for one to understand the target domain using the structure provided by the source domain. A conceptual metaphor is a conventionalized cognitive mapping of this type that is used unreflectively in everyday thinking, reasoning, and speaking. In the remainder of this essay, I will use the terms "metaphor" and "conceptual metaphor" interchangeably, unless stated otherwise.

As an example, readers of this chapter know what I am doing when I "lay the foundations of my argument" because English-speaking academics have internalized the metaphor ARGUMENTS ARE BUILDINGS, and of course no building can stand without a solid foundation (the use of small caps to indicate conceptual metaphors is a convention established by Lakoff and Johnson [1980]). If one thinks for a moment about the language we use in discussing research, one will see that it is actually very difficult for us to even think about scholarly discourse without using more general and abstract metaphors, such as MENTAL PROCESSES ARE PHYSICAL PROCESSES. This is exactly the point. The use of concrete experience to conceptualize and reason about more abstract phenomena is a fundamental mechanism of human cognition.

Most of us notice the novel metaphors that make poetry so concise and meaningful, but we also use hundreds of conventional metaphors unconsciously and automatically in everyday thinking and communicating. These conventional metaphors are part of the cognitive unconscious of our culture. Metaphors that are rooted in basic bodily experience, such as ANGER IS HEAT, may be universal (see Kövecses 2002). However, other metaphors vary significantly across cultures because people have different experiences: they live in a variety of environments and have different economies, histories, cultures, and technologies. Nevertheless, cross-cultural variation in conceptual metaphors is limited by the fact that all humans live on the earth and share the same basic physiology. So even though humans readily recognize correlations in diverse realms of experience, we simply cannot create conceptual metaphors that lack a foundation in bodily experience and direct perceptions of the world or secondhand knowledge of it. Thus, conceptual metaphors are neither universal and objective nor radically relative and subjective.

Cognitive linguistics is a subfield of linguistics that focuses on the conceptual imagery expressed in everyday language use. Three findings of this field suggest that expressions of conceptual metaphor should have the same structure in everyday speech and material culture: (1) speech expresses conventional metaphors in a coherent and systematic way; (2) this systematicity derives from the nature of metaphor and not language per se; and (3) speech is only one medium through which metaphors are expressed. Based on these facts, it appears reasonable to propose that the conceptual metaphors of a community can become embedded in its language and materialized in the form, decoration, and use of the objects its members create. If in fact metaphor is a common denominator between language and material culture, we have an opportunity to relate protolanguages to archaeological complexes by studying the metaphors that are embedded in these two forms of human expression.

Metaphor in Linguistic Prehistory

In 1990, Eve Sweetser presented a landmark study of Indo-European perception verbs that showed that historical changes in the meanings of these words follow a regular pattern, generally from concrete to abstract. Verbs for the physical act of seeing regularly came to refer to knowledge and intellection (e.g. Greek *eîdon*, "see," → English *idea*); verbs for the physical act of hearing came to refer to listening or obeying (Greek *klúo*, "hear," → English *listen* and Danish *lystre*, "obey"); verbs for the act of smelling or tasting came to refer to personal likes or dislikes (the Latin root meaning "touch" → English *taste*, from the French *tâter*, "to touch or try"); and verbs for touch came to refer to emotions or feelings (Classical Greek *aísthe: ma*, "object of perception" → Modern Greek "feeling, emotion") (Sweetser 1990). From these patterns, Sweetser hypothesized that for several millennia, people in Indo-European speech communities have utilized the metaphor THE MIND IS THE BODY to conceptualize cognitive and emotional aspects of experience in terms of physical sensation.

Sweetser thus showed that semantic change in one particular area of the lexicon was not haphazard or idiosyncratic but rather followed a regular pattern, the basis of which was a specific conceptual metaphor.

Sweetser did not examine whether the mind-as-body metaphor is part of the cultural inheritance of Indo-Europeans or is in fact universal. It is quite possibly universal, as it draws upon basic biological experiences that all humans share. What is more important for present purposes, however, is that Sweetser's methods can be used to reconstruct metaphors that are not so universal and may in fact be restricted to specific ancestral speech communities. This in turn creates opportunities for correlating archaeology and language by interrelating protometaphors embedded in language with those expressed in material culture. In this section I will first outline several methods for reconstructing protometaphors through historical semantic analysis. I will also illustrate each method using examples from Kiowa-Tanoan languages (language data sources are listed in Table 6.4).

The first method for reconstructing protometaphors is through etymology, especially the concepts brought together in coining compound words. Conceptual metaphors often provide the motivation for linking dissimilar concepts in coining new terms. Because the purpose of language is communication, it would be counterproductive to coin a new term based on a novel metaphor. It would be more effective to make use of widely shared if not conventional metaphors. Thus, we can infer that a metaphor implied by the "literal" translation of a compound word was conventional in the speech community at the time the term was coined. An example of this from Tewa is the word tʼúpʰáʔdiʔ. This word is used today to describe a pitched roof (Martinez 1982), but it analyzes literally as "basket of timbers" (tʼún, "coiled basket" + pʰe, "stick, timber," + di, "of"). The etymology of this word thus indicates that the metaphor ROOFS ARE BASKETS existed in the Tewa speech community at the time this term was coined, regardless of whether or not this concept remains active in Tewa culture today.

The second aspect of language that allows the reconstruction of protometaphors is polysemy, or the relationships among multiple senses of words. Metaphor is often involved in extending the senses of a word, in which case the metaphor will be apparent in the related meanings. In this case, we can infer that the metaphor was conventional in the speech community at the time the extended senses of the word became conventional. An example, again drawn from Tewa, is the multiple senses of p'o:kwin. The core sense of this word is "lake" because this is its primary meaning in Tewa and the word incorporates the Tewa term for water (p'o:). Yet the Tewa term can also be applied to the emergence place, a kiva, or a ceremonial bowl. The reason for this is that in Tewa belief, the original people emerged from a lake at the beginning of time and the kiva is a representation of this emergence place (cf. p'o:kwikhoyi "lake roof-hatch"). In addition, the primary object of male ceremonial leaders in Tewa villages is a ceremonial bowl (p'o:kwingéh, "lake-place"; p'o:kwisą̈ʔą̈wéh, "lake-bowl") that is filled with water and used to represent p'o:kwin during ceremonies. Also, the souls of Tewa people are believed to become ancestral cloud-beings (ókhuwa, "cloud-being"; cf. okhúwá, "cloud") after death and to dwell under the surface of lakes. Tewas in fact refer to the dead as p'o:wąhą, which translates literally as "water-wind-breath" (Laski 1958). A ruin, then, is the dwelling place of ancestors who have become clouds, and thus it is appropriate to consider ruins p'o:kwin as well. The metaphor that links these multiple senses together is ANCESTORS ARE WATER, and this concept must have been present in the Tewa speech community at the time these extended senses of p'o:kwin developed.

The third aspect of language through which one can reconstruct conceptual metaphors from linguistic data is semantic change in specific words within a language family. This method is an extension of the polysemy approach, but in this case one pays attention to semantic change within cognate sets across the languages of a language family. Metaphor is again commonly involved in the replacement of an older sense of a word by a newer sense. So when the older and newer senses can be identified through comparison of cognates, one can posit the metaphor that motivated the change among speakers of the innovative language. For example, it is clear that the metaphor PEOPLE ARE CORN has some antiquity within the Kiowa-Tanoan language family because the meanings of Kiowa-Tanoan terms for body parts appear to have been extended to parts of the corn plant over time. For example, the Proto-Kiowa-Tanoan word *kʰoy originally referred to skin or hide, but it also refers to corn husk in Tewa (see Ortman 2009). Additional reflexes of PEOPLE ARE CORN are scattered throughout Kiowa-Tanoan dialects. For example, the Tewa corn mother, a perfect ear of corn wrapped with feathers and beads, is called kʰųlųŋʔaa, or "corn-clothed" (Parsons 1974 [1929]; Robbins et al. 1916), and Jemez kį, "child," can also mean "seed," "grain," or "bean." These examples illustrate that metaphorical relationships among people and corn have been part of Pueblo culture for quite some time.

As very little historical linguistic study has focused specifically on conceptual reconstruction using the methods outlined here, the strengths and limitations of such work still need to be worked out through review of and debate about the results of specific studies. Several caveats are initially apparent. First, conceptual reconstruction is subject to the same methodological issues involved in all linguistic reconstruction, including the replacement of vocabulary, the limitations of the data, and the abilities of the analyst. Second, no studies have been done to determine how faithfully or regularly the metaphors of a speech community actually become embedded in its language. So at this point we cannot rule out the possibility that at least some conventional metaphors of past speech communities have faded without leaving a residue in descendant languages. Third, no studies have been done to examine how readily metaphors spread across language boundaries, whether metaphors involving certain domains are more or less likely to spread, or whether it is possible to distinguish the natal language in which a metaphor was invented from the languages into which it was adopted. Fourth, as is the case for all linguistic reconstruction, conceptual reconstruction can yield information only about the relative age of a metaphor. To establish the absolute time depth of a reconstructed metaphor, one must rely on correlations with the archaeological record. Fifth, when working with poorly documented languages, it can be difficult to distinguish polysemic words, which potentially reflect a metaphor, from homonyms, which represent distinct words that are phonetically similar as an accident of history.

Finally, if the goal is to relate protolanguages to archaeological complexes, only certain metaphors are likely to be effective. For example, Kövecses (2002) shows that the human body is a near-universal source domain for metaphors, and thus we might expect to find metaphors that use the body as a source domain embedded in most languages. Other aspects of the world, including the weather, seasons, plants, and animals, have experiential properties that can potentially be perceived in similar ways by people in the same environment, even if they have different languages and cultures. Such entities may therefore become source domains of similar metaphors independently in several languages. It is also important to recognize that certain metaphors are more likely than others to be transmitted along with technological innovations and thus will not be especially useful. For example, PEOPLE ARE CORN is common among maize agricultural societies of North America and is documented in the ethnographic literatures of the Hopi (Black 1984), Tewa (Ortiz 1969), Huichol (Shelton 1996), Nahua (Sandstrom 1991), Mixtec (Monaghan 1995), and Maya (Carlsen 1997). Due to its widespread distribution, this metaphor is of little use for correlating archaeology and language.

The metaphors that are most likely to be useful, then, are those that incorporate material culture items as either source or target domains. In addition, metaphors involving relatively new objects relative to the time depth of the attempted correlation are more likely to be restricted to a single language or group of closely related languages. People create and use objects within specific cultural traditions, and archaeologists can find these objects, define their distributions in time and space, and learn quite a bit about the technology and social relations involved in making and using them. Also, as we shall see, it is now possible to identify metaphors that utilize material culture in the archaeological record directly.

Metaphor in Archaeology

The identification of metaphor in language is relatively straightforward, but for the purposes of this chapter, the critical question is whether such metaphors can be identified reliably using archaeological evidence, independent of ethnographic analogy or linguistic reconstruction. Recent work shows that it is in fact possible to do this by comparing archaeological expressions of a proposed metaphor to the structure of metaphoric expressions in figurative speech. Research on figurative speech in cognitive linguistics suggests six generalizations about the structure of metaphoric expressions that ultimately derive from the ways humans manipulate mental imagery (see Ortman 2000, 2008a, 2009). Table 6.1 presents these properties and an example of each in everyday American English. These generalizations are critical because they provide something like "grammatical" rules for metaphoric expressions in material culture. In other words, material expressions of a proposed metaphor should not contradict these rules if the metaphor really was conventional in the minds of the people who created these artifacts. If one analyzes a corpus of material culture in terms of a given metaphor hypothesis and finds that expressions of the proposed metaphor are consistent with the structure of figurative thought in general, then it can be said that one has supported that hypothesis. A researcher can also reject this hypothesis based on patterns that are inconsistent with this structure. The process is more involved than that of identifying metaphors embedded in language, and the approach may be possible only for well-preserved and well-studied archaeological records, but I believe it is possible to make strong inferences regarding material metaphors following this methodology.

Example: POTTERY VESSELS ARE BASKETS

In the following paragraphs I illustrate how one can reconstruct conceptual metaphors from archaeological evidence by reviewing my previous work on a metaphor that was routinely expressed in the material culture of Ancestral Pueblo people of the Mesa Verde region in the U.S. Southwest (Figure 6.1). The linguistic affinity of this archaeological complex is also the focus of the case study linking archaeology and language that follows.

Table 6.1. Six properties of conceptual metaphor

Property	Brief Explanation	English example
Directionality principle	Conceptual metaphor is a cognitive, point-for-point mapping of image-schematic structure from a concrete source domain to an abstract target domain.	TIME IS MONEY, but money is not time.
Superordinate principle	Metaphors exist at the superordinate level of classification but are expressed at the basic level of concrete imagery.	Expressions of LIFE IS A JOURNEY involve different modes of transportation: "his marriage is off track"; "she is drifting."
Invariance principle	Image-schematic properties of the source domain that contradict properties of the target domain are not mapped.	LIFE IS A JOURNEY, but you cannot go back and take the other "fork in the road" later.
Constitutive principle	Metaphors do more than express the results of thinking; they constitute conventionalized ways of thinking and reasoning.	POLITICS IS WAR: "give ground," "attack," "defend," "strategize," "army of volunteers," etc.
Blending principle	Multiple source domains can be combined for mapping onto a single target when they share image-schematic structure.	"Brainstorming" is a useful activity, even though a storming brain is fanciful.
Experiential principle	Metaphors derive from the concrete bodily experiences of individuals in specific physical and social contexts.	ANGER IS HEATED FLUID IN A CONTAINER: Your body temperature rises when you get "steaming mad" and "blow your top."

The Ancestral Pueblo occupation of the Mesa Verde region (A.D. 600–1280) occurred in two roughly 300-year cycles with a century of low population density in between (Varien et al. 2007). The second cycle began in the early decades of the A.D. 1000s and continued until A.D. 1280, when Pueblo people left the region permanently. Throughout this second cycle, Mesa Verde region pottery was decorated in a thoroughly geometric style that featured designs in black paint on a white-slipped surface. Many researchers have noted parallels between the painted designs on this pottery and the woven objects recovered from contemporaneous cliff dwellings in southeast Utah and in Mesa Verde National Park (e.g., Brew 1946; Holmes 1886; Nordenskiold 1979 [1893]). I have studied these correlations and found abundant evidence that this stylistic unity derived from a conceptualization of painted pottery vessels as woven objects, especially coiled and plaited baskets (Ortman 2000). Patterns in Mesa

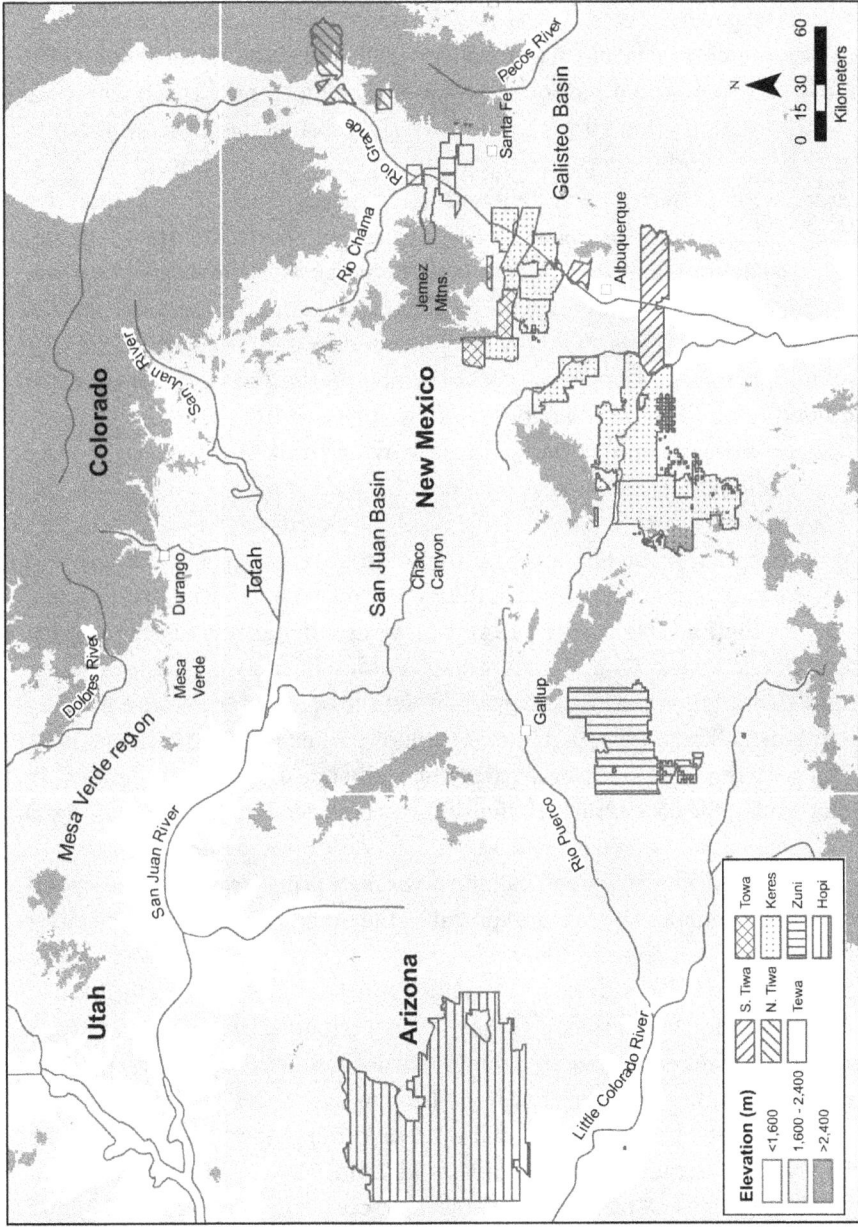

Figure 6.1. The Mesa Verde region and contemporary Pueblo lands in the U.S. Southwest.

Verde pottery designs exhibit the structure we would expect to find under the hypothesis that pottery surfaces were imagined as baskets. I summarize this evidence below (also see Ortman 2000, 2009).

The first generalization concerning the structure of metaphoric expression, the *directionality principle*, states that conceptual projection usually proceeds from a relatively structured source to a more abstract target. This is why TIME IS SPACE but space is not time; *Spring* can be just around the corner, you can be *sitting* just around the corner, but you cannot be sitting *spring* from me. Mesa Verde region pottery is consistent with this principle because more than two dozen features of woven objects, including incidental details, surface textures, design structures, and specific motifs that emerge as by-products of various weaving methods, are represented by analogs in painted pottery decoration. These correspondences could not have resulted from weavers inventing new weaving methods to represent painted pottery designs as woven textures. In addition, each of these analogous features appeared in pottery designs only after appearing first in weaving. Thus, weaving must have been the source domain and pottery the target domain of this metaphor.

The second generalization, which I call the *superordinate principle*, states that conceptual metaphors exist in the brain at relatively abstract levels of categorization but are expressed at the basic level of concrete mental imagery. Thus, in English, LIFE IS A JOURNEY, but we usually express the concept using concrete images of planes, trains, and automobiles, as in "his career is off track." Mesa Verde pottery is consistent with this principle because imagery from four different weaving methods—coiled basketry, plaited basketry, non-loom weaving, and loom-based weaving—all appear in pottery designs. In other words, the conceptual relationship was between pottery and weaving as craft media, not between specific vessel forms and/or weaving methods.

The third property, which I call the *invariance principle*, states that aspects of a source domain that are contradicted by the inherent structure of the target domain are not mapped. This is why even if LIFE IS A JOURNEY and we can "choose the path less traveled," we cannot go back to this fork in the road at a later date and choose the other path. Even if a road exists before and after a person has traveled it, time only moves forward, and thus it would make no sense to map the fact that one can go back to a fork in a road and take the other path onto our experience of life. Mesa Verde pottery is consistent with this principle because, although aspects of loom-woven cloth were incorporated into designs painted on vessel interiors (see below), rim decorations and framing patterns on pottery derive solely from basketry and not from warp-weft weaves. This is expectable because loom-based weaving does not produce actual containers, as basket-weaving does.

The fourth property, which I call the *constitutive principle*, states that a conceptual metaphor is not just a way of expressing thought but is in fact a conventionalized way of thinking and reasoning. In other words, everyday thinking and reasoning normally occurs through the operation of conventional metaphors. This is why it is very difficult to conceive of time without using the framework provided by space or of intellectual argument without the framework of a building. Our literal understanding of concepts such as space and argument are actually quite impoverished. Metaphor helps us "flesh out" these concepts so that we can think and reason about them in more detail (Lakoff and Johnson 1999). Mesa Verde pottery is consistent with this principle because 90 percent of all pottery vessels were decorated using textile imagery over a two-century period (A.D. 1060–1280) and innovations in pottery painting that became popular throughout this period can all be traced back to weaving innovations.

The fifth property, which I call the *blending principle*, states that two conceptual domains with equal inherent structure can be blended to produce new concepts that are physically impossible but conceptually coherent (Fauconnier 1997; Fauconnier and Turner 1994). This is why you can have a "brainstorming" session with your colleagues, even though a storming brain is literally ridiculous. The connection between thunderstorms and brain activity that motivates this concept is electricity, which occurs in the form of lightning in storms and firing synapses in the brain. This correspondence promotes the blending of additional conceptual structure, making it possible to imagine a lightning bolt as a "flash of insight." Mesa Verde pottery is consistent with this principle because designs created in warp-weft weaves were transferred to pottery surfaces via blending with basket imagery. As a result, framing patterns, which represent the texture of coiled baskets, are common on vessels with "banded" designs derived from coiled basketry but rare on pottery vessels with "draped" designs derived from plaited basketry.

Finally, the sixth property, which I call the *experiential principle*, states that metaphors are grounded in the direct bodily experiences of individuals in a given social, cultural, and environmental context. This is why the concept of a computer virus is possible only in a society that knows about both computers and viruses. Mesa Verde pottery is consistent with this principle because there is regional variation in pottery designs that correlates with potters' exposure to different weaving industries: pottery designs derived from loom-woven cotton cloth are more common in areas where cotton was actually grown and woven into fabrics, whereas pottery designs derived from coiled and plaited basketry are more common in areas where cotton was not grown and most fabrics were imported.

The archaeological patterns reviewed above clearly illustrate all six generalizations about the structure of metaphoric expressions identified in cognitive linguistic research. If this concept was *not* conventional among the creators of the Mesa Verde archaeological complex, the likelihood of an analyst identifying so many patterns consistent with these principles as they relate to the specific metaphor proposed would seem to be quite low. Based on this evidence, then, the inference that decorated pottery vessels were viewed as mirror images of woven objects, especially baskets, appears quite secure. In addition, based on the pervasiveness of weaving imagery in Mesa Verde pottery and the number of generations over which this metaphor structured pottery design, it appears likely that this concept was conventional, widely shared, and used unreflectively. One might therefore expect this metaphor to have influenced the language of Mesa Verde people.

With methods for reconstructing conceptual metaphors from archaeological and linguistic evidence in hand, I now turn to a case study that pulls together many of the examples discussed to this point.

Mesa Verde Archaeology: A Case Study

In my previous work I have focused on the decipherment of several metaphors that are expressed in the archaeological record of the Mesa Verde region in southwest Colorado and southeast Utah. The Ancestral Pueblo inhabitants of this region created the famous Mesa Verde archaeological complex (Noble 2006; Varien and Wilshusen 2002), which culminated in massive stone pueblos and cliff dwellings, including Sand Canyon Pueblo and Cliff Palace, and then suddenly ended with migration of the entire remaining population around A.D. 1280 (Lipe 1995; Varien et al. 2007). The most recent population estimates for the Mesa Verde region suggest that more than 20,000 people had migrated or died by the end of this occupation (Varien et al. 2007). The central question that has occupied archaeologists since the nineteenth century is what the fate of this population was. Because it is most likely that some Mesa Verde people died in place and others dispersed to the southeast, south, and southwest, perhaps the more appropriate question is whether the language of Mesa Verde people was ancestral to any extant Pueblo language or group of languages.

In the following case study I provide an affirmative answer to this question by reconstructing and correlating metaphors expressed in Mesa Verde material culture and modern Pueblo languages. First, I will summarize the results of previous research indicating that a variety of phenomena were conceptualized using container metaphors in Mesa Verde culture. Then I will examine

Pueblo language data for evidence of the metaphorical expressions apparent in Mesa Verde material culture. I will show that these metaphorical expressions are all embedded in the Tewa language but not in other Pueblo languages. This suggests that an ancestral form of Tewa was spoken in the Mesa Verde region at the time of the final migrations.

Table 6.2 summarizes the evidence supporting my deciphering of several metaphors that were expressed in Mesa Verde material culture of the A.D. 1200s. Each of these metaphors utilized container imagery as the source domain. I have presented reconstructions of these metaphors in previous publications (Ortman 2000, 2006, 2008a, 2009; Ortman and Bradley 2002), and readers interested in the details should consult these sources. Because each of these metaphors is somewhat generic, it will prove useful to break each one down into a list of specific metaphorical expressions (Table 6.3). A brief accounting of these expressions follows.

As I discussed earlier in this chapter, the pottery style of the Mesa Verde complex was thoroughly geometric and derived from a conceptualization of painted pottery vessels as woven objects (Ortman 2000), especially coiled and plaited basketry. I have also found that cooking pots were manufactured using techniques analogous to those used in coiled and twined basketry and present basket-surface textures in clay (Ortman 2006, 2009).

Mesa Verde people also conceptualized buildings as containers (Ortman 2008a). For example, the central symbolic structure of each household was a round, subterranean kiva (Figure 6.2d). Among the buildings on which decoration is preserved, a common theme is a painted geometric band design identical to the designs painted on the interior surfaces of pottery bowls. A number of granaries were decorated as pottery seed jars, and the cribbed roofs of most kivas mirror the appearance and construction of an overturned coiled basket.

The world also appears to have been conceptualized as nested containers in Mesa Verde culture. A second common theme of architectural mural decoration consists of dado patterns where the lower portion is red, the upper portion is tan to white, and sets of projecting triangles and dots run along the boundary between the two colors. Representations of the sun and moon in the upper field of some of these compositions demonstrate that dado murals depict the horizon with projecting landforms. This landscape imagery is combined with container imagery in a number of compositions (Figure 6.2e–f). Woven fabrics appear in the sky of landscape murals inside several structures that appear to have been used for calendrical observation of the sun and moon (Malville and Munson 1998; Newsome 2005), and landscape imagery is combined with pottery-bowl and basket imagery in several kivas, suggesting that

Table 6.2. Container metaphors in Mesa Verde material culture

Property	POTTERY VESSELS ARE BASKETS (Ortman 2000)	BUILDINGS ARE CONTAINERS (Ortman 2008a)	THE WORLD CONSISTS OF CONTAINERS (Ortman 2008a)	THE COMMUNITY IS A SERVING BOWL (Ortman 2009; Ortman and Bradley 2002)
Directionality principle	Incidental details and surface textures of weavings are represented on pottery; analogous features appear first in weaving and later in pottery.	Pottery designs were painted on buildings but architectural imagery was not painted on pots.	Physiographic features not represented on pottery or basketry.	Serving-bowl imagery expressed in village architecture but village architecture not represented on bowls.
Superordinate principle	Imagery from four different weaving methods, including coiled basketry, plaited basketry, nonloom weaving, and loom-based weaving, was mapped onto pottery.	Pottery bowls were mapped onto pit-structure walls, coiled baskets onto pit-structure roofs, and seed jars onto granaries.	Loom weaving mapped onto celestial motion; coiled basket mapped onto sky; pottery bowl mapped onto earth; ollas and mugs mapped onto emergence place.	Bowls mapped onto plazas and villages.
Invariance principle	Rim decorations and framing patterns on pottery derive from coiled basketry and not from loom-based weaving.	Banded pottery-design motifs were transferred to walls; all-over pottery-design motifs were not.	Blended landscape/container imagery occurs primarily on interior walls of buildings.	Houses built outside the enclosing walls are oriented north to south rather than inward.
Constitutive principle	Designs using nontextile imagery are rare; cooking pot construction techniques correspond with coiling and twining.	Kiva roofs were normally constructed to look like coiled baskets, even though it was not functionally necessary.	Loom-weaving imagery used to model celestial motion.	Villages were planned or modified to correspond with a pottery-bowl image; the central spring area was left undeveloped.
Blending principle	On pottery, framing patterns are common in "banded" layouts from coiled basketry but rare in "draped" layouts from plaited basketry.	Designs on walls derived from pottery, which in turn derived from blended weaving imagery.	Container and landscape imagery blended in mural paintings.	The imagery of people and corn are blended together in serving-bowl villages.
Experiential principle	Regional variation in pottery designs correlates with the exposure of potters to different weaving industries.	A number of correspondences exist between the form and use of containers and the form and use of buildings.	Properties of earth, sky, and celestial motion correspond to basketry, pottery, and loom weaving, respectively.	Properties of canyon-rim settings, villages, and community organization correspond to the manufacture, form, and use of pottery serving bowls.

Table 6.3. Expressions of container metaphors in Mesa Verde material culture

---

POTTERY VESSELS ARE BASKETS
POTTERY BOWLS ARE COILED/PLAITED BASKETS
COOKING POTS ARE COILED/TWINED BASKETS

BUILDINGS ARE CONTAINERS
GRANARIES ARE SEED JARS
KIVA WALLS ARE POTTERY BOWLS
KIVA ROOFS ARE COILED BASKETS

THE WORLD CONSISTS OF CONTAINERS
THE SKY IS WOVEN
THE EARTH IS A POTTERY BOWL
THE UNDERWORLD IS A WATER-FILLED VESSEL

THE COMMUNITY IS A POTTERY VESSEL
VILLAGES ARE POTTERY BOWLS
PLAZAS ARE POTTERY BOWLS

---

kivas were imagined as microcosms of a world consisting of an earthen pottery bowl below and a woven vegetal basket sky above (Ortman 2006, 2008a, 2009). In addition, it appears that pottery vessels were used to represent the underworld. Many Ancestral Pueblo kivas contain a small round hole in the floor aligned with the hearth. This feature is called the *sipapu*, after the Hopi term, and represents the path of emergence from the underworld. During the A.D. 1200s, these features were often created using an olla neck or a mug with the bottom broken out. This suggests that the underworld was conceptualized as a pottery vessel containing water.

Finally, during the middle A.D. 1200s, Mesa Verde people developed a distinctive type of village architecture that presented the community as a pottery serving bowl. These villages were built around canyon heads containing springs and had a distinctive roundish bowl shape (Figure 6.3). The plazas within these villages were also roundish and in some cases concave. Finally, there is strong evidence that the inhabitants of these villages participated in communal feasts and maintained communal food stores to a much greater extent than did the inhabitants of earlier villages (Ortman 2009; Ortman and Bradley 2002; Potter and Ortman 2004). Thus, the form and use of pottery bowls in daily domestic life appears to have become a model for community organization and architecture during the final decades of occupation.

An important point about the archaeological evidence summarized here is that the suite of container imagery expressed in A.D. 1200s Mesa Verde material culture forms a coherent complex only in the Mesa Verde region. With this knowledge in mind, I now examine modern Pueblo languages to

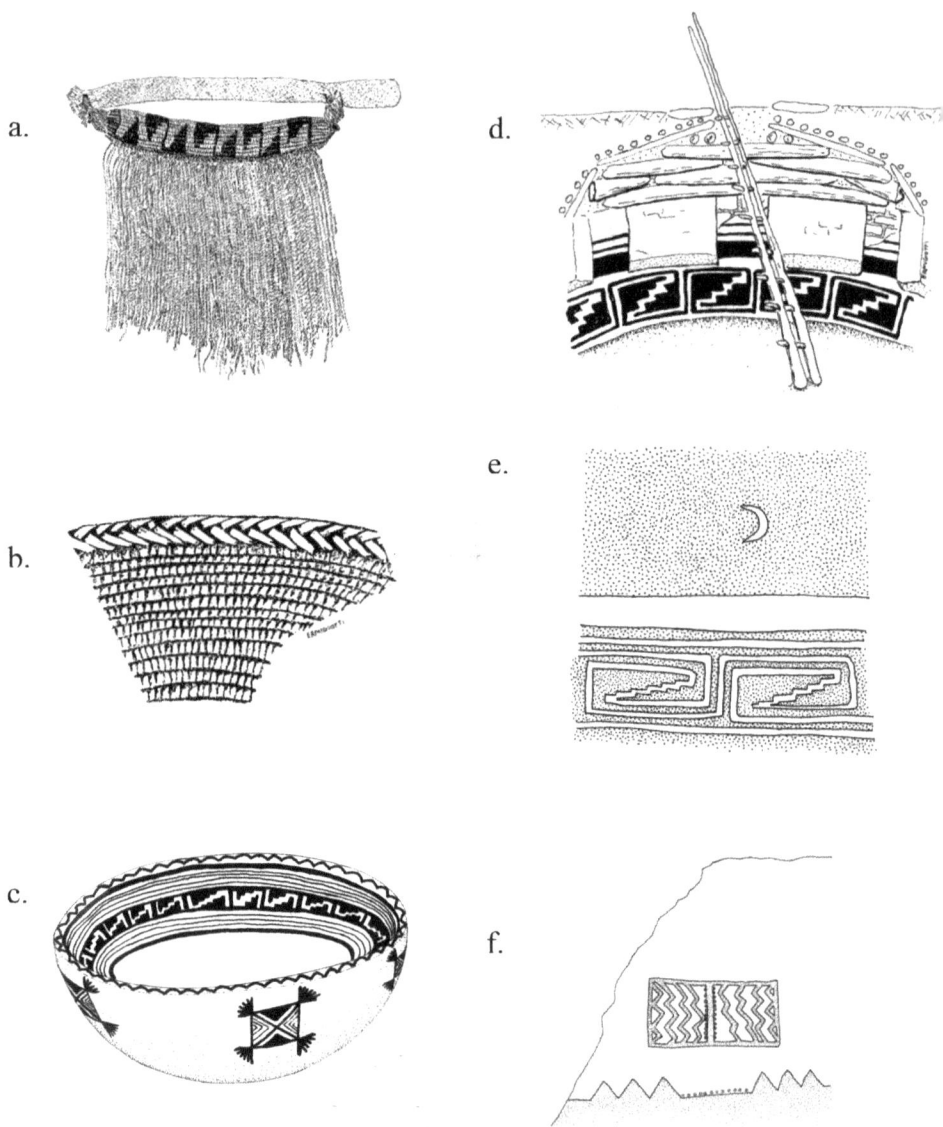

Figure 6.2. Container imagery in Mesa Verde region material culture. a) plain-weave skirt; b) coiled basket; c) painted bowl with band design and blanket motif on exterior; d) cutaway of kiva with pottery band mural and cribbed roof; e) kiva mural combining pottery-band design below and sky imagery above; f) horizon scene with blanket image in the sky.

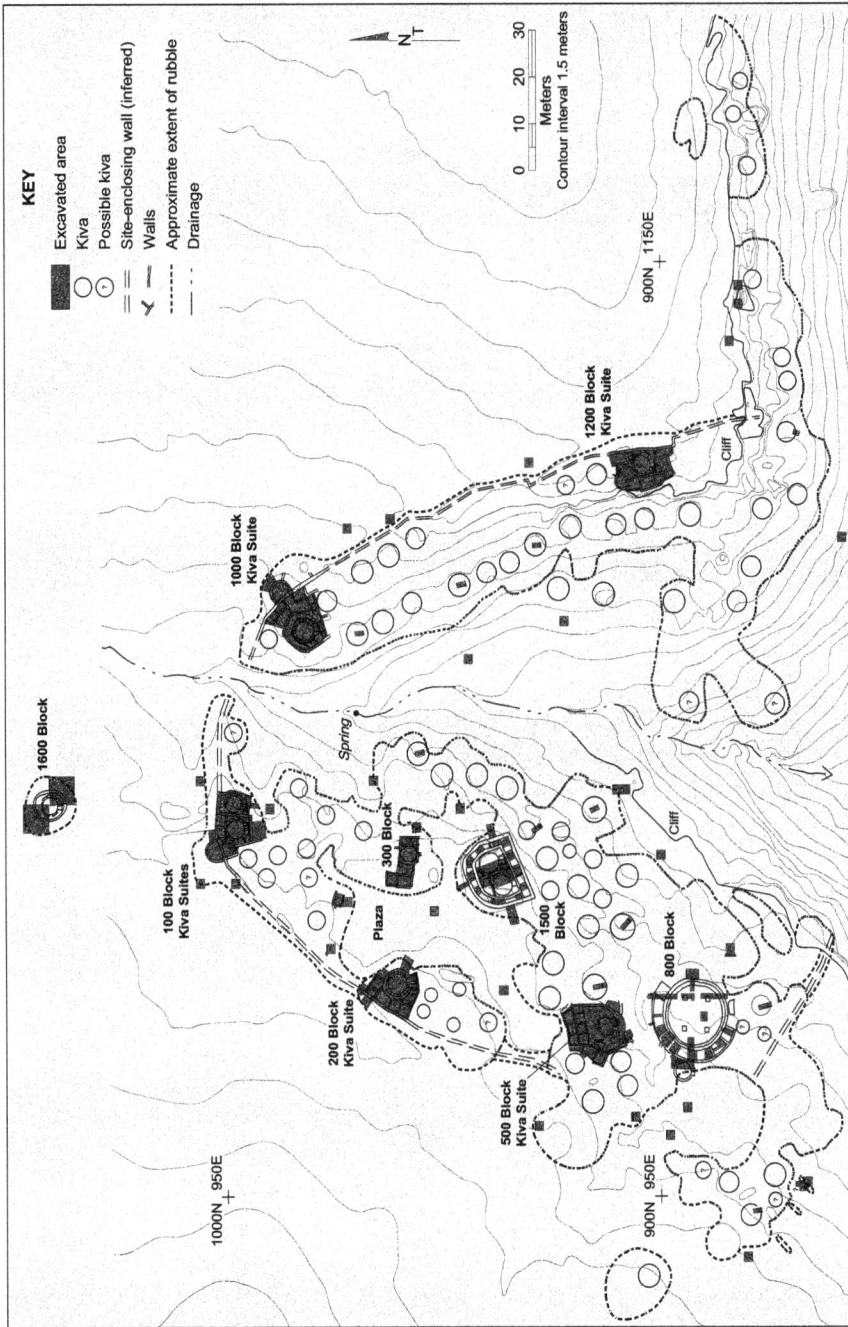

Figure 6.3. Sand Canyon Pueblo: an example of a bowl-shaped canyon-rim village.

determine how widely linguistic residues of these material metaphors are embedded in Pueblo languages. If in fact this complex of metaphors is embedded in only one language, it would suggest that Mesa Verde Puebloans spoke an earlier version of this language.

To evaluate the extent to which Mesa Verde container metaphors are embedded in modern Pueblo languages, Table 6.4 compiles vocabulary related to the source and target domains of these metaphors across seven Pueblo languages: Taos, Isleta, Tewa, Towa, Keres, Hopi, and Zuni. It is important to note that these data reflect only what I have been able to glean from the sources cited at the bottom of the table and that I have a much deeper knowledge of the Tanoan languages than I do of the others. It is likely that additional relevant words and meanings of words are missing from the extant literature or are beyond my expertise to identify. It is also likely that more extensive mining of the ethnographic literature and published Native-language texts would turn up additional relevant data. As a result, it is possible that additional evidence of embedded metaphors exists in these languages but is not apparent in the table. However, despite these problems, a close look at the table reveals that nearly all the metaphorical expressions identified in the Mesa Verde archaeological complex do have reflexes in the Tewa language, whereas the existing data suggest other Pueblo languages contain little to no evidence for most of these expressions.

POTTERY VESSELS ARE BASKETS is embedded in most of these languages. It may be implied by the Taos compound t'iod-mulu-, which appears to refer equally to a fired-clay water jar or a pitch-lined basket. It is also clearly implied by the Tewa word for pottery, nat?ú, which is a compound of nan, "earth, clay," and t?ú, "coiled baskets." The existence of this word indicates that the implied metaphor was active in the Tewa speech community when this word was coined. A Keres term for medicine bowl ('uwaist'a'nih), which appears to analyze as "pottery basket-bowl," may also indicate that this metaphor was once active in the Keres speech community. Finally, a Zuni term for cooking pot recorded by Cushing (1883), wo liak'ia te'ni tuliaton-e, appears to analyze as "coiled pottery cooking basket" and suggests that POTTERY VESSELS ARE BASKETS was once active in this speech community as well.

The remaining Mesa Verde metaphors are embedded almost exclusively in Tewa. KIVA ROOFS ARE COILED BASKETS is reflected directly in the Tewa word for "pitched roof," t'úpʰá?di? (t?ún, "coiled basket," + pʰe, "stick, timber," + di, "of"), despite the fact that the roofs of kivas in protohistoric Tewa sites in New Mexico do not have the cribbed basket-shaped appearance of older Mesa Verde kiva roofs. KIVA WALLS ARE POTTERY BOWLS is also implied by the multiple senses of p'o:kwin. As mentioned earlier, the original sense of p'o:kwin is "lake," but this term is also used to refer to the emergence place, a kiva, and a ceremonial bowl. These extended senses form what Lakoff (1987) calls a semantic chain. In Tewa belief, the first people emerged from beneath the surface of a lake (ʔOkhąngep'o:kwinge, "sandy lake place"), so the first link in this chain is THE UNDERWORLD IS A LAKE. The second link is provided by the kiva, which is taken as a model for the lake of emergence. Linguistic evidence of THE LAKE IS A KIVA can be seen in the compound p'o:kwi-khoyi, "lake roof-hatch" (cf. khoyi, "roof-hatch of a kiva"). Finally, the lake is modeled as an actual container: a water-filled bowl (p'o:kwingéh, "lake-place," or p'o:kwisą̨ʔą̨wéh, "lake-bowl") is used to represent p'o:kwin in ceremonies (Laski 1958; Ortiz 1969). These metaphors, which reflect connections between pottery bowls, kivas, and the underworld in Mesa Verde material culture, are embedded as a group only in Tewa.

THE SKY IS WOVEN is expressed in Tewa by póvitsą̨ąwą́ʔiʔtʔún, "dew basket" (póvi, "flower, cloud" + tsą̨ąwą́ʔiʔ, "blue-green," + tʔún, "coiled basket"), a term for the sky used in poetry (Spinden 1933) and in a song performed during the basket dance (Kurath 1970). This term clearly reflects the imagery of weaving associated with the sky in Mesa Verde material culture. THE EARTH IS A POTTERY BOWL is also reflected in the Tewa form bé:ʔe~bú:ʔú, "small~large low roundish place." This alternation reflects a pattern of sound symbolism that developed in Tewa after it became a distinct language and in which the manner of articulation of vowels reflects the size of entities (Harrington 1910; Ortman 2008b). Thus, one might expect bé:ʔe~bú:ʔú, "small~large low roundish place" to have descended from a single ancestral form, and in fact this ancestral form turns out to be the Proto-Tanoan word *búlu, "pottery bowl" (Ortman 2009). Thus, among Tewa-speakers, THE EARTH IS A POTTERY BOWL was involved in the application of an old word for "pottery bowl" to bowl-shaped topographic features.

Finally THE COMMUNITY IS A POTTERY VESSEL is reflected in additional meanings attached to bé:ʔe~bú:ʔú:. The original meaning of Proto-Tanoan *búlu survives in the Tewa form be:, "pottery bowl," and bú:ʔú is also used to refer to villages and to plazas (e.g., P'oqwogeʔimbú:ʔú, "San Ildefonso [water cuts down through] plaza"; Harrington 1916). Bú:ʔú is also compounded with pín, "heart, middle" to form a more formal term for plaza, búpíngéh (lit. "large bowl of the heart/middle"). Although the Tewa and Taos words for "plaza" contain cognate forms for "heart" and may imply Proto-Tiwa-Tewa *pian-, "plaza, heart-middle place," metaphoric reflexes of Proto-Tanoan *búlu are not apparent in Tiwa or Towa. These data thus suggest that even if the middle-place aspect of plazas dates from Proto-Tanoan times, the container aspect is a Tewa innovation. All of this indicates that THE COMMUNITY IS A

Table 6.4. Lexical data from seven Pueblo languages

Domain	Taos	Isleta	Tewa	Towa	Keres	Hopi	Zuni
Pottery, bowl	mulu- "pottery" t'įęn- "dish" t'ɨodene "round thing, bowl"	búru "pottery bowl" pˀakwimp'a "medicine bowl" pˀahwié-'ai "ceremonial bowl" (lit. "lake-place")	be: "pottery bowl, vessel, fruit" pˀo:kwingéh "ceremonial bowl" (lit. "lake-place") sˀwéh "dish, pot" pˀo:kwisą̈ˀą̈wéh "lake-bowl" natˀú "pottery" (Lit. "earth-baskets")	bɨ́dó "round, fat, chubby" tʸa:bɨ "sacred (pottery) bowl"	*wadyu'unih* "pottery, water bowl" *'waist'i* "bowl," *'uwaist'a'nih* "medicine bowl" (lit. "bowl-basket")	*tsaqapta*	*te-*"pot, deep container"
Cooking pot	łol-múlu "pot"		sæ-nbé : "cooking pot"	*gyídá* "pot"	*'adaushih, gúmásáwá*	*siivu*	*wo liak'ia te'ni tuliaton-e* (lit. "coiled pottery cooking basket")
Olla	t'ɨodmulu- "water jar, basket"	p'abúru "olla" (cf. *p'a* "water")	p'o:nbe: "olla" (cf. *p'o:* "water")	gíbǽ "olla"	*sbu na* "jug"	*kuysivu*	*i mush ton-e*
Basket	tˀęną "coiled basket" pûotˀę́ną "yucca-basket (plaited)"	*łicha* "coiled basket" tʰɨa-churina "meal-sifter" šuri "yucca basket"	t'ún "(coiled) basket" pʰa:yo "plaited yucca sifter basket" (cf. pʰa: "yucca")	t̓į̂:pove "basket-flowers" *weshi* "basket" kʸá:lǽ "plaited yucca sifter basket"	*'uuta'nih, gúyást'í*	*tuulewni* "basketry"	*tsi-le*
Kiva	tʰɨtane "kiva" tuła "big-house" tɨoto'óna "ceremonial chamber" cuwitʰɨna "gathering-house"	túłá "old house, pithouse, kiva"	teˀi "kiva" pˀo:kwin "lake, kiva, ruin" pˀo:kwikhoyi "lake kiva roof-hole"	ɦô:wā "kiva" (cf. ɦó:- "inside, room")	*chidya, kaatc, mauharo kai* "underworld house" (cf. *ai'tcin* "house, wooden slat altar")	*kiva, kihe* "building"	*kiwtsi*
Roof, viga	ik'ɨo-to "ceiling, roof" k'ɨo "on top" tʰɨ-łówǫ- "viga" (house + ło- "wood" + wo "pole")	k'ɨa-chu "roof" k'ɨa-tit "on top of" łą́wa "viga"	pʰéhpúˀ ɟ "ceiling" whaˀkˀayd̲i "room-top" tˀúpʰáˀdiˀ "pitched roof" ("basket-timber-of") pˀo:kwikhoyi "lake kiva roof-hole" tepʰéh "viga" (lit. "house-	ǽtʸā "viga" (tʸê "stick, wood")	*wakaiyanistiawtsa* "Milky Way, kiva roof" (lit. "way-above-earth-beam")	*kits'ovi* (cf. *kiihu* "house") *kivats'ovi* "kiva roof"	*ta po an-e, te yala* "roof of the emergence place" (*te* + *yala* "mountain, to

	Taos	Isleta	Tewa	Towa	Keres	Hopi	Zuni
village	t̂i- "house, building, room, to live, dwell"	nàuty, try "community, home, pueblo"	holɨ village (cf. t̂i- "there-stand-at"); ʔǫ̀ywįŋc "village" ("there-stand-at"); ʔǫ̀ywįŋ "to stand"; ʔąywįŋ "to grow in a standing position"	bu˙ village, plaza, large low roundish place (cf. bɛ: "pottery, bowl, fruit"); ti:yò "home, place where we live"	háusт̂i	kii̇soŋ, kiihu	hiia erone (lit. "many springing up")
Heart, plaza	píana "heart, middle"; pían̓o "plaza, middle of a circle"	pia "heart"; pían̓ad "center middle"; nap'ahia "place, town, plaza"; p'ahia "well"	pín "heart"; píngéh "middle" (géh "place"); búpíngéh (bú:'ú + píngéh)	pé: "heart"; fíǫ:pítá "plaza"; pó't'u "plaza, middle, center"; pó'k'a "in the middle"; fíǫ:lá "inside a circle, in the plaza"	kà' ka·dyi "square, plaza"	kiisonvi, tivongyapaveè (lit. "dance-display-place")	
Sky	p'ápina (cf. p'a "water")	p'apúnyi, nąp'ápųi "sky"	makowa "sky"; póvitsą̀wą́'ʔ'ʔ'ún "dew basket" (póvi "flower, cloud" + tsą̀wą́'ʔʔ' "blue-green" + t'ún "coiled basket")	ho:yị "sky"; wa:pa "sky"; wa:pa-gwahǫ́š "Milky Way" (lit. "sky-backbone")	húwaka	tokpela	a'po yan-e (lit. "stone roof")
Earth, Canyon, Valley	pǫ'ona "the earth, ground, world"	pǫ:, paire "valley"	bé:'ʔe~bú:'ú, "small~large low roundish place" (from Proto-Tanoan *búlu "pottery bowl")	pe:keta "earth"; wà:wá "arroyo"; pǽ:wámi "valley" (lit. "river-valley")	gáisbisa "world"; hárác'i· "land, earth"	sikya "canyon", tuuwaponyava "earth" (lit. "sand-altar display")	'áwiteli "the earth" (a·witen "fourth" + tè'hulikwin "womb")
Emergence Place	Cip'op'ùntha "eye-water-dark-at"; p'oxwiane "lake"	Šip'ap'ùn'ʔai "water-black-at"; p'ahwi:re "lake"	Sip'op̂e; p'o:kwin "lake, kiva, ruin"	Wawanatutu "Shipapu"	Shipap'	Sípàapuni	Ci'papo'lima

Sources: Taos Cardfile, George L. Trager Papers, University of California, Irvine; Parsons (1936)

Isleta: Harrington 1920; Frantz and Gardner 1995

Tewa: Harrington 1909, 1916; Martinez 1982; Spinden 1933

Towa: Harper 1929; Laurel Watkins personal communication 2008, Yumitani 1998

Keres: Stirling 1942; Davis 1964; White 1962

Hopi: Hill 1998; Sekaquaptewa and Washburn 2004; Whorf 1953

Zuni: Cushing 1886; Newman 1958; Bunzel 1992

SERVING BOWL influenced the Tewa language after it became distinct from other Tanoan languages.

Summary and Conclusions

Table 6.5 summarizes current evidence for expressions of Mesa Verde metaphors in Pueblo languages, based on my analysis of the data in Table 6.4. These data show that the complex of container metaphors identified in the Mesa Verde archaeological complex is enshrined in the modern Tewa language. Because of the detailed nature of these correspondences and the fact that several of these metaphors are not expressed in protohistoric Tewa material culture, it is difficult to imagine how these metaphors could have become embedded in the Tewa language if it had never been spoken in the Mesa Verde region. These correspondences thus make a strong case that the Mesa Verde complex was created by people who spoke an early form of Tewa and that the Tewa language was brought to the Rio Grande by immigrants from the Mesa Verde region in the A.D. 1200s.

It is equally important to note that the Mesa Verde container metaphor complex is not clearly enshrined in any other documented Pueblo language. POTTERY VESSELS ARE BASKETS does appear to have been widespread and perhaps reflects the widespread occurrence of the Mesa Verde style of decoration over a broad area between A.D. 1000 and 1280. Also, THE UNDERWORLD IS A WATER-FILLED VESSEL may predate the separation of Tiwa and Tewa as separate languages because this concept is also embedded in Isleta, where a water-filled pottery bowl (p'akwimp'a, "medicine bowl"; p'ahwié-'ai, "ceremonial bowl," lit. "lake-place") is used to represent the lake of emergence, as it is in Tewa communities. However, the remaining concepts are not expressed in a precise way in any other Pueblo language. This is not to say that different metaphors are not embedded in these languages. As examples, the Zuni term a'po yan-e, "sky" (lit. "stone roof") evokes the imagery of an overturned stone bowl, and several terms from Keres present buildings and altars as microcosms. Nevertheless, the specific metaphors these terms imply do not reflect those of the Mesa Verde complex or of the Tewa language. This second conclusion, based on negative evidence, strengthens the conclusion reached on the basis of positive evidence that the Mesa Verde complex was created by Proto-Tewa-speakers.

Several points arise from these conclusions. First, it appears that the metaphors enshrined in the Tewa language are expressed more thoroughly in the Mesa Verde region than they are in the Rio Grande, where Tewa-speakers live today. For example, ancestral Tewa villages in the Rio Grande are not

Table 6.5. Expressions of Mesa Verde container metaphors in modern Pueblo languages

Metaphor	Taos	Isleta	Tewa	Towa	Keres	Hopi	Zuni
POTTERY VESSELS ARE BASKETS	Yes	No	Yes	?	Yes	No	Yes
KIVA WALLS ARE POTTERY BOWLS	No	No	Yes	No	No	No	No
KIVA ROOFS ARE COILED BASKETS	No	No	Yes	?	No	No	No
VILLAGES ARE POTTERY BOWLS	No	No	Yes	No	No	No	No
PLAZAS ARE POTTERY BOWLS	No	No	Yes	No	No	No	No
THE SKY IS WOVEN	No	No	Yes	No	?	No	No
THE EARTH IS A POTTERY BOWL	?	Yes	Yes	?	?	No	No
THE UNDERWORLD IS A WATER-FILLED VESSEL	?	Yes	Yes	No	No	No	No

bowl shaped and do not occur in bowl-like physiographic settings. Rather, the houses in these villages are arranged to form rectilinear plazas and occur on benches above major floodplains (Anschuetz 2005; Fowles 2004). This pattern supports the notion that metaphors reconstructed through etymology, polysemy, and semantic change reveal residues of past conceptual systems that may persist in a language only as semantic fossils if the culture of its speakers has changed over time.

Second, recent material culture of other Pueblo communities expresses Mesa Verde metaphors more extensively than is suggested by their languages. For example, Hopi six-directions altars use a terraced medicine bowl to represent the world (Hieb 1979). This appears to be an expression of THE EARTH IS A POTTERY BOWL, but I have not been able to find any corresponding evidence of this conception embedded in the Hopi language. One possible interpretation of this evidence is that the use of a pottery bowl to represent the earth was brought to Hopi by Tewa-speaking immigrants at some point in the past.

This example illustrates why it is problematic to trace speech communities backward using correspondences between archaeological evidence and ethnographic ritual practices or poetry. Cultural diffusion can occur with relatively minor contact between peoples, whereas the semantic structure of a language can be transmitted only in cases of long-term intensive contact combined with extensive bilingualism (Ross 1997). Thus, the metaphors embedded in a language are a stronger reflection of linguistic heritage than are the metaphors expressed in current practices and discourse. This is especially true within a culture area, where one would expect extensive diffusion of practices but not necessarily the metaphors beneath the surface.

If this trial application appears promising, there are several directions one might pursue. For students of Pueblo history, it would be worthwhile to examine the conceptual metaphors of other Ancestral Pueblo archaeological complexes to see if they are different from the Mesa Verde expressions and whether they are embedded in other Pueblo languages. There is also more linguistic field work to be done to compile lexical data across Pueblo languages in an effort to determine whether the semantic patterns identified in this preliminary study hold up to further scrutiny. Finally, it would be worthwhile to examine other lines of evidence related to the speech-community history suggested by this study (cf. Cordell 1995; Ortman 2009).

A number of more general studies should also be pursued. Ethnographic studies of the extent to which metaphors expressed in everyday discourse become embedded in language would be extremely helpful for the type of research proposed here, as would studies concerning the ease with which conceptual metaphors spread between speech communities, either through language directly or through other forms of figurative expression. Also, the conditions under which this method is the most useful for correlating archaeology and language should be worked out through examination of additional cases. Finally, a great advantage of the method developed here is that it suggests a direction in which linguists and archaeologists could join forces to study the evolution of conceptual systems in nonliterate societies. The realizations that both lexical semantics and material culture are regular and structured and that conceptual metaphor is the basis of this structure offer tremendous opportunities for the development of a historical anthropology of nonliterate societies. The ability to identify past episodes of population movement on the basis of archaeolinguistic expressions of conceptual metaphors is an important step in this direction.

Acknowledgments

This paper is an outgrowth of a presentation at the Fifth World Archaeological Congress in Washington, D.C. I would like to thank Lloyd Anderson for encouraging my participation in this conference and for encouraging me to pursue publication. I would also like to thank Graciela Cabana and Jeff Clark for inviting me to attend the interdisciplinary migration workshop and to contribute to the resulting volume. Scott Evans and Paul Ermigiotti rendered the line drawings in Figure 6.3.

References

Anschuetz, K. F.
2005   Landscapes as Memory: Archaeological History to Learn from and Live by.
        In *Engaged Anthropology: Research Essays on North American Archaeology,*
        Ethnobotany, and Museology, edited by M. Hegmon and B. S. Eiselt, pp. 52–72.
        Anthropological Papers, Museum of Anthropology, University of Michigan
        no. 94, Ann Arbor.
Anthony, D. W.
2007   *The Horse, the Wheel, and Language: How Bronze-Age Riders from the Eurasian*
        Steppes Shaped the Modern World. Princeton University Press, Princeton, N.J.
Beekman, C. S., and A. F. Christensen
2003   Controlling for Doubt and Uncertainty Through Multiple Lines of Evidence: A
        New Look at the Mesoamerican Nahua Migrations. *Journal of Archaeological*
        Method and Theory 10(2):111–164.
Bellwood, P. S.
2005   *First Farmers: The Origins of Agricultural Societies.* Blackwell Publishing, Ox-
        ford.
Bellwood, P. S., and C. Renfrew (editors)
2003   *Examining the Farming/Language Dispersal Hypothesis.* McDonald Institute
        for Archaeological Research, Cambridge.
Black, M. E.
1984   Maidens and Mothers: An Analysis of Hopi Corn Metaphors. *Ethnology* 23(4):
        279–288.
Blench, R, and M. Spriggs (editors)
1997   *Archaeology and Language I: Theoretical and Methodological Orientations.*
        Routledge, London.
1998   *Archaeology and Language II: Archaeological Data and Linguistic Hypotheses.*
        Routledge, London.
1999a   *Archaeology and Language III: Artefacts, Languages, and Texts.* Routledge,
        London.
1999b   *Archaeology and Language IV: Language Change and Cultural Transformation.*
        Routledge, London.
Brew, J. O.
1946   *Archaeology of Alkali Ridge, Southeastern Utah.* Papers of the Peabody Mu-
        seum of American Archaeology and Ethnology, vol. 21. Harvard University,
        Cambridge.
Bunzel, R.
1992   *Zuni Ceremonialism.* University of New Mexico Press, Albuquerque.
Campbell, L.
1998   *Historical Linguistics: An Introduction.* MIT Press, Cambridge, Mass.
Carlsen, R. S.
1997   *The War for the Heart and Soul of a Highland Maya Town.* University of Texas
        Press, Austin.

Carr, C.

1995   A Unified Middle-Range Theory of Artifact Design. In *Style, Society, and Person: Archaeological and Ethnological Perspectives*, edited by C. Carr and J. E. Neitzel, pp. 171–258. Plenum Press, New York.

Clark, J. J.

2001   *Tracking Prehistoric Migrations: Pueblo Settlers Among the Tonto Basin Hohokam*. Anthropological Papers of the University of Arizona no. 65. University of Arizona Press, Tucson.

Cordell, L. S.

1995   Tracing Migration Pathways from the Receiving End. *Journal of Anthropological Archaeology* 14:203–211.

Cushing, F. H.

1886   A Study of Pueblo Pottery as Illustrative of Zuni Culture Growth. In *4th Annual Report of the Bureau of Ethnology*, pp. 467–521. Smithsonian Institution, Washington, D.C.

Dakin, K., and S. Wichman

2000   Cacao and Chocolate. *Ancient Mesoamerica* 11(1):55–75.

Davis, I.

1959   Linguistic Clues to Rio Grande Prehistory. *El Palacio* 66(June):73–84.

1964   *The Language of Santa Ana Pueblo*. Anthropological Papers no. 69, Bureau of American Ethnology. Smithsonian Institution, Washington, D.C.

Ellis, F. H.

1967   Where Did the Pueblo People Come From? *El Palacio* 74(3):35–43.

Fauconnier, G.

1997   *Mappings in Thought and Language*. Cambridge University Press, Cambridge.

Fauconnier, G., and M. Turner

1994   *Conceptual Projection and Middle Spaces*. Report 9401, UCSD Department of Cognitive Science, University of California, San Diego, La Jolla.

Ford, R. I., A. H. Schroeder, and S. L. Peckham

1972   Three Perspectives on Pueblo Prehistory. In *New Perspectives on the Pueblos*, edited by A. Ortiz, pp. 19–40. University of New Mexico Press, Albuquerque.

Fowler, C. L.

1972   Some Ecological Clues to Proto-Numic Homelands. In *Great Basin Culture Ecology: A Symposium*, edited by D. D. Fowler, pp. 105–121. Desert Research Institute Publications in the Social Sciences. vol. 8. University of Nevada, Reno.

1983   Some Lexical Clues to Uto-Aztecan Prehistory. *International Journal of American Linguistics* 49(3):224–257.

Fowles, S. M.

2004   Tewa Versus Tiwa: Northern Rio Grande Settlement Patterns and Social History, A.D. 1275 to 1540. In *The Protohistoric Pueblo World, A.D. 1275–1600*, edited by E. C. Adams and A. I. Duff, pp. 17–25. University of Arizona Press, Tucson.

Frantz, D., and D. Gardner
1995   Southern Tiwa Lexicon: Isleta. Manuscript in possession of the author.
Friedel, D., L. Schele, and J. Parker
1993   *Maya Cosmos: Three Thousand Years on the Shaman's Path*. Quill/William Morrow, New York.
Gregory, D. A., and D. R. Wilcox (editors)
2008   *Zuni Origins: Toward a New Synthesis of Southwestern Archaeology*. University of Arizona Press, Tucson.
Hale, K., and D. Harris
1979   Historical Linguistics and Archeology. In *Handbook of North American Indians*, vol. 9, *Southwest*, edited by A. Ortiz, pp. 170–177. Smithsonian Institution, Washington, D. C.
Harper, B. W.
1929   *Notes on the Documentary History, the Language, and the Rituals and Customs of Jemez Pueblo*. M.A. thesis, University of New Mexico.
Harrington, C. T.
1920   Isleta Language: Texts and Analytical Vocabulary. In *The Papers of John Peabody Harrington in the Smithsonian Institution, 1907–1957*, Part 4, *Southwest*. Reel 36, Frames 399–516. Kraus International, Millwood, N.Y.
Harrington, J. P.
1909   Notes on the Piro Language. *American Anthropologist* 11:563–594.
1910   An Introductory Paper on the Tiwa Language, Dialect of Taos, New Mexico. *American Anthropologist* 12:11–48.
1916   Ethnogeography of the Tewa Indians. In [H. D. Holmes], *Twenty-Ninth Annual Report of the Bureau of American Ethnology to the Secretary of the Smithsonian Institution, 1907–8*, pp. 29–618. Smithsonian Institution, Washington, D.C.
Hieb, L. A.
1979   Hopi World View. In *Handbook of North American Indians*, vol. 9, *Southwest*, edited by A. Ortiz, pp. 577–580. Smithsonian Institution, Washington, D.C.
Hill, J.
2001   Proto-Uto-Aztecan: A Community of Cultivators in Central Mexico? *American Anthropologist* 103(4):913–934.
2007   Otomanguean Loan Words in Proto-Uto-Aztecan Maize Vocabulary? Manuscript in possession of the author.
Hill, K. C. (project director)
1998   *Hopi Dictionary*. University of Arizona Press, Tucson.
Holmes, W. H.
1886   A Study of the Textile Art in Relation to the Development of Form and Ornament. In J. W. Powell, *Fourth Annual Report of the Bureau of Ethnology to the Secretary of the Smithsonian Institution, 1882–83*, pp. 189–252. Smithsonian Institution, Washington, D.C.

Kaufman, T., and J. Justeson
2007   The History of the Word for Cacao in Ancient Mesoamerica. *Ancient Mesoamerica* 18(2):193–237.

Kirch, P. V., and R. C. Green
2001   *Hawaiki, Ancestral Polynesia: An Essay in Historical Anthropology*. Cambridge University Press, Cambridge.

Kövecses, Z.
2002   *Metaphor: A Practical Introduction*. Oxford University Press, New York.

Kurath, G. P. (with the aid of A. Garcia)
1970   *Music and Dance of the Tewa Pueblos*. Museum of New Mexico Research Records no. 8. Museum of New Mexico Press, Santa Fe.

Lakoff, G.
1987   *Women, Fire, and Dangerous Things: What Categories Reveal About the Mind*. University of Chicago Press, Chicago.
1993   The Contemporary Theory of Metaphor. In *Metaphor and Thought*, edited by A. Ortony, pp. 202–251. 2nd ed. Cambridge University Press, Cambridge.

Lakoff, G., and M. Johnson
1980   *Metaphors We Live By*. University of Chicago Press, Chicago.
1999   *Philosophy in the Flesh: The Embodied Mind and Its Challenge to Western Thought*. Basic Books, New York.

Lamb, S. M.
1958   Linguistic History in the Great Basin. *International Journal of American Linguistics* 24(2):95–100.

Laski, V.
1958   *Seeking Life*. American Folklore Society, Philadelphia, Pa.

Lipe, W. D.
1995   The Depopulation of the Northern San Juan: Conditions in the Turbulent 1200s. *Journal of Anthropological Archaeology* 14(2):143–169.

Madsen, D. B., and D. Rhode (editors)
1994   *Across the West: Human Population Movement and the Expansion of the Numa*. University of Utah Press, Salt Lake.

Mallory, J. P.
1989   *In Search of the Indo-Europeans: Language, Archaeology, and Myth*. Thames and Hudson, New York.
1997   The Homelands of the Indo-Europeans. In *Archaeology and Language I: Theoretical and Methodological Orientations*, edited by R. Blench and M. Spriggs, pp. 93–121. Routledge, London and New York.

Malville, J. M., and G. E. Munson
1998   Pecked Basins of the Mesa Verde. *Southwestern Lore* 64(4):1–35.

Martinez, E.
1982   *San Juan Pueblo Tewa Dictionary*. San Juan Pueblo Bilingual Program, San Juan Pueblo, New Mexico.

Mera, H. P.
1935   *Ceramic Clues to the Prehistory of North Central New Mexico.* Laboratory of Anthropology Technical Series, Bulletin 8. Laboratory of Anthropology, Santa Fe, N.M.

Merrill, W. L., R. J. Hard, J. B. Mabry, G. J. Fritz, K. R. Adams, J. Roney, and A. C. MacWilliams
2009   The Diffusion of Maize to the Southwestern United States and Its Impact. *Proceedings of the National Academy of Science, U.S.A.* 106(50):21019–21026.

Miller, W. R.
1986   Numic Languages. In *Handbook of North American Indians*, vol. 11, *Great Basin*, edited by W. L. d'Azevado, pp. 98–107. Smithsonian Institution, Washington, D.C.

Monaghan, J.
1995   *The Covenants with Earth and Rain: Exchange, Sacrifice, and Revelation in Mixtec Sociality.* University of Oklahoma Press, Norman.

Moore, J. H.
1994   Putting Anthropology Back Together Again: The Ethnogenetic Critique of Cladistic Theory. *American Anthropologist* 96(4):925–948.
2001   Ethnogenetic Patterns in Native North America. In *Archaeology, Language, and History: Essays on Culture and Ethnicity*, edited by J. E. Terrell, pp. 31–56. Bergin and Garvey, Westport, Conn.

Newman, S.
1958   Zuni Dictionary. *International Journal of American Linguistics* 24(1), part 2.

Newsome, E.
2005   Weaving the Sky: The Cliff Palace Painted Tower. *Plateau* 2(2):28–41.

Noble, D. G. (editor)
2006   *The Mesa Verde World.* School of American Research Press, Santa Fe, N.M.

Nordenskiöld, G.
1979 [1893]   *The Cliff Dwellers of the Mesa Verde, Southwestern Colorado: Their Pottery and Implements.* Rio Grande Press, Glorieta, New Mexico.

Ortiz, A.
1969   *The Tewa World: Space, Time, Being and Becoming in a Pueblo Society.* University of Chicago Press, Chicago.

Ortman, S. G.
2000   Conceptual Metaphor in the Archaeological Record: Methods and an Example from the American Southwest. *American Antiquity* 65(4):613–645.
2006   Ancient Pottery of the Mesa Verde Country: How Ancestral Pueblo People Made It, Used It, and Thought About It. In *The Mesa Verde World*, edited by D. G. Noble, pp. 101–110. School of American Research Press, Santa Fe, N.M.
2008a   Architectural Metaphor and Chacoan Influence in the Northern San Juan. In *Archaeology Without Borders: Contact, Commerce, and Change in the U.S. Southwest and Northwestern Mexico*, edited by L. Webster and M. McBrinn,

pp. 227–255. Proceedings of the 2004 Southwest Symposium. University Press of Colorado, Boulder.

2008b   Action, Place and Space in the Castle Rock Community. In *The Social Construction of Communities: Studies of Agency, Structure and Identity in the Prehispanic Southwest,* edited by M. D. Varien and J. M. Potter, pp. 125–154. AltaMira Press, Walnut Creek, Calif.

2009   *Genes, Language and Culture in Tewa Ethnogenesis, A.D. 1150–1400.* Ph.D. dissertation, School of Human Evolution and Social Change, Arizona State University, Tempe.

Ortman, S. G., and B. A. Bradley

2002   Sand Canyon Pueblo: The Container in the Center. In *Seeking the Center Place*, edited by M. D. Varien and R. H. Wilshusen, pp. 41–80. University of Utah Press, Salt Lake City.

Parsons, E. C.

1936   *Taos Pueblo.* General Series in Anthropology no. 2. George Banta, Menasha, Wisc.

1974 [1929]   *The Social Organization of the Tewa of New Mexico.* Memoirs of the American Anthropological Association no. 36. Kraus Reprint, Millwood, N.Y.

Potter, J. M., and S. G. Ortman

2004   Community and Cuisine in the Prehispanic American Southwest. In *Identity, Feasting, and the Archaeology of the Greater Southwest,* edited by B. J. Mills, pp. 175–193. University Press of Colorado, Boulder.

Reed, E. K.

1949   Sources of Rio Grande Culture and Population. *El Palacio* 56:163–184.

Renfrew, C.

1987   *Archaeology and Language: The Puzzle of Indo-European Origins.* Cambridge University Press, Cambridge.

Robbins, W. W., J. P. Harrington, and B. Freire-Marreco

1916   *Ethnobotany of the Tewa Indians.* Bureau of American Ethnology Bulletin no. 55. Smithsonian Institution, Washington, D.C.

Ross, M.

1997   Social Networks and Kings of Speech-Community Event. In *Archaeology and Language I: Theoretical and Methodological Orientations*, edited by R. Blench and M. Spriggs, pp. 209–261. Routledge, London.

1998   Sequencing and Dating Linguistic Events in Oceania: the Linguistics/Archaeology Interface. In *Archaeology and Language II: Correlating Archaeological and Linguistic Hypotheses,* edited by R. Blench and M. Spriggs, pp. 141–173. Routledge, London.

Rouse, I.

1986   *Migrations in Prehistory: Inferring Population Movement from Cultural Remains.* Yale University Press, New Haven, Conn.

Sandstrom, A. R.
1991   *Corn Is Our Blood: Culture and Ethnic Identity in a Contemporary Aztec Indian Village*. University of Oklahoma Press, Norman.

Sapir, E.
1949 [1916]   Time Perspective in Aboriginal American Culture: A Study in Method. In *Selected Writings of Edward Sapir in Language, Culture, and Personality*, edited by D. G. Mandelbaum, pp. 46–60. University of California Press, Berkeley.

Sekaquaptewa, E., and D. Washburn
2004   They Go Along Singing: Reconstructing the Past from Ritual Metaphors in Song and Image. *American Antiquity* 69(3):457–486.

Shelton, A. A.
1996   The Girl Who Ground Herself: Huichol Attitudes toward Maize. In *People of the Peyote: Huichol Indian History, Religion, and Survival*, edited by S. B. Schaefer and P. T. Furst, pp. 451–467. University of New Mexico Press, Albuquerque.

Spinden, H. J. (translator)
1933   *Songs of the Tewa*. Published under the auspices of the Exposition of Indian Tribal Arts, New York.

Stark, M. T. (editor)
1998   *The Archaeology of Social Boundaries*. Smithsonian Institution Press, Washington, D.C.

Stirling, M. W.
1942   *Origin Myth of Acoma and Other Records*. Bureau of American Ethnology Bulletin no. 135. Smithsonian Institution, Washington, D.C.

Sweetser, E.
1990   *From Etymology to Pragmatics: Metaphorical and Cultural Aspects of Semantic Structure*. Cambridge University Press, Cambridge.

Thompson, J. E. S.
1970   *Maya History and Religion*. University of Oklahoma Press, Norman.

Trager, G. L.
1946   An Outline of Taos Grammar. In *Linguistic Structures of Native America*, pp. 184–221. Viking Fund Publications in Anthropology no. 6, New York.
1967   The Tanoan Settlement of the Rio Grande Area: A Possible Chronology. In *Studies in Southwestern Ethnolinguistics*, edited by D. H. Hymes, and W. E. Bittle, pp. 335–350. Mouton & Co., The Hague.

Varien, M. D., S. G. Ortman, T. A. Kohler, D. M. Glowacki, and C. D. Johnson
2007   Historical Ecology in the Mesa Verde Region: Results from the Village Project. *American Antiquity* 72(2):273–299.

Varien, M. D., and R. H. Wilshusen (editors)
2002   *Seeking the Center Place: Archaeology and Ancient Communities in the Mesa Verde Region*. University of Utah Press, Salt Lake City.

Wendorf, F., and E. K. Reed

1955   An Alternative Reconstruction of Northern Rio Grande Prehistory. *El Palacio* 62(5–6):131–173.

White, L. A.

1962   *The Pueblo of Sia, New Mexico*. Bureau of American Ethnology Bulletin no. 184. Smithsonian Institution, Washington, D.C.

Whorf, B. L.

1953   Linguistic Factors in the Terminology of Hopi Architecture. *International Journal of American Linguistics* 19(2):141–145.

Yumitani, Y.

1998   *A Phonology and Morphology of Jemez Towa*. Unpublished Ph.D. dissertation, University of Kansas.

7

Power, Agency, and Identity

Migration and Aftermath in the Mezquital Area of North-Central Mexico

CHRISTOPHER S. BEEKMAN AND ALEXANDER F. CHRISTENSEN

Cabana and Clark ask in their introductory chapter, "Why migration?" For our part, the theoretical value of migration lies in its exaggeration of the otherwise common event of culture contact. This forefronts fundamental questions about the relationship between biology and ethnicity and the factors affecting the material expression of cultural identity. The central discipline of our inquiry is archaeology, which has long sought to develop techniques for distinguishing migration from other possible explanations for changes in material culture. But when the problem is defined theoretically rather than methodologically (e.g., Blench et al. 2008), the failure of past approaches is understandable. Migration is not a unitary phenomenon and does not have a single material correlate or formula. Given its dynamic nature, migration itself is not even visible to archaeologists and it is instead the changed situation at the destination that we are actually interpreting. It is thus the social practices created or disturbed by a migration rather than migration itself that are visible in the archaeological record. What archaeological studies of migration require is a middle-range theory for different social strategies (Raab and Goodyear 1984). We cannot do this if all forms of movement are treated in the same way.

For these reasons we accept the editors' theoretical definition of migration as a "one-way residential relocation to a different 'environment'" but argue that archaeology must be complemented with other datasets to distinguish the many ways this can occur. In this chapter we use a case study from late pre-Columbian Mesoamerica (specifically highland Mexico) to investigate the central role of identity after a migration brought together more than one substantial cohesive community across ethnic and linguistic boundaries. In the spirit of this volume, we draw upon additional linguistic, biological, and ethnohistorical data to understand our case study. We will present our theoretical and methodological orientation, discuss the evidence we use to infer that a migration took place in north-central Mexico, and use that inference to interpret shifting patterns of identity in the wake of that migration.

Assumptions, Theoretical Orientation, and Methodological Approach

Much of the research on migration by archaeologists focuses on aligning biological populations with ethnolinguistic groups and/or with material remains, typically in early farming populations lacking authoritative power structures. Attempts to correlate material, ethnic, linguistic, and biological datasets present one set of problems when studying less complex societies (e.g., Bellwood and Renfrew 2003; Matson and Magne 2007; Renfrew 1987). However, complex societies present a social environment in which institutions based on inequalities can more forcefully promote or resist the use of different languages, religious beliefs, or lifeways and produce a lack of concordance among datasets (see Heggarty 2007, 2008 for linguistic examples). The study of migration in ancient complex societies thus forms a bridge between most archaeological studies of migration and the distinct population movements in the modern world.

Our perspective situates the social practices of individuals and groups within political, ideological, and economic formations; we argue that their decisions regarding migration and its aftermath are made with reference to those broader structures. This is especially evident in the decision to express group identity. Archaeologically speaking, people can actively use material culture to situationally express their social identities (Hodder 1977, 1979). Individuals can emphasize or deemphasize ethnicity, for example, by changing clothing, ceramic or house types, language, or behavior to better meet social goals while interacting with other groups (Barth 1969; Wobst 1977; see Hamerow 1997 for an archaeological case). Even so, the individual will seriously consider only a limited number of choices based on their understanding of acceptable behavior (Bourdieu 1992; Jones 1997). We are less likely to create new identities than to adopt, modify, or reject ones that already exist. Furthermore, ethnicity is not the only form of identity; it is selectively expressed alongside gender, age, kinship, class, nationality, and so forth at different times and in different social contexts (e.g., Berreman 1972). Whether the choice to express identity differently is accompanied by an internal sense of changed identity is another question.

When migration brings different groups into closer contact with one another, it is the nature of this interaction that impacts the decisions to express or not express that particular form of identity (e.g., Collett 1987). Archaeologists must therefore study the social and environmental context to understand the causes and results of migration rather than use migration to explain a material culture pattern. In our prior work (Beekman and Christensen 2003), we used a coordinate and contextual approach to migration that integrates linguistic, archaeological, ethnohistorical, and biological data and makes use of their various strengths and weaknesses. We studied a migration by first bracketing the time period using different datasets and then analyzing the material remains within that period following the perspective outlined above. This necessitated a more dense treatment of the contextual data, though we were still directed by generalized theoretical principles.

Some of our methodological assumptions were implicit in our earlier work and we wish to make them explicit here using a series of studies by Stone (2003, 2005; Stone and Lipe in press) as a framework. Starting from assumptions very similar to ours, Stone used examples from the American Southwest to define and illustrate major structural factors that should lead to varying degrees of emphasis upon group identity in the wake of migration. Her factors that encourage greater expression of ethnic identity are (1) size and cohesion of the migrants relative to the indigenous population, especially with regard to how difficult it is for the migrants to insert themselves into the new milieu and obtain access to space and resources; (2) more rigid social categories among both migrants and indigenes; and (3) lack of prior contact between the migrants and the group in the destination area.

Hence, large and complex groups that are able to reestablish their prior social structures (the "recovery of community" that Shami [1993] describes), are more directly in competition with their new neighbors, and have had little prior contact with the inhabitants of their migration destination are the most likely to express group identity openly. Small groups such as individuals or households that slip in easily among populations with whom they had prior contact, are largely outnumbered by the indigenes, and are expected to conform to local social roles are more likely to assimilate quietly. When identity is further paired with linguistic difference, the additional barrier to communication can enhance some differences between migrants and local populations. On the other hand, Clark (this volume) describes the possibility of a syncretic accommodation between migrants and indigenous populations, perhaps in situations of relative parity or interdependence. He describes a case in which the initial strategies among both migrants and locals were to strongly express opposing identities in ceramics and architecture, accompanied by suggestions of social tensions. Within a century, a new and syncretic material culture emerged in the area even as population decline left both groups struggling to maintain independent social institutions. While Clark does not describe a strict ethnogenesis, this nonetheless suggests that transculturation could occur and that a more stable accommodation between the two groups could emerge in time.

Our case study takes place within a more socially complex milieu than that investigated by Stone or Clark and that affects the variables for interaction and provides additional motives for both emigration and immigration (see also Ogundiran 2009; Usman 2009). For instance, political persecution or dissidence was frequent and therefore a common motive for emigration, as cited in Mesoamerican indigenous records (Beekman and Christensen 2003). Alternately, while immigration policy as understood today did not exist (e.g., Fahrmeier et al. 2003), political authorities had much to gain by attracting populations to their cities through public statements of ideology. This was demonstrated in Mesoamerica through the use of state-sponsored art programs as mass media. Larger considerations such as the location of migrants within core-periphery networks may also provoke migration and impact the ensuing conditions of interaction (Beekman and Christensen 2003). Social complexity also influences Stone's variables for migrant-indigene interaction. Social categories may define access to property or rights (Brumfiel 1994) and are likely to be more strongly defined and less flexible than in the American Southwest. Higher demographic profiles may make competitive relationships more likely as immigration pushes local populations closer to resource limits. Furthermore, the presence of centralized polities opens the door for Marxist models of ethnicity. Migration puts a potentially disadvantaged population alongside a more established one, and migration has long been recognized as contributing to hierarchical relationships (Kopytoff 1987). The state may promulgate ethnic stereotypes, increasing the possibility of resistance. Although this should result in strongly expressed identities, extensive persecution may cause groups to minimize identities that may in turn reemerge later as social conditions change. Finally, the relative prestige associated with one language or another or one ethnic group or another presents individuals and groups with social ideals to be emulated. The possibilities sketched here require further exploration, but we will refer to several of them as we consider our example of a migration in north-central Mesoamerica.

How Do We Know That a Migration Took Place and When It Took Place?

The northern extent of Mesoamerican complex societies coincides largely with the presence of the minimum rainfall needed for maize agriculture as the primary resource base (Figure 7.1), making this frontier a potentially shifting

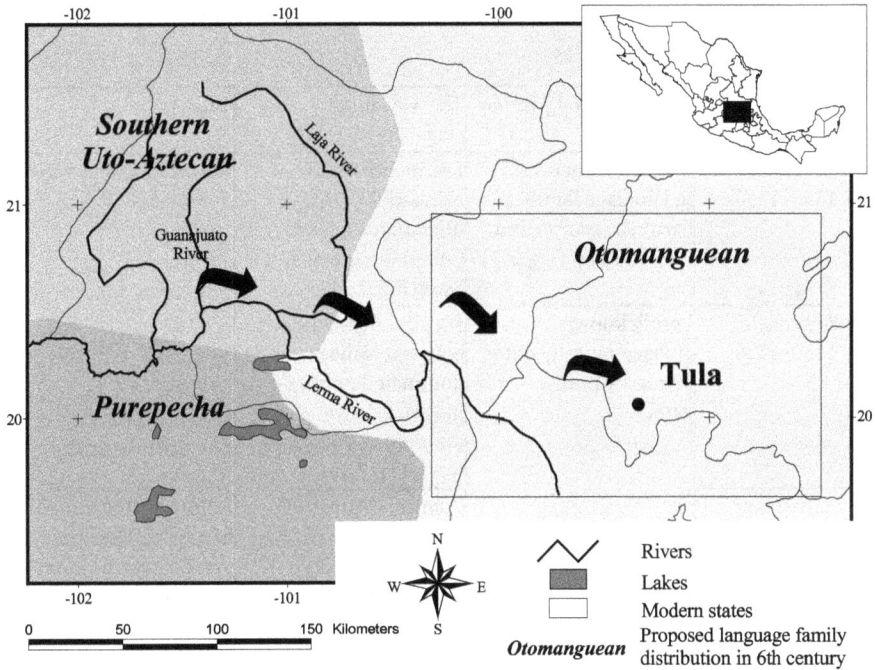

Figure 7.1. Proposed distribution of language families across the northern frontier of Mesoamerica at the time of the migration. Inset box around Tula shows the area covered in Figure 7.2.

one (Armillas 1969). The Mezquital Valley in the state of Hidalgo lies just 75 km north-northwest of Mexico City and at the southern edge of this frontier. Otomi has been spoken throughout the valley since at least the Spanish Conquest to today, while a smaller population of Nahuatl-speakers was known from the eastern Mezquital in the sixteenth century (Gerhard 1993). Early colonial archives (see Table 7.1 for time periods) demonstrate that Otomi was used for documents in the western Mezquital and Nahuatl in the east (Christensen 2002; Figure 7.2). Otomi pertains to the Oto-Manguean language family, which exhibits a largely continuous distribution from central through southern Mexico, suggesting a long period of diversification in its current locations (Winter et al. 1984). The major branches of Oto-Manguean are each centered on a highland valley with a lengthy archaeological tradition, and Oto-Manguean languages have likely been spoken continuously there since the earliest permanent settlements. By contrast, linguists are largely in agreement that Nahuatl is a comparatively late introduction into central Mexico from its nearest Southern Uto-Aztecan relatives to the northwest (see Dakin

Table 7.1. Schematic representation of the archaeological, ethnohistoric, and linguistic data at different scales

Mesoamerican Time Periods	North-Central Mexico (Fig. 7.1)	The Mezquital (Fig. 7.2–7.5)	Tula
Early Colonial A.D. 1520–1650	Spatial distinction in language families between western and eastern Bajío (Fig. 7.1)	Distinction in use of Nahuatl for written documents in east, Otomi documents in west (Fig. 7.2)	Ethnic hierarchy—Nahua dominance
Late Postclassic A.D. 1150–1520	Poorly known archaeologically but primarily hunter-gatherers	Political distinction between Nahua-dominated polities in east, Otomi-dominated polities in west (Fig. 7.3)	
Early Postclassic A.D. 850–1150		Political distinction between Nahua-dominated Tula polity in east, unincorporated Otomi in west (Fig. 7.4)	Ethnic distinction and hierarchy; changing expressions in ceramics, residential space, and trade links but single public architectural locus
Epiclassic A.D. 650–850	Multiple small polities across the region experiencing localized population growth and collapse. Spatially distinct expression of identity in portable material culture, architectural forms, and long-distance contacts between western Bajío and eastern Bajío (Fig. 7.1).	Expressed difference between Tula-related sites in east and Xajay-related sites in west (Fig. 7.5)	Accommodation with unexpressed differences in ethnicity; single ceramic complex but two separate public architectural loci
Late Classic A.D. 550–650	Multiple small polities across the region; spatially distinct expression of identity in portable material culture, architectural forms, and long-distance contacts between western Bajío and eastern Bajío (Fig. 7.1)	Migrants in hills with diverse Bajío-related material culture distinct from Teotihuacan-related material culture of sites in plains	
Classic A.D. 200–550		Teotihuacan-related sites	

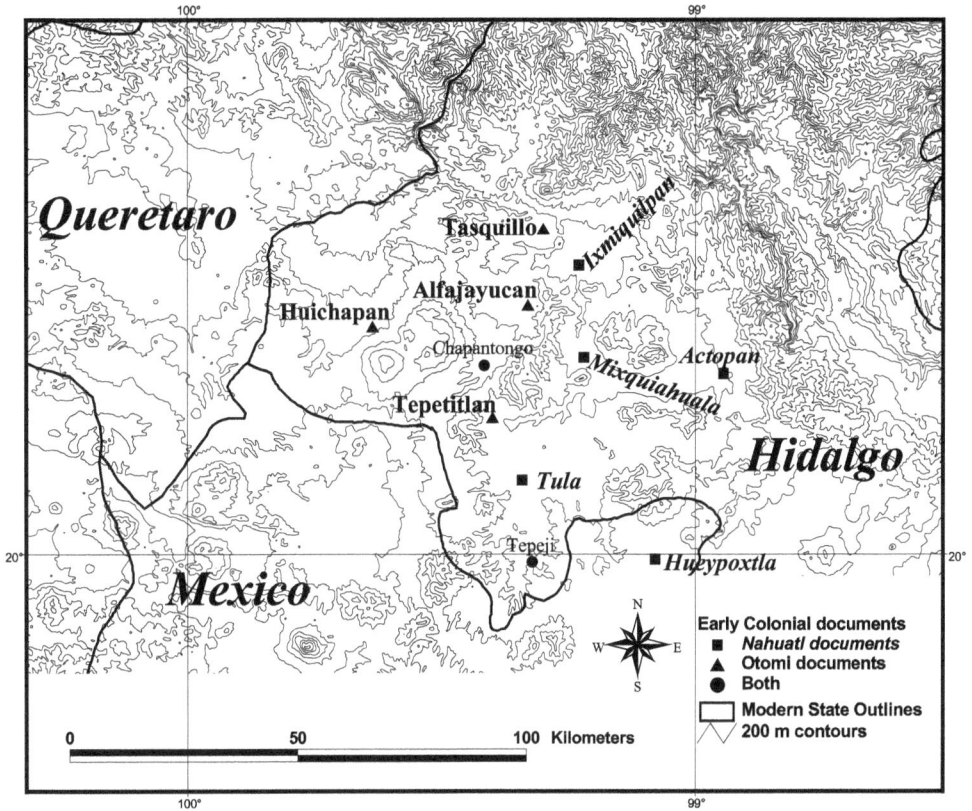

Figure 7.2. Early Colonial (A.D. 1520–1650) language use in the Mezquital Valley according to parish records (based on Christensen 2002).

and Wichmann 2000; Kaufman and Justeson 2007). Nahuatl has disappeared from the Mezquital Valley since the conquest while numerous dialects of Otomi remain, further highlighting the ephemerality of Nahuatl and the established nature of Otomi in the valley .

Linguists do not have widely accepted chronometric methods of fixing the arrival of Nahuatl and must usually rely upon dated inscriptions. Possible Nahuatl loanwords appear in southern Mesoamerican inscriptions from A.D. 650 to 750 (Macri and Looper 2005). More tentatively, rebus writing exists that suggests that Nahuatl speech is known from two central Mexican Epiclassic cities (Dakin and Wichmann 2000; Wichmann 1998). Claims for a still earlier presence for Nahuatl begin to founder at this point, as they are based on the presence of just three dated loanwords whose linguistic association is under dispute (Dakin and Wichmann 2000; Kaufman and Justeson 2007).

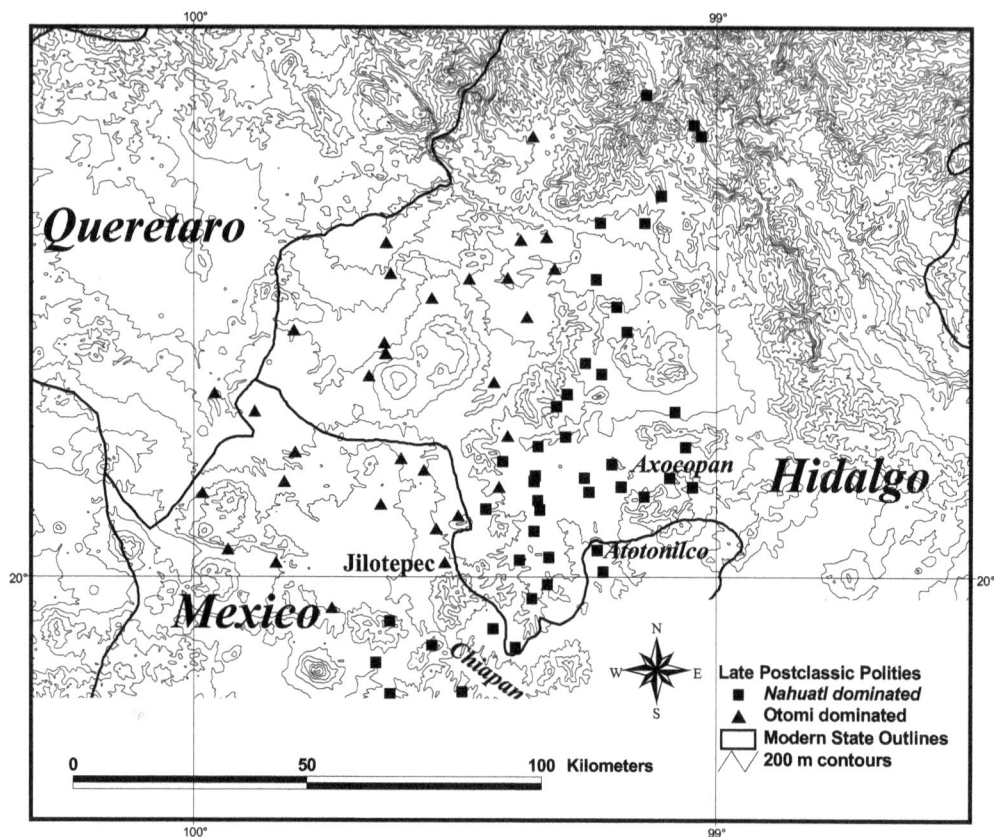

Figure 7.3. Late Postclassic (A.D. 1150–1520) political geography in the Mezquital Valley (based on Smith and Berdan 1996).

Biological evidence provides another perspective and supports physical migration as one mechanism of language expansion. Nonmetric and metric skeletal data document a significant population influx into central Mexico from the northwest sometime during the Classic to Early Postclassic (Beekman and Christensen 2003) or Epiclassic to Early Postclassic (González-José et al. 2007). DNA analyses from the important Tula site in the Mezquital Valley suggest members of a different population by at least the Early Postclassic (Fournier and Vargas Sanders 2002; Vargas Sanders and Salazar Campos 1998), although the very general data presentation and the small sample sizes and their undisclosed context do not allow further consideration.

Ethnohistoric texts add considerably more detail. Late Postclassic political geography in the Mezquital closely coincides with the use of Otomi and Nahuatl in colonial-era written records (Figure 7.3). The towns of the western

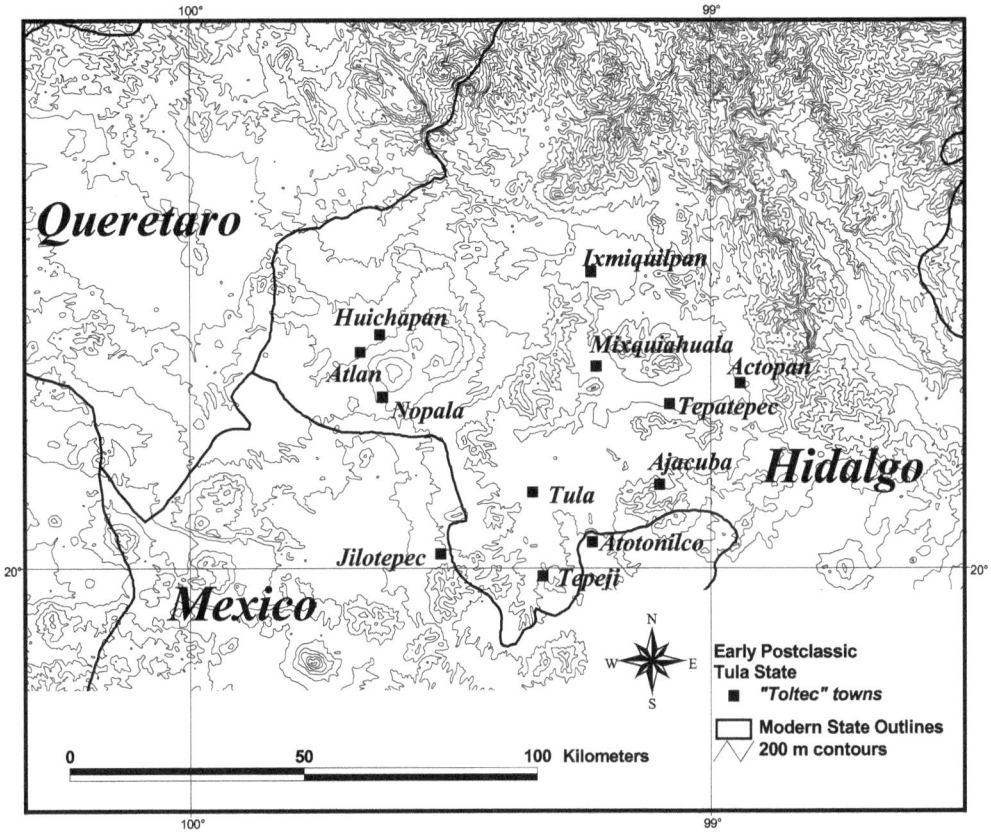

Figure 7.4. Ethnohistoric reconstruction of settlement associated with the northern portion of the Early Postclassic (A.D. 850–1150) Tula polity (based on Davies 1977).

Mezquital paid tribute to one kingdom where Otomi was the dominant language, while the eastern Mezquital was divided up into three provinces where Nahuatl formed the status language for written texts (Gerhard 1993; Smith and Berdan 1996). But one must keep in mind that this is elite language use, not the spoken language of the entire region.

This pattern of linguistic dominance, in turn, has still deeper roots in the Early Postclassic. During this period, the eastern Mezquital became home to a major regional polity based at Tula. According to a diversity of Native documents (summarized in Paredes Gudiño 1990) and widespread agreement among ethnohistorians, Tula was a multiethnic city dominated by Nahuatl-speakers. Nahuatl place names, shared gods and myths, and other ties speak to the strong cultural links between this "Toltec" state and the succeeding Nahua societies of central Mexico. Indigenous documents present numerous

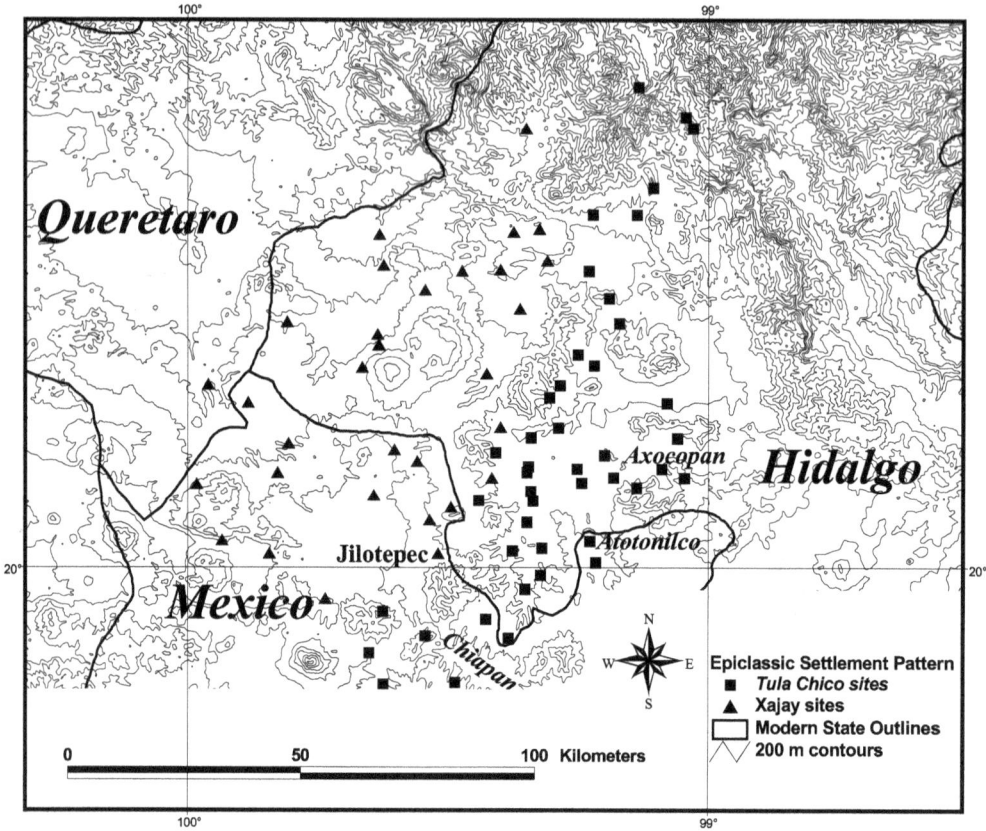

Figure 7.5. Relevant archaeological settlement in the Mezquital Valley during the Epiclassic period (A.D. 650–850) (based on several sources listed in text).

redactions of the city's founding, using Native calendrics to give various possible Epiclassic or Early Postclassic dates for the event (Paredes Gudiño 1990). Many remain skeptical of the historicity of these dates (Smith 2007), and in any case Nahuatl may have been introduced prior to the foundation of Tula. The boundaries of the Tula polity, as reconstructed through ethnohistoric analysis (Davies 1977), correspond very closely to those of political and linguistic dominance already introduced (Figure 7.4). The founding of Tula will play a central role in our analysis.

The Migration in the Epiclassic: Data from the Source

Contact-period linguistic data put the nearest Southern Uto-Aztecan languages, of which Nahuatl should have been a neighbor, in northeast Jalisco, western Guanajuato, and the southeast edge of the Sierra Madre Occidental

(Figure 7.1) (Barragan Trejo and Yáñez Rosales 2001; Herrera Muñoz and Quiroz Moreno 1991; Hill 2001; Moctezuma Zamarrón 2001). One of these languages, Cazcan, is even considered a variant of classical Nahuatl. Our archaeological understanding of a part of this area, known as the Bajío for its low-lying valleys, wetlands, and lakes, continues to improve, and we can make some tenuous suggestions about the origin of the migrants. Similar public architecture based on enclosed patios and ceramic complexes of red on buff and postfiring engraved types are found across the region (e.g., Cárdenas García 1999; Castañeda López et al. 1988), but two general material culture spheres have been identified for the Classic period (A.D. 200–650) (Brambila 1993, Figure 7.5; summarized in Wright Carr 1999). The western sphere incorporates more orange ceramics, larger sites on hilltops with agricultural terraces, more complex variations on the enclosed patios, columned architecture, greater use of cut stone in all sites, and contacts with western Mexico. The eastern sphere incorporates more redwares and white-striped ceramics, greater use of cobbles for architecture in all but the largest sites, valley-floor agriculture, and contacts with central Mexico.

The north-south dividing line between these distinct forms of material expression lies between the Guanajuato and Laja rivers, strikingly close to the sixteenth-century border between the range of Southern Uto-Aztecan languages mentioned above and the range of Oto-Manguean languages in eastern Guanajuato and Querétaro (Figure 7.1) (Moctezuma Zamarrón 2001). At the time of European contact, these groups were hunter-gatherers and occasional agriculturalists, but they likely are descendants of earlier farming populations. Assuming some territorial stability, this distribution suggests that the migrant Nahuatl-speakers came from western Guanajuato and that the migrants traversed a straight-line distance of up to 200 km before arriving in the Mezquital, likely dislodging or incorporating Oto-Manguean-speakers in the process. Similar incursions were being made across the Lerma River into other states (Beekman 1996; Beekman and Christensen 2003; Michelet et al. 2005) at similar times, so the Mezquital was not the only targeted destination. Unfortunately, we do not have a sufficiently refined chronology to evaluate the tempo of the migration.

We do have a likely motive for the migrants. Paleoclimatological data accumulated over the past 25 years form a chain of sequences across the Mexican highlands, including the Bajío (Metcalfe and Davies 2007). One of the clearest patterns is the gradual desiccation over the Classic period, reaching a peak in the period A.D. 700–1200, which two of the principal researchers describe as "probably the driest of the Holocene" (Metcalfe and Davies 2007:169). A lake core from Laguna Azteca just east of the Mezquital shows an opposing process toward greater humidity during this same time period (Metcalfe and Davies 2007), suggesting a pull factor attracting migrants from the Bajío toward the Mezquital Valley. There are conflicting claims as to whether the Bajío experienced a peak of occupation and political centralization (e.g., Castañeda López et al. 1988) or a rapid decline after A.D. 700 (Filini and Cárdenas 2007). There was substantial volatility in settlement at this time and sites such as Cerrito de Rayas (Ramos de la Vega and Crespo 2004), La Gloria (Moguel Cos and Sánchez Correa 1988), Plazuelas, Cañada de la Virgen (Castañeda López et al. 2007), Barajas (Pereira et al. 2001), and El Cerrito (Crespo 1991) each experienced a brief spike of occupation followed by abandonment. The evidence at the destination indicates that entire social communities made the move and that community leaders likely made the decision to migrate. This process was as much social as it was environmental, and some major sites in the neighboring mountains fluoresced well into the Postclassic, supported by cinnabar and red-ochre mining (Herrera Muñoz and Quiroz Moreno 1991; Mejía 2005).

There is suggestive evidence for the route and mode of migration. A long band of semi-desert in northeastern Guanajuato forms a wedge separating agricultural populations to the north and south as it angles down through central Querétaro and into the northern Mezquital. Archaeological surveys have found virtually no evidence of sedentary populations in this area (Viramontes Anzures 2000). This would have restricted the movement of migrating farmers to the valleys between this band and the Lerma River, and the river itself was always a likely route to follow. The evidence at their point of arrival indicates that the migrants formed cohesive groups that leapfrogged along this route, establishing a chain of social communities (Anthony 1990) rather than a continuous spread of evenly distributed population. The Mezquital received the first of these communities, but others stretched right through central Mexico and beyond (Beekman and Christensen 2003; Fowler 1989).

The Aftermath of Migration: Gradual Accommodation and a Multiethnic Identity

The sixth century A.D. in the Mezquital shows, as expected, the establishment of entire new communities whose material culture and site location differ from the indigenous settlements (Mastache and Cobean 1989; Polgar Salcedo 1998). The older towns were frontier communities associated with the urban state of Teotihuacan to the south (Díaz Oyarzabal 1980; López Aguilar 1994). The migrants, whom various scholars have argued originated in the Bajío based on artifact similarities (López Aguilar 1994; Mastache and Cobean 1989), initially settled in the hills of the southern Mezquital where they used material culture distinct from that of contemporary settlements on the valley floor (Mastache et al. 2002). The new hilltop sites described to date (particularly Cerro Magoni and La Mesa) are of short-term occupation but are quite large and internally diverse, with public buildings and residences. The La Mesa site has three distinct sectors, each with its own ceremonial architecture (Mastache and Cobean 1989). These settlements incorporated multiple communities with their own social institutions, though they may have been separate during the physical process of migration. They moved into a controlled social landscape that had little room for new migrants with few local social ties, and the migrants may have found it easier to settle with one another in the less-hospitable hilltops.

Mastache and colleagues (Mastache et al. 2002; Mastache and Cobean 1989) describe the new settlements as varying greatly from one to the next. They have disparate residential architecture in the form of isolated round or square houses using a slab construction technique and distinct architectural forms such as columned halls and sunken patios. The inhabitants made use of a wide range of architecture and ceramics, pointing to diverse origins for the migrants (Mastache et al. 2002). Ceramics show variation from one site to the next as well. These authors have argued that the migrants came from the Bajío on the basis of similarities in lithics, ceramics, and architecture, which we interpret more correctly as claims of affinity, but we have no reason to think those claims are false. We agree that the different lines of evidence point to an origin in western Bajío for the migrants and we also find the smaller-scale variability expressed from site to site to be of central importance. The material culture represents a tense field of competing expressed identities in these earliest migrant settlements, where the migrants were confronted with a complex social environment.

By the Epiclassic period, the new center of Tula Chico had been founded around two nuclei of formal ceremonial architecture corresponding to two social communities with their own public institutions (Mastache et al. 2002; Sterpone 2000–2001). An emerging ceramic complex known as Coyotlatelco had achieved a local conformity we interpret as a resolution of the earlier tensions. The ceramic complex is composed of red on buff, reduce-fired pottery with incised or engraved designs, and other decorative types that show general connections to the earlier pottery of the Bajío. While some subset of the ceramics and residential architecture of the immigrants continued into the Epiclassic, the material culture of the earlier indigenous residents did not. Coyotlatelco ceramics were used throughout most of the Mezquital, and we doubt that the Otomi-speaking residents had simply moved out. It is more likely that the symbolic capital of the visual corpus associated with the Teotihuacan state, which collapsed at about this time (e.g., Cowgill 2000), held no further value. Those Otomi who stayed in the Mezquital area ceased to assert their separate identity through maintaining an older material culture. The same thing happened in the former seat of power to the south, where the reduced population of Teotihuacan elaborated its own local version of the Coyotlatelco complex (Rattray 1966). There were few incentives to maintain a social identity associated with the failed former state and perhaps more than a few reasons to embrace the new arrivals.

Similar public architecture and ceramics reminiscent of Coyotlatelco extend westward (see the contributions in Solar Valverde 2006) that link source, destination, and adjacent areas of western Mexico (Beekman 1996). The distribution of the new material culture could hardly correspond strictly to the migrating peoples alone. But the Coyotlatelco-like artifacts and public architecture may cloak an ongoing process of ethnic accommodation (suggested for the Tula area by Mastache and Cobean 1989) and the expression of new identities based not only on language or ethnicity but on membership in explicitly multiethnic and perhaps political groupings. Actual language change lagged considerably behind the material expression of new identity and would not expand laterally until Nahuatl became the status language of later regimes (Beekman and Christensen 2003).

Although Tula Chico may have represented the accommodation of migrants and indigenes in a single settlement, the picture at the scale of the valley is quite different. As indicated earlier, Early Colonial written documents, Late Postclassic political geography, and the Early Postclassic Tula polity divide the Mezquital along a consistent north-south boundary (Figures 7.2–7.4). Archaeology demonstrates that a version of this boundary first appeared during the Epiclassic period, when a distinction in settlement pattern and domestic wares separated western and eastern sites in the Mezquital during Tula Chico's tenure as the urban center of the region (Figure 7.5). The western Mezquital sites extend into Querétaro and are known as the Xajay Development, while the eastern sites share Epiclassic ceramics with Tula Chico. The Xajay Development is distinguished by distinctive pottery (Crespo and Saint-Charles Zetina 1996; Solar Valverde 2001, 2002) and mesa-top ceremonial centers (Solar Valverde 2001, 2002), while the majority of the population lived on the flat bottomlands (Polgar Salcedo 1998). The eastern sites are larger and were part of a more intensely modified landscape of agricultural terraces. Their ceramic assemblages are close enough to those of Tula Chico itself that they follow the same chronological sequence (Fournier and Bolaños 2007; Solar Valverde 2001, 2002). This discontinuity does not simply correspond to groupings of indigenous Otomi to the west and Nahua migrants to the east, for recall that

Otomi-speakers should exist on either side. Rather we interpret the eastern pattern as associated with a new multiethnic Otomi-Nahuatl identity emerging around Tula Chico and being deliberately contrasted with their western neighbors.

We can compare our approach to another reconstruction of the period. Fournier and Bolaños (2007) argue for continuity in material culture corresponding to Otomi-speaking peoples in the Mezquital from the Epiclassic straight through to the present day. These authors emphasize the changes of Early Postclassic Tula (discussed below) to argue that Nahuas did not arrive in the Mezquital until that time and were essentially limited to Tula itself. We feel that this proposal clashes with the wider regional evidence for the presence of Nahuatl at an earlier date (previously discussed), but it also treats linguistic and ethnic groups as isomorphic with archaeological data and essentializes "Otomi" and "Nahuatl" material culture. We interpret Nahuas and Otomi as being present from the Epiclassic but suppressing that difference until the Early Postclassic, when some Nahuas achieve a position of political dominance. We consider this change below.

The Aftermath of Migration II: Accommodation Turns into Ethnic Hierarchy

The accommodation we envision for the eastern Mezquital ended with the burning of one of the architectural complexes at Tula Chico at the end of the Epiclassic and the expansion of the second locus into the sole political center for the city now referred to as Tula Grande (Sterpone 2000–2001). Tula Chico was left abandoned, mute testimony to a struggle of mythic proportions for succeeding generations. Mastache and colleagues (2002; Mastache and Cobean 1985; Mastache and Crespo 1982) have long seen a link between the archaeological data and a factional dispute described in stories told over the next few centuries. In these stories, Topiltzin, a wise and beneficent ruler of Tula, was tricked into public humiliation by his rival Huemac and was banished from the city in a major upset that is far more opaque in the original documents than in Mastache's reconstruction (Davies 1977).

There is nothing to specifically suggest that the factional dispute was isomorphic with Nahuatl and Otomi identities, but this is a plausible interpretation. Major shifts occurred internally toward greater categorization, by which we mean the establishment of distinct categories and dualities within Tula's archaeology during the Early Postclassic (see also Jones 1995). A set of creamwares of distinct affiliations emerged within the ceramic complex and became more important with time; contiguous apartment compounds were joined by and ultimately replaced with multistructured residential groups as more appropriate domestic space; trade in obsidian moved from western to eastern sources as old ties were abandoned and new ones were established (Mastache et al. 2002). While these changes need not correlate in any neat way with changing populations, they do indicate a rejection or reformulation of the prior multiethnic identity of the Epiclassic. The dualities in the ceramic assemblage and the residential architecture tentatively suggest that a distancing between groups took place that had not been overt before. The ethnohistoric record makes it clear that Nahua-speakers dominated the eastern Mezquital from this point on, so these changes must be interpreted in this light.

Emerging expressions of difference in the material culture were accompanied by more obvious manipulations of art and architecture for political aims. The new elites quickly adopted a mixture of traditional politics from the long-defunct center of Teotihuacan alongside a new political message (Mastache et al. 2002). Inspired by Teotihuacan, the new elites shifted Tula's site orientation and built a form of ceremonial precinct that deliberately harked back to the older state symbolism (Mastache and Crespo 1982; Mastache et al. 2002). But they also developed a new iconography that emphasized death and warrior imagery. The hybrid ideology seems to have worked, as the city as a whole grew to perhaps 40,000 people over the next few centuries. Its ruling dynasty had such high status that succeeding empires strove to establish marital alliances with it to legitimize their own political ambitions (Davies 1980). A "Toltec" identity had indeed become desirable apart from its ethnic or linguistic origins.

To summarize, worsening climatic conditions in the western Bajío during the Classic period either crippled subsistence agriculture or created such unstable social conditions that multiple communities of Nahuatl-speakers moved eastward along the Lerma River until they reached the Mezquital Valley (Figure 7.1). Faced with complex social institutions backed by the Teotihuacan state, the migrants clustered into hilltop centers. Perhaps associated with the decline of Teotihuacan, migrants and indigenes reached an accommodation in a multiethnic community at Tula Chico that preserved separate activity spaces even as they expressed a joint identity through portable material culture. A frontier between opposing expressed identities formed between Otomi-speakers in the western Mezquital and the multiethnic Otomi-Nahuatl polity to the east (Figure 7.5). This relationship ended with the destruction of Tula Chico at the end of the Epiclassic and the forging of the Toltec state (Figure 7.4). A series of dualities in the Early Postclassic archaeological record accompanied the ascendance of Nahuatl-speakers or just a faction of them. A new Toltec identity formed that symbolized civilizing influences rather than a particular language or ethnicity, although negative stereotypes of Otomi were widely promulgated at the time of the Spanish conquest (Brumfiel 1994). The linguistic predominance of Nahuatl among the elite continued in the Late Postclassic successor states in Tula's old territory (Figure 7.3) and even for a time after the Spanish conquest (Figure 7.2), before Nahuatl's eventual decline and disappearance in the Mezquital.

Conclusions

This volume's editors' definition of migration as "one-way residential relocation to a different 'environment'" encompasses a range of possible human movements that we should not expect to be equally discernible in the archaeological record. It includes, for example, the initial colonization of unoccupied lands such as the Pacific islands, the Americas, or the Australian continent. Discerning a migration in these cases is comparatively simple. But the definition also includes invading and wresting territory away from other groups (as in the European migration to the Americas) or establishing a relationship with prior claimants to the land (the most common result of migration worldwide). In complex societies, the importance of material culture for the definition of group identities is heightened and so are the social pressures to amplify or suppress visual cues. The potential range of material consequences to migration is thus too great to rely on archaeology alone.

Our example builds upon a wider-ranging case study (Beekman and Christensen 2003) that considered a series of migrations over a period of several hundred years and many thousands of square kilometers. One of the difficulties that emerged from the original study was how the visibility of a migration might vary from one place to another based upon local factors that influenced the relationship between migrants and those who came before (the "messiness" of migration discussed in Peregrine et al. 2009). Our theoretical perspective suggests that this is to be expected, and it drove us to pursue the problem here on a more local scale. Our more detailed analysis of that same late pre-Columbian migration into the Mezquital region has used theoretically derived principles to interpret complex context-specific data. Methodologically speaking, the scalar approach was one of the most productive aspects of this study. Our analysis required the wider perspective previously developed in order to correctly interpret the local situation. Without that broader picture, we might easily have reached other conclusions. Similarly, our study at the scale of the Mezquital region gave us a quite different understanding of identity politics than did the analysis of the city of Tula alone.

While the evidence for a substantial Epiclassic migration out of the Bajío continues to accumulate, there is little that *directly* ties this migration of population to the Nahuatl language. There is no Nahua artifact assemblage nor will there be, however detailed the analysis, because of the shifting and relational aspects of identity. But the linguistic, biological, and ethnohistoric evidence combined with the archaeology narrowly restrict the range of potential interpretations by rejecting other possibilities. Studies of past migration have tended to be highly empiricist, without a developed body of theory, and expectations have tended to be unrealistic as a consequence. Now that Cabana and Clark (this volume) have established a working minimal definition of migration, advancing our theoretical understanding requires us to emphasize the differences between cases. Migration among complex agrarian societies is one such variation, presenting issues that show more parallels to modern movements than to cases of migration among societies with less-institutionalized power structures and social identities.

References

Anthony, D.
1990 Migration in Archaeology: The Baby and the Bathwater. *American Anthropologist* 92:894–914.

Armillas, P.
1969 The Arid Frontier of Mexican Civilization. *Transactions of the New York Academy of Sciences*, Series 2, 31(6):697–704.

Barragán Trejo, D., and R. Yáñez Rosales
2001 Investigaciones sobre las Lenguas Indígenas en Jalisco durante el Siglo XX. *Estudios del Hombre* 13/14:61–93.

Barth, F.
1969 *Ethnic Groups and Boundaries: The Social Organization of Culture Difference.* Waveland Press, Prospect Heights, Ill.

Beekman, C. S.
1996 El complejo El Grillo del Centro de Jalisco: Una Revisión de su Cronología y Significado. In *Las Cuencas del Occidente de México: Época Prehispánica*, edited by E. Williams and P. C. Weigand, pp. 247–291. Colegio de Michoacán, Zamora.

Beekman, C. S., and A. F. Christensen
2003 Controlling for Doubt and Uncertainty through Multiple Lines of Evidence: A New Look at the Mesoamerican Nahua Migrations. *Journal of Archaeological Method and Theory* 10: 111–164.

Bellwood, P., and C. Renfrew (editors)
2003 *Examining the Farming/Language Dispersal Hypothesis.* McDonald Institute for Archaeological Research, Cambridge.

Berreman, G.

1972   Bazar Behavior: Social Identity and Social Interaction in Urban India. In *Ethnic Identity, Cultural Continuities and Change*, edited by G. De Vos and L. Romanucci-Ross, pp. 71–105. University of Chicago Press, Chicago.

Blench, R., M. Ross, and A. Sanchez-Mazas

2008   Methodological Issues: Linking Genetic, Linguistic, and Archaeological Evidence. In *Past Human Migrations in East Asia: Matching Archaeology, Linguistics, and Genetics*, edited by A. Sanchez-Mazas, R. Blench, M. Ross, I. Peiros, and M. Lin, pp. 3–19. Routledge, London.

Bourdieu, P.

1992   *The Logic of Practice*. Stanford University Press, Palo Alto, Calif.

Brambila, R.

1993   Datos Generales del Bajío. *Cuadernos de Arquitectura Mesoamericana* 25:3–10.

Brumfiel, E. M.

1994   Ethnic Groups and Political Development in Ancient Mexico. In *Factional Competition and Political Development in the New World*, edited by E. M. Brumfiel and J. W. Fox, pp. 89–102. Cambridge University Press, Cambridge.

Cárdenas García, E.

1999   *El Bajío en el Clásico*. Colegio de Michoacán, Zamora.

Castañeda López, C., L. M. Flores, A. M. Crespo, J. A. Contreras, T. Durán, and J. C. Saint-Charles

1988   Interpretación de la Historia del Asentamiento en Guanajuato. In *Primera Reunión sobre las Sociedades Prehispánicas en el Centro Occidente de México, Memoria*, pp. 321–355. Centro Regional de Querétaro, Instituto Nacional de Antropología e Historia, Ciudad de México.

Castañeda López, C., G. Zepeda García Moreno, E. Cárdenas García, and C. A. Torreblanca Padilla

2007   *Zonas Arqueológicas de Guanajuato, Cuatro Casos: Plazuelas, Cañada de la Virgen, Peralta y El Cóporo*. Editorial La Rana, Guanajuato.

Christensen, A. F.

2002   *Ethnicity, Caste, and Rulership in Mixquiahuala, Mexico*. Report submitted to the Foundation for Ancient Mesoamerican Studies, Inc. Available at http://www.famsi.org/reports/00066/index.html (accessed March 10, 2010).

Collett, D.

1987   A Contribution to the Study of Migrations in the Archaeological Record: The Ngoni and Kololo Migrations as a Case Study. In *Archaeology as Long Term History*, edited by I. Hodder, pp. 105–116. Cambridge University Press, Cambridge.

Cowgill, G.

2000   The Central Mexican Highlands from the Rise of Teotihuacan to the Decline of Tula. In *Cambridge History of the Native Peoples of the Americas*, vol. II, *Mesoamerica, Part I*, edited by R. E. W. Adams and M. J. MacLeod, pp. 250–317. Cambridge University Press, Cambridge.

Crespo, A. M.
1991   El Recinto Ceremonial de El Cerrito. In *Querétaro Prehispánico*, pp. 163–223. Instituto Nacional de Antropología e Historia, Ciudad de México.

Crespo, A. M., and J. C. Saint-Charles Zetina
1996   Ritos Funerarios y Ofrendas de Élite. Las vasijas Xajay. In *Tiempo y Territorio en Arqueología. El Centro Norte de México*, edited by A. M. Crespo and C. Viramontes, pp. 115–142. Serie Arqueología, Instituto Nacional de Antropología e Historia, Ciudad de México.

Dakin, K., and S. Wichmann
2000   Cacao and Chocolate: A Uto-Aztecan Perspective. *Ancient Mesoamerica* 11: 55–75.

Davies, N.
1977   *The Toltecs Until the Fall of Tula*. University of Oklahoma Press, Norman.
1980   *The Toltec Heritage: From the Fall of Tula to the Rise of Tenochtitlan*. University of Oklahoma Press, Norman.

Díaz Oyarzabal, C. L.
1980   *Un sitio Clásico del Área de Tula, Hidalgo*. Serie Arqueología, Instituto Nacional de Antropología e Historia, Ciudad de México.

Fahrmeir, A., O. Faron, and P. Weil (editors)
2003   *Migration Control in the North Atlantic World: The Evolution of State Practices in Europe and the United States from the French Revolution to the Inter-War Period*. Berghahn Books, New York.

Filini, A., and E. Cárdenas
2007   El Bajío, la Cuenca de Cuitzeo y el Estado Teotihuacano: Un Estudio de Relaciones y Antagonismos. In *Dinámicas Culturales entre el Occidente, el Centro-Norte y la Cuenca de México, del Preclásico al Epiclásico*, edited by B. Faugère, pp. 137–156. Colegio de Michoacan, Centro de Estudios Mexicanos y Centroamericanos, Zamora.

Fournier, P., and V. H. Bolaños
2007   The Epiclassic in the Tula Region beyond Tula Chico. In *Twin Tollans: Chichén Itzá, Tula, and the Epiclassic to Early Postclassic Mesoamerican World*, edited by J. K. Kowalski and C. Kristan-Graham, pp. 481–530. Dumbarton Oaks, Washington, D.C.

Fournier, P., and R. Vargas Sanders
2002   En busca de los "Dueños del Silencio": Cosmovisión y ADN Antiguo de las Poblaciones Otomies Epiclásicas de la Región de Tula. *Estudios de Cultura Otopame* 3:37–75.

Fowler, W. R., Jr.
1989   *The Cultural Evolution of Ancient Nahua Civilizations: The Pipil-Nicarao of Central America*. University of Oklahoma Press, Norman.

Gerhard, P.
1993   *A Guide to the Historical Geography of New Spain*. Rev. ed. University of Oklahoma Press, Norman.

González José, R., N. Martínez Abadías, A. González Martín, J. Bautista Martínez, J. Gómez Valdés, M. Quinto, and M. Hernández
2007 Detection of a Population Replacement at the Classic-Postclassic Transition in Mexico. *Proceedings of the Royal Society B* 274:681–688.

Hamerow, H.
1997 Migration Theory and the Anglo-Saxon "Identity Crisis." In *Migrations and Invasions in Archaeological Explanation*, edited by J. Chapman and H. Hamerow, pp. 33–44. BAR International Series 664, Archaeopress, Oxford.

Heggarty, P.
2007 Linguistics for Archaeologists. Principles, Methods and the Case of the Incas. *Cambridge Archaeological Journal* 17:311–340.
2008 Linguistics for Archaeologists: A Case Study in the Andes. *Cambridge Archaeological Journal* 18:35–56.

Herrera Muñoz, A., and J. Quiroz Moreno
1991 Historiografía de la Investigación Arqueológica de la Sierra Gorda de Querétaro. In *Querétaro Prehispánico*, edited by A. M. Crespo and R. Brambila, pp. 285–306. Colección Científica, Instituto Nacional de Antropología e Historia, Ciudad de México.

Hill, J. H.
2001 Proto-Uto-Aztecan: A Community of Cultivators in Central Mexico? *American Anthropologist* 103:913–934.

Hodder, I.
1977 The Distribution of Material Culture Items in the Baringo District, Western Kenya. *Man* 12:239–269.
1979 Economic and Social Stress and Material Culture Patterning. *American Antiquity* 44:446–453.

Jones, L.
1995 *Twin City Tales: A Hermeneutical Reassessment of Tula and Chichén Itzá.* University of Colorado Press, Niwot, Colorado.

Jones, S.
1997 *The Archaeology of Ethnicity: Constructing Identities in the Past and Present.* Routledge, New York.

Kaufman, T., and J. Justeson
2007 The History of the Word for Cacao in Ancient Mesoamerica. *Ancient Mesoamerica* 18:193–237.

Kopytoff, I.
1987 The Internal African Frontier: The Making of African Political Culture. In *The African Frontier: The Reproduction of Traditional African Societies*, edited by I. Kopytoff, pp. 3–84. Indiana University Press, Bloomington.

López Aguilar, F.
1994 Historia Prehispánica del Valle de Mezquital. In *Simposium sobre Arqueología en el Estado de Hidalgo. Trabajos Recientes, 1989*, pp. 113–123. Colección Científica, Instituto Nacional de Antropología e Historia, Ciudad de México.

Macri, M. J., and M. G. Looper
2003 Nahua in Ancient Mesoamerica: Evidence from Maya Inscriptions. *Ancient Mesoamerica* 14:285–297.

Mastache, A. G., and R. H. Cobean
1985 Tula. In *Mesoamérica y el Centro de México*, edited by J. Monjarás-Ruiz, R. Brambila, and E. Pérez-Rocha, pp. 273–307. Colección Biblioteca del Instituto Nacional de Antropología e Historia, Ciudad de México.
1989 The Coyotlatelco Culture and the Origins of the Toltec State. In *Mesoamerica After the Decline of Teotihuacan, A.D.700–900*, edited by R. A. Diehl and J. C. Berlo, pp. 49–67. Dumbarton Oaks, Washington, D.C.

Mastache, A. G., R. H. Cobean, and D. M. Healan
2002 *Ancient Tollan: Tula and the Toltec Heartland*. University Press of Colorado, Boulder.

Mastache, A. G., and A. M. Crespo
1982 Análisis sobre la Traza General de Tula, Hidalgo. In *Estudios sobre la Antigua Ciudad de Tula*, edited by A. G. Mastache, A. M. Crespo, R. H. Cobean, and D. M. Healan, pp. 11–38. Colección Científica no. 121, Instituto Nacional de Antropología e Historia, Ciudad de México.

Matson, R. G., and M. P. R. Magne
2007 *Athapaskan Migrations: The Archaeology of Eagle Lake, British Columbia*. University of Arizona Press, Tucson.

Mejía, E.
2005 La Arqueología de la Sierra Gorda de Querétaro: Una Revisión. In *Estudios Antropológicos de los Pueblos Otomíes y Chichimecas de Querétaro*, edited by M. E. Villegas Molina, pp. 146–160. Instituto Nacional de Antropología e Historia, Ciudad de México.

Metcalfe, S., and S. Davies
2007 Deciphering Recent Climate Change in Central Mexican Lake Records. *Climatic Change* 83:169–186.

Michelet, D., G. Pereira, and G. Migeon
2005 La Llegada de los Uacúsechas a la Región de Zacapú, Michoacán: Datos Arqueológicos y Discusión. In *Reacomodos Demográficos del Clásico al Posclásico en el Centro de México*, edited by L. Manzanilla, pp. 137–154. Universidad Nacional Autónoma de México, Instituto de Investigaciones Antropológicas, Ciudad de México.

Moctezuma Zamarrón, J. L.
2001 El Aporte de Wick Miller a los Estudios Comparativos de Lenguas Yutoaztecas. In *Avances y Balances de Lenguas Yutoaztecas. Homenaje a Wick R. Miller*, edited by J. L. Moctezuma Zamarrón and J. H. Hill, pp. 375–384. Instituto Nacional de Antropología e Historia, Ciudad de México.

Moguel Cos, A., and S. A. Sánchez Correa
1988 Guanajuato y Noreste de Michoacan: Algunas Apreciaciones Cerámicas. In *Primera Reunión sobre las Sociedades Prehispánicas en el Centro Occidente de*

México, pp. 223–235. Memoria, Centro Regional de Querétaro, Cuadernos de Trabajo 1, Instituto Nacional de Antropología e Historia, Ciudad de México.

Ogundiran, A.
2009 Frontier Migrations and Cultural Transformations in the Yoruba Hinterland, ca. 1575–1700: The Case of Upper Osun. In *Movements, Borders, and Identities in Africa*, edited by T. Falola and A. Usman, pp. 37–52. University of Rochester Press, Rochester, N.Y.

Paredes Gudiño, B. L. M.
1990 *Unidades Habitacionales en Tula, Hidalgo*. Instituto Nacional de Antropología e Historia, Ciudad de México.

Peregrine, P. N., I. Peiros, and M. Feldman
2009 Ancient Human Migrations. A Multidisciplinary Approach. In *Ancient Human Migrations: A Multidisciplinary Approach*, edited by P. N. Peregrine, I. Peiros, and M. Feldman, pp. 1–5. University of Utah Press, Salt Lake City.

Pereira, G., G. Migeon, and D. Michelet
2001 Archéologie du Massif du Barajas: Premières Données sur l'Évolution des Sociétés Préhispaniques du Sud-Ouest du Guanajuato, Mexique. *Journal de la Société des Américanistes* 87:265–281.

Polgar Salcedo, M.
1998 La Periferia en la Continuidad y el Colapso: Los Asentamientos del Periodo Clásico en el Occidente del Valle del Mezquital. *Arqueología* 20:41–52.

Raab, L. M., and A. C. Goodyear
1984 Middle-Range Theory in Archaeology: A Critical Review of Origins and Applications. *American Antiquity* 49:255–268.

Ramos de la Vega, J., and A. M. Crespo
2004 Reordenamiento de los Patrones Arquitectónicos del Centro-Norte de México. Del Clásico al Epiclásico. In *El Antiguo Occidente de México. Nuevas Perspectivas sobre el Pasado Prehispánico*, edited by E. Williams, P. C. Weigand, L. López-Mestas, and D. C. Grove, pp. 93–106. Colegio de Michoacán, Zamora.

Rattray, E.
1966 An Archaeological and Stylistic Study of Coyotlatelco Pottery. *Mesoamerican Notes* 7–8:87–211.

Renfrew, C.
1987 *Archaeology and Language: The Puzzle of Indo-European Origins*. Jonathan Cape, London.

Shami, S.
1993 The Social Implications of Population Displacement and Resettlement: An Overview with a Focus on the Arab Middle East. *International Migration Review* 27:4–33.

Smith, M. E.
2007 Tula and Chichén Itzá: Are We Asking the Right Questions? In *Twin Tollans: Chichén Itzá, Tula, and the Epiclassic to Early Postclassic Mesoamerican World*, edited by J. K. Kowalski and C. Kristin-Graham, pp. 579–617. Dumbarton Oaks, Washington, D.C.

Smith, M. E., and F. F. Berdan
1996   Appendix 4: Province Descriptions. In *Aztec Imperial Strategies*, by F. F. Berdan, R. E. Blanton, E. H. Boone, M. G. Hodge, M. E. Smith, and E. Umberger, pp. 265–349. Dumbarton Oaks, Washington, D.C.

Solar Valverde, L.
2001   *Epi-Classic Cultural Dynamics in the Mezquital Valley*. Report submitted to the Foundation for Ancient Mesoamerican Studies, Inc. Available at http://www. famsi.org/reports/00074/ (accessed March 10, 2010).
2002   *Interacción Interregional en Mesoamérica. Una Aproximación a la Dinámica del Epiclásico*. Tésis de Licenciatura en la Arqueología, Escuela Nacional de Antropología e Historia, Ciudad de México.

Solar Valverde, L. (editor)
2006   *El Fenómeno Coyotlatelco en el Centro de México: Tiempo, Espacio y Significado*. Memoria del Primer Seminario-Taller sobre Problemáticas Regionales, Instituto Nacional de Antropología e Historia, Ciudad de México.

Sterpone, O.
2000–2001   La Quimera de Tula. *Boletín de Antropología Americana* 37:141–204.

Stone, T.
2003   Social Identity and Ethnic Interaction in the Western Pueblos of the American Southwest. *Journal of Archaeological Method and Theory* 10:31–67.
2005   *Migration in Pre-State Societies*. Paper presented at the AAA symposium Migration and Anthropology: New Perspectives for a New Millennium, American Anthropological Association, December 3, Washington, D.C.

Stone, T., and W. D. Lipe
In press   *Standing Out Versus Blending In: Pueblo Migrations and Ethnic Marking*. In *Changing Histories, Landscapes, and Perspectives: The 20th Anniversary Southwest Symposium*, edited by Margaret Nelson and Colleen Strawhacker. University Press of Colorado, Boulder.

Usman, A.
2009   Precolonial Regions. Migration and Settlement Abandonment in Yorubaland, Nigeria. In *Movements, Borders, and Identities in Africa*, edited by T. Falola and A. Usman, pp. 99–125. University of Rochester Press, Rochester, N.Y.

Vargas Sanders, R., and Z. Salazar Campos
1998   La Migración Genética de las Poblaciones Prehispánicas: El Caso de Tula. In *Antropología e Historia del Occidente de México*, vol. 3, pp. 1671–1676. Sociedad Mexicana de Antropología and Universidad Nacional Autónoma de México, Ciudad de México.

Viramontes Anzures, C.
2000   *De Chichimecas Pames y Jonaces: Los Recolectores-Cazadores del Semidesierto Queretano*. Colección Científica, Instituto Nacional de Antropología e Historia, Ciudad de México.

Wichmann, S.

1998   A Conservative Look at Diffusion Involving Mixe-Zoquean Languages. In *Archaeology and Language II. Correlating Archaeological and Linguistic Hypotheses*, edited by R. Blench and M. Spriggs, pp. 297–323. Routledge, London.

Winter, M., N. A. Hopkins, and J. K. Josserand (editors)

1984   *Essays in Otomanguean Culture History*. Vanderbilt University Publications in Anthropology, Nashville, Tenn.

Wobst, H. M.

1977   Stylistic Behavior and Information Exchange. In *For the Director: Research Essays in Honor of James B. Griffin*, edited by C. E. Cleland, pp. 317–342. Anthropological Papers of the Museum of Anthropology no. 61, University of Michigan Press, Ann Arbor.

Wright Carr, D. C.

1999   El Bajío Oriental durante la Época Prehispánica. In *Arqueología y Etnohistoria: La Región del Lerma*, edited by E. Williams and P. C. Weigand, pp. 75–108. Colegio de Michoacán, Centro de Investigaciones en Matemáticas, Zamora.

IV

Ethnolinguistic Approaches

8

Linguistic Paleontology and Migration

The Case of Uto-Aztecan

JANE H. HILL

Migration has been a central theme in linguistic paleontology, a set of methods that uses the results of the comparative method in historical linguistics to reconstruct events, processes, and ideas in prehistory. The map of the languages of the world, grouped according to genealogical "families" or "stocks"—groups of languages defined by descent from a single common ancestral language—attests to the expansion and radiation of these common ancestors into diverse daughter linguistic communities. Indeed, the establishment of such families using the comparative method is the first step through which historical linguistics contributes to the study of migration. A remarkable new example is the language family Dene-Yeneseic (Vajda 2010), within which the Yeneseic languages of Siberia share a common ancestor with the Na-Dene languages of the Americas. If languages on the upper Yenesei River such as Ket and Kott are linguistically related to Tlingit and Eyak on the Gulf of Alaska and to Athapaskan languages from the north slope of Alaska to southeastern New Mexico, then migration—one-way residential relocation to a different environment, as conceptualized in the minimal definition presented in the introduction to this volume—was clearly an important process in the dispersal of the language family.

The languages of the Uto-Aztecan family, the topic of the present chapter, provide another vivid example. They are spoken from southern Idaho in the United States to Honduras and El Salvador and from the U.S. Los Angeles Basin to east Texas. If speakers of the protolanguage were archaic cultivators in a semi-arid environment (Hill 2001), they probably inhabited a range no larger than about 250,000 km^2 (roughly the size of the territory of the Upper Pimans in southern Arizona and northern Sonora). Thus the historic Uto-Aztecan range of approximately 2,000,000 km^2, like the immense distances involved in Dene-Yeneseic, surely attests to migrations. The linguistic evidence reviewed here shows that Uto-Aztecan migrants repeatedly developed new sets of labels for plants and animals, clearly defining the environments into which they dispersed as "new."

Locating the "homelands" where the common ancestors of language families (the protolanguages that are reconstructed using the comparative method) were spoken and tracing the routes of dispersal of the daughter groups are major preoccupations of linguistic paleontology that date at least to the eighteenth century, when scholars established the genealogical relationships between the languages of the far-flung Finno-Ugric and Indo-European families. The search for the homelands of these language families and the dispersal routes of their descendants was drawn into political debates during the emergence of modern European nation-states, stimulating scholarship by both nationalist advocates and disinterested scholars that led to increasing refinement of the methods.

All large language families probably attest to complex combinations of migration, language spread, and language shift. In language spread, a language acquires new speakers. These new speakers must, of course, be in contact with speakers of the spreading language. In language shift, the new speakers abandon their ancestral language in favor of the spreading language. In language shift, communities abandon their ancestral language in favor of the spreading forms. Language spread and language shift are major factors in the rearrangement of the linguistic map in the historic period, and these processes must also have occurred in prehistory. They are attested to by the presence of "substratum" evidence in surviving languages, such as Etruscan loanwords in Latin and its descendants (Ostler 2007) or unidentifiable but non-Uto-Aztecan words in the Takic languages of California (Bright and Bright 1976). Individual linguistic elements such as loanwords can travel far beyond the sphere of influence of speakers of their source language, even in the absence of any evidence of human movements. Indeed, Sapir (1949 [1916]) argued that these could behave exactly like any other "detachable" cultural element, such as a motif in myths or a way of hafting a projectile point. However, in prehistory, the semiotic complexes that we call "languages"—full-fledged grammatical systems with their associated sound systems and lexical inventories—could be moved around only by living speakers, who either replaced speakers of other languages or served as models for a shift to new ways of speaking. Thus, attention to migrations of speakers has never fallen out of fashion among historical linguists.

For Americanists, the classic essays of Edward Sapir provide models for the study of homelands and migrations. For instance, he pointed out that differences among pairs of Athapaskan languages in Alaska, the Yukon, and British

Columbia are as great as those between those languages and the Apachean languages of the U.S. Southwest. This suggested that the "historical center of gravity" (Sapir 1949 [1916]:457) of the family lay in the north. Sapir later (1949 [1936]) worked out this case in great detail, showing that the etymologies of four items of cultural vocabulary supported the hypothesis that the origin of the Navajo was in the north.

Kinkade and Powell (1976) illustrated linguistic-paleontological methods for tracing migrations with a case study of the linguistic prehistory of the Olympic Peninsula. They argued that a Chimakuan linguistic community that included the descendant languages Quileute in the west and Chimakum in the east was broken up by the advance of the Makah onto the peninsula, who spoke a Wakashan language with a center of gravity to the north. The Clallam and Quinault, Olympic Salish-speaking groups, are even later migrants into the region, perhaps from the east or northeast, given their close lexical similarities with Interior Salish languages.

Sapir was optimistic about our ability to determine relative dates for differentiation of descendant languages and for the antiquity of cultural vocabulary. His center-of-gravity hypothesis of 1916 assumes that related languages that are more different from one another have been separated longer than those that are more similar. Some scholars continue to refine such uniformitarian approaches to language change and differentiation (Nichols 1990). Contemporary "punctuationalists" (Dixon 1997; Nettle 1999) argue that in some historical circumstances languages differentiate with great rapidity, while in others long periods of stasis may limit differentiation. Nettle (1999) argued that the very extensive differentiation of the languages of the Americas may be due not to very great time depth, as Nichols (1990) suggested, but to explosive linguistic radiation in the initial colonization of an uninhabited continent. While work on refining lexicostatistical methods continues (Brown et al. 2008; Embleton 2000), the best way to date a reconstructed language is to link it to archaeological evidence. An example is my reconstruction of a word for "ceramic pot" in Proto-Uto-Aztecan (PUA). If this reconstruction holds up, it means that PUA could not have differentiated into daughter languages prior to the earliest appearance of ceramic technology in Mesoamerica, probably between roughly 2400 and 2100 B.C.

The limitations and strengths of historical linguistic method in the study of migration can be discussed in terms of the variables reviewed in the introduction to this volume. Linguistic data alone cannot usually distinguish among different types of migration according to variables of structure and scale, such as waves of advance across large regions driven by demographic expansion versus long-distance migration by small groups. Linguistic methods lack reliable chronological tools and cannot in themselves address the pace and tempo of migration. However, linguistic data can attest to impact variables. For instance, English is notoriously saturated with loanwords from Middle French in domains of elite modes of life. Words such as "chair" and "veal," for example, attest to hundreds of years of domination by French-speaking overlords of their English-speaking subjects in the Middle Ages. Linguistic data can contribute to arguments about distance: Sapir's demonstration that the Navajo word for "gourd" was a cognate with words for "horn" and "horn spoon" in the Athabascan languages of Alaska and Canada is a classic example in support of a case of a very long-distance migration. Occasionally, linguists can contribute to hypotheses about mode of transportation technology, as in the famous case of the Indo-European lexical complex for wheeled vehicles (Anthony 2007). But usually it is only in combination with archaeology and human biology that historical linguistics can contribute to the differential realization of the variables involved in migration (and, if we are fortunate, of the chronology of the move). For instance, linguistic-paleontological method permits me to propose a set of loanwords between Proto-Northern Uto-Aztecan (PNUA) and Proto-Kiowa Tanoan (PKT) (Hill 2008a). These include the borrowing into PNUA of PKT names for major economic plants of the Colorado Plateau that suggest clearly that PNUA-speakers saw that geographical environment as novel. However, additional details come only from interdisciplinary work. Data from the work of Matson (1991, 2003) provide a possible chronology and link to archaeological evidence. The Western Basketmaker II group, the name given to cultivators who appeared on the Colorado Plateau about 3,500 years ago, may be the Proto-Northern Uto-Aztecans, whereas the Eastern Basketmaker II group, which exhibits cultural continuities with the archaic hunter-gatherer groups of the plateau, may be the Proto-Kiowa Tanoan. Linguistic evidence alone has little to say about the scale of the contact. However, archaeological and human genetic evidence argues that the arrival of the Western Basketmaker II maize cultivators in the region did not take the form of a wave of advance but was instead the result of long-distance movements by small groups (Kohler et al. 2008). In summary, the linguistic data in themselves are incomplete, but they can add useful details to hypotheses about migration processes formulated in other disciplines.

Migrations in the Prehistory of Uto-Aztecan

In this section, I present linguistic evidence for two major episodes of migration by speakers of Uto-Aztecan and compare it to evidence from archaeology. The first episode is a migration from northwestern Mesoamerica to the

Colorado Plateau. The second is a migration from the Colorado Plateau to the coastal regions of southern California.

The Earliest Uto-Aztecan Dispersals

Fowler (1983) reconstructed the biosystematic lexicon of PUA. Confronting scholars who wanted to locate the family's homeland in north-central California or the Columbia Plateau, she argued that her reconstructed complex of names for plants and animals suggested a PUA homeland in the Gila River uplands in Arizona, New Mexico, Sonora, and Chihuahua.

My own alternative view pursues Bellwood's (1997) argument that the distribution of Uto-Aztecan suggests an expansion of "first famers." I proposed reconstructions of a PUA vocabulary for maize and maize cultivation (Hill 2001), which now includes thirteen items. Recently I have proposed reconstructions of PUA lexical items for "pot" and "clay" (Hill 2008b). Using the Wörter und Sachen (word and thing) method of linguistic paleontology, I argue that if such cultural vocabulary can indeed be reconstructed for PUA, then at a minimum, maize cultivation and the production of ceramics were known to its speakers and their community must have been located in a region where and at a time when maize and pottery are attested to archaeologically. The northwestern quadrant of Mesoamerica around 2000 B.C. satisfies these criteria and includes highland regions that exhibit the plant-animal complex that Fowler (1983) reconstructed for PUA.

The PUA vocabulary for maize and pottery appears to include Oto-Manguean loanwords. This is additional evidence for a PUA homeland in northwest Mesoamerica, since the distribution of the Oto-Manguean language family extends no farther north and west than the Mexican states of Queretaro, Guanajuato, and San Luis Potosi, the northern limits of the Oto-Pamean branch. The PUA forms that I believe to be loans are shown in (1), below. The symbols "V" and "C" mean "unspecified vowel" and "unspecified consonant," respectively. The symbol "7" stands for the glottal stop. The symbol "/" means that the proto-root exhibited both sounds, depending on the grammatical function.

(1) Diagnostic Proto-Uto-Aztecan Cultural Vocabulary
    a. PUA **sunu* "maize, ear of ripe corn"
    b. PUA **kumi/a* "to chew on corn or parched corn, corn"
    c. PUA **sa7a* "pot"
    d. PUA **kapam* "pot"; **kasV* "pot, bowl"
    e. PUA **sokV* "mud, clay"
    f. PUA **kwiraC* "mud, clay"

These words resemble items with the same meanings reconstructed for Proto-Oto-Manguean (POM) and for Proto-Chinantecan (PCh). (The latter is probably too late as a source but is included to stand in for Proto-Oto-Chinantecan [POCh], which has not been reconstructed.) These are shown in (2), below. Where Rensch (1976) and Kaufman (1990) have both reconstructed a form, I have given both reconstructions.[1] Note that at the date most specialists assign to POM, about 4000 B.C., there was no pottery in Mesoamerica. I believe that the POM words in items c and d in (2) meant something like "to cook, to heat, to boil in a container" at that period, but making the case for that suggestion lies beyond the scope of this chapter.

(2) Diagnostic Oto-Manguean Cultural Vocabulary
    a. POM **se(n) "corn, ear of corn" (Rensch 1976); **sa(a7)ai(n) "ear of ripe corn" (Kaufman 1990)
    b. POM **kwe "corn, ear of corn" (Rensch 1976); **kwau "corn" (Kaufman 1990)
    c. POM **su "pot, olla" (Kaufman 1990)
    d. POM **kwa "pot, olla, bowl" (Rensch 1976)
    e. PCh *sa7L "mud, earth" (Rensch 1989)
    f. PCh *gwa:7H "earth, dirt, adobe" (Rensch 1989); POM**kwa "dirt, mud, adobe" (Rensch 1976); POM **kwi(n) "clay, mud, earth" (Rensch 1976)

The forms in (1) exhibit initial consonant alternations between **s and **k(w/u). These are extremely rare in UA ([1] includes almost all known examples) but are well attested to in the Oto-Manguean languages, appearing in many pairs of words in diverse semantic domains beyond those shown in (2) (Rensch 1976). PCh doublets like those in (2)e, *sa7L "mud, earth," and (2)f, *gwa:7H "earth, dirt, adobe," show that the alternation must have survived through the POCh stage. However, the **s/**kw alternation is not attested to in the Oto-Pamean languages, the northwestern-most subfamily of Oto-Manguean (Bartholomew 1965). Therefore, POCh is the latest stage of Western Oto-Manguean from which the loans could have come. Kaufman (1990) dated POCh to about 2000 B.C., by which time pottery is attested to in the Tucson Basin (Thiel and Mabry 2006) and probably at Puerto Márquez, Guerrero (Adams 2005; Brush 1965). POCh is thus a likely source for the OM loanwords in PUA. Kaufman (1990) proposed a range for POCh extending no farther north and west than approximately Queretaro. The PUA homeland may have been just north of that region.

In Hill (2008a), I identified linguistic evidence for contact between PNUA and PKT. I proposed seven loans from PNUA into PKT, four of these in the domain of maize; six loans of names for important economic plants of the Colorado Plateau from PKT into PNUA; and four possible PKT words for major game animals borrowed into PNUA. The plant names include economic plants, such as pinyon pine, acorn-bearing oaks, wild onion, yamp, and sego lily, that may have been important for survival in a climatic regime that was distinctly hostile to maize cultivation.

In summary, linguistic evidence, using the reconstruction of cultural vocabulary and the identification of the sources of loanwords, suggests that PUA was spoken as far south as Queretaro, while PNUA-speakers were on the Colorado Plateau in the Four Corners region. These results attest to a Uto-Aztecan migration but provide few details about the accompanying variables or stages. Archaeological evidence can help. First, the pace of the migration was extremely fast. By 2100 B.C., maize cultivators making simple pottery were living in the Tucson Basin (Thiel and Mabry 2006), and by 1500 B.C. (Wills 1995) and perhaps by 1900 B.C. (Smiley 1994), maize cultivators clearly related to the Tucson Basin cultivators were on the Colorado Plateau. Archaeological and human genetic evidence also suggest that this very rapid move was not motivated by the demographic pressure that is often assumed for early farmers, since there is no evidence for a Neolithic demographic transition in the region until the middle of the first millennium A.D. (Kohler et al. 2008).

Uto-Aztecan Migrations into California

The NUA-speaking peoples include Hopi in the Four Corners region and speakers of the "Takic" languages in southern California,[2] Tübatulabal in the southern Sierra Nevada, and the Numic languages of the Great Basin. The NUA languages are almost certainly descended from a single common ancestor, since the descendant languages share several phonological innovations as well as many lexical items that are not found in the southern UA languages (Hill 2008a). PNUA-speakers, like their PUA ancestors, were apparently maize cultivators (Hill 2008a).

Fowler (1972, 1983) used the reconstructed NUA biosystematic lexicon to suggest the homeland and patterns of dispersal of the sub-branches, especially Numic. This chapter adds new reconstructions and focuses on migrations into southern California of speakers of Takic languages. The botanical lexicon is of special utility, because some plants have restricted geographical ranges that limit the range of hypotheses about migration routes. In addition, plant names that reconstruct to descendant stages rather than to the PUA protofamily show that Uto-Aztecan-speaking migrants understood that they were encountering new environments, and often those speakers apprehended moves into new environments and often developed new labels for their distinctive flora.

I locate the earliest appearance of each reconstructed name in the Takic botanical lexicon: in PUA itself, in PNUA, in Proto-Takic (PT), and, finally, in a sub-branch of Takic, Proto-Cupan (PC) (Bright and Hill 1967; Munro 1990). Among the items at each stage, I discuss those that are "diagnostic"; that is, those that restrict hypotheses about the geographical location of the speakers who used those words.

A cautionary note is required. The reconstruction of the meanings of pro-tolanguage plant names is usually imprecise, so only a few reconstructed plant names can be assigned reconstructed meanings that are useful for tracing mi-grations or establishing homelands. Thus it is important to spot floristic com-plexes rather than single plants. Even though this criterion is to some degree satisfied here, the reconstructions must be regarded as a set of hypotheses that should be further tested.

The Takic Botanical Vocabulary. Eleven Takic plant names can be traced to PUA sources. These names, mainly for genera of very wide distribution such as *Pinus* and *Phragmites*, do not help us trace the migration routes, so I do not list them. Twenty-nine Takic plant names trace only to Northern Uto-Aztecan. The presence in this vocabulary of loans from PKT (three of them appear in Takic) suggests that the PNUA community must have been located at least for a while in the Four Corners region (Hill 2008a). However, the evi-dence in (3) suggests that PNUA-speakers ranged as far west as the extreme western tributaries of the Colorado, which include the Virgin River and the Las Vegas Wash. This evidence moves us closer to Fowler's (1972, 1983) sug-gestion that the NUA homeland was in the southern foothills of the Sierra Nevada and the adjacent Mojave Desert.

(3) Diagnostic Takic Plant Names from Proto-Northern Uto-Aztecan
  a. *Echinocactus polycephalus*, cottontop cactus: PNUA **nïkwaa-*
  b. *Prosopis pubescens*, screwbean, tornillo: PNUA **kwiya~*kwinaya.* At-tested to only in Cahuilla and Kawaiisu, so this is not secure for NUA but may be a loanword.
  c. *Prosopis* spp., mesquite: PNUA **7oo-*
  d. *Salvia columbariae*, chia: PNUA **pasi/a-*

The word for *Prosopis* in (3)c, probably designating *P. glandulosa*, the west-ern honey mesquite, exhibits excellent cognacy and meaning similarity in all NUA subgroups except Hopi. Evidence from packrat middens attests that *Prosopis* grew along watercourses in the Mojave Desert during a relatively cool and damp climatic regime between 3490 and 2640 B.P. (Koehler and Ander-son 1995). By 1970–1440 B.P. the climate was like that of today, with *Prosopis* narrowly restricted to the lower, non-ephemeral watercourses in the Mojave.

P. glandulosa is restricted on the Colorado Plateau to the lower Virgin River basin and definitely did not extend into the Great Basin during the relevant period. There are no traces of *Prosopis* in the White Mountains even in the latest middens (ca. 2,000 to 3,000 years ago) (Jennings and Elliott-Fisk 1993).

No word for *Prosopis* is attested to in Hopi. Hopi *öösö* might reflect *öö-söhö* ("mesquite-grass"). However, its dictionary definition ("a plant, it is grayish green and sprouts from the ground and lies flat") does not sound like mesquite. Mesquite does not grow at Hopi, and consultants for the *Hopi Dictionary* (Hopi Dictionary Project 1998) claimed not to know a name for it. This raises the question of whether the Hopi represent a subgroup of Northern Uto-Aztecans that did not move to the west or whether, as Sutton (2000) proposed, they are descendants of a return migration from the Virgin River region.

Along with *Prosopis glandulosa*, the three other plants in (3) appear to be also restricted to the western drainages of the Colorado. These are (3)a *Echinocactus polycephalus*, (3)d *Salvia columbariae*, and (3)b *Prosopis pubescens*; the last is not securely established for PNUA. The Virgin River drainages are at the western extreme of the distribution of the Western Basketmaker II group, and the region provides a floristic complex that is a reasonable match to the Northern Uto-Aztecan (NUA) lexicon I have identified as well as to the one Fowler (1983) proposed.

Several reconstructed PNUA names may designate plants that are not found in the Mojave Desert and the southern Sierra Nevada but that do appear on the Colorado Plateau. These are *Prunus virginiana* var. *demissa*, *Allium cernuum* (a loan from PKT [Hill 2008a]), and *Artemisia tridentata*. However, related species are found in regions in the Mojave Desert and the southern Sierras that Fowler (1972, 1983) has suggested as a likely NUA homeland, so her proposal cannot be ruled out.

Twenty-five plant names reconstruct to Proto-Takic. Among these are four that support Fowler's (1972, 1983) proposal that the homeland for the Takic peoples was in the hot deserts of southeastern California. These names are shown in (4). Especially significant here is (4)a, *Ferocactus cylindraceus*, California barrel cactus, which has a very restricted distribution in the Colorado Desert and adjacent mountains. *Opuntia basilaris* (4)b and *Opuntia acanthocarpa* (4)c are more widespread in the California deserts, appearing also in the Mojave. The test plant Fowler invoked, *Washingtonia filifera*, California fan palm, (4)d, is fairly widely distributed in the southern California and Arizona deserts and is found as well in southern Nevada and in Death Valley. The appearance at the Proto-Takic level of names for "hot desert" vegetation permits us to suggest an "earliest date" for that stage. Packrat mound evidence shows that the plants in (4) do not appear in the California deserts until 2800 B.P. (Koehler and Anderson 1995).

(4) Diagnostic Proto-Takic Plant Names
  a. *Ferocactus cylindraceus*, California barrel cactus, PT **kupa-*. Possibly NUA, cf. Kawaiisu *kuwavi-bï*, *Echinocactus polycephalus*, but this may be a loan from Takic.
  b. *Opuntia acanthocarpa*, buckhorn cholla, PT **muta-* (Fowler [1972:209] lists Numic **mïca-*, hedgehog cactus, *Opuntia erinacea*, as a possible cognate but this is not a regular correspondence for NUA, so may be a loan or a different item entirely).
  c. *Opuntia basilaris*, beavertail cactus, PT **mana-*
  d. *Washingtonia filifera*, California fan palm, PT **maaxwa-*

A Proto-Takic migration into a range that included hot deserts invites a consideration of motivation. One possibility for a pull factor is the resources periodically made available by the lacustrine episodes of Lake Cahuilla. The earliest Late Holocene lacustrine episode documented by Waters (1983) occurred between 2300 and 2285 B.P., suggesting a possible earliest date for the formation of Takic groups. However, the lake was dry by A.D. 1, and lacustrine episodes did not begin again until A.D. 600–700. This dry period could have motivated the Takic shift in the direction of the Pacific Coast.

Among the Takic subgroups, I look only at the Cupan branch, the southernmost Takic group. The Proto-Cupan (PC) plant-name inventory of 36 items suggests that the PC community formed in the uplands to the west of the Desert Cahuilla rather than in the easternmost extension of the Cupan range around Indio, California. Thus, the ethnographically identified Desert Cahuilla of the Colorado Desert may be a secondary formation, a late return migration to the hot desert environment, again possibly pulled by a lacustrine episode of Lake Cahuilla.

With the exception of a word for *Larrea tridentata* (creosote bush), which is probably a late loan from Cahuilla into Luiseño and thus not a valid PC etymon, and a word for "mesquite beans," which could have been a trade item, no names for hot-desert plants appear in PC that are not also attested for Proto-Takic. The *Larrea tridentata* word permits an earliest date for the loan, since this plant, a key hot-desert indicator, does not appear in the Mojave desert until 1990 B.P. (Thorne 1986), although it may be present slightly earlier in the Coachella Valley. Some of the diagnostic upland flora names reconstructed for PC are shown in (5).

5) Diagnostic Proto-Cupan Plant Names
  a. *Eriogonum fasciculatum*, buckwheat: PC **hulaqala*

b. *Hesperoyucca whipplei*, yucca: PC **panáa-l*

c. *Heteromeles (Photinia) arbutifolia*, toyon: PC **7asha-wï-t*

d. *Prunus ilicifolia, P. helissofolius*, chokecherry: PC **chami-sh*

e. *Quercus engelmanii*, white oak: PC **tïva$a-*

f. *Quercus dumosa*, blue oak, scrub oak: PC **pawi-sh*

g. *Salvia carduacea*, thistle sage: PC **palnV-t*

The Archaeology of the Takic Spread. The diagnostic plant names reviewed above suggest the following migrations: west from the Four Corners region across the Colorado Plateau to the western drainages of the Colorado, including the Virgin River, then south into hot deserts, probably the southern Mojave Desert and the Colorado Desert of California, and then into the uplands to the west. This section explores the possibility of correlation with the archaeological record. Sutton et al. (2007) propose that NUA-speakers were in the western Mojave Desert by 3000 B.C. The evidence presented here suggests that this is much too early. For instance, there is no mesquite in that area until about 1500 B.C. Furthermore, if the PNUA are the Western Basketmaker II, as Matson (2003, 1991) suggested and as supported by the PNUA-PKT loan complex (Hill 2008a) and by the presence of maize vocabulary in Takic (Hill 2010), this is geographically, chronologically, and culturally inconsistent with the proposal by Sutton et al. (2007). In my view, a more likely manifestation of early PNUA in the west are the maize cultivators identified in the Las Vegas Basin at 2300 B.P. by Ahlstrom and Roberts (2008). Lyneis (1995) cites a date of 2250 B.P. (uncalibrated) at Willow Beach on the Colorado River in Arizona just below Hoover Dam. These dates are more consistent with the data from reconstructed botanical complexes matched with packrat mound evidence, which locates the western edge of NUA in this region. If the Las Vegas basin and Willow Beach cultivators are indeed elements of the differentiating NUA, they probably represent moves by very small groups, since this is well before the southwestern "Neolithic demographic transition" Kohler et al. (2008) identified.

Sutton et al. (2007:243) suggest that Proto-Takic and other NUA subgroups were differentiated by about 1000 B.C. This is very early for the hot-desert vegetation attested to in reconstructed Proto-Takic plant names. My data here are more consistent with the proposal by Sutton (2000:298) that the Takic diversification and spread began around A.D. 1. The dating of the arrival of Takic groups on the southern California coast has been controversial; some scholars continue to support a mid-Holocene date[3] and others argue for much more recent ones. While McCawley (1996) notes that a date as late as A.D. 700 for Takic arrival on the Pacific coast has been proposed, it is likely that the

Takic had arrived by A.D. 500, a period when Grenda (1997:20) notes "clear changes" in the archaeological record in southern California west of the Coast Ranges.

Conclusion: Strengths and Limitations of Linguistic Approaches

While historical linguists have for hundreds of years invoked "migrations" to explain the distribution of languages on the map, the discipline has included relatively little attention to the detailed structure of processes of human move- ment. This is partly because linguistic data alone simply does not permit de- termination of distinctive realizations of the variables of migration outlined in the introduction to this volume. However, I hope I have shown here that linguistic data can contribute to the contemporary study of migration. Along with clear evidence of long-distance human movements, the cultural recogni- tion of "new environments" shows up clearly in the data presented here. When environments are construed as "new," their crucial components can receive new labels. Thus linguistic data can establish, within the minimal definition outlined for this volume, that a migration indeed occurred. This demonstrates that linguistic data can inspire investigation from other disciplines. Further- more, I have suggested that by adding refinements and details, linguistic data can usefully constrain the interpretation of archaeological and genetic data in the study of migration.

Notes

1. Note that Rensch (1976) does not provide reconstructed glosses. Those I have provided here are informally based on the semantic range of the glosses in his cognate sets.

2. I am no longer sure that "Takic" is a valid genealogical unit. However, working out the implications of this idea is beyond the scope of this chapter, which uses the conventional classification.

3. I dismiss suggestions that Takic peoples have been in California since the Middle Holocene (8,000 to 5,000 years ago) as incompatible with the linguistic evidence.

References

Adams, R. E. W.
2005   *Prehistoric Mesoamerica*. University of Oklahoma Press, Norman.
Ahlstrom, R. V. N., and H. Roberts
2008   Who Lived on the Southern Edge of the Great Basin? In *The Great Basin*, edited by C. S. Fowler and D. D. Fowler, pp. 129–136. School for Advanced Research Press, Santa Fe, N.M.

Anthony, D.

2007 *The Horse, the Wheel, and Language*. Princeton University Press, Princeton, N.J.

Bartholomew, D. A.

1965 *The Reconstruction of Otopamean (Mexico)*. Unpublished Ph.D. dissertation, University of Chicago.

Bellwood, P.

1997 Prehistoric Cultural Explanations for Widespread Linguistic Families. In *Archaeology and Linguistics: Aboriginal Australia in Global Perspective*, edited by P. McConvell and N. Evans, pp. 123–134. Oxford University Press, Melbourne.

Bright, W., and M. Bright

1976 Archaeology and Linguistics in Prehistoric Southern California. In *Variation and Change in Language: Essays by William Bright,* edited by A. S. Dil, pp. 189–205. Stanford University Press, Stanford.

Bright, W., and J. H. Hill

1967 Linguistic History of the Cupeño. In *Studies in Southwestern Ethnolinguistics,* edited by D. H. Hymes and W. Biddle, pp. 352–391. Mouton and Company, The Hague.

Brown, C. H., E. W. Holman, S. Wichmann, and V. Velupillai

2008 Automated Classification of the World's Languages: A Description of the Method and Preliminary Results. *STUF–Language Typology and Universals* 61(4):285–308.

Brush, C. E.

1965 Pox Pottery: Earliest Identified Mexican Ceramic. *Science* 149:194–195.

Dixon. R. M. W.

1997 *The Rise and Fall of Languages*. Cambridge University Press, Cambridge.

Embleton, S.

2000 Lexicostatistics/Glottochronology: From Swadesh to Sankoff to Starostin to Future Horizons. In *Time Depth in Historical Linguistics* (Vol. 1), edited by C. Renfrew, A. McMahon, and L. Trask, pp. 143–66. The McDonald Institute for Archaeological Research, Cambridge.

Fowler, C. S.

1972 *Comparative Numic Ethnobiology*. Unpublished Ph.D. dissertation, University of Pittsburgh.

1983 Lexical Clues to Uto-Aztecan Prehistory. *International Journal of American Linguistics* 49:224–257.

Grenda, D. R.

1997 *Continuity and Change: 8,500 Years of Lacustrine Adaptation on the Shores of Lake Elsinore. Archaeological Investigations at a Statified Site in Southern California*. Technical Series 59, Statistical Research, Inc., Tucson.

Hill, J. H.

2001 Proto-Uto-Aztecan: A Community of Cultivators in Central Mexico? *American Anthropologist* 103:913–934.

2008a   Northern Uto-Aztecan and Kiowa-Tanoan: Evidence for Contact Between the Proto-Languages? *International Journal of American Linguistics* 74:155–88.

2008b   La Prehistoria Lingüística de los Pueblos Yuto-Nahuas. Paper presented at the Ninth Annual Meeting of the *Encuentro sobre la Lingüística en el Noroeste*, Hermosillo, Sonora, México.

2010   New Evidence for a Mesoamerican Homeland for Proto-Uto-Aztecan. *PNAS* 107(11):E33. Electronic document, www.pnas.org/cgi/doi/10.1073/pnas.0914473107, accessed September 20, 2010.

Hopi Dictionary Project

1998   *Hopi Dictionary/Hopìikwa Lavàytutuveni: A Hopi-English Dictionary of the Third Mesa Dialect*, edited by K. C. Hill. University of Arizona Press, Tucson.

Jennings, S. A., and D. L. Elliott-Fisk

1993   Packrat Midden Evidence of Late Quaternary Vegetation Change in the White Mountains, California-Nevada. *Quaternary Research* 39:214–221.

Kaufman, T.

1990   Early Otomanguean Homelands and Cultures: Some Premature Hypotheses. *University of Pittsburgh Working Papers in Linguistics* 1:91–136.

Kinkade, M. D., and J. V. Powell

1976   Language and the Prehistory of North America. *World Archaeology* 8:83–100.

Koehler, P. A., and R. S. Anderson

1995   Thirty Thousand Years of Vegetation Change in the Alabama Hills, Owens Valley, California. *Quaternary Research* 43:238–248.

Kohler, T. A., M. P. Glaude, J.-P. Bocquet-Appel, and B. M. Kemp

2008   The Neolithic Demographic Transition in the Southwest. *American Antiquity* 73:645–670.

Lyneis, M.

1995   The Virgin Anasazi, Far Western Puebloans. *Journal of World Prehistory* 9:199–241.

Matson, R. G.

1991   *The Origins of Southwestern Agriculture*. University of Arizona Press, Tucson.

2003   The Spread of Maize Agriculture into the Southwest U.S.A. In *Examining the Farming/Language Dispersal Hypothesis*, edited by P. Bellwood and C. Renfrew, pp. 341–346. McDonald Institute for Archaeological Research, Cambridge.

McCawley, W.

1996   *The First Angelinos: The Gabrielino Indians of Los Angeles*. Malki Museum Press, Banning, Calif.

Munro, P.

1990   Stress and Vowel Length in Cupan Absolute Nouns. *International Journal of American Linguistics* 56:217–250.

Nettle, D.

1999   Linguistic Diversity of the Americas Can be Reconciled with a Recent Colonization. *Proceedings of the National Academy of Sciences, USA* 96(6):3325–3329.

Nichols, J.

1990 Linguistic Diversity and the First Settlement of the New World. *Language* 66:475–521.

Ostler, N.

2007 *Ad Infinitum: A Biography of Latin*. Harper Press, London.

Rensch, C. R.

1976 *Comparative Otomanguean Phonology*. Language Science Monographs, vol. 14. Indiana University Press, Bloomington.

1989 *An Etymological Dictionary of the Chinantec Languages*. Summer Institute of Linguistics, University of Texas at Arlington, Dallas, Tex.

Sapir, E.

1949 [1916]   Time Perspective in Aboriginal American Culture History: A Study in Method. In *Selected Writings of Edward Sapir*, edited by D. G. Mandelbaum, pp. 389–462. University of California Press, Berkeley.

1949 [1936]   Internal Linguistic Evidence Suggestive of the Northern Origin of the Navaho. In *Selected Writings of Edward Sapir*, edited by D. G. Mandelbaum, pp. 213–224. University of California Press, Berkeley.

Smiley, F. E.

1994 The Agricultural Transition in the Northern Southwest: Patterns in the Current Chronometric Data. *Kiva* 60:165–189.

Sutton, M.

2000 Prehistoric Movements of Uto-Aztecan Peoples Along the Northwestern Edge of the Southwest: Impact on Southwestern Populations. In *The Archaeology of Regional Interaction*, edited by M. Hegmon, pp. 295–316. University of Colorado Press, Boulder.

Sutton, M. Q., M. E. Basgall, J. K. Gardner, and M. W. Allen

2007 Advances in Understanding Mojave Desert Prehistory. In *California Prehistory: Colonization, Culture, and Complexity*, edited by T. L. Jones and K. A. Klar, pp. 229–246, Altamira Press, Lanham, Md.

Thiel, J. H., and J. A. Mabry (editors)

2006 *Rio Nuevo Archaeology 2000–2003: Investigations at the San Agustin Mission and Mission Gardens, Tucson Presidio, Tucson Pressed Brick Company, and Clearwater Site*. Technical Report no. 2004-11. Center for Desert Archaeology, Tucson, Ariz.

Thorne, R. F.

1986 A Historical Sketch of the Vegetation of the Mojave and Colorado Deserts of the American Southwest. *Annals of the Missouri Botanical Garden* 73(3):642–651.

Vajda, E. J.

2010 A Siberian Link with Na-Dene Languages. *Anthropological Papers of the University of Alaska*, New Series, 5(1–2):10–77.

Waters, M. R.
1983 Late Holocene Lacustrine Chronology and Archaeology of Ancient Lake Ca-
      huilla, California. *Quaternary Research* 19:373–387.
Wills, W. H.
1995 Archaic Foraging and the Beginning of Food Production in the American
      Southwest. In *Last Hunters, First Farmers: New Perspectives on the Prehistoric
      Transition to Agriculture*, edited by T. D. Price and A. B. Gebauer, pp. 215–242.
      School of American Research Press, Santa Fe, N.M.

9

A Numic Migration?
Ethnographic Evidence Revisited

CATHERINE S. FOWLER

Ethnographic approaches to the study of migration have generally focused on defining motivating factors, such as changes in demographic or economic conditions, and on processual factors, such as communication networks or family structures that have facilitated documented population shifts, both gradual and rapid (Kearney 1986). In essence, they more often ask questions such as why and how such shifts occurred than if they occurred at all. However, when dealing with migrations in prehistory, the latter question is equally significant, as it would be an idle exercise to look for motivations and mechanisms if a migration could not be identified in the first place. In the following, I revisit the ethnographic data that have been cited in support of the hypothesis that speakers of ancestral Numic languages of the Uto-Aztecan family migrated or expanded into their present positions in the Great Basin of western North America at some time in the recent past (ca. 1,000 years ago). Although still controversial (and still a hypothesis), the case and its problems may be of broader interest to those interested in migration studies.

The Numic migration/expansion hypothesis is an old one that has been approached from linguistic, archaeological, ethnographic, and (most recently) bioanthropological perspectives. Although in this case the ethnographic data cited are not particularly persuasive in and of themselves, there may be good reasons for why this is so. I argue that particularly in a region such as the Great Basin, with its harsh semi-desert environment, and where the hallmarks of indigenous peoples and cultures throughout time have been their flexibility and mobility, ethnographic data are likely to be among the weakest brought to bear in migration studies. However, they are still important in any conjunctive approach to the problem, especially in offering potential motivations and processual insights and alternative factors to consider. I further suggest that if progress is to be made on the Numic migration/expansion hypothesis in the future, it will likely come from additional detailed micro-scale studies rather than the macro-scale approaches that have characterized much of the work thus far. The work also takes on a new relevance because this hypothesis is contentious for present-day descendants of speakers of the Numic languages. They see more in it than an academic exercise; arguments involving significant practical issues such as land rights and repatriation and challenges to traditional beliefs are tied to its tenets.

The Numic Migration/Expansion Hypothesis

The Numic migration/expansion hypothesis is nearly 100 years old and has generated well over 100 papers and a book (Madsen and Rhode 1994) tied to its most-often-cited articulation, that of linguist Sydney Lamb in 1958. Lamb proposed, based primarily on linguistic evidence (distributional, internal), that there had been a relatively recent (ca. 1,000 years ago) expansion of speakers of at least the northern tier of Numic languages of Uto-Aztecan from a homeland in or near Death Valley in southern California (Figure 9.1). The fan-shaped distribution, characterized by the greatest linguistic diversity at the point of the fan and significantly less to the north and northeast across the Great Basin, looked peculiarly like a case of "rapid expansion" (i.e., migration) into the region. Linguist Edward Sapir had suggested the same in 1916 (Sapir 1916). Subsequently linguist Wick Miller (1966, 1986) as well as various others concurred from the same but also different perspectives. The archaeological record for the region shows several points of discontinuity that seem to fit this interpretation, especially in the west, where the distinctive Lovelock Culture appears to have been "replaced" around 1000 C.E., and in the east, where Ancestral Puebloan and Fremont sites appear to have been abandoned at a roughly comparable period. In the central area, both archaeological continuity and discontinuity have been proposed, but the situation is made difficult by a lack of stratified sites and clearly diagnostic artifacts.[1] The ethnographic data for all regions have been read to show both continuity and discontinuity to the present, depending on which aspects are emphasized (see Madsen and Rhode 1994 for a general overview). Data from biological anthropology, particularly DNA, are relatively new to the discussion, and so far the data are minimal and support mixed positions (see for example, Cabana et al. 2008; Kaestle and Smith 2001; Johnson and Lorenz 2006).

Through the years, most linguists have remained true to Lamb's original hypothesis, but today they are less certain about the timing. Archaeologists and ethnologists also remain basically supportive, at least for an expansion out of the lower one-third to one-half of the historic range of speakers of the Numic languages, but less so as to whether the evidence and distributions in the

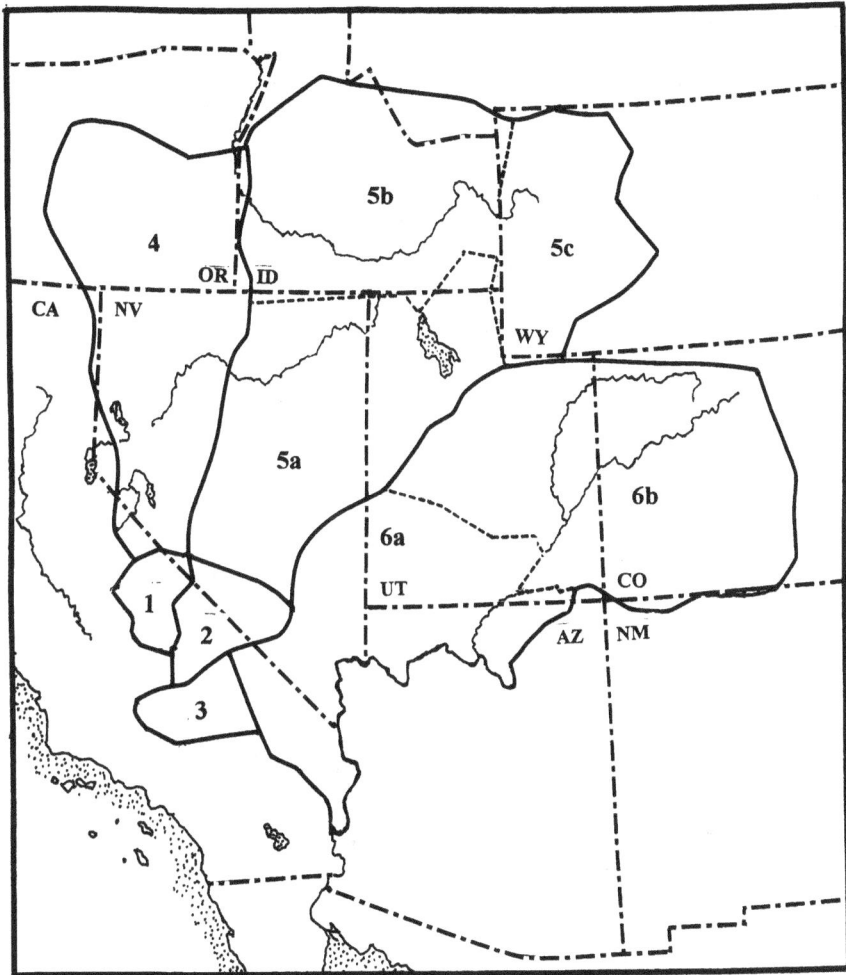

Figure 9.1. Distribution of Numic Languages (numbers 1–5) with some common cultural divisions (a–c): (1) Mono [includes Owens Valley Paiute]; (2) Panamint; (3) Kawaiisu; (4) northern Paiute; (5) Shoshone [5a, Western Shoshone; 5b, Northern Shoshone; 5c, Eastern Shoshone]; (6) Ute [6a, Southern Paiute-Chemehuevi; 6b, Ute]. After *Handbook of North American Indians, Vol. 11 (Great Basin)* (see Miller 1986 and Sutton 1993).

remaining regions represent population replacements or in situ developments (Rhode and Madsen 1994:214–215). Unfortunately, unlike the archaeological and bioanthropological records, which should see significant advances in the future, the ethnographic record for the region is less likely to change appreciably. Thus, to be helpful, additional ethnographic contributions to the topic will have to come from new perspectives on mostly existing data.

Migration: Some Working Definitions

At the symposium that generated this volume (see Introduction), the presenters worked on several key concepts that we hoped would clarify our thinking about these events in prehistory. In some cases, the results and questions raised have been discussed previously in the Numic case (see Madsen and Rhode 1994); but in others they have been less well explored. Starting with a minimal definition of migration as a "one-way residential relocation [of at least one individual] to a different 'environment,'" we were asked to consider several related questions about our particular case study and dataset: (1) the structure and scale of the migration; (2) possible motivations; (3) the impact or ways the impact might be determined; (4) the distance(s) involved (geographical, environmental, social, linguistic, genetic); and (5) the mode and technology that might be implied or demonstrated. Although ethnographic data may not be relevant to all these questions, they can and have contributed in the Numic case to several of these points. Unasked, and significant in this particular case, is the distinction between a migration and an expansion. The Numic hypothesis has been called both, but more often the term expansion or spread is used, likely because in this particular region there are no abrupt breaks in the geographic contiguity of the Numic languages (except for the Comanche). In addition, with the inherent mobility and flexibility of its peoples and cultures, even though they may have "expanded" or "migrated" several hundred miles, they likely already knew a fair amount before about the areas into which they were moving, and thus the two may be indistinguishable. The region has been host to hunters and gatherers throughout its prehistory and history, and by nature, these individuals and groups make frequent "one-way residential moves to different environments." We know from the ethnographic record that they made them seasonally, often involving a round of 50 to 100 miles or more (Steward 1938), and that they frequently changed environments through the transhumance made possible by the Basin and Range topography. They moved both temporarily and permanently for visits—some lasting many years—as well as for other reasons. Individuals (and occasionally small family units) traveled widely on foot (200 to 300 miles) on an extensive network of well-developed trails. Given low population densities, people often married at a distance, creating a network of kinsmen that again extended many miles, including, in at least some cases, across language borders. These and other features complicate issues such as whether to label something as a migration or an expansion as well as the use of any analogies to the past. Some of these difficulties clearly arise in reviews of the ethnographic data in the studies cited thus far.

Past Uses of Ethnographic Data on Numic Expansion

Three primary lines of ethnographic evidence have been cited in the past in discussions of the Numic migration/expansion hypothesis. These are documentary evidence, indigenous oral traditions, descriptive data on various cultural components and dynamics, and naming (place names, ethnobiological terms)—the latter both cultural and linguistic.

Documentary Evidence

By the time the documentary record began for the Great Basin in the mid- to late 1700s, the Numic languages were largely in their present positions. However, Sutton (1986:62–63) reviewed this record for evidence of continued expansions and relocations of Numic groups in the historic period and to identify any expansionist ideology that might have motivated movements in the distant past. He found that there was evidence of quite significant expansions on nearly all the northern and southern peripheries and, further, that the data supported an inherent "militarism" as a motivating factor.

However, alternative explanations for historic expansions also have been offered for several of the best-documented cases (Chemehuevi, Northern Paiute, Northern Shoshone, Ute; see for example Knack 1994). Although this does not negate them as Numic expansions or migrations, it calls into question militarism as a prime mover and thus perhaps its applicability in analogies to the past. One example is the expansion and relocation of Chemehuevi groups in the mid- to late eighteenth century from the Las Vegas/Pahrump valleys south into the Mojave and Colorado deserts and then ultimately by the 1830s to the Colorado River (Kroeber 1959). These movements were likely the result of Mojave warfare in those regions, further exacerbated by Spanish missionization in southern California and later U.S. encroachment. The Chemehuevi fully participated in and benefited from this situation and within a generation or at most two were as many as 100 miles farther south and east than their earlier position (Kelly 1934). Some, at least, also changed their subsistence orientation from hunter-gatherers and small-scale gardeners to fully settled floodwater farmers in that same time frame (Kroeber 1925). But in this case, internal cultural flexibility and mobility may be as important to Chemehuevi relocations as any inherent militaristic ethic.

Other examples from the northern and eastern frontiers of the Numic distribution include significant territorial expansions in the 1700s tied to groups that adopted the horse and became participants in the Plains bison-hunting pattern. This involved Northern Paiute people from Oregon who were soon traveling with Northern Shoshone to become bilingual groups known as the

Bannock (Fowler and Liljeblad 1986). Similarly, by the early to mid-1700s, Northern and Eastern Shoshone people had expanded into northern Idaho and Wyoming and were well into Canada and on the upper Missouri River on raiding, hunting, and trading expeditions. They were ultimately pushed back from this "golden age" expansion by the Blackfeet, who received guns earlier than the Shoshone and used them to drive the Shoshone back south in the late 1700s (Liljeblad 1972). After adopting the horse in the early 1700s, the Comanche broke away from their Shoshone cousins in southwestern Wyoming and migrated to the southern Plains, severing the linguistic contiguity. And with the newfound mobility provided by the horse, in the 1600s, the Ute expanded their territory east of the Rockies and south to the fringes of New Spain to be in proximity to both Pueblo and Spanish villages for raiding and trading. In most cases, these range expansions and migrations involved hundreds of miles, perhaps into thinly occupied territory. Certainly most were rapid—within a generation or two—and may have had some militaristic aspects. The movements likely did not involve groups larger than 50 people and were not coordinated (except perhaps for those of the Comanche). The introduction of a major new technological system (the horse and horse gear) and the proximity of new resources (bison and non-Indian settlements) were strong motivators.

Smaller movements of individual and multifamily groups far less dependent on the horse both toward and away from a growing non-Indian presence along the Sierran and Wasatch fronts are also documented. These are also explained by the push and pull of changes in resources and the access to them brought about by non-Indian settlement (see Malouf and Findley 1986).

Thus, although several of these migrations/expansions were going on in the historic period, at present external forces seem more powerful as explanations than internal ones. Additional external and internal forces need to be proposed and explored for the distant past.

Indigenous Oral Traditions

Oral traditions can be important sources of data on migrations, although as Sapir (1916:38–39) cautions, they are prone to time distortions. But just because migration motifs are lacking in a tradition does not necessarily mean that migrations did not occur.

Oral traditions regarding the immediate past from some Great Basin groups coincide with documentary records of movements, including, for example, the Chemehuevi southern expansion (Kroeber 1959), Kawaiisu movement into southern Death Valley in the 1820s (Fowler et al. 1995), and others. Traditions set in the mythic past generally do not refer to migrations. But

Sutton (1993) suggests that there may be subtle clues in traditional tales such as creation stories, theft cycles, and other tale types that can be used in examining the Numic migration/expansion hypothesis.

1) *Creation Stories*. Most creation stories recorded for the region's peoples tend to localize the place of creation somewhere within the present group's territory: Black Mountain, Round Valley, or Long Valley for the Owens Valley Paiute; Job's Peak or Mount Grant for central Northern Paiute; Saline Valley or Death Valley for the Panamint; an island in the Great Salt Lake for some Western Shoshone; and the Pacific Ocean and western deserts for the Southern Paiute (Sutton 1993). But some of these tales do speak of subsequent movement after creation: northward for the Northern Paiute and especially the Bannock and eastward for several of the Southern Paiute groups. Sutton (1993) sees these as lending support to a proto-Numic homeland somewhere to the south of the northernmost distribution of the Numic languages. However, Liljeblad (1986), a folklorist, notes a common tendency among Great Basin peoples to localize all important stories, including creation cycles, thus perhaps reducing their value for migration studies.

2) *Theft of Pine Nuts/Fire*. Another series of stories found among most of the groups in the core of the Great Basin are the Theft of Pine Nuts and/or Theft of Fire sequences. Nearly all these tales tell of going somewhere else to obtain the needed commodity, always to the north to steal pine nuts or to the west to get fire. The thefts are accomplished by various animals, in the Time When Animals Were People. Sutton (1993) argues that these stories suggest an orientation to the north and/or east, thus supporting an original southern location for the groups.

It is interesting to note in this regard that there has been a northward expansion of nut pine species (*Pinus monophylla*, *Pinus edulis*) over the last several millennia; they reached their northernmost limits on the western (Humboldt River) and eastern (Colorado) peripheries only within the last 1,500 to 800 years. They likely were as far north as the southern Bonneville Basin in central Nevada by 6,700 years ago (David Rhode, personal communication 2005). Perhaps this expansion is being reflected in the stories. It should be investigated further as a possible pull factor in motivating some population expansions.[2]

3) *Earlier People*. Nearly all Great Basin groups tell traditional stories of other peoples or groups who were present in their territories in the indefinite past, and several writers, including Sutton (1993), have used these data as evidence for a Numic expansion. Often the others are people, but they also may be giants, cannibals, or other superhumans. They are sometimes equated with other tribes now located elsewhere. For example, the Northern Paiute equated

them with the Pit River peoples, the Klamath, or the Umatilla (Fowler and Liljeblad 1986) and the Southern Paiute/Ute with former inhabitants of archaeological pueblos and the Hopi. Some tales describe these people as "those who came before," while others tell of an overlap in time of occupation with present people (Goss 1965; Pendergast and Meighan 1959). Although most see a historical basis to the stories, thus supporting a Numic replacement of previous groups, Liljeblad (1986:655) sees them as fitting within a widespread mythological motif of supernatural encounters. He suggests that in this case myth has become history rather than the reverse.

Cultural Patterns

Various types of descriptive ethnographic data on Great Basin cultures have been used as evidence for the Numic expansion hypothesis. These include comparisons of cultural traits, studies of material culture, investigations of cultural processes, and studies of place names and ethnobiological terms. Some of these, including studies of material culture, use the archaeological record for comparisons while others are primarily synchronic.

1) *Comparisons of Cultural Traits.* The cultures of the Great Basin have been subjected to various analyses of culture traits through the years, including Culture Element Distribution surveys directed by Kroeber (1939, 1959) and trait mapping by Driver (Driver and Massey 1957; Jorgensen 1980). Most recently, Jorgensen (1994) reexamined these data for evidence of the Numic expansion/ migration hypothesis, suggesting that if a constellation of Great Basin "core" cultural features could be discerned and that if this core could be "located" geographically, this might be powerful evidence for the Numic hypothesis. Included in Jorgensen's statistical manipulation were 292 cultural variables drawn from technology, economic organization, social organization, political organization, belief systems. and ceremonial practices for 22 subgroups that spoke Numic languages. Jorgensen (1994:102) felt that the results of this approach did identify a cultural core of features with the heaviest distribution in the southwestern Great Basin, just as Lamb had suggested. Further, the core and periphery were mirrored in the internal classification of the Numic languages and correlated with certain environmental parameters. He suggested that the core fractured at some point in the past—"2,000 years ago, maybe a little more"—into a western, central, and eastern pattern (as along linguistic lines), with a later differentiation of the northern and eastern peripheral groups (Jorgensen 1994:102).[3]

2) *Material Culture.* I have analyzed ethnographic material culture based on museum collections from several Great Basin groups (Fowler 1994). I examined roughly 1,500 items with Northern Paiute, Southern Paiute, and

Western Shoshone provenance for potential ethnic markers and to see if there was a "core" material culture for the region overall that might suggest early economic adaptations. I also compared the ethnic group and core data to the archaeological records in selected areas to better define technological continuities and discontinuities.

I compared basketry, sandals, cordage and nets, fishhooks and harpoons, bows and arrows, fire hearths and drills, pipes, ground stone, pottery, gaming pieces, beads, and so forth. Within each ethnic group, a characteristic material culture could be defined, but with variant subgroup details. A technological core for the Great Basin as a whole could also be defined, although less clearly. The strongest relationships across the region were in basketry; specifically, a complex of plain and diagonal open and closed twined baskets with forms that included burden baskets, trays, bowls, and possibly seed-beaters and water bottles. This complex was characteristic of all southern and central Great Basin groups; the fewest forms were present among those on the northern and eastern peripheries who later adopted Plains technology. Techniques and forms are related to the processing of seeds, including pine nuts. The closest associations outside the region were with California, although not necessarily southern California. Bettinger and Baumhoff (1982) had earlier argued that a superior technology for processing seeds had facilitated the Numic expansion. In several areas, this complex also largely replaces previous basketry techniques and forms around 1000 C.E. (see also Adovasio and Pedler 1994).

Other items of material culture, including linear nets, cordage, and slab grinding stones and hand stones that are also part of the core are too ubiquitous in western North America to be of much help except in adding specific details for Numic subgroups. Pottery was not likely a part of the core, but a composite fire drill/hearth, a bow and foreshafted arrow, pipes, and sandals might have been. Coiled basketry seems to have a separate history within each group in the region (Fowler 1994:112–113). The overall problem with material culture is that it is highly adaptive and subject to change by diffusion. However, it seems unlikely that the twined basketry complex would diffuse widely across the region without at least some implication for the movement of people.

3) *Cultural Processes.* Knack (1994) examined Great Basin ethnographies for evidence of documented internal cultural processes (other than militarism) that might explain such a rapid directional population movement as that proposed. She looked at warfare, subsistence cycles, trade, and intermarriage patterns. Rather than north-to-south biases, she noted east-to-west or (often) circular orientations suggested by these data. Circular patterns were more typical for subsistence and east-west patterns were more typical for

trade. Marriage exchanges did not suggest any directional bias, and although there was directional movement to the north and east in the historic period, she saw the external factors already examined (non-Indian settlement, the horse) as prime motivators.

4) *Naming.* In his early essay, Sapir (1916) noted the potential for historical studies of the semantics of place names and environmentally sensitive vocabulary. Specifically, he suggested that unanalyzable or opaque place names should be indicative of longer residence in a region than those with transparent etymologies. Following this suggestion, Miller (1986:103) looked at place names among the Owens Valley Paiute, Northern Paiute, Panamint, and Shoshone for these qualities, finding more unanalyzable forms for the Owens Valley Paiute (Mono) and Panamint than for the other two. He noted further that as predicted, as distance increased from Lamb's suggested southern California homeland, fewer unanalyzable stems were found. Although Miller did not look at Southern Paiute place names, the extensive data Isabel Kelly collected suggest a similar pattern (Fowler 2009). However, the highly specific morphemes of place among the Southern Paiute that catalog unique environmental features (potholes, buttes, mesas, etc.) could also argue for time depth in the region. It is possible that some groups change their place-name nomenclature faster than others as new stories are developed (Basso 1996; Jerald Levi, personal communication 2000).

Miller (1986) also cites Liljeblad on the semantics of Idaho Northern Paiute and Shoshone names for fish species in the Snake River country as being highly transparent while the fish names of the neighboring Nez Perce are more detailed and opaque. Fowler (1972) notes similar results for names for various plants and animals in Numic languages generally. The latter are also more indicative of southern Sierran and southern Great Basin environments than of central or northern ones. Although many feel that Sapir was right about the value of nomenclature as a clue to prehistory, little is known of the internal dynamics or the rate of change of some of these naming systems.

Summary and Conclusions

Although the data cited thus far are intriguing, they do not provide sufficient evidence in themselves for the Numic hypothesis. However, the ethnographic data do contribute to the discussion, including to theories about possible motivating factors for migrations and the cultural mechanisms that facilitate them.

In their synopsis of the volume that reexamined the hypothesis, Rhode and Madsen (1994) note several points of general agreement among the ethnographic, archaeological, and linguistic data and several that remain un-resolved. *First*, there is general agreement that there was an expansion/migra-tion and that the maximum was reached relatively recently. *Second*, the area of origin is somewhere to the south of the present northern and eastern pe-riphery. *Third*, the clearest evidence for replacement of populations—largely archaeological—comes from west-central Nevada and southeastern Oregon and the Colorado Plateau, both circa A.D. 1000. *Fourth*, whether these re-placements were gradual through assimilation or rapid through displacement or movement into unoccupied territory—or both—is not clear. And *fifth*, what occurred in the central area, except for an expansion into the northern periphery, remains open to question.[4]

Beyond these points, however, a number of other questions remain, includ-ing (1) *Area of Dispersal*: Exactly how large or small and where in the south-western Great Basin was the homeland? (2) *Timing*: Was the first dispersal early (5,000 years ago), midrange (3,000 years ago), or late (1,000 years ago)? Thus far the evidence does not support either the early or midrange dates but perhaps does support a date somewhere closer to 2,000 years ago. (3) *Who*: Earlier occupants are not well accounted for, at least in part because of a dif-ference in units of analyses among the anthropological subfields. "Languages," "cultures" (archaeological or ethnographic), "ethnic/genetic units," and so forth are not the same kinds or sizes of constructs with the same behavioral implications. (4) *Why*: Motivational factors for an expansion/migration are as yet poorly understood. Some favor economic motivations driven by popula-tion increases or climate change, others suggest militarism, and yet others suggest technological innovations (the bow and arrow, seed-processing tech-niques, etc.). And last, (5) *How*: Other than the few cases that suggest replace-ment, this is the hardest to gauge and certainly the most difficult to identify archaeologically and ethnographically, given the same basic hunter-gatherer lifestyle for millennia. Most seem to agree that it is unlikely that the three sub-branches of the Numic languages moved in some sort of coordinated fashion at the same time in a kind of "ethnic wave-of-advance" (Rhode and Madsen 1994:217). But whether small family groups moved slowly in a very complex pattern that ultimately had the effect of an expansion or in the larger leapfrog patterns that are more typical of migrations or in a variety of ways is far from clear. Undoubtedly what took place was far more complex than the present evidence allows us to theorize, and considerable more energy and research (including in the newer bioanthropological approaches) will be needed to clarify the situation—if that is possible.

To these questions can be added some from the general points raised in this symposium, including the basic one of whether there was a Numic migration and whether it fits the proposed definition. The answer is that there were likely several but that they reflected an overall expansion. At present there is no way of determining if movements were unidirectional, bidirectional, or some of each. Given the ethnographic evidence for the region, the latter seems more likely. How many migrants were involved? There is no way of calculating at present, but based on the ethnographic evidence we can say that most residence groups were small and likely remained so if they moved. In terms of motivations, some historic pushes and pulls have been identified, but how they apply to the deeper past remains unknown. In terms of mode, certain technologies facilitated ethnographic adaptations, including to specific resources (seeds, pine nuts, bison), but we do not know how and when these were worked out in the past. Numic-speaking peoples crossed geographic, social, environmental, linguistic, and genetic boundaries frequently in the historic period, but again, we do not know much about the specifics of the past.

Thus, where do we go from here? Miller (1966) once remarked that he doubted that the Great Basin saw a real coordinated migration before the advent of the Mormons under Brigham Young! Following Miller's lead, it seems time to stop talking about "*the* Numic migration/expansion" and start taking a serious microapproach to all issues involved by trying to define in a much more reasoned way, and based on multiple lines of evidence, what happened in each local area and with each set of people. Then through concerted coordination, it might be easier to see the complex ebb and flow of populations, perhaps involving some migrations but perhaps also movements in several directions (Anthony 1990). Given that it is clear that no one subfield can provide all the answers, perhaps we can better fill in the many gaps in the data through a conjunctive approach. But at the same time, we must also recognize that it is likely that good data that will answer specific questions are hard to come by (i.e., stratified archaeological sites with excellent preservation; amplified local genealogical data; early individual, family, and group movement histories; detailed dialectic data; data on bi- and tri-lingualism; adequate genetic samples, etc.). I would add here that maps with lines, be they cultural, linguistic, or archaeological, also confuse more issues than they clarify by assuming some sort of homogeneity within borders and differences outside them. They certainly do not account for the cultural or linguistic reality among ethnographically known Great Basin groups. As noted earlier, the ethnography of the region presents a different picture: one of small extended to multiple family groups, locally adapted, quite mobile, marrying across boundaries and traveling fairly widely, usually speaking more than one language and occasionally recognizing natural and cultural barriers for various social and economic reasons. Similar units of people may have been characteristic in the archaeological past—but we do not know. Given the environmental conditions, whoever came and went in the distant past would likely have made similar overall cultural adaptations, but perhaps they left some unique signatures in details yet to be identified.

Perhaps by reducing matters closer to a human scale, such a micro- or local approach to the problem would also make more clear what we know and do not know about what happened in each Great Basin area and with each subgroup of people. This in turn would get us beyond a "one solution fits all" approach and allow for multiple interpretations, including perhaps some more in keeping with views among Numic descendants. Then perhaps in another twenty years the larger issue can be revisited in the hope of making more significant progress.

Notes

1. Although there are some stratified sites in the central area, they tend to be limited to Monitor and Smoky valleys (see Thomas 1994). Most also lack good preservation in layers earlier than 2000 B.C.E. of perishable artifacts, although the chipped-stone chronology is good. Aikens and Witherspoon (1986) proposed that this central area may have been the original heartland of ancestral Numic groups 5,000 to 6,000 or more years ago (see also Aikens 1994). However, this is an archaeological issue, and until additional sites with good preservation are found, little can be added further.

2. Certainly other motivations have also been proposed. Lamb (1958) originally suggested that perhaps the lure of bison to the north and east was an original impetus. There are also climatic explanations, localized vulcanism (Fowler 1972), and other motivations.

3. I cannot comment on his statistical approaches.

4. See note 1.

References

Adovasio, J. M., and D. R. Pedler
1994   A Tisket, a Tasket: Looking at the Numic Speakers through the "Lens" of a Basket. In *Across the West: Human Population Movement and the Expansion of the Numa*, edited by D. B. Madsen and D. Rhode, pp. 114–123. University of Utah Press, Salt Lake City.

Aikens, C. M.
1994   Adaptive Strategies and Environmental Change in the Great Basin and Its Peripheries as Determinants in the Migrations of Numic-Speaking Peoples. In *Across the West: Human Population Movement and the Expansion of the Numa*, edited by D. B. Madsen and D. Rhode, pp. 35–43. University of Utah Press, Salt Lake City.

Aikens, C. M. and Y. T. Witherspoon
1986   Great Basin Numic Prehistory: Linguistics, Archaeology, and Environment. In *Anthropology of the Desert West: Essays in Honor of Jesse D. Jennings*, edited by C. Condie and D. D. Fowler, pp. 7–20. University of Utah Press, Salt Lake City.

Anthony, D.
1990   Migration in Archeology: The Baby and the Bathwater. *American Anthropologist* 92:895–914.

Basso, K.
1996   *Wisdom Sits in Places*. University of New Mexico Press, Albuquerque.

Bettinger, R. L., and M. A. Baumhoff
1982   The Numic Spread: Great Basin Cultures in Competition. *American Antiquity* 47:485–503.

Cabana, G. S., K. L. Hunley, and F. A. Kaestle
2008   Population Continuity or Replacement? A Novel Computer Simulation Approach and Its Application to the Numic Expansion (Western Great Basin, USA). *American Journal of Physical Anthropology* 135:438–447.

Driver, H. E., and W. C. Massey
1957   Comparative Studies of North American Indians. *Transactions of the American Philosophical Society* 47:65–446.

Fowler, C. S.
1972   Some Ecological Clues to Proto-Numic Homelands. *Desert Research Institute Publications in the Social Sciences* 8:105–122.

1994   Material Culture and the Proposed Numic Expansion. In *Across the West: Human Population Movement and the Expansion of the Numa*, edited by D. B. Madsen and D. Rhode, pp. 103–113. University of Utah Press, Salt Lake City.

2009   What's in a Name: Southern Paiute Place Names and Landscape Perceptions. In *Landscape Ecology: Concepts of Physical and Biotic Space*, edited by L. M. Gottisfeld and E. S. Hunn. Berghahn Books, New York.

Fowler, C. S., M. Dufort, and M. K. Rusco [and the Timbisha Shoshone Historic Preservation Committee]
1995   *Residence Without Reservation: Timbisha Shoshone Land Use Patterns in Death Valley National Park, CA*. Report to the National Park Service, Washington, D.C.

Fowler, C. S., and S. Liljeblad
1986   Northern Paiute. In *Handbook of North American Indians*, edited by W. L. D'Azevedo, pp. 435–65. Smithsonian Institution, Washington, D.C.

Goss, J. A.
1965   Ute Linguistics and Anasazi Abandonment of the Four Comers Area. *Memoirs of the Society for American Archaeology* 19:73–81.

Johnson, J. R., and J. G. Lorenz
2006   Genetics, Linguistics, and Prehistoric Migrations: An Analysis of California Indian Mitochondrial DNA Lineages. *Journal of California and Great Basin Anthropology* 26:33–64.

Jorgensen, J. G.

1980 *Western Indians: Comparative Environments. Languages and Cultures of 172 Western American Indian Tribes*. W. H. Freeman, San Francisco.

1994 Synchronic Relations among Environment, Language, and Culture. In *Across the West: Human Population Movement and the Expansion of the Numa*, edited by D. B. Madsen and D. Rhode, pp. 114–123. University of Utah Press, Salt Lake City.

Kaestle, F. A., and D. G. Smith

2001 Ancient Mitochondrial DNA Evidence for a Prehistoric Population Movement: The Numic Expansion. *American Journal of Physical Anthropology* 115:1–12.

Kearney, M.

1986 From the Invisible Hand to Visible Feet: Anthropological Studies of Migration and Development. *Annual Review of Anthropology* 15:331–361.

Kelly, I. T.

1934 Southern Paiute Bands. *American Anthropologist* 36:548–560.

Knack, M. C.

1994 Some Thoughts on Cultural Processes for the Numic Expansion." In *Across the West: Human Population Movement and the Expansion of the Numa*, edited by D. B. Madsen and D. Rhode, pp. 62–66. University of Utah Press, Salt Lake City.

Kroeber, A. L.

1925 *Handbook of the Indians of California*. Bureau of American Ethnology Bulletin 78. Smithsonian Institution, Washington, D.C.

1939 *Cultural and Natural Areas of Native North America*. University of California Publications in American Archaeology and Ethnology 38. University of California Press, Berkeley.

1959 *Ethnographic Interpretations, 7–11*. University of California Publications in American Archaeology and Ethnology 47. University of California Press, Berkeley.

Lamb, S. M.

1958 Linguistic Prehistory in the Great Basin." *International Journal of American Linguistics* 24:95–100.

Liljeblad, S. S.

1972 The Idaho Indians in Transition, 1805–1960. Special Publication. Idaho State Museum, Pocatello.

1986 Oral Tradition: Content and Style of Verbal Arts. In *Handbook of North American Indians*, vol. 11, *Great Basin*, edited by W. L. D'Azevedo, pp. 641–659. Smithsonian Institution, Washington, D.C.

Madsen, D. B., and D. Rhode (editors)

1994 *Across the West: Human Population Movement and the Expansion of the Numa*. University of Utah Press, Salt Lake City.

Malouf, C. I., and J. Findlay

1986 Euro-American Impact Before 1870. In *Handbook of North American Indians*, vol. 11, *Great Basin*, edited by W. L. D'Azevedo, pp. 499–516. Smithsonian Institution, Washington, D.C.

Miller, W. R.

1966   Anthropological Linguistics in the Great Basin. *Desert Research Institute Publications in the Social Sciences and Humanities* 1:75–112.

1986   Numic Languages. In *Handbook of North American Indians*, vol. 11, *Great Basin*, edited by W. L. D'Azevedo, pp. 98–106. Smithsonian Institution, Washington, D.C.

Pendergast, D. M., and C. W. Meighan

1959   Folk Traditions as Historical Fact: A Paiute Example. *Journal of American Folklore* 72:128–133.

Rhode, D., and D. B. Madsen.

1994   Where Are We? In *Across the West: Human Population Movement and the Expansion of the Numa*, edited by D. B. Madsen and D. Rhode, pp. 62–66. University of Utah Press, Salt Lake City.

Sapir, E.

1916   *Time Perspective in Aboriginal American Culture: A Study in Method.* Geological Survey Memoir 90, Anthropological Series no. 13. Government Printing Bureau, Ottawa.

Steward, J. H.

1938   *Basin-Plateau Aboriginal Sociopolitical Groups.* Bureau of American Ethnology Bulletin 120. Bureau of Ethnology, Washington, D.C.

Sutton, M. Q.

1986   Warfare and Expansion: An Ethnohistoric Perspective on the Numic Spread. *Journal of California and Great Basin Anthropology* 8:65–82.

1993   The Numic Expansion in the Great Basin Oral Tradition. *Journal of California and Great Basin Anthropology* 15:111–128.

Thomas, D. H.

1994   Chronology and the Numic Expansion. In *Across the West: Human Population Movement and the Expansion of the Numa*, edited by D. B. Madsen and D. Rhode, pp. 56–61. University of Utah, Salt Lake City.

10

Loanword Histories and the Demography of Migration

CHRISTOPHER EHRET

This chapter has a linguistic emphasis in the sense that it focuses on a neglected set of linguistic tools and evidence that have particular potential for assessing the demic processes accompanying different migration histories. But at the same time, the chapter is necessarily multidisciplinary. Its case studies, drawn from eastern Africa, are chronologically anchored in several long-accepted correlations of particular past speech communities with particular archaeological cultures (Ambrose 1982; Ehret 1998). Systematic full linguistic reconstructions have validated the cited linguistic evidence and the reconstructed linguistic history of each community (Ehret 1971, 1980, 1991, 2001c, 2008b; Rottland 1982; Sasse 1979; Vossen 1982). These approaches have a crossover to genetics as well. In allowing assessments of the demography of particular migrations, the linguistic tools highlighted in the chapter also allow the investigator to offer testable predictions about their expected genetic signatures.

Inferring population movements from linguistic evidence has a long history in the scholarship of migration. Typically work of this kind applies a particular set of techniques and has a limited goal. It seeks to identify probable locations of the original speakers of the protolanguage of a language family or a branch of a family and trace the subsequent expansions of the descendant peoples who spread the languages of the family or branch into a succession of new lands. The range of resources scholars usually employ in this effort is narrow. The primary data are the subclassification of the family or branch and the latter-day and (where known) earlier geographical distributions of those groups and languages. In its simplest form, the scholar applies the principle of fewest moves to these bodies of evidence, asking which origin area and which migration histories of the descendant speech communities would most parsimoniously account for the latter-day distributions of the languages. More-sophisticated versions of this kind of argumentation take into account additional indicators of earlier geographical locations of societies, such as reconstructed early lexicons of material culture and the natural world, loanword evidence of contacts with other peoples over the course of the expansions of the language family, and the potential effects of geographical factors such as mountains and rivers on the routes of expansion.

But, to use a cliché, this is only the tip of the iceberg of what linguistic evidence can offer on migration history. Linguistic testimony can generate proposals about the proportional demic contribution of incomers to the already present population. It can allow inference about the social processes and changes set in motion by such an encounter. It can identify instances of gender-differentiated migration and can reveal material cultural transfers brought in by immigrant populations. Inferences of the proportional demography of population encounters as well as gendered migration raise hypotheses for testing against the findings of geneticists. These elements of change are also likely to leave indirect markers in the archaeological record, while the value of linguistic identifications of material culture transfers for the correlation of archaeology with linguistic findings goes without saying.

Word-Borrowing Categories and Their Historical Accompaniments

How does one uncover these facets of migration history from linguistic testimony? The most powerful approach is a generally neglected one: inference from patterns of sustained word borrowing over periods from several up to many generations. Different histories of population movement, demographic encounter, and language shift generate different patterns of word borrowing between the languages of the immigrants and the existing population(s). For periods where other historical documentation is lacking, one can turn this evidence around and infer the broad human historical changes that generated the loanword patterns by identifying the particular kinds of sustained borrowing that took place. Within the overall sets of loanwords borrowed over such a period of encounter, one often can then also find individual loanwords for new customs and social relations and behaviors, which reveal particular elements of the social history of migration, and for new items of material culture, which indicate accompanying new developments in economy, technology, or the like.

Table 10.1 presents a categorization of different patterns of word borrowing over time. This categorization has been put to effective use in a number of studies over the years (e.g., Spaulding 1990, for an application to early modern African history). Ehret (2011, chap. 4) provides a recent exposition of the model and the historical examples on which it was built.

Table 10.1. Categories of word borrowing

Category	How the word borrowing takes place	Parts of vocabulary in which the word borrowing occurs	Minimum duration of word borrowing
1) Single-word borrowings	Through contacts among individuals or groups belonging to two or more speech communities	An individual word for a new item of culture is adopted	A few hours or days may sometimes be enough
2A) Semantically restricted word borrowing	Through contacts of the members of one speech community with those of another	A set of words dealing with a particular field of technical or cultural knowledge is borrowed	Uncertain; possibly as little as one to two generations in some instances
2B) Grammatically restricted word borrowing	From a suppressed collection of minority populations to a dominant speech community	Interjections and some adverbs are borrowed	Uncertain, but probably as little as a century
2C) Status-restricted word borrowing	From a lower-status minority to a dominant majority speech community	Jocular, deprecatory, or tabooed vocabulary is borrowed	Uncertain, but probably two to three generations
3A) Intensive word borrowing	From a dominant majority to a coexisting economically distinctive minority speech community, or from intrusive conquering small minority to a majority people closely related in language	Borrowings take place all through vocabulary (basic words are adopted at a rate of about 1–3% per century; other vocabulary is borrowed more rapidly)	Usually about two to three centuries; just two to three generations in instances of conquest by speakers of closely related language
3B) Heavy general word borrowing	According to first pattern described in 3A but of shorter duration than two to three centuries or according to the pattern in 3C but of longer duration than two to three centuries	Borrowings take place in all parts of vocabulary *except* for basic vocabulary	If a short period of category 3A borrowing, one to two centuries; if category 3C borrowing, more than two centuries
3C) Extensive general word borrowing	From one speech community to another as part of the merging of the one community into the other (and the loss of its former language in the process)	Borrowings take place in all parts of the vocabulary *except* for basic vocabulary and terms for large animals	Uncertain, but probably about one to two centuries
3D) Light general word borrowing	From one neighboring speech community to another	A sparse, semantically diverse scatter of culture vocabulary is borrowed	Two to three generations
4) Pidginization	By a collection of distinct speech communities thrown together by historical circumstance in the same region as part of these communities' adoption of a new common language	Rapid and extensive word borrowing takes place in all parts of the vocabulary, accompanied by severe grammatical simplification of the adopted new common language	Less than one generation

Applying the Tools to Maa History: A Sequence of Case Studies

The history of the Maa peoples of eastern Africa, of whom the Maasai are the best known, provides an especially informative set of case studies in the application of these tools. The usual methods of inferring migration from linguistic evidence have already been applied multiple times to Maa history (Ehret 1971, 1974, 1983; Vossen 1988), backed up by both archaeology (Ambrose 1982) and, for recent centuries, by oral tradition and written records (Ehret 2001a). The long-term story in this case is clear.

The historical sequence for our purposes begins with the Proto-Lotuko-Maa society, dating to roughly sometime in the second half of the first millennium B.C. Both the linguistic geographical arguments and the loanword evidence of their contacts with other peoples (Ehret 1983; Ehret et al. 1974) locate the Proto-Lotuko-Maa broadly in the same expanse of the far south of modern-day Sudan where the languages of the Lotuko branch of Lotuko-Maa are still spoken today. By the early first millennium A.D. the Proto-Lotuko-Maa had diverged into two descendant societies, Proto-Lotuko and Pre-Proto-Ongamo-Maa. The detailed examinations of loanword evidence in this chapter follow the history of the Pre-Proto-Ongamo-Maa and their cultural and linguistic heirs. The exact locations of the Pre-Proto-Ongamo-Maa during the first 700 years A.D. remain uncertain, but it is probable that their lands lay broadly in or around the Turkana Basin of modern-day northwestern Kenya.

Around A.D. 700 the Proto-Ongamo-Maa moved south, settling in central Kenya in and around the Baringo Basin. Their occupation of this region has been given firm identification with the archaeological appearance of Lanet Ware in central Kenya at that period (Ambrose 1982). At an uncertain time around A.D. 1000, a farther southward migration took place, breaking up the Proto-Ongamo-Maa into two descendant societies. The southward migrants, who resettled in the plains all around Mount Kilimanjaro, gave rise to the Ongamo society of later centuries (Ehret 1971, 1974). The communities that remained behind in the Baringo Basin and neighboring areas evolved into the Proto-Maa society (Vossen 1988).

Around A.D. 1500, one set of the Maa communities began a second southward expansion out of the Baringo Basin. In the sixteenth century they followed the Rift Valley first through central Kenya and then into the plains of southern Kenya and central far northern Tanzania. In the seventeenth and eighteenth centuries they pressed farther south toward the middle of Tanzania. Most of these communities came to be known as the Maasai. The farthest south outliers formed a somewhat distinctive group with the name Parakuyu. Major bodies of oral tradition, both from the Maasai and Parakuyu and from the peoples they encountered in the new regions, back up the linguistic evidence for these latter periods of expansion (Ehret 1971, 2001a; Jacobs 1968).

The Proto–Northern Maa, who remained behind in the Baringo Basin in the A.D. 1400s and 1500s, evolved in time into the people known as the Sampuru. A second Northern Maa dialect, Camus, was adopted by a fishing and farming people living on the shores of Lake Baringo (Vossen 1988). This community most likely arose not through migration but through the adoption of North Maa speech by a preexisting economically distinct and previously Kalenjin-speaking people.

To sum up, the linguistic evidence reveals a sequence of historical periods leading down from the Proto-Lotuko-Maa period of over 2,000 years ago to the Maa societies of recent centuries:

> The Pre-Proto-Ongamo-Maa era, from the late first millennium B.C. up to roughly A.D. 700
> The Proto-Ongamo-Maa period, which ended by around A.D. 1000–1100, when the ancestors of the Ongamo separated by moving southward to the Kilimanjaro area
> The Proto-Maa period, which closed at around A.D. 1500 with the movement of the ancestral Maasai southward out of the Baringo Basin
> The era of early Maasai expansions, A.D. 1500–1800, with the divergence of the Maasai into northern, central, and southern (Parakuyu) sets of communities

Figure 10.1 presents the stratigraphy of this history in the form of a family tree of language descent from Proto-Lotuko-Maa down to Maasai. At each period of this history Ongamo-Maa languages spread into new areas (Figure 10.2). Each period was marked also by sustained episodes of word borrowing from one or more non-Ongamo-Maa languages, as is also depicted on the stratigraphy.

Two major periods of contact and interaction with neighboring non-Ongamo-Maa speech communities appear in the loanword record of the Proto-Ongamo-Maa language, one with an Eastern Cushitic people and one with a Southern Nilotic society. The Eastern Cushitic loanwords in Proto-Ongamo-Maa came from a language whose closest relationships appear to have been to the Konsoromo subgroup of Eastern Cushitic, consisting today of two branches, Oromo and Konso. The Southern Nilotic loanwords came from an extinct language belonging to its own distinct subgroup of the Southern Nilotic group.

Linguistic and archaeological evidence from all periods over the past 2,800 years consistently places Southern Nilotic peoples only in western and central

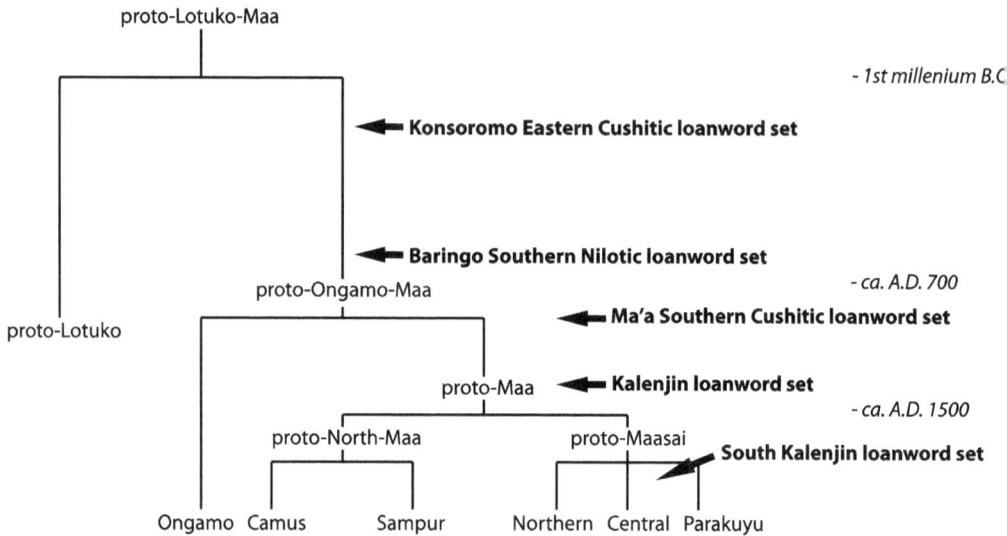

Figure 10.1. Lotuko-Maa linguistic stratigraphy.

Kenya and adjacent parts of Tanzania (Ambrose 1982; Ehret 1971, 1974, 1983; Robertshaw 1990; Robertshaw and Collett 1983). No evidence for any period since 1000 B.C. places this group of peoples farther north in Kenya than the Baringo Basin, although they did form a lasting presence in that region. In contrast, repeated extensions of Eastern Cushitic societies into northern Kenya have taken place over the past 3,000–4,000 years, but there is no evidence whatsoever that requires their presence any farther south in central and western Kenya than the Turkana Basin and Mount Kenya (Ehret 1971, 1983, 1998, 2008b; Heine et al. 1979). Given these complementary historical distributions of peoples, the likeliest conclusion is that the Eastern Cushitic contacts took place in the Turkana Basin and thus date to the Pre-Proto-Ongamo-Maa era, before the eighth century A.D. The subsequent movement of the Proto-Ongamo-Maa into Baringo, circa A.D. 700–1000, would then have brought them into encounter with longtime Southern Nilotic populations.

Archaeological evidence, though still scanty, specifically confirms the former presence of a Konsoromo-related Eastern Cushitic people in the Turkana Basin. The markers of their presence are archaeoastronomical burial sites west of Lake Turkana dating as early as 2300 B.C., the features of which replicate and reflect in specific ways the observances and beliefs still current among the Konso of far southern Ethiopia (Lynch and Robbins 1978). Ambrose (1982) has sought to link these sites to the Turkwel culture of the Turkana Basin, the better-established dates of which range in the first millennium A.D. But the

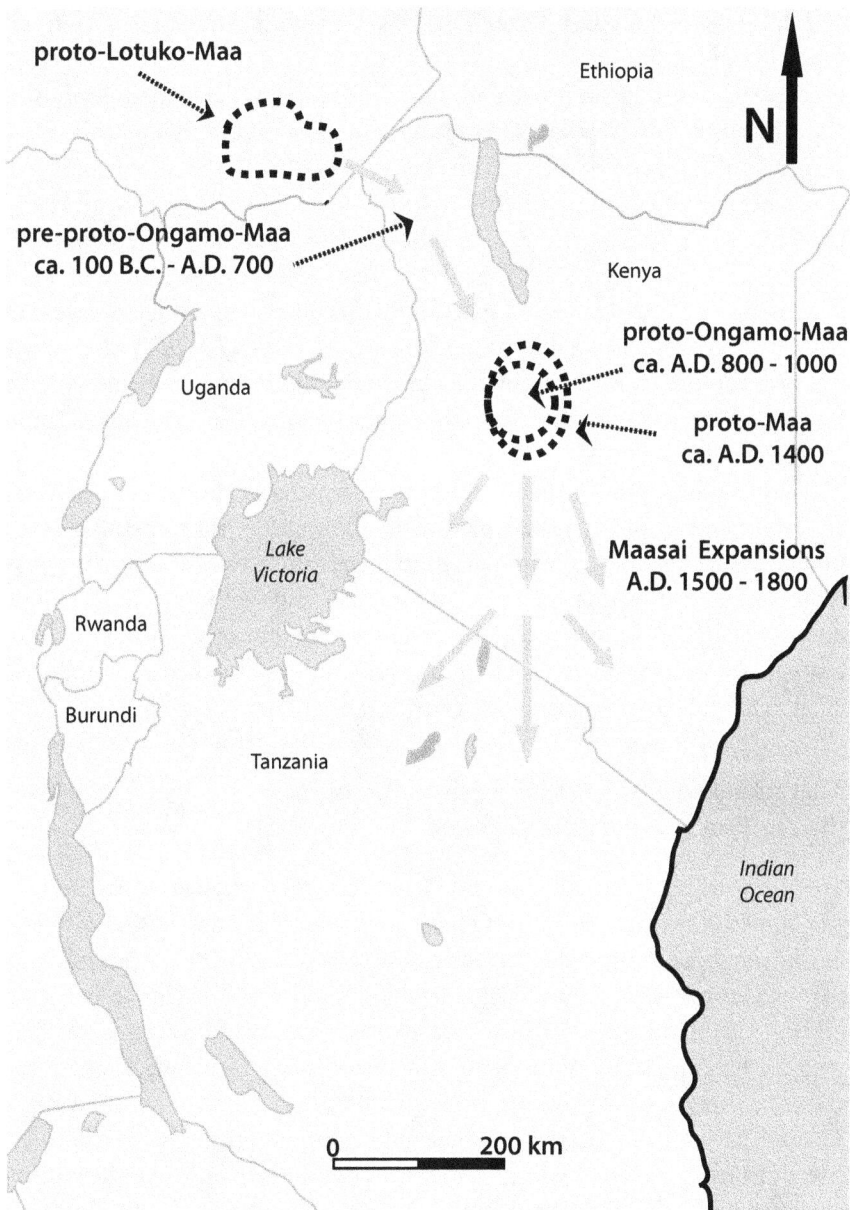

Figure 10.2. Map of Ongamo-Maa history.

more probable correlation of the Turkwel culture, considering its overall dating and distribution, would be with the Pre-Proto-Ongamo-Maa (as Lynch and Robbins 1979 argue, although they use the more general term "Nilotic" for this population).

In the succeeding Proto-Maa period, two additional extended periods of word borrowing took place. One source of loanwords in this period was a language of the Ma'a branch of Southern Cushitic.[1] The Southern Cushitic languages were brought into Kenya from the north in the late fourth and early third millennia B.C. by the first livestock-raising and cultivating peoples of East Africa (Ambrose 1982; Ehret 1998). The second major source of word borrowings in Proto-Maa was a specifically Kalenjin language of the Southern Nilotic group. The divergence of the Maasai out of Proto-Maa in around the fifteenth century and the southward advance of the Maasai language set off a last period of word borrowing into the Central Maasai dialects from Kalenjin after A.D. 1500.

The categorizations of the word-borrowing patterns at each period, along with the evidence of individual loanwords, allow us to posit something of the particular relations of language spread to migration in each case and propose the manners and features of cross-cultural exchange set in motion by these developments. This kind of argumentation makes it possible to offer predictions about what we can expect to find in archaeological record and proposals about what the differing effects on gene flow might have been.

Migration and Cross-Cultural Encounter in the Pre-Proto-Ongamo-Maa Period

The loanword set from the Lowland Eastern Cushitic language, provisionally attributed here to the Pre-Proto-Ongamo-Maa era of the first half and middle of the first millennium A.D., has the characteristics of the heavy general borrowing category (3B, Table 10.1). A heavy general set, as is true in this case (Table 10.2), characteristically includes the borrowing of some terms for large wild animals and some "peripheral" basic words, by which I mean words for common everyday noncultural meanings but ones that are not included in the Swadesh 100-word list of core vocabulary. In addition, a heavy general set consists of word borrowings across a wide variety of the semantic fields of culture and often can include some numerals. The Eastern Cushitic set in this instance does include a single "core" vocabulary item—that is, a word with a meaning from the Swadesh list, namely for "egg." Multiple borrowings of items on the 100-word list typify a stronger category of impact—intensive general borrowing (3A, Table 10.1)—but the borrowing of a single basic word is not enough by itself to count this as an intensive borrowing contact.

Table 10.2. Eastern Cushitic loanwords in the Pre-Proto-Ongamo-Maa period[a,b]

	Loanword	Eastern Cushitic Root
Core vocabulary	*-boliboli "egg"	PEC: *ɓolɓol- "egg"
Peripheral basic vocabulary	ɔl-balbal "lake"	PEC: *bal-, *balbal- "lake"
Large wild animals	ɔ-sarrai "oryx"	PEC: *sar- "species of large antelope"
	ɔl-kaldas "baboon"	PEC: *gelz- (Oromo **gald-eesa**) "baboon"
Small wild animals	ɔl-cuki "kind of mongoose"	PEC: *cuuk'- (Soomaali **shuuqshuuq**)
	ɛn-garrarrayyo "chameleon"	LEC: Oromo **garara** "chameleon"
Livestock	ɛm-balelo "lamb"	LEC: Oromo **balale** "lamb"
	*-tuala "iron cowbell"	LEC: Oromo **duwala** "iron cowbell"
	*-maal "dewlap"	PEC: *maʕal- "dewlap"
Material culture	ɛ-sɪpɪl "iron point, blade"	LEC: Oromo **sibila** "iron"
	ɛ-maro "large homestead"	PEC: *mar- "to reside" (Afar **maro** "homestead")
Numerals[c]	saal "nine"	PEC: *sagaal
	ip "hundred"	LEC: Konsoromo *d'ib-

Notes: a. Words lacking an asterisk have been recorded so far only in the Maa or only in the Ongamo branch of Ongamo-Maa.
b. PEC, Proto-Eastern Cushitic; LEC, Lowland Eastern Cushitic
c. Replaced in Ongamo by composite terms.

A typical historical context of heavy general borrowing is a period of language shift that takes place over a number of generations. The word-borrowings pass from the previously established language of the region into the language of an incoming society as local people gradually shift over to speaking the incoming language. Commonly this kind of borrowing goes along with a situation in which the established population initially formed the majority demographic component in the interaction.

No indications of a major social impact of the Eastern Cushites on the incoming Pre-Proto-Ongamo-Maa appear in the borrowing evidence. No borrowed terms for new social categories or for new rituals indicative of a significant social impact appear, at least in the presently available evidence. There is no indication as yet of the adoption of circumcision, a custom ancient among the Cushites, which became a general feature of later Ongamo-Maa cultures. If indeed, as seems the case, the Konsoromo peoples had created elaborate cycling age-grade and age-set systems by this time (Ehret 1974), these institutions surely were not taken over by the Pre-Proto-Ongamo-Maa. The Pre-Proto-Ongamo-Maa component in these actions, it can be argued, set the political and social institutional basis for absorbing Eastern Cushites into the evolving new society.

The evidence of material cultural change is not so one-sided, however. Both the Pre-Proto-Ongamo-Maa and the Eastern Cushitic participants in

Table 10.3. Baringo Southern Nilotic loanwords in Proto-Ongamo-Maa[a,b]

	Loanword	Southern Nilotic Root
Core vocabulary	-rɔra "to sleep"	PK: *rur
Peripheral basic vocabulary	*-can-ito "wild animal" (pl. stem plus POM sing. suff.)	PSNil: pl. *tyaaŋ (sing. *tyaaŋ)
Large wild animals	*-makau "hippopotamus"	PK: *makaw, also *makay
	*-njiro "rhinoceros; gray-brown color (of cow)"	PK: *njiʀ "rhinoceros"
	*-sirua "eland; eland-colored cow"	pre-PK: *siirwa "eland"
	*-inkat "wildebeest"	PSNil: *inkat
	*-motonyi "vulture"	PSNil: *motooŋ
Small wild animal	*-k-olupa "centipede"	PSNil: *ooluup-
	*-supeni "ewe lamb"	PK: *supeen
Other culture	*-sitima "wether" (C. Maasai "young ram")	PK: *setiim, also *tesiim "wether"
	*-meregec "ram" (recorded only for Maa branch)	pre-PK *merekic (PK: *meʀenkic)
	*-lɔŋo "long oval shield"	PSNil: *lɔɔŋ
	*-piron "firestick"	PSNil: *piʀoon
	*-papa "father"	PSNil: *paapaa
	*-morat- "to circumcise"	pre-PK: *moraat (PK *moraatan)
	*-murrani "young man" (age grade)	pre-PK: *muren
	*-tarakuai "juniper" (Juniperus procera)	PK: *taraɔkwa
Numerals[c]	-tikitam "twenty"	PSNil: *tiktem (PK *tiptem)
	-ɔsɔm "thirty"	PSNil: *sɔsɔm (Rottland 1982: incorrect *sasam)
	-artam "forty"	PSNil: *artam
	-ɔnɔm "fifty"	PSNil: *kɔnɔm (Rottland 1982: incorrect *kanam)

Notes: a. Words without asterisks are attested to in the available evidence only from the Maa branch of Ongamo-Maa.
b. PK, Proto-Kalenjin; PSNil, Proto-Southern Nilotic; POM, Proto-Ongamo-Maa
c. Replaced in Ongamo by composite terms

this history came into the encounter with at least some acquaintance with iron and iron implements (Ehret 2001b; see also Table 10.3). The economies of both societies appear to have been strongly pastoralist, focusing on cattle-raising. Nevertheless, at least a few words relating to iron goods and cattle passed from the Eastern Cushitic language into Pre-Proto-Ongamo-Maa. In at least one instance, the borrowed word (for "iron cowbell") reflects the probable adoption of a new implement from the Cushitic side. This implement, in particular, provides us with a potential marker to look for in the archaeology, once that work is undertaken on a more extensive scale in northwestern Kenya.

How might this encounter of an immigrant society with the existing population of the western Turkana Basin show up genetically? The earlier historical roots of the incoming Pre-Proto-Ongamo-Maa-speakers and the proposed already existing Eastern Cushites lay in two genetically distinctive regions. The long-term absorbing of the Eastern Cushites into the Pre-Proto-Ongamo-Maa society would have combined two populations, one Nilotic and Sudanic in origin and the other from the Horn of Africa. The kind of word borrowing involved here implies that overall the majority direction of gene flow may well have been from the Cushitic component. Both the Cushites and the Pre-Proto-Ongamo-Maa were already consistently patrilineal in descent and inheritance by this period of history (Ehret 2008b). If the Pre-Proto-Ongamo-Maa did form the axis around which the processes of assimilation revolved, an additional hypothesis presents itself—that there might have been a gender-differentiated gene flow that accompanied the migration and expansion of the Pre-Proto-Ongamo-Maa. A predominance of Y-chromosome ancestry in the new society may have come from the Ongamo-Maa side, and a similar predominance of the mtDNA ancestry may have come from the Cushitic side.

Migration and Encounter in the Proto-Ongamo-Maa Period

The expansion of the Proto-Ongamo-Maa speech community into the Baringo Basin brought about a second era of heavy general borrowing, this time from a Southern Nilotic language into Proto-Ongamo-Maa (Table 10.4). The sound changes and morphological differences in several cases indicate that this language did not belong to either of the existing Southern Nilotic branches, Kalenjin or Datoga, although its closest relations were probably to Kalenjin. As a heavy general borrowing set, the Southern Nilotic loanword set in Proto-Ongamo-Maa includes names of large animals as well as borrowings across a range of cultural fields. The implications are as before, that the Ongamo-Maa settlers initially formed an intrusive and probably minority element in the Baringo Basin and surrounding areas.

Table 10.4. Southern Cushitic (Maʼa) loanwords in the early Maa language[a]

	Loanword	Southern Cushitic Root
Core vocabulary	-sap-uk "big" (borrowed verb root plus Maʼa *-uk adj. suffix)	PSC *ɬaf- "to grow"
Peripheral basic vocabulary	ɔl-kɛjʊ "river; foot" (originally just "foot")	loan-translation of SC idiom, which uses the same word for "river" and "foot"
Large wild animals	ɔl-arro "buffalo"	present-day Maʼa **aro** "elephant"; earlier PSC: "large herbivore (generic)"
	e-maalo "greater kudu"	present-day Maʼa **malo**, from earlier Maʼa *maʔalo (from PSC: *maʔad-)
Small wild animals	e-suni "blue duiker"	Maʼa **soni**
	en-kumani "bush duiker"	SC: *guman- (not known in present-day Maʼa)
Residence	ɔl-manyata "young men's cattle camp, pen"	PSC: *maŋ- "enclosed area of ground" (plus SC *-at- noun suff.)
Ethnic name	*Maa "the Maa peoples"	Maʼa, self-name of the Maʼa Southern Cushites
Herding and farming	e-luaata "herd"	PSC: *ɬawa "enclosed homestead" (plus SC *-at- noun suff.)
	was "black cow with white flanks"	PSC: *wasi "colobus monkey" (which is black and white)
	en-kurma "cultivated field"	Maʼa **u-kurume** "cultivation" (from earlier *kuruma; PSC *kur- "to cultivate")
Kinship	ol-apu "mother's brother"	Maʼa **abu** (PSC: *ʔaab-)
	yeyo "mother"	PSC: *yaayo (Maʼa sound change: PSC *aay yields Maʼa *ey)

Notes: a. PSC, Proto-Southern Cushitic; SC, Southern Cushitic

Like the Eastern Cushites, the Southern Nilotes had at least some impact on Ongamo-Maa material culture, notably a military innovation: the adoption of a long, oval style of shield that was effective in protecting more of the body than older styles of shields. Unlike the Eastern Cushites, however, the Southern Nilotes appear to have had a more potent and direct social historical impact. From the Southern Nilotes the Proto-Ongamo-Maa adopted their verb for "circumcise" and their term for the young-man grade of life, the particular status that the rite of circumcision conferred upon a young man. Together these data strongly suggest that this was the period when circumcision became an established Ongamo-Maa custom and that it came to them not from Cushites but from this Baringo Southern Nilotic society.

On the other hand, once again the Ongamo-Maa component in the encounter appears to have been pivotal in the processes of social and ethnic re-identification that the Proto-Ongamo-Maa migrations into the Baringo Basin set in motion. Although they borrowed the two words connected to circumcision, the Ongamo-Maa do not appear to have taken up any other elements of the age-grade and cycling age-set systems of the Southern Nilotes. In these systems as they were practiced 1,000 to 1,500 years ago, the Southern Nilotes applied a recurring cycle of eight age-set names, initiating a new group of young men into the next named age set on the cycle at about 12- to 15-year intervals, taking more than 100 years to get back around to the first name on the cycle again (Ehret 1971). Instead, the emerging Proto-Ongamo-Maa society continued to organize social and political authority around a linear succession of age-sets (Proto-Ongamo-Maa *-aji). The mediating institution of the political and social incorporation of the Baringo Southern Nilotes into the Proto-Ongamo-Maa society would have remained the older linear style of age-set organization.

Migration and Encounter in the Proto-Maa Period

Following the divergence of Proto-Ongamo-Maa into separate Ongamo and Maa branches around 1,000 years ago, the speakers of Proto-Maa passed through two notable periods of word borrowing, one from a language of the Kalenjin branch of Southern Nilotic and the other from a Ma'a Southern Cushitic language.

The Ma'a loanword set in Proto-Maa fits the heavy general category, including both peripheral basic terms and terms for large wild animals as well as a range and variety of culture terms (Table 10.4). As a heavy general word set, these data suggest again a history in which the borrowing community, the Proto-Maa, initially formed an intrusive minority in the lands of the people from whose language the loanwords came. The borrowings include at least one cattle color term and, more intriguingly, two terms for primary kin, one of which, "mother's brother," is often a role of great importance in engaging the support of maternal relations in patrilineal societies. A single basic term (Swadesh list) meaning "big," appears among the Ma'a loanwords in Proto-Maa, but in this case the word originally borrowed would have been the peripheral basic verb for "to grow." Proto-Maa secondarily converted the borrowed verb into an adjective by adding a Maa adjective suffix to the verb.

Among the loanwords of the set, one item stands out. The immediately preceding paragraphs confront the reader with the confusing presence of two almost identical ethnic names, Ma'a and Maa, differing only in the presence of a glottal stop consonant (represented by an apostrophe) in the first name. In general, the presence of double *aa* in any word in an Ongamo-Maa language is a prima facie indicator that the word has been borrowed. Typically in the Ongamo-Maa languages, *aa* is the relic of the existence of a former glottal or pharyngeal consonant in the original word in the donor language. The Ongamo-Maa languages, lacking such consonants, simply deleted them in borrowing, leaving behind the vowels on each side of the lost consonants. Two clear examples are the Proto-Ongamo-Maa word for "dewlap" in Table 10.2 and the Proto-Maa term for "greater kudu" in Table 10.4, each of which is a loanword from a Cushitic language in which a pharyngeal consonant was present. The conclusion dictated by the linguistic considerations is that the ethnic self-name *Maa is itself a borrowing, specifically of the name the Ma'a Southern Cushites gave themselves, and that it belongs to the heavy general set of Ma'a loanwords in Proto-Maa. (The ethnonym Maasai is an additional borrowing of what was historically an alternative pronunciation of the same name: see endnote at the end of this chapter for more on this point.)

How did such a word borrowing come about? At the least, the maintenance of an ethnic name across a period of shift to an entirely different language implies major demographic and social continuity across the transition. One possible history is that an existing Southern Cushitic Ma'a community, under pressure from encroaching groups of Proto-Maa-speakers, allied with those groups against other neighboring peoples. By making alliance with the in-migrating Proto-Maa, the Ma'a could have domesticated the threat to social stability of the migrants. The linguistic consequence of these relations was the adoption of the intruders' language as a new common tongue of the allied groups. But the persistence of the ethnic name across the period of language shift suggests that the former Ma'a people remained the majority and the focal element in the social historical processes involved.

The Southern Nilotic impact on the Proto-Maa, in contrast, fits a different category, 3C, extensive general borrowing (Table 10.5). The borrowings characteristic of this category commonly include terms for small wild animals, peripheral basic words, and a wide range of cultural lexicon but differ from heavy general borrowing in that they do not include core vocabulary or names of large animals. Extensive general borrowing often involves the merging over a period of generations of people of an existing majority society into an inmigrating society. Alternatively, a borrowing set of this kind can be generated by an extended period of close interactions with an initially dominant and more prestigious neighboring people.

A combination of indicators suggests that both kinds of history may have been involved, in this instance sequentially. Several borrowed Kalenjin age-grade-connected terms reveal that the Proto-Maa took up the full Southern Nilotic age-grade system at this period, along with the military deployment of young men in warrior age-set bands (*e-sirit* and *ol-porror*) and the adoption of the associated warrior ethos (ɛn-kanyıt) (Table 10.4). These changes look very much like prestige acquisitions that were adopted from militarily more potent neighbors. Other loanwords within the set indicate Kalenjin influences on medicine, religion, and kinship, along with the Proto-Maa adoption of several new features of material culture. In the case of the new features of military culture, these would have had practical consequences for empowering the Proto-Maa against Kalenjin encroachment on their lands. The Proto-Maa maintenance of the older pattern of linear age-set successions—as their retention of the older Ongamo-Maa term *-aji* for this type of age set implies—shows that they grafted the military cultural acquisitions onto their existing political basis. Developments from A.D. 1500 onward suggest that, in the end, blending the new military capacities with the existing political foundation shifted the balance of power to the Proto-Maa. At the close of the Proto-Maa period, around the fifteenth century, these combined institutions were fully in place among their Maasai descendants as they began a new era of major expansions southward out of the Baringo Basin.

Which period of Proto-Maa interaction with their neighbors came first? The available linguistic evidence does not overtly resolve this issue. The different natures of the migrations and encounters revealed by the two bodies of language evidence do, however, suggest a probable relative chronology. The degree of accommodation and demographic and social continuity implied in the evidence for the shift of the Maʾa Southern Cushites to the Proto-Maa language make it unlikely that the Proto-Maa who were involved in these interchanges yet had the sharp power advantage that the military innovations

Table 10.5. Kalenjin loanwords in the early Maa language[a]

	Loanword	Kalenjin Root
Peripheral basic vocabulary	-misimis "to be dark"	PK *miis "to make dark"
	ol-terit "dust"	PK *terit
Small wild animals	o-suyyani "wild dog"	PK *suiyɑɑn
	ɔl-kɔrɔi "colobus monkey"	PK *kɔrɔɔi
Environment	ɔŋata, aŋata "plains"	PK *ɔŋata
Livestock	aros "cow with black-and-white-spotted underbody"	PK *ɑɑruus "dappled, mostly blue-gray cow"
	keri "cow with black stomach and white back"	PK *keri "black-and-white striped"
	ɛsonya "fat cut of meat"	PK *suun- plus PK noun suffix –ia
Other material culture	ɔl-murɔnya "razor"	PK *morɔŋa
	o-sosian "stick for cleaning out calabashes"	PK *soosiɑɑn
	ɛ-mɔɔtian "quiver"	PK *mɔɔt- plus SNil noun suffix *-yaan
	ɛ-sampʊr "pouch"	PK *sɑɑmpʊr "kind of hide sack"
	ɔl-kɛsɛn "baby sling"	PK *kɛsɛn "to carry (child) on the back"
	ɛn-anka "cloth"	PK *aanka
Society and beliefs	ɛn-kanyit "honor, duty, obligation, warrior ethos"	PK *kɑɑɲit
	ɔl-payyan "elder" (age grade)	PK *pɑɑyɑɑn
	ol-poror "age set"	PK *poror
	e-sirit "age-set band"	PK *sirit
	ɛn-tɔmɔnɔni "pregnant woman" (pl. ɪn-tɔmɔnɔk)	PK *tɔmɔnɔ ~ *tomono
	-sai "to pray"	EMK *sɑɑi ~ *saai (PK *sɑɑʀ ~ *saaʀ)
	-sakut "to work magic on"	PK *saakut "medicine; to work magic on"
	ɛ-sɛtan "magic"	PK *seetan "amulet"
	ɔl-akui "grandfather"	PK *akuy
	koko "grandmother"	PK *kooko

Note a. SNil, Southern Nilotic; PK, Proto-Kalenjin: EMK, Elgon-Mau Kalenjin would have given them. The melding of Kalenjin military practices and ethos into Proto-Maa political culture are thus likely to have come about subsequent to or overlapping with the merger of Ma'a Southern Cushites and the Proto-Maa, perhaps not fully taking hold until shortly before the end of the Proto-Maa period around 1500, when those advantages helped propel the southward migration of their Maasai descendants out of the Baringo Basin.

The advance of the early Maasai southward through central southern Kenya into central northern Tanzania between A.D. 1500 and 1700 set in motion another period of encounter of the Central Maasai with the South Kalenjin peoples already inhabiting those areas (Ehret 1971). The types of words borrowed into Central Maasai conform to the pattern of a heavy general interaction, but one of foreshortened duration. It includes peripheral basic terms and terms for large wild animals and a range of cultural words, but the set is small (Table 10.6). The incorporation of the preexisting South Kalenjin people into the advancing Maasai society must have proceeded rapidly, with the processes taking possibly as few as three or four generations to complete. In at least one instance, an existing Kalenjin alliance group apparently shifted over as a whole from Kalenjin to Maasai ethnic self-identification, as shown by their preservation down to the present of a Kalenjin name for themselves. An interesting feature of the new borrowing set, distinguishing it from all previous Ongamo-Maa and Maa word borrowing from Southern Nilotes, is the consistent adoption of nouns in a particular Kalenjin grammatical form, the so-called secondary form.

Time and Attrition in Word Borrowing Categories

An evident feature, if one compares cases, is that the sizes of loanword sets can differ even for the same category of borrowing. The historically more recent sets tend to be larger even for the same category of borrowing. This is an artifact of elapsed historical time and the effects of subsequent episodes of word borrowing. Because languages are always changing, the passage of time leads to attrition of earlier lexemes and development of new words in place of old, even if no new expansions took place. New episodes of word borrowing often lead also to replacement of older borrowed words by new borrowings. Through both of these processes, words adopted in a previous period may drop from use entirely, shrinking the overall size of the discoverable loanword set, or they may drop out in one branch but still be preserved in the other. (As one might expect, the earliest loanword sets, Tables 10.1 and 10.2, show the most effects of this kind.) A foreshortened period of borrowing can also

Table 10.6. South Kalenjin loanwords in Central Maasai dialects[a]

	Loanword	Kalenjin Root
Peripheral basic vocabulary	en-taritiki "small bird (generic)"	PK: *tariitik "birds" (plural secondary form)
Large wild animal	ɛn-tarakuet "impala" (regular Maasai epenthetic k)	PSNil and PK: *taruweet (singular secondary form)
Culture lexemes	ɔl-mɔɔkɪ "young ox"	South Kalenjin: *mɔɔk "calves" (EMK *mooik, PK *moorik (plural secondary form)
	il-meeki "cultivating people"	PK: *mee- "person without cattle" (plural secondary form)
	Il-Kaputiei "name of Maasai alliance group"	South Kalenjin and EMK: *kaputyey "people/place of the warthog" (PK *kaputyer)
	en-tereet "cooking pot"	PK: *tereet (singular secondary form)
	ol-kirisiet "smith's hammer"	South Kalenjin *kirisieet (PK: kirisueet) (singular secondary form)
	en-tiaponkit "slag"	Nandi **tɑponkiɑt** (singular secondary form) (this meaning has not been collected for other Kalenjin dialects)

Note: a. PK, Proto-Kalenjin; EMK, Elgon-Maa Kalenjin; PSNil, Proto-Southern Nilotic truncate the quantity of word borrowings, as in the example of the late-period migration of the Central Maasai into formerly South Kalenjin lands.

These considerations call attention to a crucial criterion. The key to identifying different categories of borrowing and therefore the migrational, demographic, and cultural histories they represent is not the sheer number of borrowings discoverable but their semantic distributions through the lexicon. Loanword sets from early periods will be smaller in overall numbers of identifiable loans because of attrition and replacement over time, but enough of their original semantic distributions and characteristics often survive to enable identification of the borrowing category to which they belonged.

Assessing the Demic Components of Migration

The histories of the spread of the Ongamo-Maa languages illustrate a variety of resources that go beyond the usual kinds of linguistic evidence. In particular, by uncovering the patterns and the individual components of word borrowing one can illumine the demic composition of migration events and enrich the evidence for seeking the archaeological correlates of language spread.

The first expansion considered, that of the Pre-Proto-Ongamo-Maa into the Turkana Basin, can be argued from the evidence of word borrowing to have brought together in one society an intrusive demographic component of early Nilotic ancestry from the southern Sudan with an existing and probably majority element of Eastern Cushitic, and thus Horn of Africa, genetic background. The subsequent expansion around the eighth century of the Proto-Ongamo-Maa south into the Baringo Basin brought an additional significant and probably majority element of Southern Nilotes into this genetic mix. The Southern Nilotic populations of that period, as their linguistic evidence separately shows (Ehret 1971, 1974), would already have incorporated a major genetic component of Southern Cushitic background into their own earlier Nilotic ancestry from the southern Sudan. The linguistic evidence predicts that if burial sites of this age are identified eventually and ancient DNA studies prove possible, these populations should show a significant component of Nilotic ancestry, a Southern Cushitic component, and a more-attenuated element of Eastern Cushitic ancestry.

For the interpretation of the genetic history of more recent Maa populations, however, such findings, though of value in their own right, would be of small consequence. The word-borrowing evidence of Proto-Maa, as interpreted here, suggests a discontinuity in the record after around A.D. 1000. It proposes that the Proto-Maa were a primarily Ma'a Southern Cushitic population who adopted the language of a minority Ongamo-Maa component of mixed Eastern Cushitic and Nilotic ancestry.

The two succeeding eras of population expansions—of the Proto-Maa more widely in the Baringo Basin and then of their Maasai offshoot southward through central southern Kenya and central northern Tanzania—each incorporated large demic components of Southern Nilotic background. The word-borrowing evidence generated by these migration histories leads to the expectation that the chief genetic components of the modern-day Maasai should include two different major Southern Cushitic elements, one derived from the Kalenjin side and the other from the Maa side of the encounter; Sudan Nilotic elements, especially mediated through the Kalenjin demic component; and possibly some genetic signatures left over from the very early incorporations of Eastern Cushites. The extant modern Ma'a populations, as the likely nearest relatives of the proposed major founding Proto-Maa demic component, stand out as particularly in need of fuller genetic research.

To return to the issues raised at the beginning, linguistics offers a very wide range of tools and techniques to uncover and probe histories of migration, not to speak of human social history more generally. For the most part, scholars have engaged only a few of the possible approaches. A key aim of this chapter is to bring attention to the much wider prospects still to be engaged by this kind of work in all parts of the world. The long-term patterns of word borrowing over periods of multiple generations are a neglected body of evidence that can be especially productive in discovering and assessing the demic processes and the social and material cultural developments of particular eras of migration and in offering testable predictions about the expected correlative archaeological and human genetic outcomes. The case studies presented here bring into view something of the range of arguments that one can make and conclusions one can draw from this kind of testimony.

Notes

1. The double *aa* of the ethnonym Maasai shows that this term, like Maa, is of loanword origin. It is surely simply an alternate form of the name Ma'a. The *s* had to have already existed in the original borrowed shape, because its presence cannot be explained by Maasai grammatical processes. The known phonological history of the Ma'a Southern Cushitic language, however, does provide a ready explanation for it. In the early Ma'a language, words could end in either a consonant or a vowel. At some point in the history of Ma'a a sound-change rule came into effect, changing all *a* at the end of words to *e*. Later in time, a second sound change came into being that deleted all consonants at the ends of words (Ehret 1980). Wherever the vowel preceding the lost final consonant was an *a*, that *a* became the final sound in the word. The presence of

a rather than **e* at the end of the name Ma'a therefore tells us that there once used to be an additional consonant after that *a*. The doublet Maa and Maasai reveals that the lost consonant was **s* and that the name **Ma'a* came from a still earlier shape, **Ma'as*, in the period before the operation of the rule that deleted final consonants. The Ma'a language as spoken in the early twentieth century had quite a number of noun doublets just like this, with alternative pronunciations generated by the fact that one form of the word originally had a final vowel and the other did not.

References

Ambrose, S.
1982   Archaeology and Linguistic Reconstructions of History in East Africa. In *The Archaeological and Linguistic Reconstruction of African History*, edited by C. Ehret and M. Posnansky, pp. 138–146. University of California Press, Berkeley, Los Angeles.

Ehret, C.
1971   *Southern Nilotic History: Linguistic Approaches to the Study of the Past*. Northwestern University Press, Evanston, Ill.
1974   *Ethiopians and East Africans: The Problem of Contacts*. East African Publishing House, Nairobi.
1980   *The Historical Reconstruction of Southern Cushitic Phonology and Vocabulary*. Reimer, Berlin.
1983   Population Movement and Culture Contact in the Southern Sudan, c. 3000 B.C. to A.D. 1000. In *Culture History in the Southern Sudan*, edited by J. Mack and P. Robertshaw, pp. 19–48. Memoire 8. British Institute in Eastern Africa, Nairobi.
1991   Revising the Consonant Inventory of Proto-Eastern Cushitic. *Studies in African Linguistics* 22(3):211–275.
1998   *An African Classical Age: Eastern and Southern Africa in World History, 1000 B.C. to A.D. 400*. University Press of Virginia, Charlottesville.
2001a   The Eastern Kenya Interior, 1500–1800. In *African Historians and African Voices*, edited by E. S. Atieno Odhiambo, pp. 33–46. P. Schlettwein Publishing, Basel.
2001b   The Establishment of Iron-Working in Eastern, Central, and Southern Africa: Linguistic Inferences on Technological History. *Sprache und Geschichte in Afrika* 16/17:125–175.
2001c   *A Historical-Comparative Reconstruction of Nilo-Saharan*. Rüdiger Köppe Verlag, Cologne.
2008a   Reconstructing Ancient Kinship in Africa. In *Early Human Kinship: From Sex to Social Reproduction*, edited by N. J. Allen, H. Callan, R. Dunbar, and W. James, pp. 200–231. Blackwell, Oxford.
2008b   Yaakuan and Eastern Cushitic: A Historical Linguistic Overview. In *Semito-Hamitic Festschrift for A. B. Dolgopolsky and H. Jungraithmayr*, edited by G. Takacs, pp. 128–141. Dietrich Reimer, Berlin.

2011   *History and the Testimony of Language.* University of California Press, Berkeley, Los Angeles.

Ehret, C., T. Coffman, L. Fliegelman, A. Gold, M. Hubbard, D. Johnson, and D. Saxon.

1974   Some Thoughts on the Early History of the Nile-Congo Watershed. *Ufahamu* 3(1):9–27.

Heine, B., F. Rottland, and R. Vossen

1979   Proto-Baz: Some Aspects of Early Nilotic-Cushitic Contacts. *Sprache und Geschichte in Afrika* 1:75–91.

Jacobs, A.

1968   A Chronology of the Pastoral Maasai. *Hadith* 1:10–31.

Lynch, B. M., and R. H. Robbins

1978   Namoratunga: The First Archaeoastronomic Evidence in Sub-Saharan Africa. *Science* 200:766–768.

1979   Cushitic and Nilotic Prehistory: New Archaeological Evidence from North-West Kenya. *Journal of African History* 20:319–328.

Robertshaw, P.

1990   *Early Pastoralists of South-western Kenya.* British Institute in Eastern Africa, Nairobi.

Robertshaw, P., and D. Collett

1983   A New Framework for the Study of Early Pastoral Communities in East Africa. *Journal of African History* 24:289–301.

Rottland, F.

1982   *Die südnilotischen Sprachen: Beschreibung, Vergleichung und Rekonstruktion.* D. Reimer, Berlin.

Sasses, H.-J.

1979   The Consonant Phonemes of Proto-East-Cushitic: A First Approximation. *Afroasiatic Linguistics* 7(1):1–67.

Spaulding, J.

1990   The Old Shaiqi Language in Historical Perspective. *History in Africa* 17:283–292.

Vossen, R.

1982   *The Eastern Nilotes: Linguistic and Historical Reconstructions.* D. Reimer, Berlin.

1988   *Towards a Comparative Study of the Maa dialects of Kenya and Tanzania.* Buske, Hamburg.

V

Bioanthropological Approaches

11

Identifying Archaeological Human Migration Using Biogeochemistry

Case Studies from the South-Central Andes

KELLY J. KNUDSON

Innovative new theoretical and methodological developments are dramatically changing the ways anthropologists identify and understand migration. By using biogeochemical techniques from the physical sciences, archaeologists and bioarchaeologists can now identify migration in the migratory individuals *themselves* rather than relying on proxies. More specifically, analyzing the biogeochemical composition of tooth enamel and bone that formed at different times throughout an individual's life can provide information about that individual's place of residence during the formation of enamel or bone. By combining these strontium isotope data with other lines of evidence, we can now reconstruct the complexities of human migration in the past. First I discuss the role of biogeochemistry in elucidating archaeological migration, including a definition of migration and the variables discussed here. This is followed by an introduction to strontium isotope analysis that includes discussion of the advantages and disadvantages of this approach. I then present a case study of archaeological migration in the Tiwanaku polity of the South-Central Andes to illustrate how these techniques can contribute to migration studies.

Understanding Migration through Biogeochemistry

Biogeochemistry by itself can identify only the change in an individual's long-term place of residence, which I refer to here as residential relocation. To identify migration, which I define here as the one-way change in residence from one site or region to another site or region perceived as different, other lines of evidence must be used to appropriately contextualize the movement and identify different "environments" as defined by the people moving. Here, it is also important to note that biogeochemistry can identify movement between different "environments" only if they are geologically distinct but that different geologic zones may or may not have been perceived as "different environments" by past inhabitants.

Biogeochemical techniques to identify archaeological migration rely on the comparison of the biogeochemical values in dental and skeletal elements that formed at different times over an individual's lifetime. If these values change when comparing the various dental and skeletal elements, then one can infer that an individual moved from one geologic or environmental zone during her or his lifetime. Therefore, anthropologists can now identify migration in the individuals who moved, which provides a robust, independent line of evidence to identify and understand migration in the archaeological record.

Researchers in fields as diverse as archaeology, biology, geology, and paleontology utilize the fact that different geologic environments have different radiogenic strontium isotope ratios to answer a wide variety of questions (Hoppe 2004; Kennedy et al. 1997; van der Merwe et al. 1990). In archaeology, most strontium isotope analyses address human migration (see overview in Bentley 2006). Strontium substitutes for calcium in hydroxyapatite, the mineral component of enamel and bone, during development (Carr et al. 1962; Dolphin and Eve 1963). The ratio of the radiogenic isotope of strontium, ^{87}Sr, and one stable isotope of strontium, ^{86}Sr, found in an individual's bone and teeth directly reflect ^{87}Sr/^{86}Sr found in the plants, animals, and water that she or he consumed, which reflect the isotope ratios found in the soil and bedrock of that geologic region (see overview in Bentley 2006). While tooth enamel does not remodel or incorporate new elements after it has formed, bone continually regenerates. Thus, differences in strontium isotope ratios in human tooth enamel and bone can be used to identify migration and the geologic origins of immigrants (Ericson 1985, 1989; Ezzo et al. 1997; Krueger 1985; Price et al. 1994).

Advantages and Disadvantages of Strontium Isotope Analysis

A key advantage of strontium isotope analysis is the identification of migration from the physical remains of the individuals that moved. This avoids the associative inferences between material culture, language, and people that are necessary to migration arguments in archaeology and linguistic anthropology. In addition to focusing on the movement of people rather than artifacts, which may be transported by other mechanisms than migration (i.e., exchange, emulation), biogeochemistry allows the examination of migration at the scale of the individual. Rather than examining past migration over the course of decades or centuries, as in many archaeological studies, biogeochemistry allows a very intimate and fine-grained investigation of single migrants over the course of a few years or months. This emphasizes migrants as agents rather than migrants as groups associated with the large-scale processes that are the composite of many individual actions. This is particularly important when scholars are interested in examining the scale of migration as well as its structure, as individual migrants can be identified.

However, biogeochemical techniques are useful only for identifying first-generation migrants. Although descendent populations may derive their identity from ancestral immigrant groups, these individuals will appear local to the region from a biogeochemical perspective. In these cases, other lines of evidence must be used to examine migration and population relationships over a longer biological timescale. Also, biogeochemical techniques can identify movement only between geologically distinct zones; as discussed in Chapter 1 (Cabana and Clark, this volume), this may or may not be considered migration by the migrants themselves. Analyzed bone or tooth enamel must not be changed by postdepositional, or diagenetic, contamination, that must be identified and monitored. Although bone is susceptible to diagenetic contamination from the burial environment, tooth enamel is more resistant (Budd et al. 2000; Hedges 2002; Kohn et al. 1999; Lee-Thorp 2002; Montgomery et al. 1999; Nelson et al. 1986; Price et al. 1992; Shellis and Dibdin 2000; Sillen 1989). Finally, the consumption of large amounts of strontium from nonlocal food or water sources could cause local individuals to exhibit nonlocal biogeochemical signatures. Radiogenic strontium isotope analysis cannot be used to determine paleodiet and cannot distinguish between an individual who moved from another geologic zone and an individual who ate large quantities of strontium from high-strontium imported foods. However, other lines of evidence can clarify the consumption of imported foods, including faunal and botanical analyses and paleodietary studies based on light stable isotopes such as carbon and nitrogen.

Archaeological Migration in the South-Central Andes: A Case Study of the Tiwanaku Polity

A key question in Andean archaeology involves the development of expansive states or empires, particularly before the well-known Inka empire (ca. A.D. 1400–1532). Much of this debate has focused on the Tiwanaku polity of the Middle Horizon (ca. A.D. 500–1000). In the South-Central Andes, Tiwanaku-style artifacts are found throughout what are now the Moquegua and Ilo valleys of southern Peru, the Azapa Valley and San Pedro de Atacama oasis of northern Chile, and the Lake Titicaca Basin and the Cochabamba valleys

Figure 11.1. Map of the South Central Andes with Tiwanaku-affiliated sites and regions discussed in the text. When available, mean radiogenic strontium isotope ratios of modern small-mammal enamel and bone provide proxies for the bioavailable strontium isotope signatures in each region.

of Bolivia (Figure 11.1) (e.g., Goldstein 1992, 1996; Kolata 1993a; Torres and Conklin 1995). Based on genetic analyses, residential architecture, and domestic and mortuary artifact assemblages, scholars have argued that sites such as Chen Chen in the Moquegua Valley of southern Peru and Coyo Oriental, Coyo-3, and Solcor-3 in the San Pedro de Atacama oasis of northern Chile are Tiwanaku colonies. At Chen Chen, for example, biodistance analysis of cranial nonmetric traits and ancient DNA analysis of archaeological human material have demonstrated close genetic relationships between the site's inhabitants and Tiwanaku (Blom 2005a; Blom et al. 1998; Lewis and Stone 2005). Similarly, the mortuary ceramics, wooden artifacts, and textiles from Chen Chen are in Tiwanaku styles (Goldstein 1992, 2005; Kolata 1993a). In San Pedro de Atacama, the presence of Tiwanaku-style mortuary textiles led Oakland Rodman to argue that "there were most likely many people physically present whose original home was the Bolivian altiplano . . . [and that] foreign Tiwanaku groups coexisted with local populations and were buried in spatially integrated, though partially segregated bounded cemeteries" (1992:336). Alternatively or additionally, the Tiwanaku-affiliated sites may have housed local populations who adopted Tiwanaku-style material culture as they articulated with this large and powerful polity (e.g., Torres-Rouff 2008).

To test the hypothesis that Tiwanaku-affiliated sites were in fact Tiwanaku colonies that were populated by immigrants from the Lake Titicaca Basin where Tiwanaku itself is located, strontium isotope analysis was performed on archaeological human remains from Middle Horizon sites in the South-Central Andes (Figures 11.1, 11.2). Here, I present new data that complements previously published work on the Tiwanaku polity in the South-Central Andes (Knudson 2008; Knudson and Price 2007; Knudson et al. 2004). Briefly, strontium isotope analysis was performed on an approximately 10 percent random sample of adults from the following Tiwanaku-affiliated sites: Chen

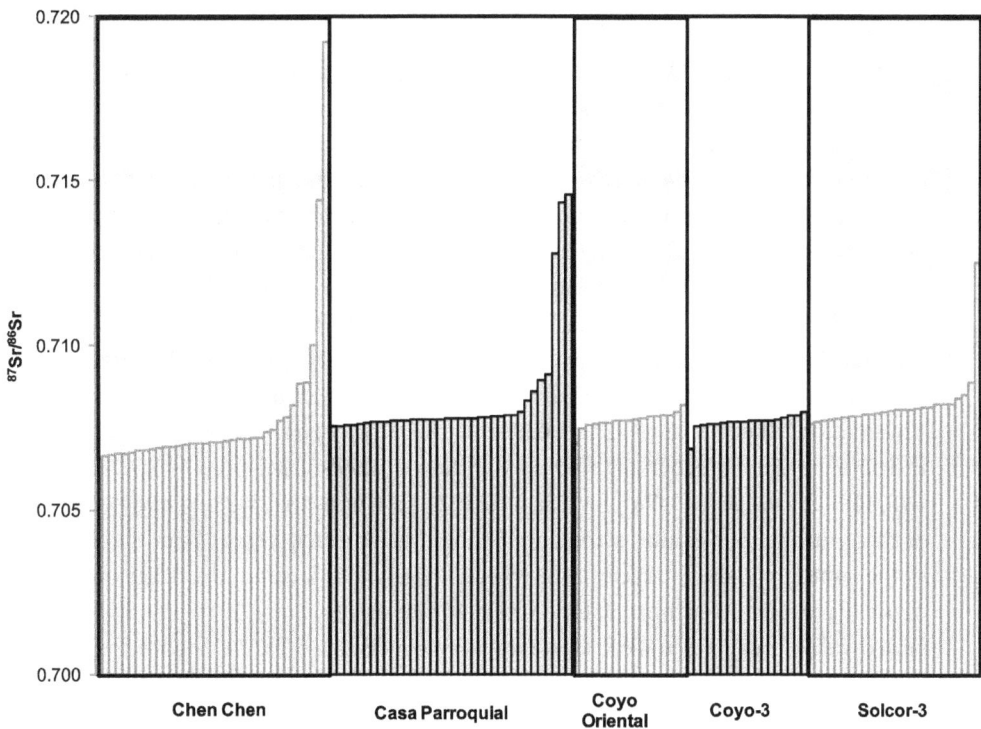

Figure 11.2. Strontium isotope data for archaeological human tooth enamel and bone from Tiwanaku-affiliated sites in the South Central Andes.

Chen in the Moquegua Valley of southern Peru and Casa Parroquial, Coyo Oriental, Coyo-3, and Solcor-3 of the San Pedro de Atacama oasis of northern Chile (Figures 11.1, 11.2). The site of Tiwanaku itself is not included in this dataset because much of its mortuary population consists of dedicatory offerings and victims of sacrifice and as such may not provide an accurate picture of the site's inhabitants. Archaeological context, strontium sources in the diet, regional geology, sampling strategy, and laboratory methods are discussed in detail elsewhere (Knudson 2008; Knudson and Price 2007; Knudson et al. 2004).

Defining Local and Nonlocal Strontium Isotope Values

One of the most important issues in the use of biogeochemical techniques to understand archaeological residential relocation is the definition of local and nonlocal isotopic signatures. Many strontium isotope studies use faunal samples as proxies of the bioavailable strontium in a given geologic zone or zones. While regional geologic data and strontium isotope ratios from bedrock and soil samples can give valuable isotopic information, faunal proxies provide a better indicator of the bioavailable strontium in a given region (Bentley 2006; Evans and Tatham 2004; Price et al. 2002). Ideally, faunal samples can be collected in situations in which the animals are fed high-strontium foods from the same field systems as the studied human population, thereby closely approximating the radiogenic strontium isotope ratios in the human diets. One commonly used definition of a local signature is the mean of the modern and/ or archaeological faunal samples at two standard deviations (Price et al. 2002).

    Using this definition, the local ranges used in this study are $^{87}Sr/^{86}Sr =$ 0.7059–0.7066 in the Moquegua Valley, $^{87}Sr/^{86}Sr = 0.7091$–0.7102 in the Tiwanaku Valley, and $^{87}Sr/^{86}Sr = 0.7074$–0.7079 in the San Pedro de Atacama oasis. According to these definitions, there are four clear outliers at the Tiwanaku-affiliated site of Chen Chen in the Moquegua Valley (M1-3840 [$^{87}Sr/^{86}Sr = 0.708843$], M1-S/NB092 [$^{87}Sr/^{86}Sr = 0.709995$], M1-0036 [$^{87}Sr/^{86}Sr = 0.714404$], and M1-2947 [$^{87}Sr/^{86}Sr = 0.719211$]) (Knudson 2008). While two of these individuals exhibit strontium isotope ratios much higher than those in the southern Lake Titicaca Basin where Tiwanaku is located, the other individuals exhibit strontium isotope ratios within or very close to the modern faunal values near Tiwanaku. These data are consistent with the theory that there was a small number of first-generation Tiwanaku immigrants at Chen Chen. However, based on the strontium isotope data, the mortuary population at Chen Chen also contains large numbers of individuals who were likely born in the Moquegua Valley and, based on material culture, were affiliated with the Tiwanaku polity and likely descended from earlier migrants. Interestingly, material culture, cranial modification, tomb type, and tomb location all fail to distinguish these migrants from others buried at Chen Chen (Knudson 2008; Knudson and Blom 2009). These individuals were likely not local individuals affiliated with the Huaracane archaeological culture, given the absence of non-Tiwanaku material culture at Chen Chen.

In the San Pedro de Atacama region, no individuals with strontium isotope signatures within the Lake Titicaca Basin values were buried in the cemeteries of Coyo Oriental, Solcor-3, or Coyo-3 (Knudson 2007, 2008; Knudson and Price 2007). Although there is a mix of Tiwanaku-style and Atacameño-style material culture in these cemeteries, no first-generation migrants from the Lake Titicaca Basin were present. When combined with material culture and data about cranial modification style, these data suggest an example of identity redefinition by local Atacameños who adopted Tiwanaku material culture rather than a case of archaeological migration (Knudson and Blom 2009). In addition, new data show that one individual buried in the cemetery of Casa Parroquial exhibits a strontium isotope signature that may be from the Lake Titicaca Basin. Because Casa Parroquial graves contain exquisite Tiwanaku-style gold artifacts, this may be a case where small numbers of higher-status individuals migrated from the Lake Titicaca Basin and coexisted with a much larger Atacameño population that was converted to Tiwanku ideology. The preponderance of Atacameño-style material culture, Atacameño cranial modification styles, and mortuary treatment support the hypothesis that the majority of individuals buried in the San Pedro de Atacama cemeteries were local Atacameños (Torres-Rouff 2002, 2008).

Using modern faunal values to determine the local ranges of the study regions and then interpreting the data based on those regions has certain advantages. It is important that faunal values provide an independent measure of bioavailable strontium isotope ratios in the study regions. In addition, when using modern domesticated fauna, the strontium sources in the diets of the animals can be determined accurately rather than estimated, as they currently are for archaeological faunal samples.

However, using modern and archaeological faunal data to define the local range in each region also has disadvantages. For example, at the Moquegua Valley site of Chen Chen, four individuals have strontium isotope ratios much higher than the local range as defined by modern fauna. However, none of the 25 individuals analyzed from Chen Chen exhibit strontium isotope ratios that are within the local range as defined by modern fauna (Knudson 2008). It is unlikely that all of these individuals are immigrants to the site and simplistic to define these individuals as such. While the modern faunal values are a very useful guide (Bentley 2006; Evans and Tatham 2004; Price et al. 2002), they cannot be used to identify migrants based on minute differences in $^{87}Sr/^{86}Sr$ values. It is more likely that the local fauna represent the bioavailable strontium in modern diets, which is similar but not identical to the bioavailable strontium in the archaeological human diets.

Similarly, as at Chen Chen, some individuals exhibit strontium isotope ratios that are just outside of the San Pedro de Atacama local range as defined by modern fauna. This is particularly apparent at the cemetery of Solcor-3, where 14 out of 26 samples have strontium isotope ratios that are higher or lower than the range of $^{87}Sr/^{86}Sr = 0.7074–0.7079$ as defined by modern fauna. However, only one sample is substantially higher and likely represents an individual who lived in a different geologic zone during enamel formation in the first years of life (F1681, SC3-0050, $^{87}Sr/^{86}Sr = 0.712522$) (Torres-Rouff and Knudson 2007). Rather than a large cemetery of immigrants, it is more likely that the mortuary population at Solcor-3 represents a population who consumed strontium from a different part of the oasis and that the bioavailable strontium sources in the diet of the modern and archaeological fauna used to determine a local range were more similar to the strontium sources consumed at Coyo Oriental and Coyo-3.

Given the advantages and disadvantages of using faunal samples as proxies for the bioavailable strontium in a study region, a number of scholars are exploring additional, complementary ways to determine which individuals in a given dataset should be considered local to a given region. In some cases, an archaeological human population of known geographic origin can be used to define local for a given region (e.g., Bentley et al. 2007; Knudson and Tung 2007; Tung and Knudson 2008). However, this technique is not appropriate for this dataset, given the lack of a local human population of known origin.

In some populations it is appropriate to assume that archaeological human bone values represent the local strontium isotope signature, since bone values reflect the bioavailable strontium consumed during the last years of life, presumably in the areas where individuals resettled after migration and were ultimately buried. At Chen Chen, mean human bone $^{87}Sr/^{86}Sr = 0.707195 ±$ 0.000651 (1σ, n = 10) (Knudson 2008; Knudson and Price 2007), so a local range defined as the mean human bone value plus or minus two standard deviations would be $^{87}Sr/^{86}Sr = 0.7059–0.7085$. Using this range, only four of the enamel samples would be classified as nonlocal (M1-3840 [$^{87}Sr/^{86}Sr = 0.708843$], M1-S/NB092 [$^{87}Sr/^{86}Sr = 0.709995$], M1-0036 [$^{87}Sr/^{86}Sr = 0.714404$], and M1-2947 [$^{87}Sr/^{86}Sr = 0.719211$]); these are the same outliers discussed previously. In San Pedro de Atacama, mean human bone $^{87}Sr/^{86}Sr = 0.70818 ± 0.00034$ (1σ, n = 9), so a local range defined as the mean human bone value plus or

Table 11.1. Descriptive statistics for strontium isotope data for archaeological human tooth enamel and bone from Tiwanaku-affiliated sites

	Complete Dataset	Trimmed Dataset
Moquegua Valley		
Mean	0.707790	0.707103
Standard Error	0.000412	0.000086
Median	0.707031	0.707004
Standard Deviation	0.002436	0.000480
Sample Variance	5.9E-06	2.3E-07
Kurtosis	15.64	5.38
Skewness	3.83	2.11
Minimum	0.706562	0.706562
Maximum	0.719211	0.708850
Count	35	31
San Pedro de Atacama		
Mean	0.708065	0.707815
Standard Error	0.707815	0.000031
Median	0.707754	0.707749
Standard Deviation	0.001203	0.000299
Sample Variance	1.45E-06	8.92E-08
Kurtosis	19.36	4.25
Skewness	4.35	0.96
Minimum	0. 706845	0. 706845
Maximum	0. 714565	0. 708939
Count	97	92

minus two standard deviations would be $^{87}Sr/^{86}Sr$ = 0.7075–0.7089. Using this definition, only one individual at Solcor-3 (SC3-0050 [$^{87}Sr/^{86}Sr$ = 0.712522]) and six individuals at Casa Parroquial would be classified as nonlocal. However, it is possible that some individuals spent most of their adult lives in a different geologic zone and returned to their birthplace just before or after death; this would complicate the use of human bone values to determine the "local" strontium isotope signature in this dataset. In fact, at least one individual buried at Chen Chen (M1-1600) had an enamel strontium isotope value consistent with strontium from the Moquegua Valley yet had a bone strontium isotope value that was consistent with the Lake Titicaca Basin (Knudson 2008).

Descriptive statistics can also be used to evaluate the datasets from the Moquegua Valley and the San Pedro de Atacama region. As Table 11.1 shows, the complete datasets for each region are both variable and leptokurtic. However, when the four outliers from Chen Chen and the five outliers from the San Pedro de Atacama region are removed, both datasets become more normally distributed, with means and medians that are closer than in the complete datasets. As Wright (2005) noted, "One might expect skeletal $^{87}Sr/^{86}Sr$ to be normally distributed at an archaeological site where there is good reason to believe that the majority of the population were born locally, [and] that all individuals consumed foods grown on the same soils." This complementary approach provides an additional way to define the local strontium isotope signature at a given site.

Residential Relocation and Political Integration in the Tiwanaku Polity

Strontium isotope analysis can be used to identify the geographic origin of individuals buried at Tiwanaku-affiliated sites in the South-Central Andes. These data can then be used to reconstruct the nature of Tiwanaku influence during the Middle Horizon and the role of residential relocation and migration in the Tiwanaku polity. Here, I define residential relocation as an individual's long-term change in residence. This movement can be intentional, as when an individual permanently moves from one site or region to another, or unintentional, as when an individual is captured in warfare or forcibly moved to another site. Strontium isotope data used alone can identify Tiwanaku residential relocations. However, by incorporating multiple lines of anthropological evidence, Tiwanaku migration can be elucidated as well. The key variables in understanding Tiwanaku migration are structure, scale, motivation, and impact.

At Chen Chen there is clear evidence that migrants from the southern Lake Titicaca Basin lived and were buried at the site in cemeteries. The mortuary population at Chen Chen exhibit cranial modification styles consistent with an affiliation with the Tiwanaku polity (Blom 2005b; Blom et al. 1998) and were buried with Tiwanaku-style material culture that included ceramics, wooden spoons, and textiles (Goldstein 1990, 1998, 2005; Goldstein and Owen 2001; Goldstein and Rivera 2005). In addition, ancient DNA and biodistance analyses of the individuals buried at Chen Chen show that the mortuary population was closely related to individuals buried in the Tiwanaku heartland (Blom 2005a; Lewis et al. 2007; Lewis and Stone 2005). Together, these data demonstrate that the individuals buried at Chen Chen migrated from the Lake Titicaca Basin and retained close ties to the Tiwanaku polity. The motivation for migration to Chen Chen was most likely to gain access to ritually important agricultural crops such as maize, which does not grow well in the high-altitude Lake Titicaca Basin where Tiwanaku is located (Goldstein 1989, 1993, 2005; Kolata 1992, 1993a).

However, the presence of at least two first-generation Tiwanaku migrants at Chen Chen does not suggest a large or constant flow of people from the Lake Titicaca Basin to Chen Chen, and it is more likely that a small Tiwanaku-derived population migrated to Chen Chen. The presence of first-generation migrants from the Lake Titicaca Basin at Chen Chen supports models of the Tiwanaku polity as an expansionist state or empire (Goldstein 1992, 1993; Kolata 1992, 1993b; Ponce Sanginés 1972; Stanish 2003) or a vertical archipelago (Lynch 1989; Mujica et al. 1983), in which the Tiwanaku polity established a series of multiethnic productive colonies, based on John Murra's (1972) concepts of Andean verticality. However, multiple lines of evidence, including the strontium isotope data, increasingly support the diasporic model of Tiwanaku influence in the Moquegua Valley, in which individuals affiliated with the heterarchical and segmentary Tiwanaku polity settled in Moquegua but were not sent by the state as colonists (Goldstein 2000, 2005).

In contrast, while there is evidence for some residential relocation in the San Pedro de Atacama oasis, the nature of Tiwanaku influence did not include direct colonization and migration. Strontium isotope analysis did not identify *any* individuals who had lived in the Lake Titicaca Basin as children and then migrated to San Pedro before burial in the cemeteries of Coyo-3, Coyo Oriental, or Solcor-3. However, one individual may have lived in the Lake Titicaca Basin before burial in Casa Parroquial. This implies that local Atacameños adopted attributes of Tiwanaku material culture that strengthened economic and/or religious ties. Given the prevalence of portable, ritually important Tiwanaku-style artifacts in San Pedro de Atacama (e.g., Llagostera et al. 1988; Oakland Rodman 1992; Torres 1987; Torres and Conklin 1995), the strontium isotope and material culture data support a model of Tiwanaku influence in San Pedro de Atacama that involves shared ideologies but not migration. Instead, most inhabitants of the oasis incorporated aspects of Tiwanaku mortuary identity in addition to Atacameño identity (Knudson and Blom 2009; Torres-Rouff 2008).

Conclusion

Strontium isotope analysis can be used to identify residential relocations and the geographic origin of individuals in the archaeological record. While bone remodels and it can be used to identify place of residence in the years before death, tooth enamel elucidates the geographic origins during the first years of life. Despite the promise of strontium isotope analysis for studies of archaeological residential relocation, anthropologists are continuing to refine this technique, focusing particularly on the definition of local strontium isotope signatures using proxies for bioavailable strontium isotope signatures and descriptive statistics. When combined with multiple lines of evidence, strontium isotope analysis can be very useful for the study of archaeological migration. This provides a powerful tool for examining the structure and scale of migration and, with other contextualized data, the motivations and impacts of migratory events. Migration can then be used to understand sociopolitical development and core-periphery interactions in the Andes and beyond.

Acknowledgments

This project was funded by the National Science Foundation (BCS-0202329 and SBR-9708001), the Latin American Studies Department at the University of Wisconsin at Madison, the Geological Society of America, and the Institute for Social Science Research and the School of Human Evolution & Social Change at Arizona State University. I am also very grateful to Dr. Paul Fullagar of the Geochronology and Isotope Geochemistry Laboratory at the University of North Carolina at Chapel Hill and Drs. Ariel Anbar and Gwyneth Gordon of the W. M. Keck Foundation Laboratory for Environmental Biogeochemistry for their expertise in isotopic analysis and their generosity in granting laboratory access and in analyzing samples. At the Archaeological Chemistry Laboratory at Arizona State University, numerous laboratory technicians contributed to this project. Finally, I thank the editors of this volume for their invitation to participate and the editors and contributors to the volume and to the 2005 American Anthropological Association symposium and the 2006 Cross-Disciplinary Approaches to Migration conference for their thought-provoking research.

References

Bentley, R. A.
2006   Strontium Isotopes from the Earth to the Archaeological Skeleton: A Review. *Journal of Archaeological Method and Theory* 13(3):135–187.
R. A. Bentley, H. R. Buckley, M. Spriggs, S. Bedford, C. J. Ottley, G. M. Nowell, C. G. Macpherson, and D. G. Pearson
2007   Lapita Migrants in the Pacific's Oldest Cemetery: Isotopic Analysis at Teouma, Vanuatu. *American Antiquity* 72:645–656.
Blom, D. E.
2005a A Bioarchaeological Approach to Tiwanaku Group Dynamics. *Us and Them: Archaeology and Ethnicity in the Andes*, edited by R. M. Reycraft, pp. 152–182. Costen Institute of Archaeology, Los Angeles.
2005b Embodying Borders: Human Body Modification and Diversity in Tiwanaku Society. *Journal of Anthropological Archaeology* 24(1):1–24.

Blom, D. E., B. Hallgrímsson, L. Keng, M. C. Lozada, and J. E. Buikstra
1998   Tiwanaku "Colonization": Bioarchaeological Implications for Migration in the Moquegua Valley, Peru. *World Archaeology* 30(2):238–261.

Budd, P., J. Montgomery, B. Barreiro, and R. Thomas
2000   Differential Diagenesis of Strontium in Archaeological Human Dental Tissues. *Applied Geochemistry* 15:687–694.

Carr, T. E. F., G. E. Harrison, J. F. Loutit, and A. Sutton
1962   Movement of Strontium in the Human Body. *British Medical Journal* 2:773–775.

Dolphin, G. W., and I. S. Eve
1963   The Metabolism of Strontium in Adult Humans. *Physics of Medical Biology* 8(2):193–203.

Ericson, J. E.
1985   Strontium Isotope Characterization in the Study of Prehistoric Human Ecology. *Journal of Human Evolution* 14:503–514.
1989   Some Problems and Potentials of Strontium Isotope Analysis for Human and Animal Ecology. *Stable Isotopes in Ecological Research*, edited by P. W. Rundel, J. R. Ehleringer, and K. A. Nagy, pp. 254–269. Springer-Verlag: New York.

Evans, J. A., and S. Tatham
2004   Defining "Local Signature" in Terms of Sr Isotope Composition using a Tenth-to Twelfth-Century Anglo-Saxon Population Living on a Jurassic Clay-Carbonate Terrain, Rutland, UK. *Forensic Geoscience: Principles, Techniques, and Applications* 232:237–248.

Ezzo, J. A., C. M. Johnson, and T. D. Price
1997   Analytical Perspectives on Prehistoric Migration: A Case Study from East-Central Arizona. *Journal of Archaeological Science* 24:447–466.

Goldstein, P.
1989   *Omo, a Tiwanaku Provincial Center in Moquegua, Peru.* Unpublished Ph.D. dissertation, University of Chicago.
1990   La Ocupación Tiwanaku en Moquegua. *Gaceta Arqueológica Andina* V (18/19):75–104.
1992   Tiwanaku Temples and State Expansion. *Latin American Antiquity* 4:22–47.
1993   House, Community and State in the Earliest Tiwanaku Colony: Domestic Patterns and State Integration at Omo M12, Moquegua. *Domestic Architecture, Ethnicity, and Complementarity in the South-Central Andes*, edited by M. S. Aldenderfer, pp. 25–41. University of Iowa Press, Iowa City.
1996   Tiwanaku Settlement Patterns of the Azapa Valley, Chile: New Data, and the Legacy of Percy Dauelsberg. *Dialogo Andino* 14/15:57–73.
1998   Moquegua y el Imperio Tiwanaku. In *Moquegua: Los Primeros Doce Mil Años*, edited by K. Wise, pp. 45–58. Policrom, Arequipa, Peru.
2000   Communities Without Borders: The Vertical Archipelago and Diaspora Communities in the Southern Andes. In *The Archaeology of Communities: A New World Perspective*, edited by M. A. Canuto and J. Yaeger, pp. 182–209. Routledge, London.

2005   *Andean Diaspora: The Tiwanaku Colonies and the Origins of South America Empire*. Gainesville, University Press of Florida.

Goldstein, P., and B. Owen

2001   Tiwanaku en Moquegua: Las Colonias Altiplánicas. In *Huari y Tiwanaku: Modelos vs. Evidencias, Segunda Parte*, edited by P. Kaulicke and W. H. Isbell, pp. 139–169. La Pontificia Universidad Católica del Perú, Lima.

Goldstein, P., and M. Rivera

2005   Arts of Greater Tiwanaku: An Expansive Culture in Historical Context. In *Tiwanaku: Ancestors of the Inka*, edited by M. Young-Sánchez, pp. 150–185. University of Nebraska Press, Lincoln.

Hedges, R. E.

2002   Bone Diagenesis: An Overview of Progress. *Archaeometry* 44(3):319–328.

Hoppe, K. A.

2004   Late Pleistocene Mammoth Herd Structure, Migration Patterns, and Clovis Hunting Strategies Inferred from Isotopic Analyses of Multiple Death Assemblages. *Palaeobiology* 30(1):129–145.

Kennedy, B. P., C. L. Folt, J. D. Blum, and C. P. Chamberlein

1997   Natural Isotope Markers in Salmon. *Nature* 387:766.

Knudson, K. J.

2007   La Influencia de Tiwanaku en San Pedro de Atacama: Una Investigación por los Isótopos del Estroncio. *Estudios Atacameños* 33:7–24.

2008   Tiwanaku Influence in the South Central Andes: Strontium Isotope Analysis and Middle Horizon Migration. *Latin American Antiquity* 19(1):3–23.

Knudson, K. J., and D. E. Blom

2009   The Complex Relationship between Tiwanaku Mortuary Identity and Geographic Origin in the South Central Andes. *Bioarchaeology and Identity in the Americas*, edited by K. J. Knudson and C. M. Stojanowski. University Press of Florida, Gainesville.

Knudson, K. J., and T. D. Price

2007   Utility of Multiple Chemical Techniques in Archaeological Residential Mobility Studies: Case Studies from Tiwanaku- and Chiribaya-Affiliated Sites in the Andes. *American Journal of Physical Anthropology* 132(1):25–39.

Knudson, K. J., T. D. Price, J. E. Buikstra, and D. E. Blom

2004   The Use of Strontium Isotope Analysis to Investigate Tiwanaku Migration and Mortuary Ritual in Bolivia and Peru. *Archaeometry* 46(1):5–18.

Knudson, K. J., and T. A. Tung

2007   Using Archaeological Chemistry to Investigate the Geographic Origins of Trophy Heads in the Central Andes: Strontium Isotope Analysis at the Wari Site of Conchopata. In *Archaeological Chemistry: Analytical Techniques and Archaeological Interpretation*, edited by M. D. Glascock, R. J. Speakman, and R. S. Popelka-Filcoff, pp. 99–113. American Chemical Society, Washington, D.C.

Kohn, M. J., M. J. Schoeninger, and W. W. Barker
1999   Altered States: Effects of Diagenesis on Fossil Tooth Chemistry. *Geochimica et Cosmochimica Acta* 63(18):2737–2747.

Kolata, A. L.
1992   Economy, Ideology, and Imperialism in the South-Central Andes. In *Ideology and Pre-Columbian Civilizations*, edited by A. A. Demerest and G. W. Conrad, pp. 65–86. School of American Research Press, Santa Fe.
1993a   *The Tiwanaku: Portrait of an Andean Civilization*. Blackwell, Oxford.
1993b   Understanding Tiwanaku: Conquest, Colonization and Clientage in the South Central Andes. In *Latin American Horizons*, edited by D. S. Rice, pp. 193–223. Dumbarton Oaks Research Library and Collections: Washington, D.C.

Krueger, H. W.
1985   *Sr Isotopes and Sr/Ca in Bone*. Poster paper presented at Biomineralization Conference, Airlie House, Warrenton, Va.

Lee-Thorp, J.
2002   Two Decades of Progress Towards Understanding Fossilization Processes and Isotopic Signals in Calcified Tissue Minerals. *Archaeometry* 44(3):435–446.

Lewis, C. M., Jr., J. E. Buikstra, and A. C. Stone
2007   Ancient DNA and Genetic Continuity in the South Central Andes. *Latin American Antiquity* 18(2):145–160.

Lewis, C. M., and A. C. Stone
2005   MtDNA Diversity at the Archaeological Site of Chen Chen in Perú. In *Biomolecular Archaeology: Genetic Approaches to the Past: Proceedings from the 19th Annual Visiting Scholar Conference*, edited by D. M. Reed, pp. 47–60. Southern Illinois University Press, Carbondale.

Llagostera, A., C. M. Torres, and M. A. Costa
1988   El Complejo Psicotrópico en Solcor-3 (San Pedro de Atacama). *Estudios Atacameños* 9:61–98.

Lynch, T. F.
1989   Regional Interactions, Transhumance, and Verticality: Archaeology Use of Zonal Complementarity in Peru and Northern Chile. *Michigan Discussions in Anthropology* 8:1–11.

Montgomery, J., P. Budd, J. Evans, and B. Barreiro
1999   LA-ICP-MS Evidence for the Distribution of Lead and Strontium in Romano-British, Medieval and Modern Human Teeth: Implications for Life History and Exposure Reconstruction. In *Metals in Antiquity*, edited by S. M. M. Young, A. M. Pollard, P. Budd, and R. A. Ixer, pp. 290–296. Archaeopress, Oxford.

Mujica, E. J., M. A. Rivera, and T. F. Lynch
1983   Proyecto de Estudio sobre la Complementaridad Economica Tiwanaku en los Valles Occidentales del Centro-Sur Andino. *Chungará* 11:85–109.

Murra, J. V.

1972   El "Control Vertical" de un Máximo de Pisos Ecológicos en la Economía de las Sociedades Andinas. In *Visita de la Provincia de Leon de Huanuco en 1562*, vol. 2, edited by J. V. Murra, pp. 429–476. Universidad Nacional Hermilio Valdizan, Huanuco, Perú.

Nelson, B. K., M. J. DeNiro, M. J. Schoeninger, D. J. de Paolo, and P. E. Hare

1986   Effects of Diagenesis on Strontium, Carbon, Nitrogen, and Oxygen Concentration and Isotopic Concentration of Bone. *Geochimica et Cosmochimica Acta* 50:1941–1949.

Oakland Rodman, A.

1992   Textiles and Ethnicity: Tiwanaku in San Pedro de Atacama, North Chile. *Latin American Antiquity* 3(4):316–340.

Ponce Sanginés, C.

1972   *Tiwanaku: espacio, tiempo, y cultura*. Academia Nacional de Ciencias de Bolivia, La Paz.

Price, T. D., J. Blitz, and J. A. Ezzo

1992   Diagenesis in Prehistoric Human Bone: Problems and Solutions. *Journal of Archaeological Science* 19:513–529.

Price, T. D., J. H. Burton, and R. A. Bentley

2002   The Characterization of Biologically Available Strontium Isotope Ratios for the Study of Prehistoric Migration. *Archaeometry* 44(1):117–136.

Price, T. D., C. M. Johnson, J. A. Ezzo, J. Ericson, and J. H. Burton

1994   Residential Mobility in the Prehistoric Southwest United States: A Preliminary Study Using Strontium Isotope Analysis. *Journal of Archaeological Science* 21:315–330.

Shellis, R. P., and G. H. Dibdin

2000   Enamel Microporosity and Its Functional Implications. In *Development, Function and Evolution of Teeth*, edited by M. F. Teaford, M. M. Smith, and M. W. J. Ferguson, pp. 242–251. Cambridge University Press, Cambridge.

Sillen, A.

1989   Diagenesis of the Inorganic Phase of Cortical Bone. In *The Chemistry of Prehistoric Human Bone*, edited by T. D. Price, pp. 211–228. Cambridge University Press, Cambridge.

Stanish, C.

2003   *Ancient Titicaca: The Evolution of Complex Society in Southern Peru and Northern Bolivia*. University of California Press, Berkeley.

Torres, C. M.

1987   The Iconography of the Prehispanic Snuff Trays from San Pedro de Atacama, Northern Chile. *Andean Past*. 1: 191-245.

Torres, C. M., and W. J. Conklin

1995   Exploring the San Pedro de Atacama/ Tiwanaku Relationship. In *Andean Art: Visual Expression and Its Relation to Andean Beliefs and Values*, edited by P. Dransart, pp. 78–108. Avebury Press, Aldershot, UK.

Torres-Rouff, C.
2002   Cranial Vault Modification and Ethnicity in Middle Horizon San Pedro de Atacama, Chile. *Current Anthropology* 43(1):163–171.
2008   The Influence of Tiwanaku on Life in the Chilean Atacama: Mortuary and Bodily Perspectives. *American Anthropologist* 110(3):325–337.
Torres-Rouff, C., and K. J. Knudson
2007   Examining the Life History of an Individual from Solcor 3, San Pedro de Atacama: Combining Bioarchaeology and Archaeological Chemistry. *Chungará* 39(2):235–257.
Tung, T. A., and K. J. Knudson
2008   Social Identities and Geographical Origins of Wari Trophy Heads from Conchopata, Peru. *Current Anthropology* 49(5):915–925.
van der Merwe, N. J., J. A. Lee-Thorp, J. F. Thackeray, A. Hall-Martin, and F. J. Kruger
1990   Source-Area Determination of Elephant Ivory by Isotopic Analysis. *Nature* 346:744–746.
Wright, L. E.
2005   Identifying Immigrants to Tikal, Guatemala: Defining Local Variability in Strontium Isotope Ratios of Human Tooth Enamel. *Journal of Archaeological Science* 32(4):555–566.

12

Migration in Anthropological Genetics

ALAN G. FIX

Migration, as have many ordinary language terms, has been defined in several senses in biology, biological anthropology, and anthropological genetics (see Fix 1999). Biologists tend to study migration from both an ecological and an evolutionary point of view. Thus biologist Hugh Dingle focuses on behavior as the defining criteria—migration is "persistent and straightened-out movement effected by the animal's own locomotory exertions" (1996:25)—and applies it to cyclical long-range movements such as the annual migrations of many bird species. For this reason, this definition excludes daily ranging behavior and presumes movement into new habitats. Biologists see migration as different from dispersal, which is the one-way movement of organisms to a new environment (Dingle 1996). Such one-way movement is therefore an outcome, or result, of the behavior of migration. In contrast, biological anthropologists see migration more in terms of the outcome: migration is "one-way movement of organisms to a new environment" (see Cabana and Clark, this volume). Such migration can be long range—such as a range expansion, colonization, invasion, or demic diffusion (Cavalli-Sforza et al. 1993; Weiss 1988)—or short range, encompassing movements of individuals, families, or somewhat larger groups to neighboring groups.

One consequence of migration is the evolutionary effect of gene flow. Gene flow, or the diffusion of genes between breeding populations, is one of the four forces of evolution (with mutation, natural selection, and genetic drift) that affects the frequency, spatial pattern, and spread of genes in human populations. Therefore, migration as the *cause* of gene flow plays a central role in anthropological genetic theory, and gene flow produces spatial distributions of gene frequencies. For instance, a typical spatial pattern of gene frequencies known as isolation by distance is the result of limited gene exchange (via migration) with increasing geographic distance between local populations.

Although movement, or the process of migration, leads to gene flow and gene flow can lead to patterned gene distributions, inference often goes the other way: process is inferred from gene distributions. With the triumph of the neutral theory of molecular genetic variation, much research in current anthropological genetics attempts to trace the population history of migration using molecular markers, or genetic variants presumably not subject to natural selection. These markers are presumed to have originated by mutation, increased in frequency through genetic drift, and then been dispersed via prehistoric migration. It is assumed that the present distribution of molecular markers provides information about presumed migrations.

The actual behavior of migrating, the basis of Dingle's (1996) definition, is usually left unspecified in genetic studies. Somehow populations split and components migrate off to new habitats, taking their genes with them. Daughter populations remain isolated and diverge genetically. The long-term consequence of this process is a species divided into branches, like a tree. Much of the efforts of contemporary human molecular geneticists go toward constructing branching tree diagrams (also dendograms or cladograms) to reconstruct population histories, including the history of our entire species (e.g., Cavalli-Sforza et al. 1994). Unfortunately, anthropologists seem unconcerned about their lack of knowledge of the ecology of migrating. For example, Bellwood and Renfrew (2002), in presenting the emerging synthesis of the new discipline of archaeogenetics (population history inferred from molecular genetics), conspicuously fail to include the comparative ethnography and demography that would provide this perspective. In the absence of such comparative data, migration is often invoked simply on the basis of shared traits.

Among humans, mobility and migration show clear associations with socioeconomic factors, population density, and other factors such as ecology (Fix 1999). Yet there is a serious problem with inference based on ethnography: it is in present time and records the events and consequences of short-term activities. Nevertheless, it is worth remembering that local short-term activities can have long-term global consequences. For example, near-neighbor migration can lead to isolation and genetic differentiation, keeping regional sets of populations in one evolutionary system (Weidenreich 1946).

John Moore (1994) has argued that populations of conspecifics are always capable of exchanging genes or fusing with neighbors and/or of migrating to new areas and exchanging genes or fusing with previously distant groups. Separated courses of evolution can reunite and genetic divergence evolved in semi-isolation can be homogenized. He views the process of human evolutionary change as a braided course of anastomosing river channels that he has termed ethnogenesis. This contrasts with a view of human population history as separated branches of a tree, produced by a series of population fissions, migrations to new ranges, and isolation followed by genetic divergence among daughter populations (Cavalli-Sforza et al. 1994).

Moore's (1994) critique of tree-branching models of population history is strongly grounded in ethnographic and ethnohistoric research. Detractors argue that inferring the past from the ethnographic present is not always appropriate (for example, Wobst's [1978] phrase "the tyranny of the ethnographic record"). The root of the problem is that not all events of significance are recorded in the necessarily short-term records of ethnography and ethnohistory. The bolide from space that putatively wiped out the dinosaurs is not a daily occurrence; thus, theory should not be bound by the known record. However, as Moore retorts, "without the inductive discipline imposed by uniformitarianism, theorists are free to construct whatever bizarre theories they might find agreeable, on whatever basis" (1994:931).

The upshot is that if we are to understand the past, some representation of population structure and process must be employed. This does not rule out rare cataclysmic events or large-scale migrations, for that matter, but it does mean that implicit, unexamined analogies ("bizarre theories") should not be produced to simply fit the data. For example, the fact that some modern agricultural societies show very high annual rates of population increase does not mean that *all* food-producers expand—or did expand—blitzkrieg-like (c.f. Cavalli-Sforza et al. 1993).

With these ideas in mind, an extended case study of the Semai Senoi of Malaysia will be used to examine and evaluate some of the payoffs, problems, and pitfalls of studying migration from the perspective of anthropological genetics.

Case Study: The Semai Senoi Peoples (Orang Asli) of Malaysia

The Orang Asli ("original people" in the Malay language) are indigenous people of the Malay Peninsula comprising three groups: Semang foragers, Senoi farmers, and Melayu Asli farmer-traders (Benjamin 1985). The Semai are the largest population of Senoi (see Dentan [1968] for an ethnography and Fix [1982, 1995, 2000] for population genetic history). Intensive fieldwork with the Semai Senoi from 1968 to 1969 and again in 1987 has allowed me to document migration and gene flow at the ethnographic scale of current and recent events. The process of testing inferences about migration on a larger spatial and temporal scale will be illustrated by arguments about the origins of the Orang Asli as a whole. Finally, I will examine long-term scenarios of range expansion using recent data on the Orang Asli and the Southeast Asian region more generally.

Local Migration among the Semai

The Semai living on the eastern flank of the Main Range in Peninsular Malaya during my period of fieldwork were long-fallow swidden farmers who supplemented their diet and income through hunting, fishing, and collecting forest products. I spent some eight months in 1968 and 1969 censusing and collecting genealogies, individual migration histories, and village histories (among other things) to characterize the Semai population structure and understand the pattern of genetic microdifferentiation within the region. In my study region, the population of some 776 was distributed in seven settlements ranging in size from 50 to 272 people. Population density was relatively low (two to three persons per km^2) (Fix 1982, 1999).

Movement of individuals and groups between settlements was frequent for a variety of reasons, including postmarital residence and political (unresolved disputes) and/or economic reasons. When groups moved, they were usually comprised of families, a pattern I have called kin-structured migration (Fix 1978).

This fieldwork was conducted over a relatively short period of time and within a small region, allowing me to describe local migration in great detail (see Fix 1999 for more examples from other populations). Based on census data alone, it as possible to document the birthplaces of individuals, providing information on movement (or not) to an individual's current residence. Table 12.1 shows such data for married pairs from the study region. The same data also allow measures of parent-offspring differences in birthplace, a measure of intergenerational movement. These data can be represented in matrix form (Table 12.2), showing the probabilities of an offspring who was born in

Table 12.1. Birthplaces of Semai Senoi married pairs[a]

Settlement	Nr	Ns	Settlement Endogamous	Region Endogamous	Region Exogamous
A	272	117	0.453	0.888	0.112
B	69	19	0.210	0.946	0.054
C	107	37	0.054	0.648	0.352
D	54	34	0.147	0.824	0.176
E	107	33	0.182	0.847	0.153
F	117	79	0.304	0.721	0.279

Note: a. Adapted from Fix (1999:36:Table 2.2).

Table 12.2. Backward stochastic migration matrix for Semai Senoi data, showing the probabilities of an offspring born in a row settlement having a parent born in a column settlement[a]

Settlement	Pop. Size	A	B	C	D	E	F	G
A	449	0.601		0.065	0.009		0.011	0.189
B	82	0.085	0.171	0.049	0.146			0.159
C	114			0.298	0.018	0.026		0.061
D	70				0.430	0.200		0.057
E	139	0.007		0.029	0.208	0.575		0.029
F	26	0.039					0.115	0.403
G	153	0.105		0.007	0.007	0.007	0.019	0.705

Note: a. Adapted from Fix (1999:63:Table 3.1).

a row settlement having a parent born in a column settlement (see Fix 1999 for details). Migration matrix analysis, one of several classic models of human migration and population structure, uses such data to predict genetic patterns among populations after sufficient generations to achieve equilibrium (Bodmer and Cavalli-Sforza 1974).

The ethnographic recording of genealogies and settlement histories provides another avenue for reconstructing migration patterns in contemporary and recent populations. Figure 12.1 is a genealogy showing the descendants of an immigrant (at the top of the figure) from a neighboring Orang Asli group (probably Temuan); this individual entered the local Semai population toward the end of the nineteenth century. This date corresponds with a series of incursions by Indonesian Malay raiders in the area that are historically documented (Milner 1978). Furthermore, this genealogy accounts for some 36percent (18 of 50 individuals) carriers of ovalocytosis (Southeast Asian ovalocytosis, or SAO), which is otherwise rare in Semai populations (Fix 1995). This example demonstrates the link between the direct measurement of migration rates based on demographic data from contemporary populations to the "backward" inference of such migration based on shared alleles between populations. In this case, gene flow (migration) can be demonstrated directly from genealogical and historical data and provides an explanation for the presence of the ovalocytosis allele among the Semai.

The more common approach in anthropological genetics is to infer migration (or some shared history) from observed genetic similarities. In this case, such inference would seem straightforward: where neighboring populations share the same gene variant but in differing frequencies, gene flow is the most likely cause.

Such migration between adjacent populations has been extensively documented in the ethnographic and demographic literature (see Fix 1999). These

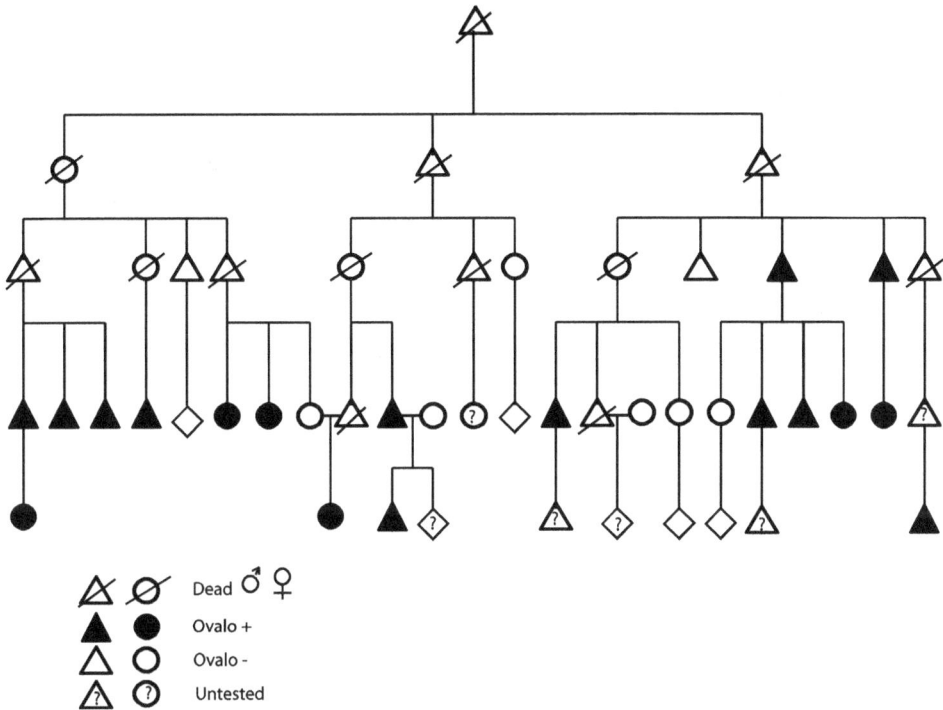

Figure 12.1. Migrant genealogy and genealogical distribution of SAO allele.

studies show that short-range movement over one or a few generations is the normal pattern. This kind of local migration is the basis for several classic population genetics models (e.g., isolation by distance and stepping-stone and migration matrices). These patterns of genetic exchange have predictable consequences for genetic variation and are often invoked to explain spatial patterns of allele frequencies.

Regional Migration among the Orang Asli and Long-Term Migration in Greater Southeast Asia

Looking at the larger temporal and spatial scale of the history of the Orang Asli in the Malay Peninsula and then in Southeast Asia generally, we can ask whether long-term movements (migrations, invasions, population replacements, and even the original colonization of the region) can be discerned from the genetic data on the human populations.

The origins of the three Orang Asli groups have been interpreted as a successive series of migrations (Carey 1976). The most ancient brought the ancestors of the present-day Semang foragers to the peninsula. Later waves introduced farming Senoi ancestors (including those of the Semai), who were followed by the farming-trading Melayu Asli. Although this explanation for present-day cultural (and biological) diversity hearkens back to the *Kulturkreislehre* school of cultural diffusion, in some measure it continues to have support among current scholars (e.g., Peter Bellwood [1993]). An alternative model was put forward by Geoffrey Benjamin (1976, 1985), who argued that cultural differentiation arose in situ on the peninsula through a process of competitive economic displacement.

How might we test these competing hypotheses? Benjamin's (1976) model was based partly on the pattern of shared languages among the Orang Asli (all are speakers of Mon-Khmer languages of the Austroasiatic family) and a sociocultural argument for a kind of competitive displacement among the economies and cultures of the three groups. The alternative migration idea, as championed by Bellwood (1993), ascribes the expansion of Austroasiatic-speaking rice farmers via demic diffusion from a homeland in China through Southeast Asia down to the Malay Peninsula. Thus, range-expanding Senoi agriculturalists would have displaced the original hunter-gatherer Semang inhabitants from some of their lands. The linguistic similarity between Senoi and Semang would have come about through adoption of farmer languages by the foragers on the model of the Agta of the Philippines and the Pygmies of central Africa (Headland and Reid 1989).

Neither the linguistic nor the cultural/archaeological data provide an un-equivocal test; both hypotheses can account for the distributions. Although one might not accept Bellwood's (2002) view that languages can expand only by the movement of their speakers, there can be no argument about genes be-ing intrinsic to migrants. What do genes tell us? Unfortunately, not enough to definitively resolve the question (Fix 1995, 2000, 2002).

Classical genetic loci, including blood groups, enzymes, and structural proteins such as hemoglobin, have been used to construct tree-branching diagrams meant to represent genetic affinities among a series of sampled pop-ulations. Genetic similarity thus implies a common evolutionary history of populations. Unfortunately, such trees offer little evidence that bears on Orang Asli origins and migrations. For example, Cavalli-Sforza et al. (1994) included the Semai among a number of other Southeast Asian populations in a tree based on 31 classical molecular markers. They are shown as clustering closest to the Zhuang, a Tai-speaking ethnic group of South China, whereas they are quite distant from the Khmer, the contiguous population of Cambodia with whom they share a close linguistic tie. Interestingly, another tree diagram con-structed from a different set of classical markers and a somewhat different set of Southeast Asian populations contrasts significantly from Cavalli-Sforza et al.'s (1994) tree diagram, linking Semai and Khmer closely and separating this cluster from other populations (Saha et al. 1995). Neither study includes data from other Orang Asli groups.

This comparison of datasets and subsequent interpretations illustrate some pitfalls of genetic inference for the history of populations. Tree diagrams are constructed from matrices of genetic similarity/difference. If all loci are marking the same history of population fission, migration, isolation, and random differentiation, then all diagrams should be identical. However, this may not always be the case. Consider the fact that one of these trees includes hemoglobin E (HbE) (Flatz 1967; Livingstone 1985). It turns out that HbE confers some resistance to malaria so that this nonneutral allele attains high frequency in several mainland Southeast Asian populations (including the Khmer), and, for the same reason, it confers malarial resistance in the Semai. Not surprisingly, then, Khmer and Semai show strong genetic affinity in a tree diagram based on HbE distribution. Shared ancestry as part of the widespread Austroasiatic-speaking (Mon-Khmer) mainland Southeast Asian population may explain the presence of this allele among the Semai, but its significantly high frequency surely depends on natural selection.

Similarly, the historical evidence discussed above records the introduction of another adaptive allele, ovalocytosis, via migration from a Melayu Asli group (see Figure 12.1). In this case, however, a common population history between Semai and other populations with high frequencies of SAO is less likely an explanation than for HbE. While HbE is found in mainland Southeast Asia, SAO occurs in a wide swath from coastal Papua New Guinea through island Southeast Asia (Fix 1995). Among the southern Semai, we perhaps find an adaptive allele protecting against malaria in the process of being introduced from a neighboring population (Melayu Asli), who likely received the gene through intermarriage with trading partners, Austronesian-speaking Malays, seafarers ranging over the entire extent of the islands. SAO demonstrates a *link* (gene flow) with island Southeast Asia but does not necessarily show the *origins* of Orang Asli from this region. The cause of high frequencies of SAO in coastal New Guinea and Melayu Asli (and among some local Semai populations) is malarial selection. A few migrants would be sufficient to spread the allele, and where advantageous, it increased in frequency.

Indeed, without historical or genealogical information, it may be difficult to demonstrate that gene flow is the cause for the presence of an allele in a population. Recent work (Ramos-Kuri et al. 2005) has identified exactly the same 27 base-pair deletion that characterizes SAO in Mexico. A colleague suggested the Manila galleon as a source of transportation, but it is not impossible to rule out a new mutation as an alternative explanation for this sporadic

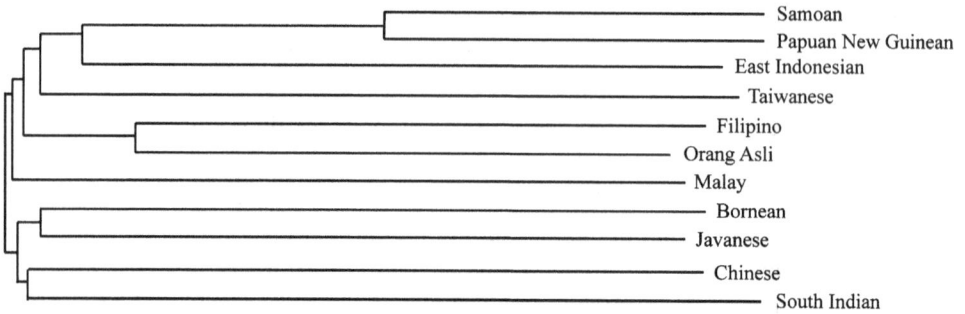

Figure 12.2. Tree diagram based on mtDNA lineages (haplotypes) and the 9bp deletion for eleven Asian populations (from Melton et al. 1995:Figure 2). Scale: genetic distance.

occurrence. Thus, multiple causal factors must be considered if we are to understand any genetic distribution. As a consequence, "history may not be read simply from gene trees" (Fix 2000:16).

A problem with classical loci is their lack of specificity. As Majumder (2005:293) notes, "Since genes move as people move, the commonly used method to trace trails of human migration is to identify *specific genetic signatures* in the source population and look for these signatures in extant populations along the suspected migration route" (emphasis added). It would appear that the molecular signature of SAO (the deletion of a particular sequence of DNA) would satisfy this requirement. But a similar deletion genotype, the famous 9bp deletion in the COII/tRNA^{Lys} intergenic region of the mitochondrial DNA (mtDNA) genome that is the basis of the Polynesian motif (as well as haplogroup B, a common Native American lineage), is quite widespread, and several origins of the basic deletion have been posited (Schurr and Wallace 2002; Watkins et al. 1999).

Even where we may presume a common mutational origin, molecular genetic markers may only record *ancient* history over a wide geographic region. Neither HbE nor SAO can be used to characterize or differentiate Senoi or Orang Asli ethnic populations; rather, they demonstrate shared histories and gene flow on a spatial scale from eastern India to Papua New Guinea.

Similarly, the mtDNA 9bp deletion has a wide distribution including among the Semai Senoi, where 37 percent of individuals in Melton et al.'s (1995) sample demonstrate the deletion. Melton and colleagues (1995) propose that the original deletion occurred perhaps 60,000 years ago and was subsequently widely spread through Southeast Asia. Moreover, a tree diagram (Figure 12.2) based on this and other markers on the mitochondrial genome has deep branches extending far back to an ancestral form, indicating that these divisions among populations are *all* ancient.

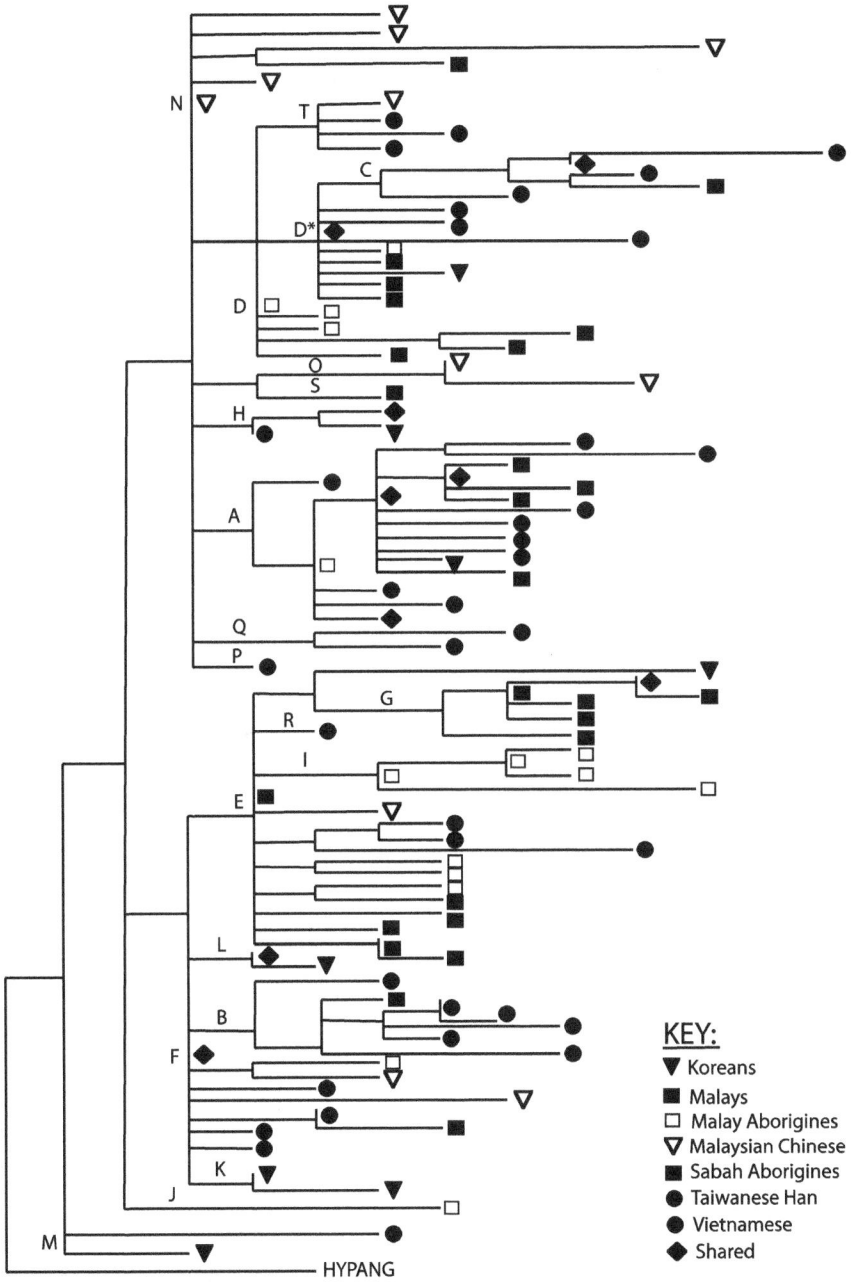

Figure 12.3. Genealogy of Southeast Asian mtDNA lineages. Symbols designate ethnic origin of the lineage (adapted from Ballinger et al. 1992:Figure 2).

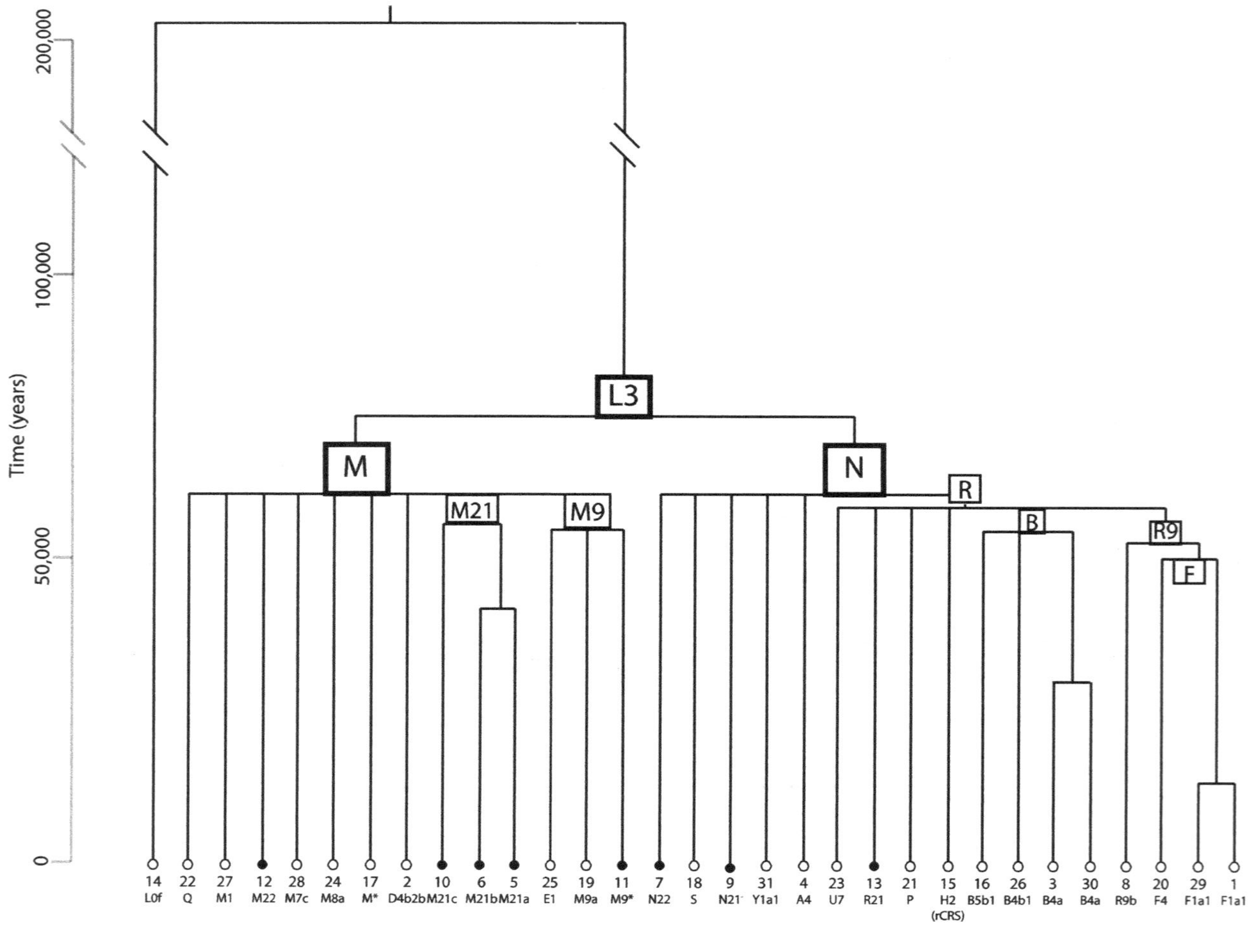

Figure 12.4. Tree diagram based on mtDNA lineages of 260 Orang Asli (all subgroups; from Macauley et al. 2005).

This conclusion is reinforced by the independently constructed mtDNA tree diagram of Ballinger et al. (1992) (Figure 12.3). Some 33 Orang Asli of various ethnicities (but probably mostly Semai Senoi) are located in almost every branch of this tree. Some Orang Asli mtDNA lineages are very similar to those found in present-day Sabah indigenes, Koreans, Vietnamese, and Malays. Again, the mtDNA data do not uniquely mark origin(s), differentiate subgroups (Semang, Senoi, or Melayu Asli), or demonstrate population movements of the Orang Asli.

More recently, Macaulay and colleagues have analyzed mtDNA from 260 Orang Asli from all three subgroups and claim that it supports a single, rapid coastal settlement of Asia (Macaulay et al. 2005). Figure 12.4 shows Macaulay et al.'s (2005) resulting mtDNA tree diagram. The basal mtDNA lineage, L3 (the African clade ancestral to M and N), is estimated to be approximately 84,000 years old, with M and N originating circa 63,000 years ago. These dates, if correct, would suggest that lineages M and N (and the nearly contemporary R) were carried by the original anatomically modern *Homo sapiens* migrants who dispersed from Africa. Note that the terminal lineages represented as filled circles in Figure 12.4 indicate Orang Asli. Macaulay and colleagues (2005:1035) interpret this to mean that the Orang Asli "harbor 'relict' mtDNA lineages with time depths of ~44,000 to 63,000 years. Their restricted distribution makes it very likely that these lineages diverged around that time within mainland southeast Asia." The Orang Asli would thus be relict populations (Forster and Matsumura 2005) preserving ancient mtDNA signatures of the first colonization of southern Eurasia by modern humans. In this scenario, the Orang Asli survived in a "glacial refuge," avoiding later "waves of replacement . . . during the late Holocene" (Macaulay et al. 2005:1035).

Interestingly, all three subgroups of Orang Asli show relict lineages (although only one Semai was typed—the rest of the Senoi sample were Temiar). This may constitute evidence for the in situ differentiation hypothesis of Orang Asli origins discussed above or may only be an indication of gene flow among these populations after their successive arrival in the Peninsula. Once again, we are left with no unequivocal conclusion regarding ancient migration.

Conclusions

Migration is an often-invoked concept in anthropological genetics. Ethnographic and historical data that document migration are central to understanding spatial genetic patterns. Over larger spatial and longer temporal scales, gene distributions are often presumed to be the result of migrations and dispersions. However, as the Semai Senoi case study has demonstrated, other evolutionary forces, including natural selection (e.g., HbE and SAO), may play important roles that determine genetic spatial patterns. Further, in the absence of data, we do not know whether the form of migration is group displacements or simple the trickle of local marital exchanges. Even the rapidly evolving mitochondrial genome seems to record the initial colonization of the region rather than subsequent migrations. Rapidly proliferating molecular markers and new methods have increased the ability of anthropological geneticists to infer past migrations. However, a better understanding of the process of human movement must be gained if we are to read history from the genes.

References

Ballinger, S. W., T. G. Schurr, A. Torroni, Y. Y. Gan, J. A. Hodge, K. Hassan, K.-H. Chen, and D. C. Wallace
1992   Southeast Asian Mitochondrial DNA Analysis Reveals Genetic Continuity of Ancient Mongoloid Migrations. *Genetics* 130:139–152.

Bellwood, P.
1993   Cultural and Biological Differentiation in Peninsular Malaysia: The Last 10,000 Years. *Asian Perspectives* 32:37–60.
2002   Farmers, Foragers, Languages, Genes: The Genesis of Agricultural Societies. In *Examining the Farming/language Dispersal Hypothesis*, edited by P. Bellwood and C. Renfrew, pp. 17–28. Oxbow Press, Oxford.

Bellwood, P., and C. Renfrew
2002   *Examining the Farming/Language Dispersal Hypothesis*. Oxbow Press, Oxford.

Benjamin, G.
1976   Austroasiatic Subgroupings and Prehistory in the Malay Peninsula. In *Austroasiatic Studies*, edited by P. N. Jenner, L. C. Thompson, and S. Starosta, pp. 37–128. University of Hawaii Press, Honolulu.
1985   In the Long Term: Three Themes in Malayan Cultural Ecology. In *Cultural Values and Tropical Ecology in Southeast Asia*, edited by K. Hutterer and T. Rambo, pp. 219–278. Center for South and Southeast Asian Studies, Ann Arbor, Mich.

Bodmer, W. F., and Cavalli-Sforza, L. L.
1974   The Analysis of Genetic Variation Using Migration Matrices. In *Genetic Distance*, edited by J. F. Crow and C. Denniston, pp. 45–61. Plenum, New York.

Carey, I.
1976   *Orang Asli: The Aboriginal Tribes of Peninsular Malaysia*. Oxford University Press, Kuala Lumpur.

Cavalli-Sforza, L. L., P. Menozzi, and A. Piazza
1993   Demic Expansions and Human Evolution. *Science* 259:639–646.

1994   *The History and Geography of Human Genes*. Princeton University Press, Princeton.

Dentan, R. K.

1968   *The Semai: A Nonviolent People of Malaya*. Holt, Rinehart and Winston, New York.

Dingle, H.

1996   *Migration: The Biology of Life on the Move*. Oxford University Press, Oxford.

Fix, A. G.

1978   The Role of Kin-Structured Migration in Genetic Microdifferentiation. *Annals of Human Genetics* 41:329–339.

1982   Genetic Structure of the Semai. In *Current Developments in Anthropological Genetics: Ecology and Population Structure*, edited by M. H. Crawford and J. H. Mielke, pp. 179–204. Plenum, New York.

1995   Malayan Paleosociology: Implications for Patterns of Genetic Variation Among the Orang Asli. *American Anthropologist* 97:313–323.

1999   *Migration and Colonization in Human Microevolution*. Cambridge University Press, Cambridge.

2000   Genes, Language, and Ethnic Groups: Reconstructing Orang Asli Prehistory. *Bulletin of the Indo-Pacific Prehistory Association* 19:11–16.

2002   Foragers, Farmers, and Traders in the Malayan Peninsula: Origins of Cultural and Biological Diversity. In *Forager-Traders in South and Southeast Asia: Long Term Histories*, edited by K. D. Morrison and L. L. Junker, pp. 185–202. Cambridge University Press, Cambridge.

Flatz, G.

1967   Hemoglobin E: Distribution and Population Dynamics. *Humangenetik* 3:189–234.

Forster P., and Matsumura S.

2005   Did Early Humans Go North or South? *Science* 308:965–966.

Headland, T. N., and L. A. Reid

1989   Hunter-Gatherers and Their Neighbors from Prehistory to the Present. *Current Anthropology* 30:43–51.

Livingstone, F. B.

1985   *Frequencies of Hemoglobin Variants: Thalassemia, the Glucose-6-Phosphate Dehydrogenase Deficiency, G6PD Variants, and Ovalocytosis in Human Populations*. Oxford University Press, New York.

Macaulay V., C. Hill, A. Achilli, C. Rengo, D. Clarke, W. Meehan, J. Blackburn, O. Semino, R. Scozzari, F. Cruciani, A. Taha, N. K. Shaari, J. M. Raja, P. Ismail, Z. Zainuddin, W. Goodwin, D. Bulbeck, H.-J. Bandelt, S. Oppenheimer, A. Torroni, and M. Richards

2005   Single, Rapid Coastal Settlement of Asia Revealed by Analysis of Complete Mitochondrial Genomes *Science* 308:1034–1036

Majumder, P. P.

2005   Southward Ho! *Journal of Biosciences* 30:293–294.

Melton T., R. Peterson, A. J. Redd, N. Saha, A. S. M. Sofro, J. Martinson, and M. Stoneking
1995   Polynesian Genetic Affinities with Southeast Asian Populations Identified by mtDNA Analysis. *American Journal of Human Genetics* 57:403–414.

Milner, A. C.
1978   A Note on "the Rawa." *Journal of the Malaysian Branch of the Royal Asiatic Society* 51:143–148.

Moore, J. H.
1994   Putting Anthropology Back Together Again: Ethnogenetic Critique of Cladistic Theory. *American Anthropologist* 96:925–948.

Ramos-Kuri, M., J. C. Farga, J. Zuniga, M. T. A. Guerrero, J. Granados, and F. J. Estrada
2005   Molecular Demonstration of SLC4A1 Gene Deletion in Two Mexican Patients with Southeast Asian Ovalocytosis. *Human Biology* 77:399–405.

Saha, N., H. W. Mak, J. S. H. Tay, J. A. M. A. Tan, P. S. Low, and M. Singh
1995   Population Genetic Studies among the Orang Asli (Semai Senoi) of Malaysia: Malayan Aborigines. *Human Biology* 67:37–57.

Schurr, T. G., and D. C. Wallace
2002   Mitochondrial DNA Diversity in Southeast Asian Populations. *Human Biology* 74:431–452.

Watkins, W. S., M. Bamshad, M. E. Dixon, B. Bhaskara Rao, J. M. Naidu, P. G. Reddy, B. V. R. Prasad, P. K. Das, P. C. Reddy, P. B. Gai, A. Bhanu, Y. S. Kusuma, J. K. Lum, P. Fischer, and L. B. Jorde
1999   Multiple Origins of the mtDNA 9-bp Deletion in Populations of South India. *American Journal of Physical Anthropology* 109:147–158.

Weidenreich, F.
1946   *Apes, Giants, and Man. Chicago*: University of Chicago Press, Chicago.

Weiss, K. M.
1988   In Search of Times Past: Gene Flow and Invasion in the Generation of Human Diversity. In *Biological Aspects of Human Migration*, edited by C. G. N. Mascie-Taylor and G. Lasker, pp. 130–166. Cambridge University Press, Cambridge.

Wobst, H. M.
1978   The Archaeo-Ethnology of Hunter-Gatherers or the Tyranny of the Ethnographic Record in Archaeology. *American Antiquity* 43:303–309.

13

Continuity and Change in Anthropological Perspectives on Migration

Insights from Molecular Anthropology

DEBORAH A. BOLNICK

Historically, anthropological discussions of migration have focused on migration as both a source and form of major change. The term "migration" has been used most frequently to refer to mass population movements over large distances and across sociocultural boundaries (Cabana 2002; Clark 2001). In most cases, it is assumed that these movements involve well-defined groups with distinct cultural and biological traits (Burmeister 2000). This characterization of migration suggests that immigrants to a new area will be clearly identifiable as foreigners, and Andresen has argued that "to demonstrate migration it is necessary to discover . . . a foreign group in the suspected immigration area" (2000:554). Many anthropologists also associate migration with population replacement, as in Rouse's description of migration as when "the people of one area expands into another area, replacing the latter's population" (1986:13). These formulations of migration clearly emphasize the association between migration and change: migrants experience change when they move from one physical and social environment to another and they produce change in the geographic region where they eventually settle.

As Cabana (this volume; 2002) argues, this conceptualization of migration (i.e., migration as a source and form of change) reflects the role that it has traditionally played in studies of human prehistory. In archaeological research, migration has generally been considered in the context of material culture change, as an explanation for discontinuities in the archaeological record. Similarly, in studies of prehistoric skeletal remains, physical anthropologists have often proposed migrations to account for changes in skeletal morphology over time. Migration hypotheses of this sort were especially popular among the culture historians and racial typologists of the early twentieth century (for example, see Childe 1925; Hooton 1930; and Parker 1916), but they have also played a role in more recent studies. Thus, while other sources of change certainly exist (e.g., cultural diffusion, in situ development, genetic drift, natural selection), migration has frequently served as a ready explanation for cultural and biological change in studies of human prehistory.

In this chapter, I consider the study of migration in molecular anthropology in light of these broader traditions. I examine how molecular anthropologists investigate migration, and I draw upon examples from genetic studies of Native Americans to illustrate the benefits and limitations of such research. I discuss two case studies in detail to show how molecular anthropology can yield important insights about both the process and impact of migration.

Migration Studies in Molecular Anthropology

Anthropologists have traditionally approached the study of prehistoric migration by examining archaeological remains, skeletal traits, linguistic patterns, and ethnographic evidence. Over the past few decades, the development of new techniques in molecular biology has made it possible to investigate past migrations using genetic data. Molecular anthropologists focus on the genetic correlates of migration, which exist because migrants alter the genetic makeup of the population at their destination when they settle and reproduce. In other words, the movement of people is accompanied by the movement of genes (known as gene flow), and this gene flow has a significant impact on the patterns of genetic variation among human populations. Those patterns comprise another important source of information about past population movements.

Genetic studies are also useful because they can help circumvent some of the problems that commonly arise in other anthropological studies. For example, many bioarchaeological studies focus on skeletal morphology, but skeletal traits are influenced by both genetic and environmental factors, making it difficult to determine the precise causes of morphological trait variation. In contrast, noncoding genetic loci are not directly influenced by environmental factors. Studies of these loci can therefore help separate the biological effects of migration from patterns produced by life history, environmental adaptation, and cultural practice (all of which may be confounded in studies of skeletal morphology). Similarly, it can sometimes be difficult to pinpoint the causes of cultural or linguistic patterns. When genetic data are considered in conjunction with cultural, linguistic, and archaeological evidence, it becomes easier to distinguish the effects of migration from the effects of trade, cultural diffusion, linguistic borrowing, and in situ innovation.

Molecular anthropologists rarely provide an explicit definition for "migration" in their studies, but the term is commonly used to refer to any type of movement that leads to gene flow. This definition comes from the field of population genetics, as does the practice of quantifying migration as the number of individuals who move from one population to another in a given generation. Because this understanding of migration differs from the minimal definition used in this volume (i.e., a one-way residential relocation to a different "environment"), I will use the term "movement" in the rest of this chapter to refer to what population geneticists (and many molecular anthropologists) call migration.

In general, molecular anthropologists employ two related methods to infer past human movements. Both begin with an analysis of the genetic composition of two or more populations to assess the genetic similarities and differences among them. While some similarities may be the result of chance or natural selection, similarities in the noncoding regions of the genome usually reflect shared ancestry among populations (i.e., the populations are derived from the same ancestral population) and/or the exchange of genes via the movement of individuals between populations. Several analytical approaches have been developed to determine the most likely cause(s) of genetic similarity, and these methods can estimate the number of individuals who moved from one place to another (Beerli and Felsenstein 1999, 2001; Hey and Nielsen 2004; Nielsen and Wakeley 2001; Slatkin 1985).

In the first of the two methods used to infer past human movements, molecular anthropologists compare contemporaneous populations from different geographic regions. Genetic similarities suggest that gene flow once connected the populations in those regions. For example, molecular anthropologists have conducted genetic studies of Native Americans and other populations from around the world to investigate the initial migration of people into the Americas (e.g., Achilli et al. 2008; Eshleman et al. 2003; Fagundes et al. 2008; Kitchen et al. 2008; Schurr 2004; Wang et al. 2007). Present-day Native Americans appear most genetically similar to indigenous populations in south-central Siberia (near Lake Baikal), so these studies suggest that the ancestors of Native Americans migrated from that region of Asia to the Americas (Derenko et al. 2001; Karafet et al. 1999; Schurr 2004). Because this method relies on genetic data from contemporaneous populations, either extant or ancient populations could be examined to infer past population movements.

In contrast, the second method requires genetic data from at least some ancient populations. In this approach, molecular anthropologists compare populations inhabiting the same geographic region but at different points in time. Genetic similarities in different populations suggest that there has been genetic continuity through time, making it unlikely that biologically distinct people moved into the region at some point in the past. If, however, significant genetic differences are observed, then the genetic data are consistent with the hypothesis of past immigration (and perhaps population replacement). An example of this approach is Kaestle and Smith's (2001) study, which uses genetic data from prehistoric and extant Native Americans in western Nevada to test the hypothesis that Numic-speakers migrated into the Great Basin and replaced the previous inhabitants of that area. Kaestle and Smith find significant genetic differences between the extant and ancient populations, so they conclude that the genetic data support the Numic expansion hypothesis. Thus, genetic *dissimilarity* is taken as evidence of population movement in this method, whereas genetic *similarity* indicates movement in the first method used to infer past human movement.

Even though molecular anthropologists usually define migration differently than the definition in this volume, the methodology described here is still compatible with this volume's definition and can be used to inform our understanding of several key variables. For example, molecular anthropology research can shed light on the structure and scale of migration by providing estimates of the number of migrants (see the case studies below for examples) and by indicating whether one or both sexes migrated (see the second case study below). The demographic impact of migration can also be assessed by determining how a migration affected the genetic makeup of the populations involved (as in the second method described above). Finally, genetic data may sometimes help reconstruct the distance migrants traveled. If studies of contemporaneous populations identify a potential source population, then the distance traveled can be estimated as the geographic distance between that source population and the migrants' destination. This estimate assumes that the source population has not moved since the migration in question, an assumption that will be discussed in more detail below.

It should be noted that genetic studies of migration cannot tell us about other key variables, such as the mode of migration or the motivations that led individuals to move from one location to another. Nor can genetic data clarify some aspects of a migration's structure, such as whether migrants moved in one large group or many small groups or whether the migration occurred over a long or short time span. Perhaps most important, though, we must remember that it can be difficult for molecular anthropologists to distinguish relatively permanent residential relocations (i.e., migrations) from temporary visits, which can also have a genetic impact if visitors leave behind genes (in the form of offspring) when they return home. If such visits are infrequent, then it is unlikely that they will significantly alter allele frequencies in the receiving population (especially if neutral alleles, or alleles not subject to natural selection, are studied). Evidence of significant gene flow will therefore indicate past migration in most cases, but the appropriateness of this assumption must be evaluated on a case-by-case basis.

Other limitations constrain what we can learn about past migrations from molecular anthropology. First, because it is easier to extract and analyze DNA from living individuals, the majority of genetic studies have compared extant populations from different geographic regions (i.e., the first approach described above). However, studies of extant populations provide information about only prehistoric migrants who still have descendants alive today. Any migrant who had no offspring (or whose lineage subsequently went extinct) will not be detected with this approach. Consequently, these studies cannot conclusively answer many questions about past migrations. As an example, consider the numerous genetic studies of extant Native Americans that have been conducted to investigate the initial peopling of the Americas (listed above). Even though virtually all these studies suggest that the founding population(s) migrated from Asia to the Americas, these studies cannot exclude the possibility that some prehistoric migrants came from elsewhere but left no living descendants.

Similarly, studies of extant populations provide information about where related groups live today, but they cannot tell us exactly where the ancestors of those people lived in the past. The ancestral population might have occupied the same region as one (or more) of the present-day populations, but it could have also lived in a completely different location. For instance, as mentioned earlier, many studies suggest that the ancestors of Native Americans came from south-central Siberia because extant Native Americans are most genetically similar to the present inhabitants of that region. While this scenario is certainly plausible, it is also plausible that the common ancestors of Native Americans and south-central Siberians lived elsewhere (such as in an intermediate location in Asia). In that case, both descendant populations would have migrated away from their shared ancestral lands. Since the genetic data are compatible with both scenarios, these studies cannot determine exactly where the founding population(s) lived before moving into the Americas.

Finally, just as cultural, linguistic, and morphological data can be misinterpreted, so can genetic data. The genetic signal of a past migration might be missed, especially if it has been obscured by subsequent changes in the DNA. Genetic patterns might also appear to indicate a past migration when they instead reflect natural selection or genetic drift (random changes from one generation to the next). Computer simulations can help us evaluate alternative explanations (e.g., Cabana et al. 2008), but incorrect inferences may still be drawn in some cases.

Despite these limitations, molecular anthropology can yield important insights about both the process and impact of migration. In particular, genetic data can be used to explore forms of migration that are less well studied, such as the small-scale, short-range, and incremental movements of individuals. These types of migration have received relatively little attention in the anthropological literature on the subject because it has traditionally focused on long-distance mass migration. However, small-scale migrations (involving isolated individuals or small groups), short-range migrations (occurring over shorter geographic distances), and incremental migrations (occurring in a stepwise fashion) can all have an impact. Such migrations influence the culture, language, and biological makeup of a region even in the absence of mass migration and population replacement. Furthermore, the importance of individuals and small groups moving *within* the bounds of established social networks (but still across some kind of sociocultural boundary) should not be discounted. Indeed, ethnographic, historical, and archaeological evidence all suggest that mass migration has been relatively rare; rather, most human movements have involved isolated individuals or families and have occurred within existing social networks (Adams et al. 1978; Burmeister 2000).

While we cannot hope to reconstruct every small-scale, short-range, or incremental migration in prehistory, we can examine the cumulative effects of such movements. In the two case studies below, I show how molecular anthropology can illuminate the effects of small-scale movements and migration on a localized scale, both of which have had a significant impact on the genetic structure of human populations.

Case Study 1: Migration and Cultural Exchange Among the Hopewell

For more than a century, archaeologists have studied a set of widespread but variable archaeological remains from the Middle Woodland period (100 B.C.–A.D. 400) in eastern North America (Figure 13.1A). These Hopewell assemblages are most common in Ohio, Illinois, and Indiana and are characterized by nonutilitarian grave goods made from imported materials, complex burial mounds, elaborate mortuary-processing facilities, and large geometric earthworks (Brose and Greber 1979; Carr and Case 2006; Charles and Buikstra 2006). These assemblages are thought to represent the remains of an interregional interaction sphere that connected local communities via trade networks and periodic ritual gatherings at corporate spaces. Despite these interactions, Hopewell communities did not belong to a single widespread culture. Substantial variability has been documented, for example, in the size of corporate ceremonial centers, in the nature of local Hopewell rituals, and in the composition of populations involved at any given site. This diversity

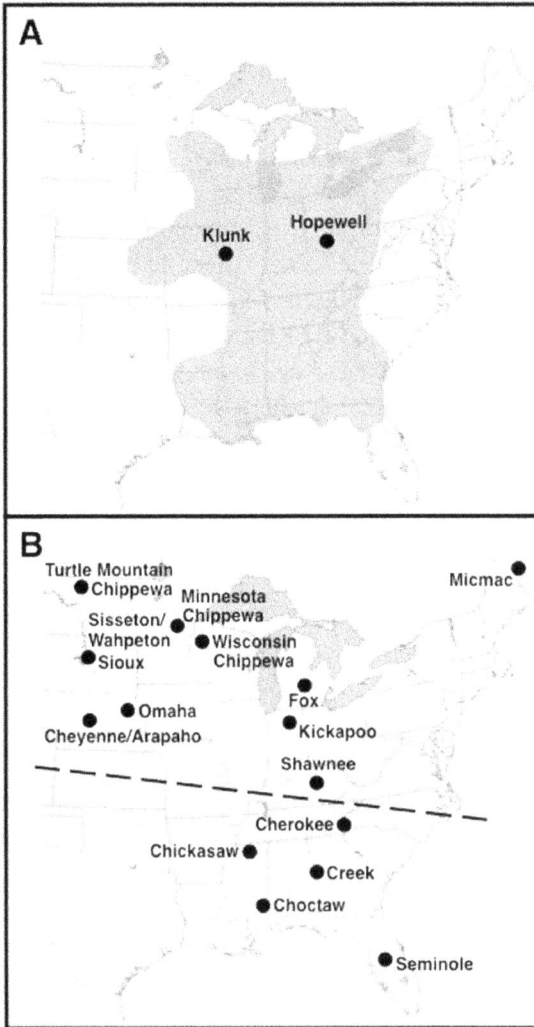

Figure 13.1. A: Locations of the sampled Hopewell sites and the approximate geographic range of the Hopewell phenomenon (shaded). B: Locations of the sampled populations in early historic times. The dashed line separates the northeastern and southeastern culture areas.

suggests that extensive cultural variation existed among Hopewell communities, both over time and across space.

While many aspects of the Hopewell phenomenon are now well understood, questions still remain about whether migration and gene flow accompanied the cultural exchange between Hopewell communities. Bioarchaeologists have examined cranial variation in Illinois and Ohio Hopewell populations to address this question, but the results have been contradictory. Jamison (1971) identified morphological similarities between some Illinois and Ohio Hopewell populations, whereas Reichs (1975) and Johnston (2002) found significant differences between roughly contemporaneous populations from the two regions. The findings of these studies may also be confounded by the fact that cranial variation reflects both genetic and nongenetic factors. Thus, it remains unclear if migration and gene flow connected the Middle Woodland communities in Illinois and Ohio.

To help address this question, Bolnick and Smith (2007) examined mitochondrial DNA (mtDNA) variation between two Hopewell burial populations from Illinois and Ohio. Mitochondrial DNA is maternally inherited, so it provides a measure of matrilineal relatedness between individuals and populations. In this study, mtDNA was extracted and analyzed from the skeletal remains of 39 individuals buried at the Pete Klunk Mound Group. This mortuary site is located on a bluff overlooking a large Middle Woodland habitation site on the Illinois River in Calhoun County, Illinois. The burial mounds were excavated in 1960–1961 (Perino 1968), and the remains of approximately 370 individuals were assigned to a Middle Woodland component dating to 175 ± 75 B.P. (Crane and Griffin 1963). Mound burial was the primary form of Middle Woodland mortuary activity, and the skeletal series at this site corresponds to a "typical" cemetery population but with a low frequency of the youngest individuals. These findings suggest that most community members were buried at the site, so this skeletal series is thought to be representative of the local population (Buikstra 1976).

Our analysis also included mtDNA data previously collected from 34 individuals interred in Mound 25 of the Hopewell mound group in Ross County, Ohio (Mills 2003). The Hopewell mound group is located at the epicenter of the Ohio Hopewell phenomenon, and radiocarbon and obsidian hydration dates from Mound 25 range from 78 B.C. to A.D. 398 (Carr and Case 2006). Both sets of ancient DNA data were collected using appropriate methods to ensure the authenticity of the data (Kaestle and Horsburgh 2002).

To investigate whether gene flow occurred between the two communities, we analyzed the mtDNA dataset using four methods for estimating gene flow: the rare alleles method (Slatkin 1985), the maximum likelihood program MIGRATE (Beerli and Felsenstein 1999, 2001), the likelihood/Bayesian program MDIV (Nielsen and Wakeley 2001), and the likelihood/Bayesian program IM (Hey and Nielsen 2004). The rare alleles method considers only allele frequencies, whereas the latter three methods take into account the ancestral relationships among alleles. MDIV and IM also explicitly model the effects of population divergence from a common ancestral population *and* the per-generation migration rate after that divergence.

Each method provided an estimate of the number of breeding individuals who moved between the two communities in each generation (N_em). The mean of these estimates is 39.9 individuals per generation; the median is 7.7

individuals per generation. While these numbers are not very large, population genetics theory suggests that $N_e m >1$ is sufficient to prevent genetic differentiation due to genetic drift (Slatkin 1985; Wright 1931). These results therefore indicate significant levels of gene flow between the two communities, and they demonstrate that genetic exchange accompanied the cultural exchange between Middle Woodland communities involved in the Hopewell phenomenon.

The genetic data do not specify whether this gene flow stemmed from residential relocations (migrations) or temporary visits, but migration seems the more likely source. The two sites are more than 400 miles apart, so it is unlikely that enough people made transient visits between them to produce the observed levels of gene flow. If migration did occur, the evidence suggests that it was not a single mass migration but rather repeated migrations of individuals or small groups over multiple generations. These individuals may have moved directly between the two sampled communities, but the observed genetic patterns could also be due to the cumulative effects of short-range and incremental migrations, perhaps via regional mating networks (Carr and Case 2006). Either way, these movements played an important role in shaping the genetic structure of the two communities.

Case Study 2: Migration and Postmarital Residence in Eastern North America

This second case study focuses on the individualized and short-range movements that accompany marriage in many human societies. While marital practices are highly variable, marriage often results in a change of residence for one spouse. In matrilocal societies, men leave the household or community in which they were raised to join that of their wife. In patrilocal societies, on the other hand, women move from their own household or community to that of their husband. While the exact movement varies from individual to individual and often occurs over a relatively short distance, these movements may still influence the cultural practices, languages, and patterns of genetic variation in human societies.

To investigate the impact of postmarital residence practices on human genetic structure, Bolnick et al. (2006) examined the patterns of mtDNA and Y-chromosome variation in eastern North America. As noted earlier, mtDNA is maternally inherited, so it reflects maternal relationships and female gene flow. In contrast, the male-specific region of the Y chromosome is strictly paternally inherited, so it can be used to assess paternal relationships and male gene flow. The 15 extant Native American populations that were sampled for this study are shown in Figure 13.1B, and they can be divided into two culture areas (the Southeast and Northeast). Populations from the southeastern culture area exhibited matrilineal kinship systems and matrilocal postmarital residence in the recent past, whereas populations from the northeastern culture area generally exhibited patrilineal kinship systems and patrilocal postmarital residence.

Our analyses showed that the patterns of mtDNA and Y-chromosome variation differed between the two culture areas. Specifically, the maternally and paternally inherited loci exhibited opposite patterns of genetic differentiation among populations. Mitochondrial DNA allele frequencies differed significantly among populations from the southeastern culture area, whereas populations from the northeastern culture area generally exhibited similar mtDNA frequencies. Accordingly, the Φ_{ST} summary statistic indicated a high level of mtDNA differentiation among populations in the Southeast ($\Phi_{ST} = 0.19$) but low mtDNA differentiation in the Northeast ($\Phi_{ST} = 0.06$). The Y-chromosome analysis, on the other hand, found greater genetic similarities among southeastern populations than among northeastern ones. Y chromosomes therefore indicated low differentiation among populations in the Southeast ($\Phi_{ST} = 0.04$) and high differentiation among populations in the Northeast ($\Phi_{ST} = 0.12$).

Differences in the genetic structure of males and females were assessed using the parameter N_V, which is calculated as $(1/\Phi_{ST}) - 1$ (Cavalli-Sforza and Bodmer 1971). Different N_V values reflect different rates of gene flow between populations and/or different breeding population sizes (Destro-Bisol et al. 2004). The Φ_{ST} values for the Northeast produced a ratio of mtDNA to Y chromosome N_V of 2.14, which indicates female gene flow and/or a female breeding population that was more than twice that of males. In contrast, the Φ_{ST} values for the Southeast produced a N_V ratio of 0.19, suggesting that male gene flow and/or the male breeding population was approximately five times greater than that of females in this area.

We also measured the rate of male and female gene flow among populations using the maximum likelihood program MIGRATE (Beerli and Felsenstein 1999, 2001). For each pair of populations, MIGRATE estimated the number of breeding males and females who moved between the two populations in each generation ($N_e m$). Male gene-flow estimates were based on the Y-chromosome data; female gene-flow estimates were based on the mtDNA data. The estimates for specific pairs of populations were quite variable, but male gene flow was generally higher in the Southeast than in the Northeast (mean Southeast $N_e m = 1.43$ vs. mean Northeast $N_e m = 0.77$). In contrast, female gene flow was generally higher in the Northeast than in the Southeast (mean Northeast $N_e m = 11.07$ vs. mean Southeast $N_e m = 3.86$).

These data show that asymmetric patterns of male and female gene flow have affected the genetic structure of Native American populations in eastern North America. Significantly, these patterns correlate precisely with past postmarital residence practices. As noted earlier, populations from the southeastern culture area exhibited matrilocality (Hudson 1976), in which males moved from their own household or community to that of their wife after marriage. Matrilocal systems therefore facilitated male movement and gene flow in each generation while fostering mtDNA differentiation. On the other hand, the populations from the northeastern culture area that we sampled all exhibited patrilocality (Mason 1981), which facilitated female movement and gene flow while augmenting Y-chromosome differentiation. These correlations show that postmarital residence practices have greatly influenced the genetic structure of human populations.

Because postmarital residence changes involve individualized movements and relatively short distances, anthropologists often do not consider them migrations. However, postmarital residence changes are permanent residential relocations, and the movements studied here did cross both sociocultural and linguistic boundaries. These movements therefore meet the definition of migration in this volume, and this study shows that individualized and localized migration can have a significant genetic impact. In fact, because the postmarital residence systems of many Native American populations changed during the nineteenth and twentieth centuries (Eggan 1937; Perdue 1989), the effect of marriage-related migration is great enough that it can be detected for at least five to six generations after practices have shifted (assuming a generation length of 30 years).

Conclusions

Although migration studies in molecular anthropology have a number of limitations, they can yield important insights about the process and impact of migration. In particular, they can help us reconstruct the structure and scale of past migrations and they allow us to assess a migration's impact on the genetic composition of the populations involved. They also show that it is important to investigate less-well-studied forms of migration, such as the small-scale, short-range, and incremental movements of individuals. As the two case studies here demonstrate, such migrations can have a profound impact on the genetic structure of human populations. Indeed, the cumulative effects of such migrations may be just as significant as the effects of larger population movements.

Migration studies in molecular anthropology also provide an important reminder that migration is not always associated with upheaval and major change. Rather, some forms of migration comprise a normal part of everyday life. Migration can also be viewed as something that produces similarity rather than difference since communities become more similar to one another as a result of the genetic, cultural, and linguistic exchange that accompanies migration. Migration is therefore a source of continuity as well as change.

Acknowledgments

Thanks to the Native Americans who donated samples for genetic analysis and to Della Collins Cook and the Bioanthropology Laboratory at Indiana University for providing skeletal samples from the Pete Klunk Mound Group. The Office of Human Research Protection at the University of California, Davis approved all sampling protocols for the study of extant Native Americans from eastern North America and the extraction and analysis of ancient DNA from the skeletal samples from the Pete Klunk Mound Group.

References

Achilli, A., U. A. Perego, C. M. Bravi, M. D. Coble, Q.-P. Kong, S. R. Woodward, A. Salas, A. Torroni, and H.-J. Bandelt
2008 The Phylogeny of the Four Pan-American mtDNA Haplogroups: Implications for Evolutionary and Disease Studies. *PLoS One* 3:e1764.
Adams, W. Y., D. P. Van Gerven, and R. S. Levy
1978 The Retreat from Migrationism. *Annual Review of Anthropology* 7:483–532.
Andresen, M.
2000 Comment on "Archaeology and Migration." *Current Anthropology* 41:553–554.
Beerli, P., and J. Felsenstein
1999 Maximum-Likelihood Estimation of Migration Rates and Effective Population Numbers in Two Populations Using a Coalescent Approach. *Genetics* 152:763–773.
2001 Maximum Likelihood Estimation of a Migration Matrix and Effective Population Sizes in N Subpopulations by Using a Coalescent Approach. *Proceedings of the National Academy of the Sciences USA* 98:4563–4568.
Bolnick, D. A., D. I. Bolnick, and D. G. Smith
2006 Asymmetric Male and Female Genetic Histories Among Native Americans from Eastern North America. *Molecular Biology and Evolution* 23:2161–2174.
Bolnick, D. A., and D. G. Smith
2007 Migration and Social Structure Among the Hopewell: Evidence from Ancient DNA. *American Antiquity* 72:627–644.
Brose, D. S., and N. B. Greber (editors)
1979 *Hopewell Archaeology*. Kent State University, Kent.

Buikstra, J. E.

1976   *Hopewell in the Lower Illinois River Valley: A Regional Approach to the Study of Biological Variability and Mortuary Activity.* Monograph No. 2. Northwestern University. Evanston, Illinois.

Burmeister, S.

2000   Archaeology and Migration. *Current Anthropology* 41:539–567.

Cabana, G. S.

2002   *A Demographic Simulation Model to Assess Prehistoric Migrations.* Unpublished Ph.D. dissertation, University of Michigan, Ann Arbor.

Cabana, G. S., K. L. Hunley, and F. A. Kaestle

2008   Population Continuity or Replacement? A Novel Computer Simulation Approach and its Application to the Numic Expansion (Western Great Basin, USA). *American Journal of Physical Anthropology* 135:438–447.

Carr, C., and D. T. Case (editors)

2006   *Gathering Hopewell: Society, Ritual, and Ritual Interaction.* Springer, New York.

Cavalli-Sforza, L. L., and W. Bodmer

1971   *The Genetics of Human Populations.* Freeman, San Francisco.

Charles, D. K., and J. E. Buikstra (editors)

2006   *Recreating Hopewell.* University Press of Florida, Gainesville.

Childe, V. G.

1925   *The Dawn of European Civilization.* Kegan Paul, London.

Clark, J. J.

2001   *Tracking Prehistoric Migrations: Pueblo Settlers among the Tonto Basin Hohokam.* Anthropological Papers of the University of Arizona no. 65. University of Arizona Press, Tucson.

Crane, H. R., and J. B. Griffin

1963   University of Michigan Radiocarbon Dates VIII. *Radiocarbon* 5:228–253.

Derenko, M. V., T. Grzybowski, B. A. Malyarchuk, J. Czarny, D. Miscicka-Sliwka, and I. A. Zakharov

2001   The Presence of Mitochondrial Haplogroup X in Altaians from South Siberia. *American Journal of Human Genetics* 69:237–241.

Destro-Bisol, G., F. Donati, V. Coia, I. Boschi, F. Verginelli, A. Caglià, S. Tofanelli, G. Spedini, and C. Capelli

2004   Variation of Female and Male Lineages in Sub-Saharan Populations: The Importance of Sociocultural Factors. *Molecular Biology and Evolution* 21:1673–1682.

Eggan, F.

1937   Historical Changes in the Choctaw Kinship System. *American Anthropologist* 39:34–52.

Eshleman, J. A., R. S. Malhi, and D. G. Smith

2003   Mitochondrial DNA Studies of Native Americans: Conceptions and Misconceptions of the Population Prehistory of the Americas. *Evolutionary Anthropology* 12:7–18.

Fagundes, N. J. R., R. Kanitz, R. Eckert, A. C. S. Valls, M. R. Bogo, F. M. Salzano, D. G. Smith, W. A. Silva, Jr., M. A. Zago, A. K. Ribeiro-dos-Santos, S. E. B. Santos, M. L. Petzl-Erler, and S. L. Bonatto

2008 Mitochondrial Population Genomics Supports a Single Pre-Clovis Origin with a Coastal Route for the Peopling of the Americas. *American Journal of Human Genetics* 82:583–592.

Hey, J., and R. Nielsen

2004 Multilocus Methods for Estimating Population Sizes, Migration Rates and Divergence Time, with Applications to the Divergence of *Drosophila pseudoobscura* and *D. persimilis*. *Genetics* 167:747–760.

Hooton, E. A.

1930 *The Indians of Pecos Pueblo*. Yale University Press, New Haven, Conn.

Hudson, C. M.

1976 *The Southeastern Indians*. University of Tennessee Press, Knoxville.

Jamison, P. L.

1971 A Demographic and Comparative Analysis of the Albany Mounds (Illinois) Hopewell Skeletons. In *The Indian Mounds at Albany, Illinois*, edited by E. B. Herold, Appendix I. Davenport Museum Anthropological Papers, no. 1. Davenport Academy of Natural Sciences, Davenport, Iowa.

Johnston, C. A.

2002 *Culturally Modified Human Remains from the Hopewell Mound Group*. Unpublished Ph.D. dissertation, Ohio State University, Columbus.

Kaestle, F. A., and K. A. Horsburgh

2002 Ancient DNA in Anthropology: Methods, Applications, and Ethics. *Yearbook of Physical Anthropology* 45:92–130.

Kaestle, F. A., and D. G. Smith

2001 Ancient Mitochondrial DNA Evidence for Prehistoric Population Movement: The Numic Expansion. *American Journal of Physical Anthropology* 115:1–12.

Karafet, T. M., S. L. Zegura, O. Posukh, L. Osipova, A. Bergen, J. Long, D. Goldman, W. Klitz, S. Harihara, P. de Knijff, V. Wiebe, R. C. Griffiths, A. R. Templeton, and M. F. Hammer

1999 Ancestral Asian Source(s) of New World Y-Chromosome Founder Haplotypes. *American Journal of Human Genetics* 64:817–831.

Kitchen, A., M. M. Miyamoto, and C. J. Mulligan

2008 A Three-Stage Colonization Model for the Peopling of the Americas. *PLoS One* 3:e1596.

Mason, R. J.

1981 *Great Lakes Archaeology*. Academic Press, New York.

Mills, L.

2003 *Mitochondrial DNA Analysis of the Ohio Hopewell of the Hopewell Mound Group*. Unpublished Ph.D. dissertation, Ohio State University, Columbus.

Nielsen, R., and J. Wakeley

2001 Distinguishing Migration from Isolation: A Markov Chain Monte Carlo Approach. *Genetics* 158:885–896.

Parker, A. C.

1916 The Origin of the Iroquois as Suggested by Their Archaeology. *American Anthropologist* 18:479–507.

Perdue, T.

1989 Cherokee Women and the Trail of Tears. *Journal of Women's History* 1:14–30.

Perino, G.

1968 The Pete Klunk Mound Group, Calhoun County, Illinois: The Archaic and Hopewell Occupations. *Illinois Archaeological Survey Bulletin* 6:9–124.

Reichs, K. J.

1975 *Biological Variability and the Hopewell Phenomenon: An Interregional Approach.* Unpublished Ph.D. dissertation, Northwestern University, Evanston, Illinois.

Rouse, I.

1986 *Migrations in Prehistory: Inferring Population Movement from Cultural Remains.* Yale University Press, New Haven, Conn.

Schurr, T. G.

2004 The Peopling of the New World: Perspectives from Molecular Anthropology. *Annual Review of Anthropology* 33:551–583.

Slatkin, M.

1985 Rare Alleles as Indicators of Gene Flow. *Evolution* 39:53–65.

Wang S., C. M. Lewis, M. Jakobsson, S. Ramachandran, N. Ray, G. Bedoya, W. Rojas, M. V. Parra, J. A. Molina, C. Gallo, G. Mazzotti, G. Poletti, K. Hill, A. M. Hurtado, D. Labuda, W. Klitz, R. Barrantes, M. C. Bortolini, F. M. Salzano, M. L. Petzl-Erler, L. T. Tsuneto, E. Llop, F. Rothhammer, L. Excoffier, M. W. Feldman, N. A. Rosenberg, and A. Ruiz-Linares

2007 Genetic Variation and Population Structure in Native Americans. *PLoS Genetics* 3:2049–2067.

Wright, S.

1931 Evolution in Mendelian Populations. *Genetics* 16:97–159.

14

Migration Muddles in Prehistory

The Distinction between Model-Bound and Model-Free Methods

SUSAN R. FRANKENBERG AND LYLE W. KONIGSBERG

The study of past human migration has followed varying trajectories in bio-archaeology and paleoanthropology over the past half-century. Bioarchaeo-logical studies have used biological distance analysis to evaluate continuity of regional populations, identify external migration, and address questions of intraregional marital migration and residence patterns. These studies, sum-marized most recently in Stojanowski and Schillaci (2006), focus primarily on within-site analysis, but even this level of analysis may reveal the effects of past migrations. Steadman (2001) is a good recent example of a bioarchaeo-logical analysis that focuses on the question of migration between regions, and Konigsberg (2006) summarizes some of the additional literature relevant to the bioarchaeological study of past migrations. Past bioarchaeological studies of migration have not, however, clearly articulated a formal basis for evaluat-ing competing hypotheses of regional continuity versus wholesale migration from another region and have tended to emphasize statistical significance testing instead of estimating the population genetic patterns. Paleoanthro-pological studies of the history of modern human origins, in contrast, have generated a number of suggested approaches for looking at the question of regional continuity versus large-scale migration (e.g., Cole 1996; Eswaran et al. 2005; Konigsberg 1997; Sokal et al. 1997; Waddle 1994). Unfortunately, the paleoanthropological studies of migration face the issue of how to construct hypothetical biological-distance matrices and the problem of large estimation errors due to small sample sizes.

The disconnect between bioarchaeology and paleoanthropology in how migration should be evaluated is curious, given that both areas are often concerned with the question of regional continuity versus population re-placement, albeit on different scales. The disconnect and some of the migra-tion muddles resulting within each area can be attributed to fundamental differences in how human biological variation has been analyzed. Relethford and Lees' (1982) influential *Yearbook of Physical Anthropology* article, "The Use of Quantitative Traits in the Study of Human Population Structure," follows W. W. Howells in making a useful distinction between model-free and model-bound methods for analyzing human biological variation. Model-free methods typically look at relationships between trait data and such external factors as geography, time, linguistics, or cultural distance. These analyses are motivated in a general way by population genetic models but do not include estimation of genetic parameters in the underlying models. Model-bound methods, in contrast, adopt a particular population genetic model and then estimate one or more genetic parameters.

The distinction between model-free and model-bound methods for analyzing human population structure can be illustrated using three previously published analyses of prehistoric human data. None of these analyses is, strictly speaking, a model-bound analysis, yet they do make use of population genetic models to varying extents. The first example, Diane Waddle's (1994) work on the origin of anatomically modern *Homo sapiens*, is a model-free analysis. Waddle's analysis, graphed by Tim Cole (1996:481), compares hypothetical distance matrices from regional-continuity and replacement models to biological distances. In addition to evaluating strict single-origin and regional-continuity models, Waddle (1994) examines hybrid models with varying degrees of gene flow between different geographic regions during specific geological time periods. Despite referring to various models of population history, Waddle's approach is model free under Relethford and Lees' (1982) classification, since she was not attempting to estimate population genetic parameters.

The second study, Alan Rogers's (1995) thought experiment for evaluating the regional continuity debate in human paleontology, is an example of an analysis poised between model-free and model-bound methods. Rogers models cranial traits at two time periods in three or more regions with varying degrees of long-range migration and suggests that the bivariate correlation between cranial traits over time can be used as a measure of regional continuity. This analysis on the surface appears to be model bound, given Rogers's measure of regional continuity. However, regional continuity is not a population genetic parameter in the same sense as effective population size or migration rate.

The third analysis, Konigsberg and Blangero's (1993) simulation of the peopling of Polynesia, has some elements of a model-bound analysis. These authors simulated expected Mahalanobis distances for cranial traits under within-group kinships of 0, 0.03, 0.05 and 0.1 and compared the results with actual Mahalanobis distances calculated from W. W. Howells's craniometric data. They showed that actual distances for six craniometrics between Tolai and Moriori required abnormally high within-group kinships that could not be explained by drift alone. This study was model bound in the sense that it estimated population distances from quantitative multivariate genetic trait values and evaluated the fit of these values under population genetic models of drift, founder effect, and selection on founders. But the study did not attempt to estimate effective population sizes or migration rates, as one would expect to see in a model-bound analysis.

Theoretically, model-bound methods should be preferred over model-free methods because they explain biological variation in terms of clear, mathematically defined processes. In addition, model-free methods have relatively limited applicability in resolving questions surrounding past migration because they essentially seek ad hoc explanations for biological variation in external variables. Model-free methods also are problematic because they adopt a classic frequentist hypothesis-testing framework in a situation where specification of a null hypothesis and concepts of statistical significance are unclear. This point is amply illustrated in Cabana (2002) and Cabana et al. (2008), who showed that statistical significance cannot necessarily be used to argue for or against any particular historical scenario. Nevertheless, model-free methods for analyzing human biological variation have been more commonly applied to prehistoric data than model-bound methods for a variety of reasons. Model-free methods also have been extremely useful in demonstrating that isolation by distance models do typically hold for circumscribed regions within prehistory.

To date, the best example of a model-bound analysis in bioarchaeology is Sciulli and Mahaney's (1991) study of drift versus selection as explanations for phenotypic trends in the prehistoric Ohio Valley. In their study they were able to estimate effective population sizes after assuming selective neutrality and to estimate the amount of truncation selection necessary after assuming infinite population sizes. This study clearly demonstrates that in model-bound analyses, one can estimate population genetic parameters such as effective population size or the amount of truncation selection. In studies of past migration, it is the migration rates that are ultimately of interest. We should be careful to note that the calculation of F_{ST}, an R matrix, or the regression of distances from the centroid onto variances (Relethford and Blangero 1990) does not constitute a model-bound analysis per se. It is only with the estimation of migration rates or a migration matrix (Blangero 1990) that a bioarchaeological study of migration could truly be considered to be model bound.

Both bioarchaeological and paleoanthropological studies of past human migration point out the need for clearly defined and testable models of how measurable characteristics should behave under various migration scenarios. Unfortunately, such model-bound analyses can be difficult to apply in prehistory because many different scenarios can produce the same data outcome. For example, a biological distance matrix can be converted to a matrix of average kinship coefficients within and between demes, but this does not lead to estimation of effective population sizes or migration rates. Our goal here is to evaluate what analyses of prehistoric human population structure can tell us about past migration, given the complexity of potential migration and population histories.

To address this problem, we have adopted a quantitative genetic model following Konigsberg and Blangero (1993) and have simulated data on six quantitative traits for two demes, allowing for different migration histories. We focused strictly on quantitative genetic traits, including both metric traits and so-called nonmetric traits that can be considered as quantitative traits if we use the threshold model. Because what we have to say is motivated by quantitative genetics, it may have relatively little applicability to genetic-marker and trace-element methods. We considered the two migrational extremes of complete continuity and complete replacement and used simulation results with different scales of migration and different lengths of postmigration drift to evaluate two issues: (1) How big must a migration event be to be biologically detectable? and (2) How long after the event will it be detectable given small population size and drift?

The Quantitative Genetic Model and Simulation Method

Following the method outlined in Konigsberg and Blangero (1993), we started with two populations each with 100 individuals and followed six quantitative genetic traits. The six-by-six additive genetic variance-covariance and environmental variance-covariance matrix among traits is taken from Konigsberg and Blangero's Table 2, which they obtained using a phenotypic variance-covariance matrix from Howells's (1989) craniometric data, and the cephalometric heritabilities and additive genetic correlations among traits from Black's (1982) dissertation. For the founding generation, we simulated the environmental deviation (x_e) for each of the 200 individuals (100 within two populations) using equation (1):

$$x_e = \mathbf{E}^{1/2} z_e \qquad\qquad (1)$$

and found the additive genetic deviations (x_a) using equation (2):

$$x_a = \mathbf{G}^{1/2} z_a \qquad\qquad (2)$$

where z_e and z_a are six-by-one-column vectors of standard random normal numbers and matrices to the half-powers represent the Cholesky decompositions (matrix "square root") of the environmental variance-covariance matrix (**E**) and additive genetic variance-covariance matrix (**G**), respectively. The trait value for each individual is then the sum of the environmental and additive genetic deviations.

In the current generation, we randomly chose two individuals to be parents for each of 99 individuals within the two populations (with the possibility of selfing). We simulated the environmental deviations for these offspring using equation (1) while we simulated the additive genetic deviations for these offspring using equation (3):

$$x_{ao} = 0.5\, x_{af} + 0.5\, x_{am} + \sqrt{0.5}\,\mathbf{G}^{1/2}\, z_a \qquad (3)$$

where x_{af} and x_{am} are the simulated additive genetic deviations for the father and mother and the final term is for segregation at polygenetic loci. In each generation, we simulated one individual in each of the two populations as a founder using equations (1) and (2). We simulated this individual to represent a "systematic pressure" due to a long-range migrant (Morton 1969).

All simulations, which we ran using the GNU free software graphics and statistical package R, proceeded as outlined above for 50 generations. Based on 25 years per generation, this allowed a settling-in period of 1,250 years. This "early" period represents a period of drift and no migration other than the systematic pressure of a single founder per generation. At the end of these 50 generations, we recorded the phenotypic deviations for all individuals and then allowed for a possible migration event from one population to the other such that the immigrants replaced an equal number of individuals in the population into which they migrated. The single migration event assumed a varying number of migrants who contributed genetically to the receiving population; we set the number of migrants at 0, 10, 20, 25, 40, 50, 60, 75, 80, and 100 for various runs. We chose migrants with replacement because that model keeps the "breeding values" of migrants in the population from which they emigrated. It was thus unnecessary to simulate population growth in the population from which they migrated.

We then began the drift process anew following the previously described simulation of two regional populations with effective sizes of 100. We continued to simulate data on six quantitative traits through additional generations following the migration event and observed each population of 100 individuals at differing generational points in time. The number of generations after migration was set at 1, 2, 3, 4, 5, 10, 15, 20, 30, and 50 for each number of migrants. These values for the postmigration populations constituted a "late" period that represented a period of migration followed by genetic drift. We thus constructed the simulations to allow periods of drift with no migration, single unidirectional short-range migration events of varying sizes, and subsequent periods of drift in two geographically isolated populations subject to a low systematic pressure of long-range migration. We sampled quantitative trait values both immediately preceding migration and at specific generational times after migration.

The results of each simulation run consisted of phenotypic deviations (i.e., quantitative trait values) observed after 50 generations of drift for 100 individuals in each of two populations and observed again at some set number of generations after the migration event for 100 individuals in each of two populations. We labeled the first set of observations "E" (for early period) and the second set of observations "L" (for late period). We then used a series of calculations to make these results comparable and interpretable. First, we used the six quantitative traits from this total of 400 individuals to calculate a biological distance matrix (D^2). The D^2 matrix was then converted to a four-by-four R matrix (Harpending and Ward 1982; Relethford and Blangero 1990; Rogers and Harpending 1986). The four-by-four elements of the R matrix represented the relationships between the two populations sampled at two points in time. To calculate the R matrix we specified an average trait heritability of 0.35 (Cheverud 1988; Konigsberg and Ousley 1995). In reality, the heritability estimate was only necessary to calculate F_{ST} and acted to scale the R matrix.

We ran each simulation 100 times and averaged the R matrices, which was possible since the R matrix was a standardized variance-covariance matrix around the population centroid. We then ordinated the average R matrices using principal coordinates analysis. In other words, we used principal coordinates analysis to extract three dimensions from the four-by-four average R matrix, and the resulting three-dimensional "map" of the four populations exactly reproduced the R matrix. Finally, we used a generalized Procrustes analysis, with possible reflection and with size removed, so that we could show simulation results in similar orientations. Thus, we could average and plot the 100 rounds of simulation for any particular scenario so we could visually interpret the effect of migration on the simulated craniometric biological distances.

Simulation Results

We ran the described simulation using different scales of migration (from 0 to 100 individuals) and different lengths of postmigration drift (from 1 to 50 generations) in order to evaluate how and when past migration events might be biologically detectable in the face of small population size and genetic drift. Rather than discussing each run, we will first consider the two extreme cases of complete continuity with no migration and complete replacement with 100 migrants. We will then summarize our findings concerning the number of migrants and the number of generations by comparing the effects of the number of migrants at 1, 10, and 50 generations after migration for 0, 20, 40, 60, 80, and 100 migrants. The results are presented as ordinated three-dimensional plots of principal coordinates, or biological-distance maps, where a dashed line indicates one population, a solid line represents the other population, E is the early premigration observation after 50 generations of drift, and L is the late observation some set number of generations after the migration event. Note that migration was always unidirectional, involving genetic movement of some number of "dashed-line" migrants into the "solid-line" population.

Figure 14.1 shows the simplest case, where there are no migrants and where the populations are observed after 1, 5, 10, 20, 30, and 50 generations of additional genetic drift following the initial 50 generations. Where we recorded the phenotypic deviations for all individuals after only one additional generation of drift (as shown in the upper-left biological-distance map in the figure), the dashed-line early (E) and late (L) values are near each other, as are the solid-line early (E) and late (L) values, because the early and late samples represent a single population separated by only one generation of drift. The dashed- and solid-line populations are relatively far from one another, separated by the first principal coordinate shown on the horizontal axis, because these populations bear no genetic relationship to one another. As we proceed through time by moving from left to right and top to bottom in Figure 14.1, through 5, 10, 20 30, and finally 50 generations, we see that the late samples within each population (dashed-line and solid-line) have differentiated from the early samples because of genetic drift. This figure illustrates the rather obvious conclusion that drift has a small effect over small numbers of generations for populations with effective sizes of 100 but that the cumulative effect of drift can be large.

Figure 14.2 shows the other extreme case, where there is complete population replacement after 50 generations of drift. Here the solid-line population is replaced by 100 migrants from the dashed-line population and we recorded phenotypic deviations for all individuals after 1, 5, 10, 20, 30, and 50 additional generations of postmigration drift from left to right and top to bottom in the figure. As we are referring to the dashed-line and solid-line populations as representing regional populations, the solid-line late population here is really a dashed-line population now living in "solid-line country." Because the late solid-line population is entirely derived from the early dashed-line population, while the early solid-line population is unrelated to any other group

1 generation   5 generations   10 generations

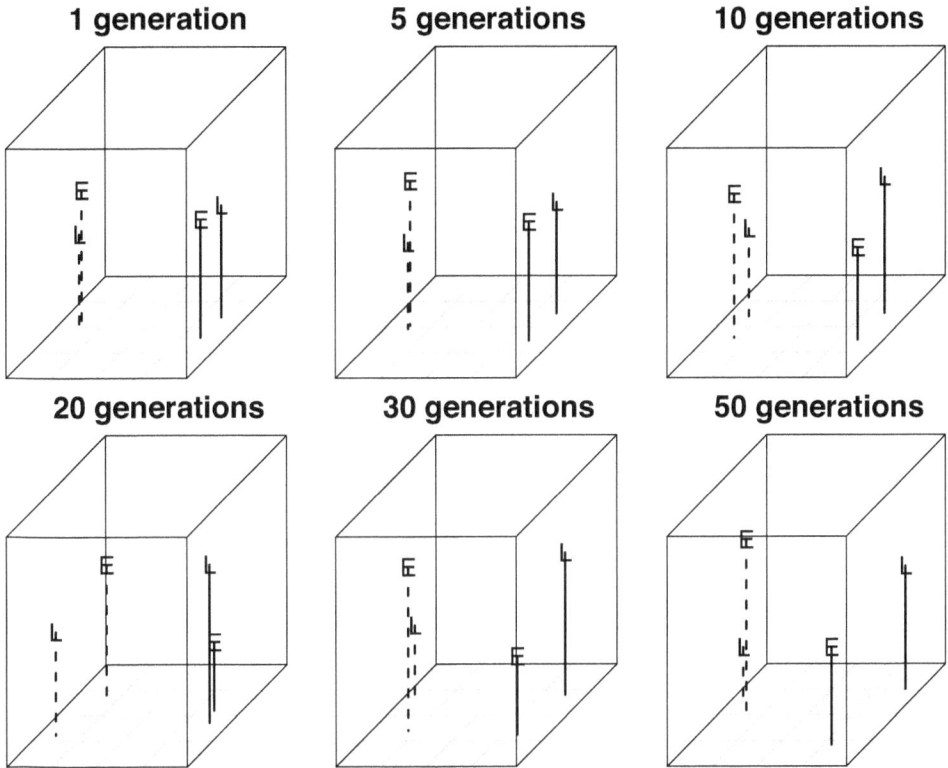

20 generations   30 generations   50 generations

Figure 14.1. Complete continuity. Biological distance maps of the simulation results for the simplest case of no migration, or complete population continuity. E indicates the value observed for each population (dashed and solid lines) after 50 generations of drift. From left to right and top to bottom across the figure, L indicates the value observed after 1, 5, 10, 20, 30 and 50 additional generations of drift.

shown, after only one generation of drift we get the biological distance map shown in the upper left of Figure 14.2. With time, again measured as 5, 10, 20, 30, and finally 50 generations, genetic drift eventually brings the populations back to a configuration that is difficult to distinguish from complete regional continuity.

Now let's consider some less extreme cases of migration. In these simulation runs, we varied the number of migrants at 20, 40, 60, and 80 individuals after 50 generations of initial drift and then examined the late-period populations after 1, 10, and 50 generations of additional postmigration drift. The results of the less-extreme simulations are presented in Figures 14.3, 14.4, and 14.5 for 1, 10, and 50 generations of postmigration drift, respectively. We have added the cases of no migration (0 migrants) in the upper-left corner and

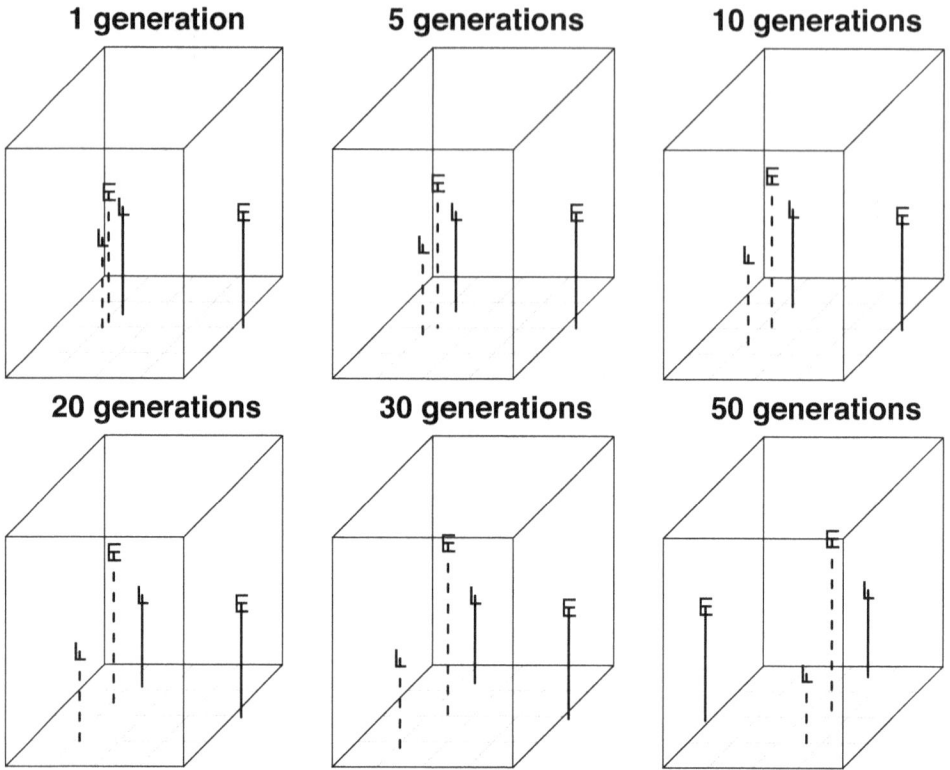

Figure 14.2. Complete replacement. Biological distance maps of the simulation results for the extreme case of complete population replacement (100 migrants). E again indicates the value observed for each population after 50 generations of drift. From left to right and top to bottom across the figure, L indicates the value observed after 1, 5, 10, 20, 30 and 50 generations of additional postmigration drift.

complete replacement (100 migrants) in the lower-right corner of each figure for comparison. The remaining four biological distance maps in each figure are arranged in order of increasing number of migrants from left to right and top to bottom.

Figure 14.3 shows the cases where after 50 generations of independent drift, 20, 40, 60, and 80 migrants from the early dashed-line population migrate to "solid-line country" and replace the equivalent numbers of individuals in the solid-line population. Each of these migration events is followed by one generation of drift. Based on these results, clear displacement of the late solid-line population toward the dashed-line population values occurs only for cases of 60 or more migrants and slight displacement occurs in the case of 40 migrants. These results suggest that migration will be difficult to catch, even soon after

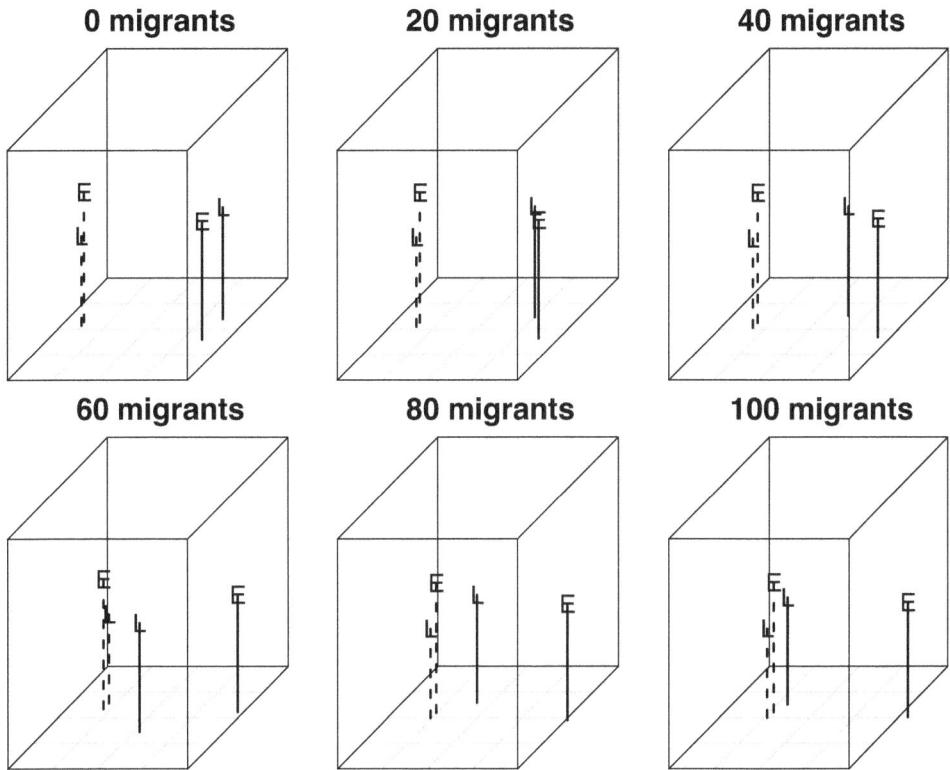

Figure 14.3. Varying numbers of migrants with one generation postmigration drift. Biological distance maps for simulations of 20, 40, 60 and 80 migrants after 50 generations of pre-migration drift and 1 generation of postmigration drift.

it has occurred, unless the relative proportion of migrants is very high. Figure 14.4 shows that if we consider these same numbers of migrants but record the late-period phenotypic deviations after 10 generations of postmigration drift, we lose some of this displacement due to drift. Finally, in Figure 14.5 we see that if we consider these same numbers of migrants after 50 generations of postmigration drift, this displacement is completely lost due to drift. Detecting biological or genetic differences due to migration consequently seems to become an impossible task when we are faced with large time spans.

Discussion

In describing studies of past human migration above, we noted the need for clearly defined testable models of how measurable characteristics should behave under various migration scenarios. We also noted that such model-bound

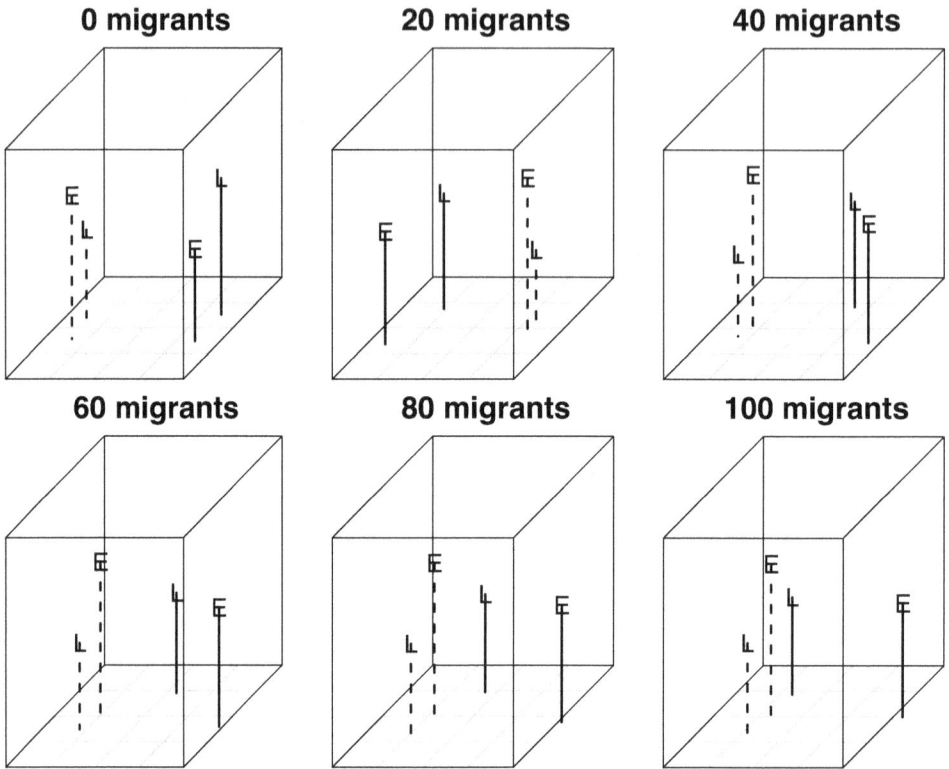

Figure 14.4. Varying numbers of migrants with ten generations postmigration drift. Biological distance maps for simulations of 20, 40, 60 and 80 migrants after 50 generations of pre-migration drift and 10 generations of postmigration drift.

analyses could be difficult to apply in prehistory because many different scenarios can produce the same data outcome. The simulation exercise presented here is intended as a first step toward a formal basis for addressing the question of regional continuity versus population replacement for bioarchaeological cases. One of the motivating questions for the simulation was what it would take to demonstrate in situ development of an archaeological culture or population rather than an externally derived one. More generally, what can model-bound analyses of prehistoric human population structure tell us about past migration, given the complexity of potential migration and population histories?

The simulation results presented here show that migration has a small or undetectable biological effect in terms of quantitative trait values when population sizes and migrant numbers are small, when migration is a single event, and when drift has a long time to operate. In the absence of a migration event,

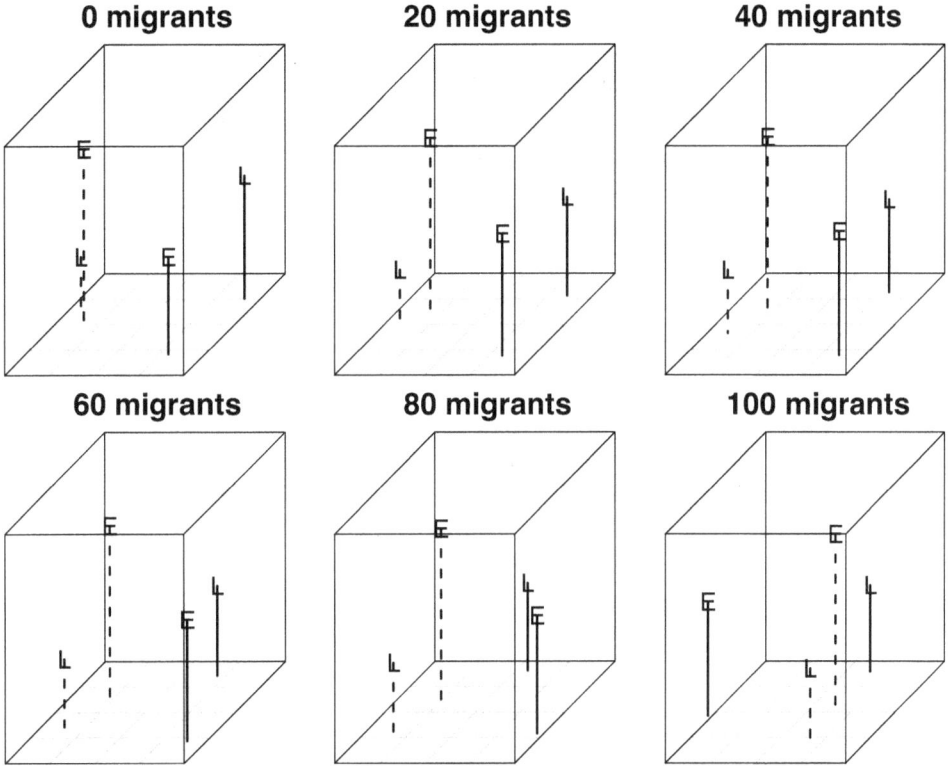

Figure 14.5. Varying numbers of migrants with fifty generations postmigration drift. Biological distance maps for simulations of 20, 40, 60 and 80 migrants after 50 generations of pre-migration drift and 50 generations of postmigration drift.

drift has a small effect over small numbers of generations for populations with effective sizes of 100, but its cumulative effect over many generations can be large. Further, in the case of complete population replacement, genetic drift can eventually bring populations back to a configuration that is difficult to distinguish from complete regional continuity. The simulation runs with varying number of migrants demonstrate that clear displacement of quantitative trait values toward the population contributing migrants occurs only when at least half of the receiving population is replaced by migrants, that such migration is difficult to catch after 10 generations of drift, and that this displacement is completely lost due to drift after 50 generations.

The simulation results also provide some answers to the question of when and how well we can detect genetic or biological effects of migration. The answer is that we cannot detect such effects very well in small populations unless migration involves a proportionately large number of individuals and we manage to measure biological variation within a few generations after migration occurs. The results do not, however, put us much closer to answering the question of whether or not we will reach a state where we can estimate effective population sizes or migration rates for prehistoric populations. The methods we present here do provide us with the tools for creating formal ways to evaluate how large a migration event must be to be biologically detectable and how long after the event it will be detectable given small population size and drift.

Conclusion

Model-bound analyses of prehistoric human population structure should be preferred over model-free methods because they explain biological variation in terms of clear, mathematically defined processes; avoid ad hoc explanations for biological variation based on such external variables as geography, time, linguistics, or cultural distance; and are not bound in a hypothesis-testing framework where a null hypothesis and concepts of statistical significance are unclear. The simulation we have presented in this chapter is one such model-bound method, rooted in quantitative genetics, that provides partial answers to questions of prehistoric migration. From the quantitative trait data that arise we can distinguish between continuity and complete replacement provided that the demes are observed fairly soon after the migration, or replacement, event. Even if replacement is incomplete (as in the case where 40 percent of the original population admixes with 60 percent of in-migrants), this migration event could be reconstructed if the demes are observed soon thereafter. Unfortunately, the amount of temporal separation between archaeological samples is typically too large to allow a clear view of past migration events from quantitative traits. Consequently, quantitative skeletal traits are but a single tool in an arsenal that must include other estimators of population or migration structure.

References

Black, S.
1982   *Quantitative Genetics of Anthropometric Variation in the Solomon Islands*. Unpublished Ph.D. dissertation, University of Auckland, New Zealand.
Blangero, J.
1990   Population Structure Analysis using Polygenic Traits: Estimation of Migration Matrices. *Human Biology* 62:27–48.

Cabana, G. S.

2002 *A Demographic Simulation Model to Assess Prehistoric|Migrations.* Unpublished Ph.D. dissertation, University of Michigan, Ann Arbor.

Cabana, G. S., K. L. Hunley, and F. A. Kaestle.

2008 Population Continuity or Replacement? A Novel Computer Simulation Approach and Its Application to the Numic Expansion (Western Great Basin, USA). *American Journal of Physical Anthropology* 135:438–447.

Cheverud, J. M.

1988 A Comparison of Genetic and Phenotypic Correlations. *Evolution* 42:958–968.

Cole, T. M.

1996 The Use of Matrix Permutation Tests for Evaluating Competing Hypotheses of Modern Human Origins. *Journal of Human Evolution* 31:477–484.

Eswaran, V., H. Harpending, and A. R. Rogers

2005 Genomics Refutes an Exclusively African Origin of Humans. *Journal of Human Evolution* 49:1–18.

Harpending, H. C., and R. Ward

1982 Chemical Systematics and Human Evolution. In *Biochemical Aspects of Evolutionary Biology*, edited by M. Nitecki, pp. 213–256. University of Chicago, Chicago.

Howells, W. W.

1989 *Skull Shape and the Map: Craniometric Analyses in the Dispersion of Modern Homo.* Harvard University Press, Cambridge, Mass.

Konigsberg, L. W.

1997 Comments on Matrix Permutation Tests in the Evaluation of Competing Models for Modern Human Origins. *Journal of Human Evolution* 32:479–488.

2006 A Post-Neumann History of Biological and Genetic Distance Studies in Bioarchaeology. In *Bioarchaeology: The Contextual Analysis of Human Remains*, edited by J. E. Buikstra and L. A. Beck, pp. 263–279. Academic Press, New York.

Konigsberg, L. W., and J. Blangero

1993 Multivariate Quantitative Genetic Simulations in Anthropology with an Example from the South Pacific. *Human Biology* 65:897–915.

Konigsberg, L. W., and S. D. Ousley

1995 Multivariate Quantitative Genetics of Anthropometric Traits from the Boas Data. *Human Biology* 67:481–498.

Morton, N. E.

1969 Human Population Structure. *Annual Reviews in Genetics* 3:53–74.

Relethford, J., and J. Blangero

1990 Detection of Differential Gene Flow from Patterns of Quantitative Variation. *Human Biology* 62:5–25.

Relethford, J. H., and F. C. Lees

1982 The Use of Quantitative Traits in the Study of Human Population Structure. *Yearbook of Physical Anthropology* 25:153–168.

Rogers, A. R.
1995 How Much Can Fossils Tell Us About Regional Continuity? *Current Anthropology* 36:674–676.

Rogers, A. R., and H. C. Harpending
1986 Migration and Genetic Drift in Human Populations. *Evolution* 40:1312–1327.

Sciulli, P. W., and M. C. Mahaney
1991 Phenotypic Evolution in Prehistoric Ohio Valley Amerindians: Natural Selection Versus Random Genetic Drift in Tooth Size Reduction. *Human Biology* 63:499–511.

Sokal, R. R., N. L. Oden, J. Walker, and D. M. Waddle
1997 Using Distance Matrices to Choose Between Competing Theories and an Application to the Origin of Modern Humans. *Journal of Human Evolution* 32:501–522.

Steadman, D. W.
2001 Mississippians in Motion? A Population Genetic Analysis of Interregional Gene Flow in West-Central Illinois. *American Journal of Physical Anthropology* 114:61–73.

Stojanowski, C. M., and M. A. Schillaci
2006 Phenotypic Approaches for Understanding Patterns of Intracemetery Biological Variation. *American Journal of Physical Anthropology* 43:49–88.

Waddle, D. M.
1994 Matrix Correlation Tests Support a Single Origin for Modern Humans. *Nature* 368:452–454.

15

Evolutionary Models of Migration in Human Prehistory and Their Anthropological Significance

KEITH L. HUNLEY

Many of this volume's chapters examine a long-standing tension in anthropology concerning the relative roles of large-scale population movements and local intergroup interactions in shaping human biological and cultural variation. This tension is reflected within the field of anthropological genetics in the debate over whether human genetic variation primarily reflects a history of serial founder effects and population movements associated with the expansion of our species out of Africa or a continuum of local groups, or demes, connected by gene flow. The serial founder effects (SFE) model sees human prehistory as a series of successive population splits and movements followed by isolation of descendent populations. It predicts that neutral genetic variation will be predominantly hierarchically patterned and that the degree of genetic similarity between any two populations will be a function of the specific pattern of population splits (see Figure 15.1, left). The continuum-of-connected-demes model envisions that whatever the early history of our species is, genetic exchange, or gene flow (GF), between local populations has since played a dominant role in shaping variation. The GF model predicts that the degree of neutral genetic similarity between any two demes will be primarily a function of the geographic distance between them.

If human genetic variation has been shaped primarily by SFE, we should be able to reconstruct important details of the deep prehistory of our species, such as the timing and order of various colonization events. In contrast, if variation was primarily shaped by GF, it would be more difficult to reconstruct details of our deep history but we should be able to learn a great deal about the social and ecological factors that govern the interactions between neighboring groups. The different models also have important implications for statistical methods used to measure and interpret human variation.

Model 1
Long-range movements and serial founder effects

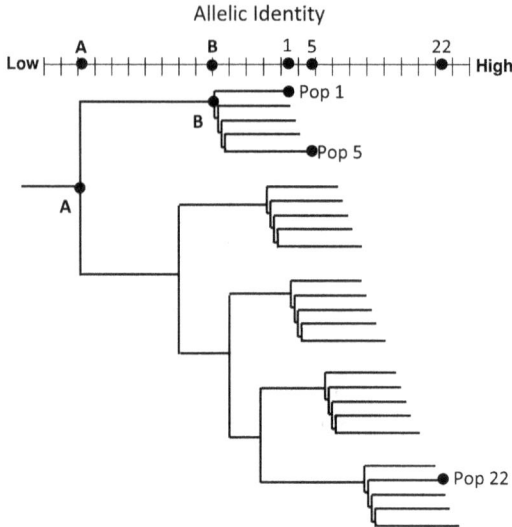

Model 2
Continuum of Connected Demes

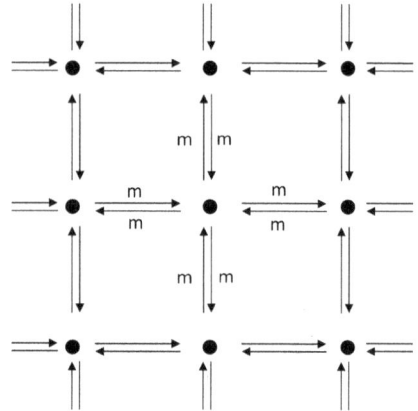

Figure 15.1. Model 1 shows one version of the serial founder effects (SFE) model. There are five regions and five populations within each region. The populations within each region formed through successive founder events from a regional founding population, and the regional founders themselves formed through successive founder events from a single ancestral population. The scale at the top shows the average level of allelic identity within and between populations that results from this serial founder effects history. The level of identity within populations corresponds to the position on the scale of the terminal position of each branch. The level of allelic identity between any two populations is the identity on the scale at the node connecting them; for example, node B for populations 1 and 5, and node A for populations 1 and 22 and populations 5 and 22.

Model 2 shows a subset of nine populations from a larger two-dimensional grid of populations that are evenly distributed across a landscape (adapted from Kimura and Weiss 1964). Each population exchanges some portion (m) of its individuals every generation with its four most immediate neighbors. As a result of this pattern of exchange, individuals in nearby populations will share more recent common ancestors than individuals in more distant populations and the degree of genetic similarity between individuals in different populations will decrease exponentially and monotonically with increasing geographic distance (Kimura and Weiss 1964; Malécot 1948).

Currently both models are more-or-less equally supported by the literature. On the one hand, published studies that use trees or clusters to describe human genetic variation support the SFE model, as do studies that measure the apportionment of genetic variation at different hierarchical levels of populations structure (e.g., Bowcock et al. 1994; Cavalli-Sforza et al. 1994; Jorde et al. 1997; Li et al. 2008; Ramachandran et al. 2005; Rosenberg et al. 2002). On the other hand, studies that emphasize the primacy of geographic proximity in determining the degree of genetic similarity among human groups support a GF model (e.g., Handley et al. 2007; Relethford 2002, 2004; Serre and Pääbo 2004).

Unfortunately, these studies have not provided clear tests to allow us to distinguish between the SFE and GF models. They analyzed similar genetic data (sometimes even the same genetic data) and in many cases they identified similar patterns of genetic variation, but they reached very different conclusions about the evolutionary causes of the patterns and their broader meaning. Clearly, methodological approaches that are capable of distinguishing between alternative evolutionary processes are sorely needed.

The first goal of this chapter is to determine the relative importance of SFE and GF in shaping the current pattern of human genetic variation. My strategy is to (1) simulate genetic data using the two models; (2) perform analyses of the simulated data that capture the different evolutionary processes underlying each model; and (3) compare the results of the analyses of the simulated data to results of identical analyses of observed genetic data collected from a large sample of people and populations. The second goal of the chapter is to explore the larger anthropological meaning of the evolutionary processes that have molded human genetic variation.

Materials and Methods

Samples and Genetic Loci

The real genetic data consist of the allele sizes for 576 autosomal microsatellite loci typed in 2,407 individuals from 107 globally distributed populations located in five major geographic regions: Africa, West Eurasia, East Asia, Oceania, and the Americas (see Figure 15.2). These microsatellite loci are highly variable and contain substantial information about the evolutionary process (Friedlaender et al. 2008; Rosenberg et al. 2005; Wang et al. 2007).

Figure 15.2. Map of population locations and migration routes assumed in the SFE model. The dashed arrows indicate secondary migrations from East Asia into Island Melanesia and then into Remote Oceania.

Measure of Genetic Variation

The measure of within- and between-population genetic variation is allelic identity, or the probability that two randomly drawn alleles from the same locus are identical (Nei 1987). If the alleles are drawn from the same local population, allelic identity is a measure of within-population variation. High values of within-population allelic identity reflect high genetic similarity among population members resulting from, for example, small population size or endogamy. If instead the alleles are drawn from different populations, allelic identity is a measure of between-population variation. High values of between-population allelic identity reflect high genetic similarity among members of different populations because of recent common ancestry and/ or marital exchange. Allelic identity is an ideal measure of genetic variation because (1) it results in a minimal loss of the information contained in the allelic data; (2) it provides an intuitive gauge of the degree of genetic similarity between individuals within and between populations; and (3) it provides clearly different predictions for the alternative models being tested here.

Computer Simulation

The simulated genetic data consist of microsatellite loci generated using a coalescent approach in the computer package SIMCOAL (Laval and Excoffier 2004). The coalescent approach permits the rapid simulation of the two models of population history using the same numbers of populations (107) and regions (5) as are in the real genetic sample. Following the simulations,

I estimated within- and between-population allelic identities from the simulated data. I plotted the identities using simple graphical methods that highlight the allelic identities at three levels of population structure: within populations, between populations within a region, and between populations in different regions. Then I compared the simulated patterns for each of the two models to the real patterns measured directly from the microsatellite loci collected from the 107 populations.

Serial Founder Effects (SFE) Model

In this model, a single ancestral population forms in Africa. This population grows and then a small portion of the population splits and migrates to a new location. The parental population persists and the new daughter population grows and splits. Eventually daughter populations colonize the other four major geographic regions in the following order: from West Eurasia to East Asia to Oceania and finally to the Americas. This pattern of population splitting is illustrated for a small number of populations in Figure 15.1.

At the within-population level, SFE predicts that, relatively speaking, allelic identity will be lowest in the original, oldest ancestral population in Africa and that it will increase steadily as each new population forms, attaining its highest value in the most recently formed population in the Americas (Ramachandran et al. 2005). At the between-population/within-region level, the model predicts a layered pattern of allelic identity. That is, the precise level of between-population identity will be a function of the specific order of branching events: populations that share a more recent common ancestor will be more similar than ones that share a more distant common ancestor. For this reason, populations within a particular region will have higher allelic identities than populations in different regions. Figure 15.1 provides several examples of the predicted level of allelic identity at the three levels of population structure.

Local Gene Flow (GF) Model

The GF model sees populations as distributed evenly over a landscape with each population exchanging a portion of its members with its immediate geographic neighbors in every generation. As a result of this pattern of exchange, individuals living in adjacent populations are likely to share more recent common ancestors than individuals living in more-distant populations, and therefore the level of allelic identity will be higher between nearby populations than between distant populations. The equilibrium version of the model, in which the location of populations and the pattern of migration has remained stable for a long time (a.k.a. isolation by distance, or IBD), predicts that allelic identities will be equal within all populations and that the level of allelic identity will

decay monotonically with increasing geographic distance between populations (Kimura and Weiss 1964; Malécot 1948). Therefore, allelic identity will be
higher between populations within regions than between populations in different regions simply because regional populations are geographically closer
to one another.

Results

SFE Model

In Figure 15.3, the leftmost panels show the real pattern of allelic identity variation, while the middle panels show the results of the SFE simulations and the
rightmost panels show the results of the GF simulations. The top three plots
(panel A) show the allelic identities within populations for the real data, SFE
simulations, and GF simulations, respectively. In both the real data and the
simulated data for SFE, allelic identities are lowest in African populations and
increase steadily with each successive founder effect. In contrast, the identities
are fairly uniform for the GF simulations.

Panel B shows the identities between populations in the same region. Neither simulated model captures exactly the same pattern as the real data. However, like the real data, the SFE model shows a layered pattern of regional
variation in which the lowest identities are between populations in Africa,
intermediate levels are between populations in Eurasia, and the highest levels
are between populations in the Americas. In contrast, there is no such layer-
ing in the simulated GF plot. Consistent with the predictions of the GF model,
geographic distance, not regional location, is the sole predictor of between-
population genetic similarity. Consistent with the predictions of the equilibrium version of the GF model (IBD), the decay in allelic identity is monotonic.

Panel C shows allelic identity between populations in different regions.
Once again, the SFE model captures the layered pattern of variation seen in
the real data, though not perfectly so, and the GF model does not. Again, for
the GF model, the sole predictor of between-population genetic similarity is
geographic distance and the decay in similarity is monotonic.

One reason for the differences between the real plots and the SFE plots is
that the simulations assume there are a *total* of 107 human populations while
the real data sample only 107 of thousands of human populations. For example,
the real African sample contains only seven Sub-Saharan African populations
and the geographic separation between them and the other 101 populations
is large. This large geographic separation is evident in the large gap between
the Sub-Saharan African layer and the other layers in panel C of the real data.

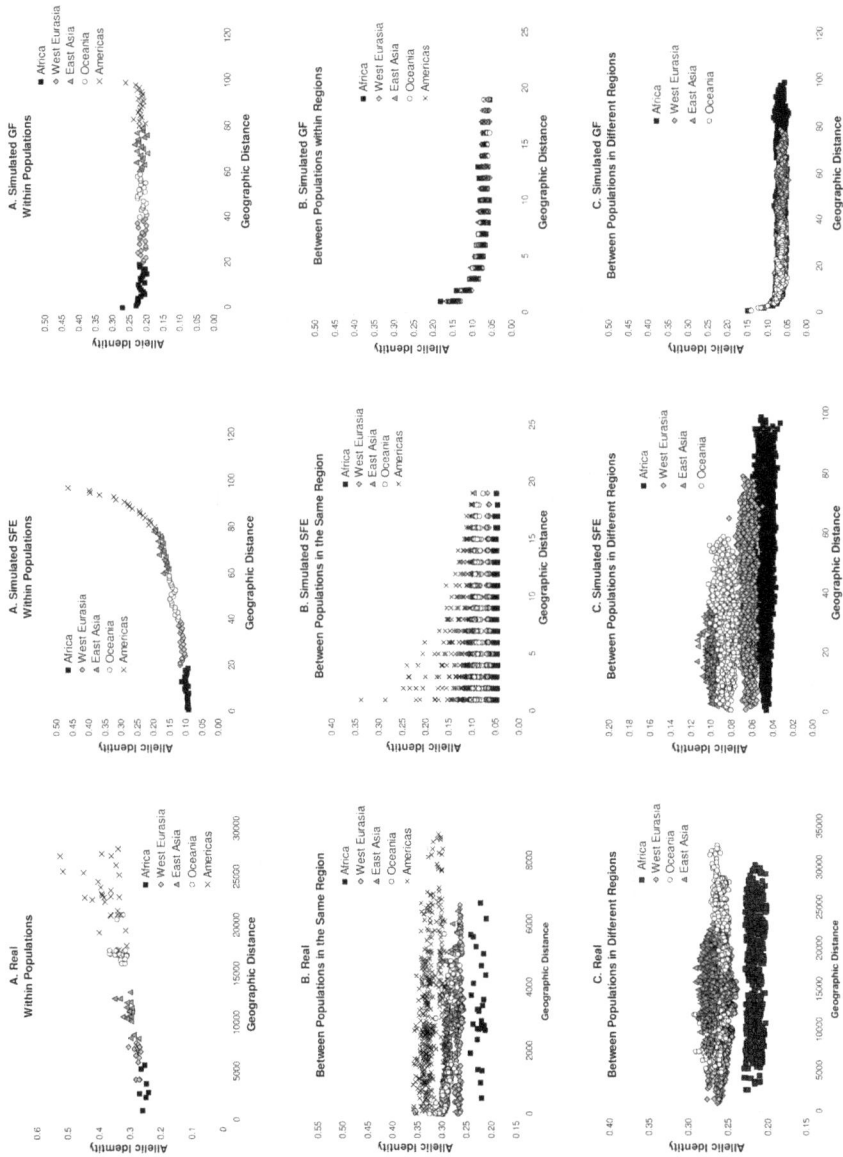

Figure 15.3. Comparisons of real and simulated data. The plots are in the following order: real genetic data, left; SFE-simulated data, middle; GF-simulated data, right. Panel A shows the within-population allelic identity. Panel B shows the allelic identity between populations in the same region. Panel C shows the allelic identity between populations in different regions. In panel A, for the real data, the populations are arrayed in order of their geographic distance from the Bantu population in Kenya; for the SFE-simulated data, by geographic distance to the founding population; for the GF-simulated data, by the geographic distance between populations. The scale for the latter two is arbitrary. All geographic distances for the real populations were computed through waypoints on land.

The simulated SFE contains no such gap. Tishkoff et al. (2009) recently published microsatellite data from a much larger set of African populations. My preliminary analysis of these data indicate that including the additional African populations eliminates the gap in the real data, resulting in even greater agreement between the real pattern and the simulated SFE pattern. That said, there are still significant differences between the SFE predictions and the real pattern that cannot be explained by uneven sampling of real data. These differences have to do mainly with populations in Oceania and are the result of two major waves of migration into the region followed by intermarriage between first- and second-wave peoples (Green 1991). Still, it is remarkable that a model as simple as the SFE one captures so much of the real pattern of human genetic variation.

Overall, the GF simulation results are inconsistent with the real pattern of allelic identity at all three levels of population structure. The SFE model does not perfectly capture the real pattern, but it clearly indicates that human genetic variation is primarily hierarchically patterned and that the pattern is broadly consistent with an African origin for our species followed by successive founder effects as we spread through Eurasia and into the Americas.

Local Genetic Exchange Within Regions

The within-region pattern of allelic identity variation in panel B of Figure 15.3 deserves further attention. Some of the difference between the real pattern and the simulated SFE pattern has to do with uneven sampling, but even after taking sampling limitations into account, the layers in the real data are more compressed than they are in the simulated data and there is some decay in allelic identity with increasing geographic distance in the real data that is absent in the simulated data. It is possible that the GF model captures the pattern of variation in allelic identity within individual regions. In this regard, it has been demonstrated that local genetic exchange is more likely to affect patterns of genetic variation at smaller geographic scales than at larger (i.e., global) scales (Wilkins and Marlowe 2006).

To explore this possibility, I examined the pattern of real allelic identity variation in the Near Oceania subregion of the Oceania sample. I chose this particular subregion because it shows the clearest evidence of a smooth decay in allelic identity with increasing geographic distance and because it has the largest number of populations located in the smallest geographic area of any region in the study. The Near Oceania subregion consists of 28 populations from Northern Island Melanesia (NIM), a grouping of five large islands and many smaller offshore islands located off the northeast coast of Papua

New Guinea (see Figure 15.2), and two populations from Papua New Guinea (Eastern Highlands and Sepik Basin).

Some background on the prehistory of the Oceanic region is relevant. As noted above, many scholars agree that there were two major long-range migrations into Oceania (Green 1991). The first occurred at least 40,000 years ago, and it probably carried the ancestors of speakers of modern-day Papuan languages to the region. The second migration occurred about 3,000 years ago, carrying the ancestors of modern-day Oceanic speakers to the region. Since that time, substantial intermarriage and linguistic exchange has occurred, as have numerous population displacements. The result is somewhat of a muddle of genetic and linguistic variation in the region that has made it difficult to reconstruct the precise details of its prehistory (Friedlaender et al. 2008; Lindström et al. 2007). The relevant question here is whether the exchange has been of sufficient magnitude or duration to result in a GF-like pattern of variation in the region.

Panel A of Figure 15.4 shows the geographic pattern of allelic identity variation for the Near Oceania sample. At first glance, the pattern looks like it conforms to the predictions of the GF model. There is a smooth decay in allelic identity with increasing geographic distance and the decay appears to be monotonic. Panel B of the figure, however, shows that there is substantial heterogeneity in within-population allelic identity. The populations in the plot are arranged from lowest to highest allelic identity. On the left side of the plot, populations are labeled by language (Oceanic and Papuan). On the right, they are labeled by whether they are located along island coasts or in their rugged interiors. The left side of the plot shows that within-population allelic identity is patterned by language, with most Oceanic-language speaking populations showing lower identity (greater diversity) than the Papuan-language speaking populations. One hypothesis for this heterogeneity is that Papuan-speaking groups trace largely to small, isolated first-wave foragers, while Oceanic-speaking groups trace to larger, less-isolated second-wave horticulturalists. An alternative hypothesis is that the heterogeneity reflects local ecology, with coastal locations supporting larger population sizes (thus more genetic diversity, which corresponds to lower allelic identity) than rugged inland locations (Friedlaender 2007). The right side of the panel B shows that this coastal-inland distinction even better captures the variation in within-population allelic identity. The lowest inland allelic identity exceeds the highest coastal identity. The primary reason for the covariation of within-population variation by language and ecology is that most populations that speak Papuan languages are located in inland regions. It is possible that Papuan-speakers were displaced

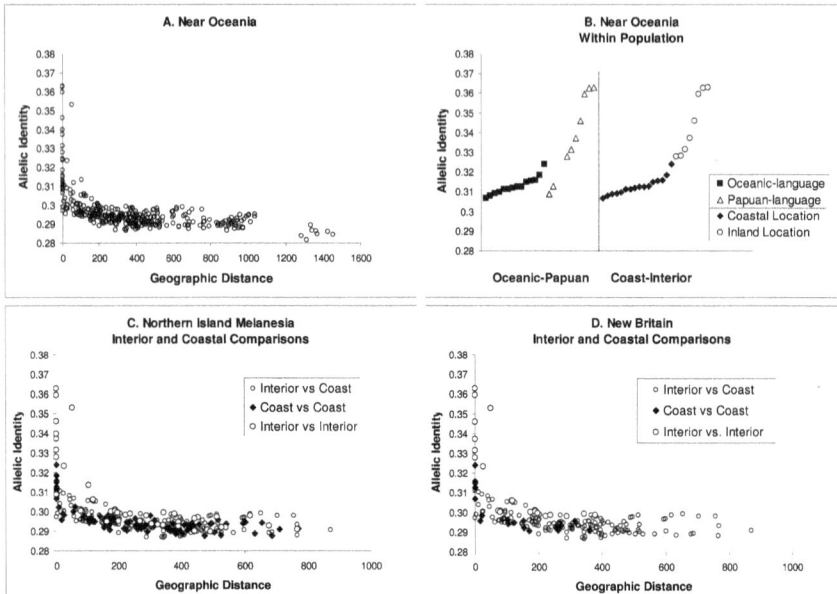

Figure 15.4. Allelic identity in Near Oceania. Panel A. Within- and between-population allelic identity versus geographic distance for 30 Near Oceania populations. Panel B. Within-population allelic identity arranged by language group (Oceanic language versus Papuan language) on the left and by ecological setting (coastal versus inland location) on the right. Panel C. Within- and between-population allelic identity versus geographic distance for 28 Northern Island Melanesian populations. Coastal vs. coastal and inland vs. inland comparisons are highlighted. Panel D. Within- and between-population allelic identity versus geographic distance for 19 New Britain populations. Coastal vs. coastal and inland vs. inland comparisons are highlighted.

to inland locations after the arrival of second-wave Oceanic-language-speakers or that Papuan languages survived only in the rugged interiors. In either case, it appears that the inland ecology supports smaller populations than the coasts.

Panel C of Figure 15.4 shows that the decay in allelic identity with increasing geographic distance is not, in fact, monotonic. Instead there are two different strata, one for comparisons of coastal populations and one for comparisons of inland populations. The distinction between coastal and inland areas is most pronounced on the largest island in the region, New Britain, shown in panel D. Coupled with the substantial heterogeneity in allelic identity within populations, these results indicate that genetic variation does not necessarily conform to the predictions of the GF model even at the most local of geographic scales.

In summary, human genetic variation is primarily hierarchal patterned at the global scale. Figure 15.5 represents this hierarchical structure as a tree. The tree was constructed using Nei's minimum genetic distances, which are computed from the allelic identities (Nei 1987), and is plotted on a scale of allelic identity. The tree structure captures the African origin for our species (i.e., the root of the tree is in Africa) and the pattern of increasing within- and between-population allelic identity away from Africa that resulted from an evolutionary history based on SFE. Others have shown that such trees provide a good representation of the pattern of human genetic variation (Long et al. 2009). However, the tree in Figure 15.5 does not perfectly capture this pattern, in part because of the history of two-wave colonization and intermarriage in Oceania and, to a lesser extent, gene flow between local populations. Gene flow has clearly occurred between nearby populations, no doubt since they originally formed, and populations have always moved, merged, emerged, and disappeared, but it takes thousands of generations for these local processes to overwrite the genetic signatures of more-ancient formative processes (Wilkins and Marlowe 2006).

Discussion

Potential Limitations of Genetic Data

It is possible that the sample locations in this study are unevenly distributed in geographic space such that populations on the borders between major geo-graphic regions are underrepresented; this may result in an overemphasis on genetic differences between populations and an underemphasis of the clinal nature of human variation (Serre and Pääbo 2004). If this were truly a prob-lem, then the hierarchical pattern identified here would be largely an artifact of sample-location bias.

For many reasons, this potential critique does not apply to this study, nor does it affect the results. First, the population samples used here do include populations from border regions—for example, in the Middle East and North Africa. These populations show the same hierarchical pattern of allelic iden-tity variation as other populations in the sample. Second, as the number of populations used in global studies has increased, support for SFE has become stronger, not weaker (DeGiorgio et al. 2009; Deshpande et al. 2009; Jakobsson et al. 2008; Ramachandran et al. 2005). The current study contains one of the largest, most widespread population samples analyzed to date. It shows that the SFE model fits the pattern of within- and among-population genetic varia-tion for this large sample exceptionally well. SFE may not fit other, unsampled

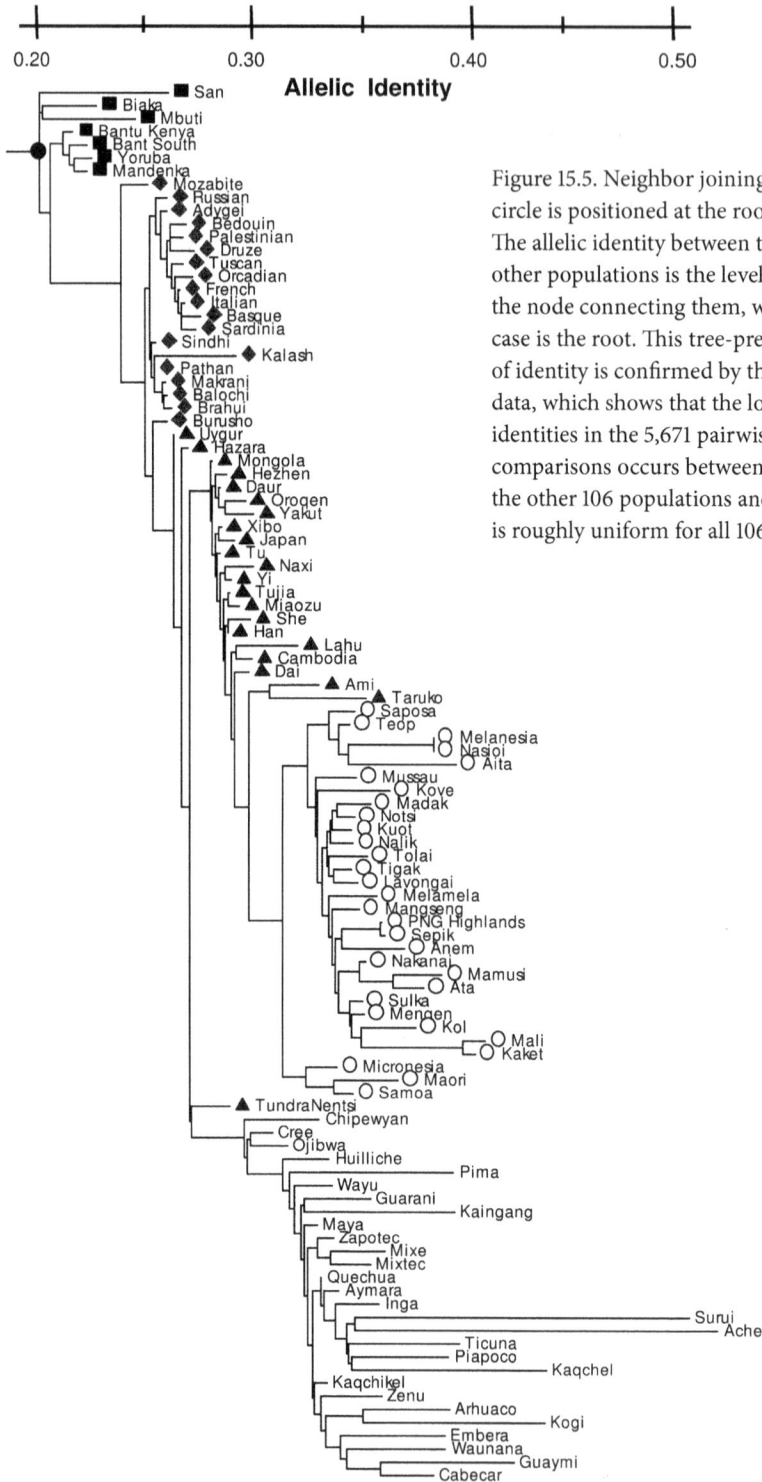

Figure 15.5. Neighbor joining tree. The black circle is positioned at the root of the tree. The allelic identity between the San and all other populations is the level of identity at the node connecting them, which in this case is the root. This tree-predicted level of identity is confirmed by the real genetic data, which shows that the lowest level of identities in the 5,671 pairwise population comparisons occurs between the San and the other 106 populations and that this level is roughly uniform for all 106 comparisons.

population data, but adding such data would not change the result for the current sample. Third, the predictions of the GF model are insensitive to the location of populations used. This is because under the equilibrium (IBD) version of the model, in which population sizes are equal and rates of intergroup exchange are uniform, the sole predictor of among-population allelic identity is geographic distance. Though non-equilibrium versions of the GF model have not been formally described, they would not predict (1) a steady increase in within-population allelic identity with increasing geographic distance from East Africa (Figure 15.3a); and (2) a lack of decay in among-population allelic identity with increasing geographic distance (Figure 15.3b, c). In contrast, these two features of the real data are predictions of the SFE model.

There are important limits, nevertheless, to what can be learned from genetic data alone. This study shows that important details of human prehistory can be reconstructed by fitting alternative evolutionary models to high-quality genetic data and then examining the causes of deviations from the predictions of the models. However, the causes of these deviations cannot be interpreted without incorporating other types of anthropological data. For example, in Near Oceania, archaeological, linguistic, and ecological data were required to assess why the two simple models failed to fully capture the observed pattern of allelic identity variation in the region (Friedlaender et al. 2008; Hunley et al. 2008). The same will be true of other locations. This study provides one clear strategy for investigating prehistory and highlights the importance of a multidisciplinary anthropological approach.

Models Matter

In the introduction to this volume, Cabana and Clark state that we study migration in order to reconstruct the past. Historical reconstruction requires an understanding of the evolutionary processes that affect variation. This is why I have concentrated on evolutionary process in this chapter. The two particular evolutionary processes I have examined here have received considerable attention from anthropological geneticists for decades precisely because of their relevance in reconstructing human prehistory. More important, I concur with Cabana and Clark (this volume) that our ultimate goal is to unravel the larger social and scientific meanings of this prehistory. Here especially, models matter.

In anthropological genetics, for example, our statistical descriptions of human genetic variation and, more important, our interpretations of those descriptions assume specific models of evolution. To take one important example, biological anthropologists reject the idea that the human species is divided into independently evolving races whose members are genetically closer to one another than they are to members of different races. The rejection is based on methods that apportion genetic variation into within- and between-group components. When these methods are applied to human genetic data, they show that only a small portion of the total variation is apportioned between so-called races. Ironically, these methods assume the only evolutionary model that could lead to the existence of races (Long and Kittles 2003), that of independently evolving groups. The rejection of race is based not on the rejection of the model but on the conclusion that races simply have not been evolving independently for long enough for the between-race differences to matter (Lewontin 1972). The problem is that this evolutionary model is wrong. Yes, human genetic variation is structured hierarchically, but that hierarchy reflects an African origin and a subsequent history of serial founder effects in which daughter groups contained a subset, not a unique set, of the genetic variation of the parent. The *meaning* of this nested-subset pattern of variation is that (1) the biological race concept is an inaccurate way to describe human genetic variation; (2) apportionments of variation cannot capture the complex nature of human evolution; and (3) most genetic changes that have occurred since we left Africa are shared by descendent groups in different geographic regions. As a result, we should expect the genetic factors underlying multifactorial traits, including multifactorial diseases that afflict millions, to be widespread and not restricted to one group or another. Finally, (4) most genetic changes on more-terminal—that is, intraregional or population—branches will appear in only a small subset of the people in those groups. This is why some Mendelian diseases are relatively more common in particular ethnic groups but still rare in those groups. None of this would be true if our evolutionary history had been different—if, for example, local gene flow had been the primary factor molding human biological variation or if human races indeed existed and had been evolving independently. If our ultimate goal is to unravel the larger social and scientific meanings of our prehistory, then models matter.

References

Bowcock, A., A. R. Linares, J. Tomfohrde, E. Minch, J. Kidd, and L. L. Cavalli-Sforza
1994   High Resolution Trees with Polymorphic Microsatellites. *Nature* 368:455–457.
Cavalli-Sforza, L. L., P. Menozzi, and A. Piazza
1994   *The History and Geography of Human Genes.* Princeton University Press, Princeton.
DeGiorgio, M., M. Jakobsson, and N. A. Rosenberg
2009   Out of Africa: Modern Human Origins Special Feature: Explaining Worldwide Patterns of Human Genetic Variation using a Coalescent-Based Serial Founder

Model of Migration outward from Africa. *Proceedings of the National Academy of Sciences USA* 106(38):16057–16062.

Deshpande, O., S. Batzoglou, M. W. Feldman, and L. L. Cavalli-Sforza
2009 A Serial Founder Effect Model for Human Settlement out of Africa. *Proceedings. Biological Sciences* 276(1655):291–300.

Friedlaender, J.
2007 Introduction: The Framework. In Genes, *Language, and Culture Change in the Southwest Pacific*, edited by J. S. Friedlaender, pp. 3–9. Oxford University Press, New York.

Friedlaender, J., F. Friedlaender, F. Reed, K. K. Kidd, J. Kidd, G. Chambers, R. Lea, J. Loo, G. Koki, J. Hodgson, D. A. Merriwether, and J. L. Weber
2008 The Genetic Structure of Pacific Islanders. *PLoS Genetics* 4(1):e19.

Green, R. C.
1991 The Lapita Cultural Complex: Current Evidence and Proposed Models. *Bulletin of the Indo-Pacific Prehistory Association* 11:295–305.

Handley, L. J., A. Manica, J. Goudet, and F. Balloux
2007 Going the Distance: Human Population Genetics in a Clinal World. *Trends in Genetics* 23(9):432–439.

Hunley, K., M. Dunn, E. Lindstrom, G. Reesink, A. Terrill, M. E. Healy, G. Koki, F. R. Friedlaender, and J. S. Friedlaender
2008 Genetic and Linguistic Coevolution in Northern Island Melanesia. *PLoS Genetics* 4(10):e1000239.

Jakobsson, M., S. W. Scholz, P. Scheet, J. R. Gibbs, J. M. VanLiere, H. C. Fung, Z. A. Szpiech, J. H. Degnan, K. Wang, R. Guerreiro, J. M. Bras, J. C. Schymick, D. G. Hernandez, B. J. Traynor, J. Simon-Sanchez, M. Matarin, A. Britton, J. van de Leemput, I. Rafferty, M. Bucan, H. M. Cann, J. A. Hardy, N. A. Rosenberg, and A. B. Singleton.
2008 Genotype, Haplotype and Copy-Number Variation in Worldwide Human Populations. *Nature* 451(7181):998–1003.

Jorde, L. B., A. R. Rogers, M. Bamshad, W. S. Watkins, P. Krakowiak, S. Sung, J. Kere, and H. C. Harpending
1997 Microsatellite Diversity and the Demographic History of Modern Humans. *Proceedings of the National Academy of Sciences USA* 94(7):3100–3103.

Kimura, M., and G. Weiss
1964 The Stepping Stone Model of Population Structure and the Decrease of Genetic Correlation with Distance. *Genetics* 49:561–576.

Laval, G., and L. Excoffier
2004 SIMCOAL 2.0: A Program to Simulate Genomic Diversity over Large Recombining Regions in a Subdivided Population with a Complex History. *Bioinformatics* 20(15):2485–2487.

Lewontin, R.
1972 The Apportionment of Human Diversity. In *Evolutionary Biology*, vol. 6, edited by T. Dobzhansky, M. Hecht, and W. Steere, pp. 391–398. Appleton-Century-Crofts, New York.

Li, J. Z., D. M. Absher, H. Tang, A. M. Southwick, A. M. Casto, S. Ramachandran, H. M. Cann, G. S. Barsh, M. Feldman, L. L. Cavalli-Sforza, and R. M. Myers
2008 Worldwide Human Relationships Inferred from Genome-Wide Patterns of Variation. *Science* 319(5866):1100–1104.

Lindström, E., A. Terrill, G. Reesink, and M. Dunn
2007 The Languages of Island Melanesia. In *Genes, Language, and Culture Change in the Southwest Pacific*, edited by J. S. Friedlaender, pp. 118–139. Oxford University Press, New York.

Long, J. C., and R. A. Kittles
2003 Human Genetic Diversity and the Nonexistence of Biological Races. *Human Biology* 75(4):449–471.

Long, J. C., J. Li, and M. E. Healy
2009 Human DNA Sequences: More Variation and Less Race. *American Journal of Physical Anthropology* 139(1):23–34.

Malécot, G.
1948 *Les Mathématiques de l'Hérédité*. Masson et Cie, Paris.

Nei, M.
1987 *Molecular Evolutionary Genetics*. Columbia University Press, New York.

Ramachandran, S., O. Deshpande, C. C. Roseman, N. A. Rosenberg, M. W. Feldman, and L. L. Cavalli-Sforza
2005 Support from the Relationship of Genetic and Geographic Distance in Human Populations for a Serial Founder Effect Originating in Africa. *Proceedings of the National Academy of Sciences USA* 102(44):15942–15947.

Relethford, J. H.
2002 Apportionment of Global Human Genetic Diversity Based on Craniometrics and Skin Solor. *American Journal of Physical Anthropology* 118(4):393–398.
2004 Global Patterns of Isolation by Distance Based on Genetic and Morphological Data. *Human Biology* 76(4):499–513.

Rosenberg, N. A., S. Mahajan, S. Ramachandran, C. Zhao, J. K. Pritchard, and M. W. Feldman
2005 Clines, Clusters, and the Effect of Study Design on the Inference of Human Population Structure. *PLoS Genetics* 1(6):e70.

Rosenberg, N. A., J. K. Pritchard, J. L. Weber, H. M. Cann, K. K. Kidd, L. A. Zhivotovsky, and M. W. Feldman
2002 Genetic Structure of Human Populations. *Science* 298(5602):2381–2385.

Serre, D., and S. Pääbo
2004 Evidence for Gradients of Human Genetic Diversity Within and Among Continents. *Genome Research* 14(9):1679–1685.

Tishkoff, S. A., F. A. Reed, F. R. Friedlaender, C. Ehret, A. Ranciaro, A. Froment, J. B. Hirbo, A. A. Awomoyi, J. M. Bodo, O. Doumbo, and others
2009 The Genetic Structure and History of Africans and African Americans. *Science* 324(5930):1035–1044.

Wang, S., C. M. Lewis, M. Jakobsson, S. Ramachandran, N. Ray, G., Bedoya, W. Rojas, M. V. Parra, J. A. Molina, C. Gallo, G. Mazzotti, G. Poletti, K. Hill, A. M. Hurtado, D. Labuda, W. Klitz, R. Barrantes, M. C. Bortolini, F. M. Salzano, M. L. Petzl-Erler, L. T. Tsuneto, E. Llop, F. Rothhammer, L. Excoffier, M. W. Feldman, N. A. Rosenberg, and A. Ruiz-Linares

2007   Genetic Variation and Population Structure in Native Americans. *PLoS Genetics* 3(11):e185.

Wilkins, J. F., and F. W. Marlowe

2006   Sex-Biased Migration in Humans: What Should We Expect from Genetic Data? *Bioessays* 28(3):290–300.

VI

Lessons from Contemporary Migration

16

Modern Perspectives on Ancient Migrations

TAKEYUKI (GAKU) TSUDA

In many ways, the recent (i.e., post-1990) renewed interest in migration among prehistorians represents an attempt to overcome the shortcomings of previous research: instead of simply using migration as a convenient explanation for sudden changes found in local material cultures, prehistorians are now developing better methods to detect and track migration. And, as this volume attests, they are also attempting to better understand migration as a complex, dynamic social process.

As more than a few scholars of prehistory have noted (e.g., Anthony 1990; Burmeister 2000), sociocultural anthropologists, geographers, and sociologists have been studying modern migration for a long time. Should the concepts and theories developed by contemporary immigration specialists be applied to the study of population movements in the distant past? Some question the relevance of modern migration because of the vast differences between contemporary and past migration (e.g., Beekman and Christensen 2003; Clark 1994; Rouse 1986). There is no doubt that migration after the Industrial Revolution has been structured by capitalist wage-labor systems, nation-states and their immigration policies, and modern transportation and communications technologies, none of which existed in ancient times.

Others argue that certain aspects of contemporary population movements do resemble those from the distant past and that studies of modern migration can provide them with an understanding of the social dynamics of migration, which in turn will help illuminate and better explain archaeological data.[1] In fact, a number of archaeologists have reviewed the findings of modern migration theory and applied them directly to their prehistoric case studies (e.g., Anthony 1990, 1997; Burmeister 2000; Cameron 1995; Chapman 1997; Duff 1998).[2]

As a sociocultural anthropologist who specializes in modern migration, I tend to concur with the latter group of archaeologists about the relevance of the present to the past. However, I argue that scholars of prehistory can learn from the present not because population movements have basically remained the same over the course of human history. Instead, my objective in this chapter is to assess from the perspective of a contemporary immigration specialist the extent to which current population movements may be different from (as well as similar to) those in the distant past. As Duff (1998) has pointed out, if archaeologists are to use theories and knowledge about modern migration to better understand the prehistoric record, they must also be aware of the aspects of migration that have been constant over human history and those that have changed, often quite dramatically. In the process, I will also reflect on whether the apparent differences between present and past are partly related to methodological limitations inherent in studying the distant past. In certain respects, humans today may migrate in somewhat similar ways as their distant ancestors.

Bridging a Temporal and Conceptual Divide in Migration Studies

Migration is a very important research topic for anthropologists because of its great significance throughout human history. Since at least 250,000 years ago, human beings have migrated vast distances to populate all corners of the globe. Despite the prevalent notion that societies became sedentary as they evolved from nomadism to agricultural villages and states, continuous migration may have been a greater part of even late prehistory than was previously believed, as Fowles (this volume) points out. Today, migration remains as significant as ever. According to United Nations estimates, the number of people living outside their country of birth or nationality doubled between 1970 and 2005 to 191 million, and the total volume of international migration will undoubtedly continue to increase in the twenty-first century.

However, with very few exceptions (e.g., Manning 2005), migration research is characterized by an unfortunate temporal divide, with virtually no collaboration between scholars who examine contemporary and those who examine prehistoric migrations. Modern immigration specialists focus exclusively on the present with little to no interest in ancient migrations (e.g., Brettell and Hollifield 2000; Castles and Miller 2003; Cohen 1995; Portes and Rumbaut 1996). Even research by historians (especially those studying Euro-American migration) mainly covers the last couple of centuries and rarely ventures farther into the past (e.g., see Daniels 1990; Diner 2000; Hoerder 2002; Takaki 1993). Meanwhile, scholars of prehistoric and ancient migrations examine population movements during or before the first millennium A.D. and generally do not engage with modern migration scholars.

This temporal division of labor in migration studies is highly problematic, if only because people have been migrating continuously across the globe since the dawn of humankind and no clean temporal or conceptual break exists between the past and present in this regard. As noted above, some archaeologists (to their great credit) have recently attempted to bridge this vast divide by turning to the literature on contemporary immigration to understand the complex social processes involved in migration instead of merely viewing it as the simple movement of people and their material cultures.

But what aspects of contemporary immigration research are the most relevant for archaeologists? Most of the issues that interest modern migration specialists either did not exist in prehistory or cannot be studied using the fragmentary material and skeletal record. These include socioeconomic causes of population movements and their impact on labor markets, migrant families, gender relationships and identities, immigration policies and politics, public and media reactions toward immigrants, migrant communities and diasporas, and immigrant citizenship and social integration.

Nonetheless, there are areas of considerable topical overlap. Clark (this volume) outlines the main issues for the archaeology of migration (beyond the basic methodological detection of migration) as its *causes* ("motivation"), the *process* of migratory movement ("logistics and organization during movement"), and its immediate social *impact* (mainly in destination areas). These are all issues that have been extensively studied by contemporary immigration scholars, and the scholars of prehistory who have drawn from the modern migration literature have mainly focused on them. I will discuss each of these topics in further detail through a comparison of the past and present in order to better illuminate the distinctiveness of prehistoric migration as well as some of its similarities with population movements today.

The Causes of Migration: Then and Now

Environmental, Economic, Demographic, and Political Pressures

A number of archaeologists, starting with Anthony (1990), have studied the contemporary immigration literature and found the "push/pull" theory (which examines the forces that "push" people out of a region and "pull" them to another region) to be quite useful in understanding why people migrated in the past. Among the various causes for ancient migrations identified by archaeologists, the most frequently cited seems to be environmental pressures. Unstable or deteriorating environmental conditions such as climatic changes, droughts, and floods as well as environmental overexploitation and resource depletion (often exacerbated by intergroup competition) pushed people out of certain geographical regions and pulled them to those that had better environmental conditions and subsistence opportunities.

Overpopulation in certain regions is also frequently cited as a migratory push factor in the prehistoric past. However, population pressures are undoubtedly intertwined with environmental factors, as regions that are resource rich will generally be able to sustain larger populations, raising the threshold at which expanding population pressures will compel people to out-migrate. The amount of population a local region can sustain also depends on the level of its inhabitants' agricultural and technological development, which may allow them to more efficiently exploit local resources and support a larger number of people. Therefore, "overpopulation" is a relative (not absolute) measure, and it is difficult to gauge when expanding populations will become unable to sustain themselves and choose to migrate (supposedly to a less-populated area).

In addition, external political conflicts with neighboring peoples (raids, wars, invasions, and other military threats) as well as internal conflicts and political disintegration often forced threatened peoples to leave or flee the region in the past. Military invasion as a form of political conflict was also an important motive for conquering peoples, who were often "pulled" to another region in order to exploit human and environmental resources and better habitats. Likewise, the political disintegration of states and civilizations not only caused out-migration, it also instigated the in-migration of populations intending to take advantage of state collapse and the resulting power vacuum (e.g., Beekman and Christensen 2003).

In the modern world, economic pressures have replaced environmental factors as the primary cause of migration as the global spread of capitalism has made wage labor the primary source of livelihood and wealth (Castles and Miller 2003; Martin et al. 2006; Massey 1999). Most international migration today consists of people from poorer developing countries that have low wages and insufficient jobs seeking better economic opportunities in richer countries abroad. The structural demand for inexpensive and exploitable immigrant labor in advanced industrialized countries continues to increase because of aging and declining populations, upwardly mobile native workers who are unwilling to perform unskilled jobs, and the need to cut production costs in the face of rising global competition (Cornelius 1998; Cornelius and Tsuda 2004; Massey 1999; Tsuda 1999b). Because wage differentials and disparities in per-capita income between rich and poor countries have become considerable, most advanced industrialized nations offer an abundant supply of relatively high-paying jobs for would-be immigrants, providing a powerful economic incentive for poorer peoples to cross national borders.

In contrast, environmental factors have largely receded as an important cause of contemporary migration. This is primarily due to the advent of modern technology, which now enables people to live and subsist in the most environmentally inhospitable areas of the world and has made them less vulnerable to the climactic changes, drought, floods, and even natural disasters that caused people to migrate in prehistoric times. Global trade and the international flow of goods, commodities, and natural resources across borders ensures that societies can thrive even if the local geographical region is too resource poor (or environmentally depleted) to sustain large human populations.[3] Therefore, although modern humans consume a vastly greater quantity of natural resources and cause much more environmental destruction than prehistoric peoples, advanced technology and economic globalization ensure that they are much less susceptible to disruptive environmental impacts. The exceptions are rural subsistence economies in the world's poorest nations (or regions), whose poverty and relative global isolation make them vulnerable to natural resource depletion, environmental instability, and famine, which can instigate out-migration in ways somewhat similar to what occurred in prehistoric societies.

In most cases, however, the economically driven nature of modern migration often disregards environmental pressures. Reviews of the literature on the causes of modern migration do not even mention environmental factors (Castles and Miller 2003; Krtiz and Zlotnik 1992; Martin et al. 2006; Massey 1999; Tsuda 1999a, 1999b). In fact, a number of contemporary migration flows are directed to the countries that are poorest in natural resources but economically rich (such as Japan, Korea, and Taiwan in Asia) as well as to the most environmentally desolate areas of the world, where jobs and economic opportunities happen to be abundant (e.g., internal migration in the United States to Phoenix, Las Vegas, and other desert cities and international migration to oil-rich Middle Eastern countries).

Although there are occasional cases where natural disasters such as massive floods and hurricanes can force people to flee the affected area, they tend to be short-term evacuations and not long-term migrations, except in cases of massive destruction (e.g., hurricane Katrina) or in poor countries that have trouble recovering from the economic devastation of natural disasters.[4] Nonetheless, such "environmental refugees" are not significant enough to become a subject of contemporary migration studies and they are not recognized by the United Nations Convention Relating to the Status of Refugees. However, as the environmental disruptions caused by global warming worsen considerably over the next several decades, we may see more environmentally instigated migrations in the future.[5] It seems that the current overexploitation and destruction of the environment may eventually reach a point where even the marvels of modern technology and the global economy will not be able to overcome the subsequent devastation.

Population (demographic) pressures remain more relevant to modern international migration than environmental factors. Generally, Third World migrant-sending countries have much higher fertility rates, expanding populations, and surplus labor, and First World immigrant-receiving countries have low fertility rates, shrinking populations, and labor shortages. As was probably the case with prehistoric migration however, it is not absolute population density that determines whether people are pushed out of a region but the economic ability of countries to sustain their populations (richer countries can support larger populaces and vice versa). As a result, migration is not always directed from more densely populated to less populated regions. In fact, some of the world's richest countries (in Western Europe and East Asia) are also the most heavily populated, and it is no surprise that much international migration is directed at these countries, often from the rural and less-populated areas of migrant-sending countries. Even in immigrant-receiving countries that have lower population densities (such as the United States), the bulk of international migration is directed toward the most heavily populated wealthy metropolitan areas (Portes and Rumbaut 1996; Waldinger and Lee 2001). Much *internal* migration within countries is also from less-populated poor rural areas to more-prosperous major urban population centers (e.g., Gaetano and Jacka 2004; Nam et al. 1990; White 1979). As is the case with environmental factors, modern migration has become somewhat detached from immediate demographic pressures and is again driven more by regional and global economic disparities.

As it was in prehistory, political conflict continues to be an important source of international migration today as significant numbers of refugees are forced to flee political, ethnic, and religious persecution as well as wars, political instability, and other conflicts (Castles and Miller 2003). The total volume of the world's refugees is considerably less than that of labor (economic) migrants,[6] indicating than human conflict has probably become a less prominent source of population movement than it was in the ancient past. However, it is often difficult to clearly differentiate between the political and economic causes of migration, since political conflict and persecution often deprive peoples of their economic livelihoods, forcing them to become de facto labor migrants, and economic problems or competition between ethnic groups often lead to political conflict that can then produce refugee flows. A similar situation may have existed in ancient times, when political conflict was often about limited local environmental or natural resources and forced out weaker groups, who lost their means of subsistence, or when resource competition led to social conflicts, leading to the out-migration of peoples seeking to escape the political turmoil.

Social Networks and Information Flows

As the literature on contemporary international migration makes clear, economic push/pull factors do not completely explain population flows. Although economic pressures are the initial factor that causes people to leave the sending country, the simultaneous conjunction of economic "push" forces in one country and "pull" forces in another does not, by itself, specify the direction of the migrant flow. When faced with economic pressures to migrate, why do people decide to move to certain advanced industrialized countries and not to others that also need immigrant labor and offer equally high wages? The answer is that labor migrants tend to head to countries to which they have personal and institutional connections and linkages that enable and facilitate their migration. Such transnational social networks allow them to gather necessary information, arrange and pay for their passage abroad, and obtain housing, jobs, and other forms of assistance in the destination country (Boyd 1989; Castles and Miller 2003; Massey 1999). Therefore, although economic forces *initiate* migration, social networks *channel* migration flows to specific countries, thus determining their destination (see Tsuda 1999a).

In addition to push/pull theories, the impact of social networks on migration patterns has been another important theoretical insight that prehistorians have gleaned from the literature on contemporary immigration. Although it is difficult to document the effect of social networks using the prehistoric material record, archaeologists have surmised that migrants generally moved to regions where they had social contacts and exchange relationships, whether through relatives, previous migrants, marriage, trade, cross-border raids, or religious interactions. Migrations also seem to have followed established trade routes in ancient times, which is consistent with contemporary migration patterns, which are often structured by capital and investment flows across national borders (Sassen 1988). When advanced industrialized nations trade with and invest in developed countries, it creates economic connections and bridges that enable labor migration from poorer to richer nations.

Once social networks are firmly established between migrant-sending and -receiving areas, they produce what modern migration specialists call "cumulative causation" (Massey 1999)—the tendency of migration flows to increase and become self-sustaining over the long run, even if the original economic causes of migration weaken somewhat. Not only do social networks reduce the risk, cost, and difficulty of migration, making people more willing to migrate under less economic pressure, they also encourage additional migration as the initial migrants in the host country pave the way for subsequent migrants by calling over and sponsoring family, kin, and acquaintances from the home country (chain migration).

Contemporary immigration specialists also note that as emigration becomes pervasive and entrenched in a sending community (especially across generations), a "culture of migration" develops in which positive attitudes and a high regard for the economic benefits of out-migration create an enduring cultural propensity for and expectation of moving abroad (Cornelius 1992; Kandel and Massey 2002; Tsuda 1999a). This is analogous to the "migration mentality" among historic Pueblo peoples, whose constant mobility was reinforced by rituals of movement in anticipation of future migrations (Fowles, this volume). This cultural glorification and normalization of migration is another reason it tends to become self-perpetuating and enduring over time.

The Migratory Process: Historical Differences or Methodological Limits?

Large-Scale and Smaller-Scale Migrations

Once people decide to migrate to a specific region, how do they do so and what does it look like? Most of the prehistoric migrations prehistorians deal with seem to be large-scale collective migrations over relatively long distances that took place over considerable periods of time. Although such population movements are still quite common today, many contemporary migrations consist of temporary or circular movements over shorter distances that are undertaken selectively by individuals. Does this analysis point to a fundamental difference in migration patterns between the past and present or is it more the result of methodological limitations in the study of prehistoric population movements?

Although a number of prehistorians differentiate between small- and large-scale migrations, they tend to focus on larger migrations that were long distance and long term. For instance, Clark (2001) defines migration as residential relocation by discrete social groups over significant economic, cultural, political, or linguistic boundaries. Others have adopted similar definitions, emphasizing its large-scale nature. In contrast, seasonal or circular short-term movements over localized areas by small groups or individuals are sometimes excluded as "not migration" or "background noise" and therefore not a subject of study (e.g., Adams et al. 1978; Cameron 1995; Duff 1998; Rouse 1986).

It may be true that migration in the distant past consisted more of relatively large collective movements by entire social groups, especially in sparsely populated areas such as the American Southwest, where entire villages or clans often seemed to move together. At other times, migration would start with smaller groups such as households, followed by cascading moves by surrounding households and then entire communities.

In contrast, we know that modern migration is rarely undertaken by entire communities or even communal subgroups but is a much more individually selective process. Only certain individuals from a community migrate (usually those with social connections abroad; e.g., see Castillo et al. 2007) and they can sometimes migrate to completely different parts of the world (again, depending on where their social networks take them), even if they are from the same local community. Migrant decision making today occurs either at the individual or household level. In the latter case, the decision is not whether the entire household should migrate but which individuals from the household should migrate (usually the husband or mature youth) (Boyd 1989). Entire households do often migrate, but usually after an initial family member first settles abroad and then calls over the spouse and children and possibly other kin as chain migrants. In most migrant-sending communities, emigrants remain only a minority of the population. Usually, young or middle-aged males are the most likely to migrate and children, older persons, and women are more likely to be left behind (e.g., Boyd 1989; Smith 2006; Tsuda 2003). Even in high-emigration areas that have experienced cumulative chain migration over generations, the eventual relocation of entire communities is quite rare.

If this distinction between the collective nature of prehistoric migrations and the individualized nature of contemporary migration is indeed historically accurate, there may be a few reasons that explain it. First, many prehistoric societies (especially simple tribal or rural village societies) were characterized by communal living and decision making (and collective movement for nomadic societies). Today, most people reside in more urbanized settings in atomized social units (usually families), living relatively independent lives and rarely making decisions collectively or communally. This is true even in rural areas.

Second, the environmental difficulties that caused prehistoric migrations were more likely to have affected entire communities rather uniformly, forcing all or most of its members to leave the area. In today's highly complex and socioeconomically stratified societies, economic difficulties affect only certain (usually poorer) segments of a local society, leading to highly selective emigration patterns. Also, the cross-border social networks that channel migration in today's globalized world are more complex, extensive, and diversified, directing different individuals and families to different overseas destinations and forcing those without such connections to stay home,[7] whereas in the distant past, their scope was probably limited to a few neighboring areas, leading to considerably less selectivity and diversity in migration patterns.

Finally, the difficulty, uncertainly, and danger of travel across land (especially over long distances) in prehistoric times probably compelled peoples to migrate collectively, whereas today, individualized international travel is comparatively safe, fast, routine, and affordable.

It also seems that prehistoric migration often covered considerable geographic distances while crossing topographic, political, and/or ethnolinguistic boundaries. Of course, "long-distance" in the ancient past probably meant a few to several hundred miles. Today, this can mean several thousand miles with the speed and relative ease of international travel. Although many large contemporary migrant flows are to neighboring countries or regions (the migration of Central Americans to the United States, Eastern Europeans to Western Europe, Arabs from North Africa to Southern Europe), a number of notable migration flows are to very distant countries (Chinese and Filipinos to the United States, Middle Easterners and Latin Americans to Western Europe). Whereas modern migratory social networks can span halfway across the globe because of advanced telecommunications and mass media networks, the limited geographical scope of prehistoric social networks probably meant that migrants could not range much beyond their immediate surrounding areas. Therefore, it seems that long-distance migration in the past was often the cumulative result of many shorter-distance migrations that took place over decades or longer (e.g., Darling et al.'s [2004] "village drift" or Ammerman and Cavalli-Sforza's [1973] "wave of advance" models) and not direct migration to distant regions, as it is today.

Much modern migration, however, is relatively short distance since the amount of internal migration within national borders is vastly greater than the volume of international migration across national borders.[8] For instance, internal migration in China alone has been estimated to be a staggering 130 million (Martin and Widgren 2002), which is 70 percent of the total volume of international migration in the entire world. Also, more refugees are internally displaced peoples than those who cross international borders.

In addition, an increasingly large number of migrants in the contemporary world are temporary economic target earners—sojourners who return home in several years with their earnings. Others return when the economic situation back home improves. In addition to the relative ease of international travel, contemporary migrants are able to more readily maintain transnational economic, social, and political connections to their homelands through the constant global movement of peoples, commodities, and information across national borders (Basch et al. 1994; Portes et al. 1999), increasing the amount of return and circular migration. Although return migration probably occurred in prehistory (e.g., Anthony 1990), it was probably far less common, especially for those who migrated in response to long-term environmental or population pressures. Long-distance travel was also far more difficult, as was maintaining social ties to the area of migrant origin, especially if the entire community had left, all of which probably discouraged temporary circular migration.

Methodological Implications

It is also possible that these apparent differences between past and present migration are partly the result of methodological difficulties and limitations inherent in studying prehistory, which causes archaeologists to prioritize large-scale migration. In fact, a bias in archaeological theory and research toward large movements of entire populations over long distances and time periods may exist, since it is likely that these were quite rare compared to more-frequent short-term, smaller-scale, and continuous migrations in localized areas such as seasonal agricultural relocations and movements attributable to trade and hunting, marriage exchanges, raids of neighboring areas, and local religious ritual.

In contrast to contemporary population movements, where even the smallest and individualized migration patterns can be directly observed and studied as they occur, archaeologists relying on fragmentary material remains can usually only detect major long-term population movements that create significant change in a region's material cultures by introducing discernibly different artifacts and settlement patterns. In contrast, short-term and localized migrations or selective and smaller individual/family migrations below the community level are difficult (and often impossible) to track (though Clark [this volume] presents a clear exception).[9] This means that only the aggregate macro-level effects of individual migratory actions can be documented through the archaeological record.

In the case of skeletal morphology, only the in-migration of relatively large and phenotypically distinct populations that partly displace or interbreed at significant levels with the local population can generally be detected. Biological anthropologists studying migration through gene flows also seem to be restricted to the study of large-scale migrations that have significant genetic effects on populations over long periods of time (see Cabana et al. 2008). Although Bolnick (this volume) encourages biological anthropologists to include short-range incremental migrations in their analyses, it seems that genetic analysis can only track the cumulative long-term effects of small-scale movements and not these individual movements themselves.

This is not to say that modern migration specialists pay sufficient attention to smaller-scale, shorter-distance migration flows either. Migration studies today are heavily focused on international migration at the expense of internal migration within national borders, despite the fact that the total volume of the latter is considerably greater. Although there are no real methodological reasons for this bias, since internal migrants stay within the country and apparently do not cross significant political, geographical, cultural, or even ethnoracial boundaries, their impact and disruptive effects are seen as less consequential than international migration, leading to a lack of scholarly interest in the topic. In fact, internal migration in advanced industrialized nations (e.g., Americans who move from California to Arizona) is not even seen as migration. The only type of internal migration that is taken seriously by scholars is rural-to-urban migration in developing countries, where migrants do cross a significant social divide (sometimes almost as significant as national borders) and where their impact can be considerable, such as in China.

Because the research of modern migration specialists (with the exception of historians) generally covers a very limited time period (sociocultural anthropologists generally do only one to two years of fieldwork), they cannot trace the long-term effect of current migratory disruptions over dozens or hundreds of years. As a result, they may easily overestimate the ultimate impact of the international migratory flows they are studying. Even the most major international migration flows do not last for more than several decades because the pool of potential migrants in the sending community is eventually depleted or the country becomes sufficiently developed and economically prosperous, significantly reducing the incentive for continued emigration. Therefore, just as scholars of prehistory are often trapped in long-term macroperspectives because of the limitations of their methodologies, contemporary immigration specialists are often restricted by the limited time frame of their research projects, making it difficult to assess whether the migrations they study will really have the significant long-term impact they anticipate.

The Social Impact of Migration: Population Replacement or Assimilation?

The impact of migration on the receiving society is the third major topic of interest among scholars of prehistory. The impression again given by the prehistoric record is that migration flows were not just large scale, they were also perhaps more disruptive to local societies than they are now and could even replace or displace the local population. In fact, Rouse (1986) defined migration as consisting of large numbers of peoples who invade and expand into a new area, replace or absorb its population, and introduce a new culture. Clark (2001:3) also refers to "serial displacements," where one in-migrating group displaces the resident population, which then migrates elsewhere and displaces others.[10] In fact, there seem to be plenty of examples in the archaeological record of entire settlements being abandoned or local communities collapsing and being replaced by new peoples, especially in the sparsely populated American Southwest (e.g., Bernardini 1998; Cameron 1995; Clark 2001; Duff 1998; Fowler, this volume; Palkovich 1996) but also in other world regions (e.g., Adams et al. 1978; Beekman and Christensen 2003).

There is also evidence of migrants ethnically coexisting and interacting with local populations in prehistoric times and eventually assimilating and intermingling with them (Clark, this volume; Cordell 1995), especially in more highly populated areas with multiethnic states (Adams et al. 1978; Beekman and Christensen 2003; Buzon et al. 2007). In fact, as Clark (this volume) puts it, migration has now come to be seen more as a "social mixer" than a cultural replacer.

In the contemporary world, there are almost no cases of migration displacing or absorbing local populaces or examples of entire regions being depopulated or repopulated. Not only is the wholesale migration of entire communities almost unheard of, but because the world is now densely populated compared to prehistoric times, immigrants are always members of a minority population that usually assimilates to its host country. Even in countries with the largest numbers of immigrants (such as the United States), the proportion of the total population that is foreign born rarely exceeds 15 percent, and even in regions within these countries where immigrants are highly concentrated (such as California), they never approach 50 percent of the local populace. However, if we look at the history of modern migration over the past few hundred years, there are cases of entire world regions being gradually depopulated and repopulated by migrant populations over centuries. The best-known examples are the colonization and peopling of the New World (and Australia and New Zealand) by waves of European immigrants, who eventually displaced and destroyed many of the original indigenous inhabitants (through war, genocide, and, most significantly, the spread of disease). Today, however, very few sparsely populated areas are left in the world that can be re-peopled.

Population replacement through migration may indeed have occurred more often in the distant past because the world was considerably less populated and collective movements of large populations (as well as invasions) were more frequent. However, this may also be partly a reflection of the inherent limitations of archaeological methods. Since archaeologists have primarily traced migrations by examining sudden shifts and changes in local material culture and settlement patterns, it may have appeared to them that a new population entered the region and largely replaced the old population and its culture. In fact, Rouse (1986) claims that because the immigration of smaller groups who were assimilated by local host populations is difficult (if not impossible) for archaeologists to detect in the material record, they can only readily study cases of large invading migrant groups that drive out or dominate local populations and thus leave a sufficient mark on the material landscape.

However, even a sudden and significant change in material culture does not necessarily mean that a local population was replaced or re-peopled by migrant newcomers. The immigrants may have been only a minority in the new region but could have attained political or ethnic/cultural supremacy and thus have had a much greater impact on its material life and settlement patterns than their smaller numbers indicated. This can sometimes become clear when the analysis of material culture is combined with other bioarchaeological indicators. For instance, Buzon's (2006) study of ancient Nubia after the Egyptian invasion indicates a high degree of Egyptianization of material culture. However, analysis of cranial morphology from burial sites shows that the Nubians were not simply displaced by the Egyptians but interbred with them, producing a biologically mixed local population.

Studying Prehistoric Migration: Methodological Issues

In this manner, although there are definitely significant differences between contemporary migration flows and those of the distant past, they may be partly a reflection of the methodological difficulties faced by archaeologists, historical linguists, and biological anthropologists who study prehistoric migrations. Since such methodological issues may make the differences between past and present migration appear more dramatic than they actually are, I would like to reflect on some of them in this final section from the perspective of a contemporary immigration specialist.

The Movement of Peoples and Artifacts: Do They Always Correlate?

There continues to be considerable uncertainty in most prehistoric cases about whether migration actually occurred, when it occurred, and where it came from (Ahlstrom et al. 1995; Beekman and Christenson 2003; Burmeister 2000; Cameron 1995; Fowler, this volume). Before prehistorians can better understand how migration functioned as a dynamic social process and compare it with the present, they must be able to first reliably detect and verify its occurrence by analyzing the fragmentary prehistoric material record (Clark 2001).

Although archaeologists have often attributed sudden and distinct changes in local material artifacts and settlement patterns to migration, it is often unclear whether they were a product of a new population migrating into the area with a different material culture or simply the diffusion of new artifacts and lifestyles into the region (through trade, acculturation from neighboring peoples, etc.).[11] In fact, there has been notable tension between migrationist and diffusionist explanations for discontinuities in the material record and it is often difficult to distinguish between the two, although trade can be eliminated as a cause of changes in material artifacts if evidence exists that they were locally produced (e.g., see Clark, this volume).

Even if diffusion can be ruled out, attempts to trace migration by examining the introduction of new artifacts (or settlement patterns) into a local region are based on a problematic assumption that migratory populations are discrete and separate ethnic groups that correspond with bounded collections of artifacts. Although certain ethnic groups can be identified with specific material styles, they are often too ambiguous or too widely distributed to be linked to a specific group (see Fowler, this volume) or they may be not be distinct enough from surrounding cultures to be readily identifiable. Especially in multiethnic settings, ethnic groups are often fluid and flexible; their boundaries are not clearly drawn and they often interact and intermarry. In this process, different ethnic groups may adopt multiple material styles, several ethnic groups may have similar material styles, and the material culture of ethnic groups often changes through in situ development or techniques adopted from other cultures. Since migrating populations often ethnically intermingle and biologically interbreed with existing ones, this admixing also creates considerable ambiguity in the material record and in skeletal morphology. In addition, a migratory group may simply choose not to emphasize its ethnic identity through material culture. In the case of contemporary migration, a neat one-to-one correspondence between peoples and material cultures simply does not exist, especially in complex multiethnic societies.

Tracking the migration of specific peoples through their artifacts also assumes that their material culture does not change during and after the migratory process. However, the material cultures and subsistence patterns of migrants are often transformed as they adapt to different cultural and local environmental conditions in their new areas of settlement, especially over the relatively long periods of time studied by archaeologists. Even if ethnic identity is preserved though language and other traditions after migration, material culture may undergo substantial change. Some archaeologists have attempted to overcome this problem by focusing on internal domestic aspects of material culture, which are supposedly less subject to change after migration, as opposed to external, public, and highly visible aspects of material culture (e.g., Burmeister 2000; Clark 2001). Indeed, modern immigrants and their descendants who have assimilated to the host society often continue to maintain ethnic cultural differences in the privacy of their homes, whether through food, language, or other traditional customs.

However, research on contemporary immigration also indicates that most of the material culture migrants bring with them often does not endure and leave a lasting mark on the host society. This may be even truer today than it was in the distant past, since most people have become consumers rather than producers of material goods in modern capitalist societies. As a result, contemporary migrants do not take most of their material implements and artifacts with them or manufacture them after migration and build their own dwellings and settlements (as their prehistoric ancestors did). Instead, they purchase all their consumer items from the host society and live in its homes and adopt its material lifestyle. As a result, material culture is often the first aspect of migrant culture to change and assimilate to the dominant society (before language, religion, customs and values, etc.). This is especially true for long-term economic migrants, who move to the host society seeking a higher (material) standard of living. Of course, immigrants continue to consume various goods, commodities, and food from their home countries (which are usually imported and sold in their immigrant communities) (e.g., see Chinchilla and Hamilton 2001; Portes and Stepick 1993; Tsuda 2003), but its material impact on the host society is quite small. Since modern migrants move into preexisting housing (instead of constructing their own), they also have a minimal impact on residential architecture patterns, except for ethnic businesses in immigrant communities (which often simply take over existing buildings with a change in signage). As immigrants become socioeconomically successful over time, they also leave inner-city neighborhoods and move to mainstream suburbs. Any continued assertion of their migrant ethnic identities through material culture is usually done during ceremonies and festivals, which feature ethnic clothes and food (which are relatively perishable from an archaeological standpoint). However, migrants often change their ethnic identities in the host society (e.g., see Tsuda 2003) and eventually assimilate to it by the second generation (Alba and Nee 1997; Gans 1997), making any initial differences in their material culture undetectable in the long run.

Although prehistoric migrants may have retained more of their material culture after relocation, somewhat similar conditions to those of modern society may have existed for those who moved to highly developed states and cities with advanced consumer economies, where their material culture was subject to much greater change and assimilation than those who lived in simple agricultural societies and manufactured most of their artifacts, tools, and homes.[12] Even in prehistory, therefore, material culture rarely remained constant between the migrant origin and destination areas (Beekman and Christensen 2003; Rouse 1986). Therefore, it is highly problematic to assume that similarities in material culture in two different locations is an indication of migration, except perhaps in cases of large migratory invasions when the conquerors imposed their homeland culture on the conquered host society (in contrast to most cases, where migrants became ethnic minorities that eventually assimilated to the dominant culture).

Historical linguists face similar issues when attempting to track ancient migrations through the distribution and dispersal of languages. Although language is one of the primary markers of ethnic difference, specific ethnic groups do not always correlate with specific languages. A variety of different groups may speak the same language, and sometimes one group speaks multiple languages. In other cases, linguistic differences between ethnic groups may not be clear or there may be too much linguistic intermixing to clearly distinguish between different groups. Therefore, documenting migratory patterns by the gradual spread of languages to new geographic areas is usually limited to the large-scale migration of its speakers over long time periods and cannot get at smaller-scale migrations of specific groups of peoples, either because they speak the same language or are not closely associated with a specific and distinct language or dialect. For instance, the current (although partial) introduction of the Spanish language into the United States is evidence of the large-scale immigration of peoples from Latin America over several generations, but is not a specific enough indicator of the smaller-scale migrations of different nationalities of Latin American peoples over shorter time periods. Although dialect differences between speakers of a certain language group usually are associated with various ethnic subgroups, they are often more prominent in the spoken rather than in the written language (on which scholars studying ancient migration must rely). In addition, smaller-scale migrations over shorter periods of time may not have a significant linguistic impact on the receiving area, especially since the immigrants are likely to assimilate to the local language within a generation or so, as is the case with contemporary immigrants.

However, tracing ancient migrations through the historical spread of a language is probably more reliable than doing so through the distribution of material artifacts, since peoples are more closely tied to their languages than they are to their material cultures. Although the introduction of new material artifacts into a certain geographical area may simply be a product of trade and diffusion (and not in-migration per se), the introduction of a new language into an area almost always indicates that a significant number of its speakers immigrated. Without migration, the linguistic diffusion between peoples living in different locations is usually restricted to the simple borrowing of words and phrases and rarely involves the wholesale importation of an entirely new language (except for a relatively small number of local peoples learning a foreign language) (see Hill, this volume). Therefore, tracking ancient migrations through the linguistic analysis of borrowed words seems to me to be less reliable, except in cases where there is clear archaeological or biological evidence that migration actually occurred (e.g., Ehret, this volume).

Historical linguists have also traced languages back in time to a specific geographical origin area of the protolanguage in order to track the migratory dispersal of its speakers (see Hill, this volume; Manning 2005; Ortman, this volume). However, such efforts remain speculative and the exact chronology of such historical reconstructions of linguistic dispersal is difficult to substantiate without corroborating evidence from archaeology or biological anthropology (see Ehret, this volume). Not surprisingly, attempts to correlate a language (or protolanguage) with specific material cultures (or ecological environments) in order to determine the chronology of its migratory dispersal are rife with problems (see Ortman, this volume).

New Methods from Biological Anthropology

In contrast to traditional archaeological and linguistic methodologies, which examine only proxies for population movement (material artifacts and languages, which do not always correlate with specific migrant groups), new bio-anthropological methods provide direct information about actual migrations through their biological traces, regardless of whether they caused changes in material culture or language. However, these new methodologies also seem to have their own limitations, which I find to be somewhat analogous to the archaeological analysis of material remains.

Bolnick (this volume) summarizes both the promises and shortcomings of genetic analysis as a way to track ancient migrations. Although this methodology directly traces human movements (instead of their artifacts), I wonder if genetic similarities between two extant populations living in different regions is a completely reliable way of detecting prehistoric migrations that took place over vast amounts of time when evolutionary genetic changes were also occurring (it seems that just as material culture can change during population movement, so can genes). It is also not always clear whether genetic variation over time in a single population is a result of a migratory inflow that introduced new genes or simply the normal process of evolutionary change and genetic drift (Cabana et al. 2008).

Perhaps a more reliable and direct way to trace ancient migrations is by analyzing the biogeochemical signatures of human skeletal remains (Knudson, this volume). By comparing the strontium or oxygen isotope ratios in individual bones and teeth with isotope signatures from surrounding geological regions (whose plants, animals, and water the individual may have consumed), this relatively new method indicates where the migrants originated. It can track small individual migrations instead of just large group movements, thus overcoming one of the critical shortcomings of gene flow and material artifact analysis. However, it has some similar limitations to material culture approaches: it can only detect relatively long-distance migrations from distinct geological regions with different isotope signatures and it cannot differentiate between those who migrated from a different region and those who simply consumed imported food and water from that region (analogous to the migration versus diffusion problem). Finally, both the gene flow and biogeochemical approaches cannot determine the causes of migration or its social impact.

Conclusion: Is Modernity Really That Different from Prehistory?

Despite the vast temporal gulf between current and prehistoric population movements, I hope this chapter has demonstrated some of the possible benefits of a closer dialogue between anthropologists studying these two epochs of human migration. Although it is usually scholars of contemporary societies who look back in time to see what the past can teach us about the present, in the case of migration, it has been scholars of the ancient past who have looked at contemporary societies to see what the present can possibility teach us about the past. I have attempted to make a small contribution to this endeavor, from the perspective of a modern migration specialist.

In contrast to those of us who study contemporary migration, prehistorians (particularly archaeologists) seemed to have initially stumbled onto the topic somewhat by default. Instead of choosing to study migration as an independent phenomenon in its own right, they mainly used it as a means to explain changes and discontinuities they found in the material record (Cabana, this volume). As the field matured and moved beyond simply attempting to detect and track population movements, some archaeologists have turned to studies of modern migration to order to better understand its actual social dynamics.

When assessing the relevance of contemporary migration flows to those from the distant past, it comes as no surprise that the differences seem to outweigh the similarities. Nonetheless, these contrastive differences can still illuminate aspects of prehistoric migration. Peoples in ancient times moved more for environmental than for purely economic reasons, and population pressures and human conflict also played a much greater role. Migrations also seemed to have been large collective movements of entire peoples that could displace or absorb local populations, and they seem to have taken place over considerable time periods and long distances. In contrast, because today's population movements are more temporary, internal, and individualized, immigrants are always ethnic minorities that assimilate to the societies where they reside.

However, this chapter has also suggested that the differences between the past and present may not be as great as they initially appear. The environmental pressures that caused prehistoric migration are analogous to the economic pressures of today. Both of them push migrants out of sending areas with poorer conditions and pull them to regions with better conditions. Throughout human history, migration has been driven by the continued search for a better livelihood and means of subsistence. In addition, social and trade networks that link migrants to other geographical regions have always directed population movements to specific destinations and have increased and sustained migration flows over time. Finally, I have also suggested that many of the apparent differences between contemporary and prehistoric migrations may also be the product of the methodological difficulties inherent in reconstructing population movements from the fragmentary prehistoric material and skeletal record. In order to overcome these limitations, it seems that archaeologists, linguists, and biological anthropologists are increasingly combining different approaches and methodologies (as well as devising new ones), each of which has its own strengths, instead of relying solely on one source of evidence. As these scholars of prehistory continue to obtain a more comprehensive understanding of ancient migrations, they may find that the overall dynamics and nature of population movement have remained relatively constant throughout human history.

Notes

1. Chapman (1997) has even argued that the experiences and knowledge that archaeologists have of modern migration influence their theorization and understanding of prehistoric migration, whether they are aware of it or not.

2. However, the literature they cite is rather outdated.

3. Most countries today actually import most of their food and natural resources, even if they are located in environmentally rich geographical areas.

4. For instance, past hurricanes and floods in Central America have caused people who lost their economic livelihood to migrate to the United States.

5. A recent military intelligence study cited by Al Gore in a speech about global warming warned of the possibility of hundreds of millions of "climate refugees" causing instability around the world ("Gore Calls for Carbon-Free Electric Power," *New York Times*, July 17, 2008).

6. At the end of 2006, there were an estimated 9.9 million international refugees (UNHCR 2007:24), which is just 5 percent of the total estimated population of international migrants. The number of internally displaced peoples (internal refugees) was 12.8 million, which is a small fraction of the total volume of the world's internal migrants.

7. Certain emigration countries such as China and the Philippines send individual migrants to most regions in the world and have large impoverished populations at the bottom of the socioeconomic ladder who do not have the means or social connections to migrate internationally.

8. This is the modern equivalent of Duff's (1998) distinction between migration within sociopolitical and physical boundaries and migrations that crossed such boundaries.

9. Rouse claims that local seasonal migration can be traced by studying tool kits and food remains from neighboring sites (1986), although he does not elaborate and is not interested in such migrations.

10. However, Clark (2001) notes that co-residence between migrants and locals occurred more often than displacement.

11. They could also be the product of local development and in situ changes, although these are usually quite gradual and not abrupt.

12. However, even in advanced states, such as those in Central Mexico, new migrants could build new types of architecture and change ceramic production, although in other cases they adopted local architectural styles (Beekman and Christensen 2003).

References

Adams, W., D. Van Gerven, and R. Levy
1978   The Retreat from Migrationism. *Annual Review of Anthropology* 7:483–532.
Ahlstrom, R., C. Van West, and J. Dean
1995   Environmental and Chronological Factors in the Mesa Verde-Northern Rio Grande Migration. *Journal of Anthropological Archaeology* 14:125–142.
Alba, R., and V. Nee
1997   Rethinking Assimilation Theory for a New Era of Immigration. *International Migration Review* 31(4):826–874.

Anthony, D.

1990   Migration in Archeology: The Baby and the Bathwater. *American Anthropologist* 92(4):895–914.

1997   Prehistoric Migration as Social Process. In *Migrations and Invasions in Archaeological Explanation*, edited by J. Chapman and H. Hamerow, 21–32. Oxford Archaeopress, Oxford.

Basch, L., N. Glick Schiller, and C. Szanton Blanc

1994   *Nations Unbound: Transnational Projects, Postcolonial Predicaments, and Deterritorialized Nation-States*. Gordon and Breach Publishers, Amsterdam.

Beekman, C., and A. Christensen

2003   Controlling for Doubt and Uncertainty Through Multiple Lines of Evidence: A New Look at the Mesoamerican Nahua Migrations. *Journal of Archaeological Method and Theory* 10(2):111–164.

Bernardini, W.

1998   Conflict, Migration, and the Social Environment: Interpreting Architectural Change in Early and Late Pueblo IV Aggregations. In *Migration and Reorganization: The Pueblo IV Period in the American Southwest*, edited by K. Spielmann, pp. 91–114. Arizona State University Anthropological Research Papers no. 51. Arizona State University, Tempe.

Boyd, M.

1989   Family and Personal Networks in International Migration. *International Migration Review* 23(3):638–670.

Brettell, C. B., and J. F. Hollifield (editors)

2000   *Migration Theory: Talking Across Disciplines*. Routledge, New York.

Burmeister, S.

2000   Archaeology and Migration: Approaches to an Archaeological Proof of Migration. *Current Anthropology* 41(4):539–567.

Buzon, M.

2006   Biological and Ethnic Identity in New Kingdom Nubia: A Case Study from Tombos. *Current Anthropology* 47(4):683–695.

Buzon, M., A. Simonetti, and R. Creaser

2007   Migration in the Nile Valley During the New Kingdom Period: A Preliminary Strontium Isotope Study. *Journal of Archaeological Science* 34(9):1391–1401.

Cabana, G. S., K. L. Hunley, and F. A. Kaestle

2008   Population Continuity or Replacement? A Novel Computer Simulation Approach and its Application to the Numic Expansion (Western Great Basin, USA). *American Journal of Physical Anthropology* 135:438–447.

Cameron, C.

1995   Migration and the Movement of Southwestern Peoples. *Journal of Anthropological Archaeology* 14:104–124.

Castillo, G., Z. Jiménez-Pacheco, and P. Pasillas

2007   Stay-at-Homes: Why Many People Do Not Migrate. In *Mayan Journeys: The New Migration from Yucatán to the United States*, edited by W. Cornelius, D.

Fitzgerald, and P. Lewin Fischer, pp. 141–149. Center for Comparative Immigration Studies, La Jolla, Calif.

Castles, S., and M. J. Miller

2003   *The Age of Migration: International Population Movements in the Modern World*. 3rd ed. Guilford Press, New York.

Chapman, J.

1997   The Impact of Modern Invasions and Migrations on Archaeological Explanation. In *Migrations and Invasions in Archaeological Explanation*, edited by J. Chapman and H. Hamerow, pp. 11–20. British Archaeological Reports International Series no. 664. Oxford Archaeopress, Oxford.

Chinchilla, N. S., and N. Hamilton

2001   Doing Business: Central American Enterprises in Los Angeles. In *Asian and Latino Immigrants in a Restructuring Economy: The Metamorphosis of Southern California*, edited by M. López-Garza and D. Diaz, pp. 188–214. Stanford University Press, Stanford, Calif.

Clark, G. A.

1994   Migration as an Explanatory Concept in Paleolithic Archaeology. *Journal of Archaeological Method and Theory* 1(3):305–343.

Clark, J. A.

2001   *Tracking Prehistoric Migrations: Pueblo Settlers Among the Tonto Basin Hohokam*. Anthropological Papers of the University of Arizona no. 65. University of Arizona Press, Tucson.

Cohen, R.

1995   *The Cambridge Survey of World Migration*. Cambridge University Press, Cambridge.

Cordell, L.

1995   Tracing Migration Pathways from the Receiving End. *Journal of Anthropological Archaeology* 14(2):203–211.

Cornelius, W.

1992   From Sojourners to Settlers: The Changing Profile of Mexican Immigration to the United States. In *U.S.-Mexico Relations: Labor Market Interdependence*, edited by J. Bustamante, C. W. Reynolds, and R. A. Hinosa Ojeda, pp. 155–195. Stanford University Press, Stanford, Calif.

1998   The Structural Embeddedness of Demand for Mexican Immigrant Labor: New Evidence from California. In *Crossings: Mexican Immigration in Interdisciplinary Perspective*, edited by M. Suárez-Orozco, pp. 114–44. Harvard University Press, Cambridge, Mass.

Cornelius, W., and T. Tsuda

2004   Controlling Immigration: The Limits of Government Intervention In *Controlling Immigration: A Global Perspective*, edited by W. A. Cornelius, T. Tsuda, P. L. Martin, and J. F. Hollifield, pp. 3–48. 2nd ed. Stanford University Press, Stanford, Calif.

Daniels, R.
1990 *Coming to America: A History of Immigration and Ethnicity in American Life.* HarperCollins, New York.

Darling, J. A., J. C. Ravesloot, and M. R. Waters
2004 Village Drift and Riverine Settlement: Modeling Akimel O'odham Land Use. *American Anthropologist* 106(4):282–295.

Diner, H. R.
2000 History and the Study of Immigration: Narratives of the Particular. In *Migration Theory: Talking Across Disciplines*, edited by C. B. Brettell and J. F. Hollifield, pp. 27–42. Routledge, New York.

Duff, A. I.
1998 The Process of Migration in the Late Prehistoric Southwest. In *Migration and Reorganization: The Pueblo IV Period in the American Southwest*, edited by K. Spielmann, pp. 31–52. Arizona State University Anthropological Research Papers no. 51. Arizona State University, Tempe.

Gaetano, A., and T. Jacka
2004 *On the Move: Women and Rural-to-Urban Migration in Contemporary China.* Columbia University Press, New York.

Gans, H.
1997 Toward a Reconciliation of "Assimilation" and "Pluralism." *International Migration Review* 31(4):875–892.

Hoerder, D.
2002 *Cultures in Contact: World Migrations in the Second Millennium.* Duke University Press, Durham, N.C.

Kandel, W., and D. Massey
2002 The Culture of Mexican Migration: A Theoretical and Empirical Analysis. *Social Forces* 80(3):981–1004.

Kritz, M., and H. Zlotnik
1992 Global Interactions: Migration Systems, Processes, and Policies. In *International Migration Systems: A Global Approach*, edited by M. M. Kritz, L. L. Lim, and H. Zlotnik, pp. 1–16. Clarendon Press, Oxford.

Manning, P.
2005 *Migration in World History.* Routledge, London.

Martin, P., M. Abella, and C. Kuptsch
2006 *Managing Labor Migration in the Twenty-First Century.* Yale University Press, New Haven, Conn.

Martin, P., and J. Widgren
2002 International Migration: Facing the Challenge. *Population Bulletin* 57(1):3–39.

Massey, D. S.
1999 Why Does Immigration Occur? A Theoretical Synthesis. In *The Handbook of International Migration*, edited by C. Hirschman, P. Kasinitz, and J. DeWind, pp. 34–52. Russell Sage Foundation, New York.

Nam, C., W. J. Serow, and D. F. Sly (editors)

1990   *International Handbook on Internal Migration*. Greenwood Press, New York.

Palkovich, A. M.

1996   Historic Depopulation in the American Southwest: Issues of Interpretation and Context-Embedded Analyses. In *Bioarchaeology of Native American Adaptation in the Spanish Borderlands*, edited by B. J. Baker and L. Kealhofer, pp. 179–197. University Press of Florida, Gainesville.

Portes, A., and R. G. Rumbaut

1996   *Immigrant America: A Portrait*. University of California Press, Berkeley.

Portes, A., and A. Stepick

1993   *City on the Edge: The Transformation of Miami*. University of California Press, Berkeley.

Portes, A., L. Guarnizo, and P. Landolt

1999   Introduction: Pitfalls and Promise of an Emergent Research Field. *Ethnic and Racial Studies* 22(2):217–237.

Rouse, I.

1986   *Migrations in Prehistory: Inferring Population Movement from Cultural Remains*. Yale University Press, New Haven, Conn.

Sassen, S.

1988   *The Mobility of Labor and Capital: A Study in International Investment and Labor Flow*. Cambridge University Press, Cambridge.

Smith, R. C.

2006   *Mexican New York: Transnational Lives of New Immigrants*. University of California Press, Berkeley.

Takaki, R. T.

1993   *A Different Mirror: A History of Multicultural America*. Little, Brown & Co., Boston.

Tsuda, T.

1999a   The Motivation to Migrate: The Ethnic and Sociocultural Constitution of the Japanese-Brazilian Return Migration System. *Economic Development and Cultural Change* 48(1):1–31.

1999b   The Permanence of "Temporary" Migration: The "Structural Embeddedness" of Japanese-Brazilian Migrant Workers in Japan. *Journal of Asian Studies* 58(3):687–722.

2003   *Strangers in the Ethnic Homeland: Japanese Brazilian Return Migration in Transnational Perspective*. Columbia University Press, New York.

United Nations High Commissioner for Refugees (UNHCR)

2007   *Statistical Yearbook 2006: Trends in Displacement, Protection and Solutions*. United Nations High Commissioner for Refugees, Geneva, Switzerland.

Waldinger, R., and J. Lee
2001   New Immigrants in Urban America. In *Strangers at the Gates: New Immigrants in Urban America*, edited by R. Waldinger, pp. 30–79. University of California Press, Berkeley.

White, J. W. (editor)
1979   *The Urban Impact of Internal Migration*. Institute for Research in Social Science, University of North Carolina, Chapel Hill.

Contributors

Christopher S. Beekman is associate professor of anthropology at the University of Colorado Denver.

Wesley R. Bernardini is associate professor of anthropology at the University of Redlands.

Deborah A. Bolnick is associate professor of anthropology at the University of Connecticut.

Graciela S. Cabana is associate professor of anthropology and director of the Molecular Anthropology Laboratories at the University of Tennessee, Knoxville.

Alexander F. Christensen is a forensic anthropologist and DNA coordinator at the Joint POW/MIA Accounting Command-Central Identification Laboratory in Honolulu, Hawaii.

Jeffery J. Clark is a preservation archaeologist at Archaeology Southwest in Tucson, Arizona, and adjunct associate professor in the School of Anthropology, University of Arizona.

J. Andrew Darling is owner and senior archaeologist/principal investigator for Southwest Heritage Research, LLC in Chandler, Arizona, and Dallas, Texas.

Christopher Ehret is distinguished professor of history and linguistics at the University of California, Los Angeles.

Alan G. Fix is professor emeritus of anthropology at the University of California, Riverside.

Catherine S. Fowler is professor emeritus of anthropology at the University of Nevada, Reno.

Severin M. Fowles is assistant professor of anthropology at Barnard College.

Susan R. Frankenberg is program coordinator of Museum Studies at the University of Illinois, Urbana-Champaign.

Jane H. Hill is a Regents' professor and professor emerita of anthropology (linguistics) at the University of Arizona.

Keith L. Hunley is assistant professor of anthropology at the University of New Mexico.

Kelly J. Knudson is assistant professor at the Center for Bioarchaeological Research, School of Human Evolution and Social Change, Arizona State University.

Lyle W. Konigsberg is professor of anthropology at the University of Illinois, Urbana-Champaign.

Scott G. Ortman is director of research and education at the Crow Canyon Archaeological Center in Cortez, Colorado.

Takeyuki (Gaku) Tsuda is associate professor of anthropology at the School of Human Evolution and Social Change, Arizona State University.

Index

www.ingramcontent.com/pod-product-compliance
Lightning Source LLC
Chambersburg PA
CBHW071729270326
41928CB00013B/2615